D0966162

INTRODUCTION

This is where we're supposed to tell you something important to prepare you for everything that follows. At least, that's what we think the word *introduction* means. It could also mean that we introduce ourselves to you. So, let's try that.

Hi! Our names are Tony and Daniel. We love God, each other, our family, and the people around us. We're Christians, which means Jesus is our Savior and Lord, and we want to grow into whatever that means for our lives. We often talk about that and other fun things around our dinner table, lying on our trampoline, or simply hanging out over a smoothie. For real . . . we both really, really like smoothies. They're simply amazing.

Anyway, welcome to our book. We didn't originally set out to "author" anything but found ourselves writing down what inspired some of the great conversations we've had at home, in the car, on walks, and just about everywhere else. Every question led to another question, which not only kept things fun but made us rethink why our original answers were what they were. The next thing we knew, we were opening up the Bible and growing together spiritually too.

That's where hearing and listening both matter and overlap. As we understand it, *listening* is better than *hearing*. Then again, maybe it's the opposite. Someone probably explained it all to us once, but we weren't paying attention. The bottom line is: paying attention matters.

What if "hearing" means you're aware a conversation is happening, while "listening" means you're considering what's been said? Maybe you'd swap those words and definitions around. Feel free. Make it a conversation starter if you want.

In the meantime, it's great to be on this journey with you. So as you get serious, have some fun! And as you have some fun, get serious! We love how this plays out in our home and are praying for what's about to happen in yours.

Together,

Tony Myles and Daniel Myles, father and son

Overview

Admit it. You've asked the question. "What will I get out of this?" Perhaps your whole family is eager to dive into something meaningful together. Then again, maybe one or more people in your home seem more cautious and skeptical than curious and open.

No worries. Wherever everyone is today *is simply where everyone is today*. Growth is possible over time as you step in the right direction and show others how to do the same. Parents have something to say to kids, kids have something to say to parents, and siblings have something to say to each other. Even better, God has something to say to all of you through each other!

It's why God wrote a book. His Bible is one story told through the Old Testament and the New Testament—kind of like a film series made of multiple movies. We're actually living out our own part of that story right now!

The Old Testament reveals that God made everything good, but people sinfully messed things up and created a need for God to save them. Each Old Testament book points forward to a Savior (Jesus) coming one day, while also showing God's blessings or discipline for the Old Testament people, based on whether they trusted Him or rebelled.

The New Testament shares Jesus' arrival on earth and everything that followed. He lived among us, taught truth, transformed people, and launched His incredible church. Many New Testament books represent letters the early Christians passed around to understand the Christian life. The last book of the Bible shows how God offers us an eternal fresh start as heaven and earth again come together, fixing everything for good.

Put all of that together, and the Bible is full of human-sized scandal, fighting, controversy, and disappointment . . . and yet also full of God-sized hope, restoration, freedom, clarity, and life. The Lord loves us even when He doesn't like the choices we make. He is consistent and committed to saving us.

Tracking so far? Feeling a bit overwhelmed? Either way, it's pretty awesome! To help you with this, we created a memorable phrase to help you understand the big message of the Bible: THERE IS HOPE:

- **Trinity:** Before there was anything, there was a Community of Someone.
- **Heritage:** God began everything and everyone in a good starting place so He could pass down His blessings to us.
- **Enemy:** God's people listened to an enemy and became an enemy—to God, one another, and even creation itself.
- **Revolution:** The Lord began His own uprising to turn things around by creating special covenants with His people meant to change the world.
- **Ego:** When humanity as a whole lost sight of how far it had drifted from God, He removed everyone's sense of control by raising up a holy nation of people who descended from His revolutionaries and had His favor.
- **Identity:** God's people strangely tried to find their uniqueness by looking like everyone else, and so the Lord allowed many of their shortsighted decisions to play out while He spoke wisdom into them to bring them back to their true intended selves.
- **Shhh:** For years, the Lord didn't reveal Himself in any way that was recorded but instead let His previous words be more than enough while creating the right timing for His arrival.
- **Hero:** Jesus Christ came to earth to live among us, inspire us with truth, reveal His kingdom, save us from sin, and unleash us into a fully alive life.
- **Opportunity:** Jesus didn't just tell us what to do but made it possible for us to seize the true life through Him and the Holy Spirit.
- **Purpose:** Just as Jesus had a purpose of transformation on earth, so has He given us the purpose of being His church and transforming the entire world.
- **Eternity:** One day heaven and earth will come together forever, and God's people will live with Him forever.

Did you see it? If you take the first letter of each of these words and put them together, you spell "THERE IS HOPE," which is the big story of the Bible. Just like life, what's in its pages isn't tame but is full of God at work while people run wild. Some of His people made destructive decisions we can learn from (maybe so we know our own temptations are just-as-messy yet just-as-capable of a turnaround).

This is why in every chapter we'll help you come back to how THERE IS HOPE in Jesus Christ for everyone. Everything we'll be sharing with you is something we took the time to learn. Keep in mind, God is still God, and we can't fully understand Him on everything. Thankfully, the important things are clear. Some Scriptures will reach your mind by touching your heart. Other Scriptures will reach your heart by touching your mind. Along the way, your family will start asking better questions that engage the soul so God's will may be done on earth as it is in heaven.

You may wonder "if" that could happen, but "what if" it could? There is hope.

So, make the most of this book by putting it where you'll see it daily, pick it up, and let God work. We've even given you a regular set of questions to ask each other every seventh day to catch up and better own what you've studied. This rhythm can really serve you well.

Don't let any hurdles stop you from pressing on. If you drop off in reading together, simply pick it up again. If a family member begins pushing back or complaining, don't grow weary in doing good. Even our loved ones who seem a little "too young to get anything out of this" or "too stuck-in-their-ways to consider anything new" will pick up things simply by being around the conversations you and the rest of the family have, so keep having those conversations! A seed that is planted today may grow into something rooted in the days to come.

Wouldn't that be fantastic? There is hope for something more meaningful than the way things are. This is more than a book. It's an invitation for your family into a real-life adventure with a real-life God. It's also a chance to be a part of something bigger than your household that involves your household. Something that could significantly impact the world and lives around you.

The Bible wasn't given to us so we'd become know-it-alls but to foster wonder and wisdom that help us know Jesus. The key is not just what happens when you open it up but in how you help each other live it out when you close its cover. One hundred years from now, the only thing that will matter is our relationship with God. If that isn't motivation, what is?

Maybe it's time to pause and pray. And then, let's get after it together!

TRINITY

Imagine you were given a huge amount of money to build a tree house. You'd have so much fun shopping for it, right? You'd want to be smart about the whole process, though. It'd be silly to focus on just buying a bunch of wood to create the "house" part without ever considering the strength of the tree you'd attach it to. Otherwise every time you tried to step into the tree house you'd wonder if it had the strength to hold you or if you'd ultimately fall down.

What you build your faith on matters too. Throughout this section, we're going to talk about some big topics regarding God. You might wonder if it's really necessary to stretch your brain like this because, in the end, God is still going to be bigger than what you can understand. Some people actually think, *I don't have time to think about who God is. I just want to start building out my faith.*

Again, remember the importance of studying the tree part of a tree house. Even though you wouldn't need to understand everything about every leaf on a tree to build something on it, you would want to know enough about its core to have the confidence to step out in faith. Get ready to feel more confident about the core of your faith!

Before there was anything, there was a Community of Someone.

1: First Things First

***IF** you could create and know every detail of what was going to happen tomorrow, would you want to?*

***WHAT IF** you were to plan my day and I was to plan your day?*

READ IT: GENESIS 1:1

Remember that one time you invented a game? Come on, everyone has invented a game, whether it was something you played with friends or by yourself. Maybe it's time to play it again.

Before you invented that game, it didn't exist, but you did. The game was dependent on you to exist and keep existing, but your existence wasn't dependent on the game to keep existing. Makes sense, right?

Keep this in mind while trying to understand God and His role in creation. Sometimes people wonder, *If God created everything, who created God?* We ask this because everything natural we see with our eyes comes from another thing that also had a beginning . . . a tree comes from the seed of another tree, which came from the seed of another tree, and so on. But for everything natural to exist, something or someone had to supernaturally exist outside of creation to create the very first things. Even the smallest atoms and molecules needed something to start them.

The Bible reveals God is behind it all, for He existed before "the beginning." We only ask, "Who created God?" when we think He is like us. But the rules don't apply to Him because He's the one who created it all, including the rules. Wow! Let that blow your mind and deepen your faith!

Clear your schedule. Spend some time really thinking about who God is and what it means that He has always existed. God makes Himself known in creation, and He will make Himself known to you.

THERE IS HOPE

You bare the mark of your Creator.*
** This is not a typo.*

Think back to the starting point of anything significant in your life, like when you bought something meaningful to you, first got into your favorite hobby, moved into a neighborhood, or formed an important relationship.

- ***IF*** that didn't happen, what would be different about your life?
- ***WHAT IF*** you looked for a way to thank God for these starting points?

2: Three-In-One

***IF** you could copy yourself and be in three different places, how would each version of you spend the day?*

***WHAT IF** you could give this power to someone else so that person could be in three different places?*

READ IT: GENESIS 1:1

Have you ever stared at a whirring ceiling fan? When a fan isn't turned on, you usually see three single blades attached to a core at the center. All of this is touchable until you flip a switch and put the fan into full motion. At this point it looks more like one big blade spinning around! Keep in mind, whether the fan is "touchable" or in motion "beyond your touch," the fan is a fan.

The Bible tells us God is our Creator, which means only One supreme being began everything and everyone. At the same time, the ancient word used in this verse that we translate as God is *elohiym*, which is a plural word. That means this single God is kind of like a three-bladed fan—you can experience His touches in your life as the Father, Son, or Spirit, who each do specific things, but you can also pull back to see how "the Lord is one" in full motion over everything. A word we use to describe all of this is that God is a *Trinity*.

This probably feels too big to think about, but that's the point. There's no way to completely understand how awesome and amazing God is! Anything we compare Him to is no comparison.

Maybe your experience so far in getting to know God has focused more on His role as a Supreme Ruler you should respect, a loving Savior you can follow, or a powerful Spirit who can guide you from within. Keep getting to know our one God as a complete Trinity, though. There is far, far more for you to learn as you realize how far, far greater He is when He is in full motion in your life!

THERE IS HOPE

God invites you into a complete relationship with Him as your complete God.

When have you thought you knew something or someone well, only to be surprised by new knowledge? Maybe it was a movie sequel's storyline or a friend's hidden talent.

- ***IF*** you never got to know the thing you learned that surprised you, what would be different in how you see that thing or person today?
- ***WHAT IF*** we did something else to know God better as a family today?

3: One-In-Three

***IF** you had an extra eye, where would you want it and what would you use it for?*

***WHAT IF** everyone had an extra eye?*

READ IT: JOHN 1:1–4

Do you have a favorite kind of pie? One popular choice is cherry, especially when it's hot and gooey. Something interesting happens when you cut into a hot cherry pie in the pan, though—every time you pull the knife out between two pieces, the insides of the pie ooze out and cover the gap between those sections. So even if you cut a hot cherry pie into three equal pieces, while it was sitting in the pan it would ooze together and still be like one complete pie. Three-in-one, yet one-in-three. *Wild, huh?*

John 1:1–4 shows how Jesus ("the Word" of God) had a specific role in creation, but He also "was God." Nothing happened "apart" from Him— He has always existed and always been connected to everything the Bible speaks of when it refers to "God." You see, God didn't create the world because He was alone or bored; He created it of the joy of the Father, Son, and Spirit being filled, complete, and connected as "one."

So is a hot cherry pie the best way to understand the Trinity? Actually, no. Like any illustration, it falls short. God isn't made up of "parts" but is three "Persons": the Father makes the plans for the world, the Son carries out the plans, and the Spirit testifies to the plans. If you still have pie on the brain, consider how a pie has taste, temperature, and color. Each of those things tells us something different about the pie, but they are each true of the whole pie—and they are never separate from each other.

Personalize all of this. If there's more to God than the piece of Him you're reaching for, what would happen if you invited *every* aspect of who He is into *every* area of your life? Let that ooze around . . . and fill in some gaps.

THERE IS HOPE

God doesn't just reveal Himself as a Trinity. He saves us as a Trinity.

When have you accomplished something as a family where each person had a specific role in getting it done?

- **IF** one person had been missing from what your family did, what would have happened?
- **WHAT IF** you each traded roles in what you did? What would have been different?

4: Father

***IF** you could film a big budget movie, what type of movie would it be and what would the story be about?*

***WHAT IF** you could choose three famous movie stars or characters to star in your movie?*

READ IT: ISAIAH 64:8

Ever run into the same person you don't know over and over again? Weird, right? If your life was a movie, you might think God was running short on cast members or was like a Hollywood director who puts his favorite family members into the shot. It actually doesn't work that way, but as creators ourselves we may assume it does.

Think about a story you wrote, told, or made a video of. As the creator, you dreamed up your characters and what happened to them. Maybe they seemed to take on a life of their own, even though in reality you controlled them all.

Sometimes people wonder if this is what our relationship with God is like. He *is* our author and creator, yet He gives us something that characters in made-up stories don't get—the ability to make choices. And God works through those choices to accomplish His will. It's just tricky to identify how much freewill He has or hasn't given us. Some people think we do whatever we want while He watches from a distance, while others believe that we can't sneeze unless God makes it happen. It's easy to settle for extreme ideas like these if we think God is more random than personal.

This is the role of the Father in the Trinity, for He is "sovereign"—the supreme power and authority over everything. He isn't a distant creator, but is personally involved in our lives. He knows the larger story and can direct us toward a better ending if we trust Him.

Bottom line? God creates and sustains everything that has existed, does exist, or ever will exist. If we had His creative power, we might do things differently. If we had His creative wisdom, though, we wouldn't change a thing.

THERE IS HOPE

We may not understand every detail about how God works, but we can connect with Him through every detail of our lives.

Think about a time when someone took control of something when others were making bad choices, like a police officer showing up in a scary situation.

- ***IF*** that person didn't use his or her authority, how might things have turned out?
- ***WHAT IF*** everyone always had to do everything you said without question?

5: Son

***IF** you had a chance to live another person's life for a day, what person would you pick?*

***WHAT IF** it meant that on that same day that person would live your life?*

READ IT: 1 JOHN 5:20

Think about your favorite restaurant, store, or vacation spot. Consider your favorite books, games, snacks, songs, movies, or sports. Have you thought about how they came to exist before you discovered them? Even if you could see the first day of something being made, you still wouldn't know where the idea for that thing or its materials began. Everything you *can* see reveals things you *can't* see through what you do see . . . you see?

Getting to know Jesus is like this because we can "see" many things about Him that tell us about what we can't see. For example, our calendars reflect how He was physically born to a young woman named Mary twenty centuries ago on earth, but He was around centuries before she was (or even the earth was). Christ has always existed and will continue to exist. When He walked around 100 percent human, He was at the same time 100 percent God. It's why in one Bible verse Jesus is referred to as the son of man and in another verse he is referred to as the Son of God.

This is more than a big thought we're to marvel at from a distance, though. Jesus personally stepped out of the comforts of hanging out with the Trinity to live among sinful people who betrayed and crucified Him. Being God, He knew this would happen, yet He did it anyway so that you could be transformed.

Get to know this larger story of the Son, and let it shape you. Not only can it impact how you know His love, but it'll change how you love others. Perhaps everything they can see in you will reveal things about Jesus that they couldn't otherwise see. See?

THERE IS HOPE

By leaving the breathtaking glory of heaven, Jesus made it possible for you to one day enter it.

Discuss some of your favorite things and what their backstories might be.

- ***IF*** you could go back in time to watch the inventor behind one of your favorite things come up with the idea, whom would you visit?
- ***WHAT IF*** you could be friends with that person? Do you think it would affect how you view your favorite thing?

6: Spirit

***IF** an expert could help you in any area of life, what would you ask for help with?*

***WHAT IF** you could become an expert at something and help others?*

READ IT: GENESIS 1:2; JOHN 14:16–17

How do you feel about watching a train go by? Sure, it can be a-m-a-z-i-n-g-l-y s-l-o-w, but some families enjoy seeing all the passing sections and make a game out of counting each car. The fun is in guessing how short or long the train is without knowing its true length. What you may expect to be a short wait can turn into a really long one, or maybe the other way around.

It's why you might sometimes see drivers who don't want to wait for the train to pass turn around to try to avoid what they can't see. This totally backfires when they drive off and it's revealed that the train was shorter than they thought, or if they head down a different street and discover that the train still blocks them even there.

But what if someone who was above the train and saw it all at once was willing to give us guidance on what to do? He might be in a helicopter and radio us, telling us to wait or turn around. He also might simply say, "Use this moment to just be still. There's actually something important happening in the space you're in right now."

The Holy Spirit plays this role in our lives. He is as much God as the Father and as the Son, which means He has a unique big-picture perspective to share with us. We may only see things "car by car" as life passes before us, but He sees the whole train all at once. Instead of radioing in from afar, He will personally come live inside of us!

Like anything, it's best to understand Him through reading the Bible and being a part of a church family. In this way you can track how He's at work in each other's lives in all the passing sections of life.

THERE IS HOPE

You are not alone. The Holy Spirit is with you everywhere you go (and everywhere you stop).

Talk about how God might have been a part of you turning something negative into a win.

- ***IF*** you had been more aware of God's presence in that moment, what else might have been different in you or how you viewed the situation?
- ***WHAT IF*** the Holy Spirit wants to speak through you into someone else who is going through something tough these days?

7: Weekly Recap

***IF** you ran a business, how would you manage everything?*

***WHAT IF** you could hire two other people to help you?*

Oh, the depth of the riches both of the wisdom and of the knowledge of God! How unsearchable his judgments and untraceable his ways! (Romans 11:33)

CATCH UP

- Who or what made you laugh recently?
- How did life feel easy or hard this past week?

RECAP

- What stood out to you from what we've read together, talked about, or attempted to do together over the past week?
- What thoughts or questions do you have from today's Bible verse?

GROW TOGETHER

- What might be the main thing God is trying to tell your family today?
- What if we did something new together or built a good habit of living out what we're learning? What might that be?

OPEN UP

- In what ways are you struggling in life or experiencing something hard?
- If we were to confess something to God as a family, what might that be?

PRAY

- Who is Jesus to you today?
- Who would like to close out our time with a simple prayer?

8: Timeless Identity

***IF** you were a superhero, how would you feel if other people gave you a superhero name you didn't choose?*

***WHAT IF** people knew your correct superhero name but would never recognize you as that superhero?*

READ IT: EXODUS 3:14

What would it be like for a stranger who's never seen you to describe details about your hair? What if that person told others those details as if they were facts? You could work to correct those rumors by personally showing others who you really are, truthfully describing yourself to the world, or letting someone who had met you describe you.

God wants us to know who He is, but that's a big hurdle since God is beyond our complete understanding. He constantly reveals His goodness, but He can't appear completely before us right now. It's why some people guess at who He is and then assume they're right.

In response, God made all the important things about Him super clear so we can clearly know Him. He reveals He's the "I AM," as if to say, "Don't stress about who you thought I was in the past or might be in the future, but get to know Me right now for who I am."

That's why we're taking the time to study God's identity. Every truth you discover about Him is like finding two pieces of a puzzle that genuinely fit together and also give you a larger understanding of the whole puzzle (which helps you more accurately start looking for your next piece).

Just remember that not being able to completely understand the full picture of who God is doesn't mean we can't truthfully know Him. Even in heaven God will be beyond our full understanding (because He'll still be God and we won't), but at least then we'll see Him face-to-face (Revelation 22:3–4). The more you personally learn about God, the more you realize there's so much more of Him to personally know! Let that wrinkle your brain just thinking about it!

THERE IS HOPE

All the opinions in the whole world about who God is won't change who He is, but one truth about who God is can change the whole world.

Name at least one thing about God that is different than humans.

- ***IF*** you could erase a lie people believe about God, what would it be?
- ***WHAT IF*** everyone you knew read the Bible every day? What is one thing they might realize about God?

9: Timeless Superiority

***IF** you could be a complete expert on three things right now, what would you choose?*

***WHAT IF** you would forget all of this in a week?*

READ IT: JOB 36:26; 38:4

There are so many things you can totally enjoy in life without totally understanding them. Like how you can order a delicious meal and fully enjoy it without knowing the restaurant's secret recipe for it. Or how you can play an instrument for years without ever mastering it, yet still enjoy making music. So many things you're regularly close to remain some kind of mystery that you can wholeheartedly live with.

Ever notice how we treat others who do things better than we do, though? We might comfortably sit on our couch while yelling at a professional athlete on TV for dropping a ball. We're tempted to laugh when a musician plays an off-key note or a professional racecar driver spirals off the track. Instead of appreciating how skilled or knowledgeable someone is, we look for and poke at their gaps.

Put all of that together, and it's no surprise why we aren't always sure what to do with the perfect superiority of God. We could spend most of our lives trying to get by or pass the next test to look slightly better than others around us, but we're nowhere close to being God's equal. We can't see what He is capable of seeing or do what He's capable of doing.

Here's what's amazing, though—God "superiority" over us doesn't prompt Him to insults but to an *invitation*. His version of love, truth, justice, and forgiveness is better than ours, and yet so many people would rather create their own flawed version than embrace His. For reasons we'll never figure out, God is longing to come closer and closer to us each day. They only way you can realize the heights you're truly capable of with Him is by wholeheartedly embracing the mystery of His superiority over your life.

THERE IS HOPE

All that you know of God isn't all of who God is. What He reveals to you in each moment is what you need in that moment.

What things do you enjoy together without completely understanding all that's involved?

- ***IF*** you knew everything about everything and there would be nothing new to discover, what would that do to your enjoyment of things?
- ***WHAT IF*** you were able to learn just one more bit of information about God? What would you want to know and why?

10: Timeless Wholeness

***IF** you always tasted every individual ingredient in a recipe instead of tasting it all mixed together, do you think you'd still like the food?*

***WHAT IF** it took you as long to eat food as it did to make it?*

READ IT: MATTHEW 28:18–20

If there's one food that should come with a cape because of how often it saves the day for busy families, it's pizza! You can chow down on it anytime and anywhere, whether you're at an all-you-can-eat pizza buffet or snacking on a single piece late at night. It's also one of the only foods you can toss random vegetables (and sometimes fruit) on top of, although most of us might prefer bacon or extra cheese. You could even eat pizza cold right out of the fridge!

One thing that can make a pizza awesome is the crust. This baked dough represents flour, salt, and yeast blended together with warm water. It'd be a little surprising to order a pizza and get a box full of sauce and cheese on top of those individual ingredients. Those ingredients are great to have separately to use to make other things, but when you are wanting pizza, you want all those ingredients blended together to make something you and others can enjoy eating.

Think about these ingredients. What does pizza sauce have that the crust does not have? What do pepperonis have that mozzarella cheese does not? Each adds things the others do not. Together they make a delicious combination. But God is not like that. The Son does not add anything the Father and Spirit are lacking. Each person of the Trinity is identical except for their roles. So instead of pizza math (1/3 + 1/3 + 1/3 = 1) it's God math. 1+1+1=1.

Just as the Lord timelessly comes together to represent Himself to us, we come together in this time to represent Him to the world. And just like an extra-large pizza, there is so much of God to go around; after chowing down on His Word, you end up full but with leftovers to spare.

THERE IS HOPE

"Father" is more than a title. "Jesus" is more than a remedy. "Spirit" is more than a mystery. God is a Person offering a relationship.

Try to remember one of your favorite meals and what ingredients you think went into it.

- ***IF*** the person who cooked that meal had just served you each of the individual ingredients on a plate, what would you have done?
- ***WHAT IF*** every restaurant in the world gave you ingredients for the meals they listed but required you to cook it yourself in their kitchen?

11: Timeless Wisdom

***IF** you could always see what would happen in five seconds, how would you live differently?*

***WHAT IF** you could also see what would happen in twenty-four hours, but only for a minute at noon every day?*

READ IT: 1 CORINTHIANS 2:7

Before video games, there was pinball! These loud, physical arcade-style games let you use "flippers" to bounce a metal ball around an angled play area while aiming for "bumpers" or other targets found high or low in the game. If you bounce the ball carelessly (or do nothing at all), it's doomed to naturally fall down and out of play. You can also "tilt" the game and lose your round if you're a wild player who shakes the machine too much. However you play, it eventually ends with you either feeling victorious or defeated based on how you used your time.

The thing about pinball is that every machine is unique in having hidden traps or opportunities to score that you won't see at first glance. You either have to learn these details the hard way by wasting a lot of money and time up front, or by turning to a more experienced player for tips. You could also learn information written down from the creator of the game that reveals what to do to achieve a victory.

Your life is like a pinball machine in that you can just end up carelessly bouncing around in a world angled against you. Thankfully, God gives you insider information through His Bible and other growing Christians who can help you make your round in this world count. Even certain things that He spoke to a certain group of people offer a big-picture nugget of wisdom that's true for all people in all times in all places. If you trust Him and what He's telling you, even situations that feel like "bumpers" set against you will help launch you into a real victory.

THERE IS HOPE

God sees you bouncing around. He's able and willing to flip what you think is a lost ball back into play before things go down the drain.

What would it mean to trust God's wisdom as a family in a particular area of life?

- ***IF*** God were to tell us that we're doing something right together as a family, what do you think He'd compliment us on?
- ***WHAT IF*** we followed God's wisdom together on something new over the next two days? What could be different about how we'd live or treat each other because of it?

12: Timeless Grace

***IF** you had a watch that beeped an hour before someone was going to hurt you in any way, how would you use it?*

***WHAT IF** this watch also showed you in detail what was about to happen?*

READ IT: 2 TIMOTHY 1:9

You've been there, right? You order some fast food based on how it looks in a picture. What you actually get looks like a garbage truck drove over it. So do you eat it as is or go up to the counter and demand something better?

It's like how in life we feel a unique joy when something turns out as we hoped or experience a special kind of sadness when things don't end up as planned. That's why the term *Plan B* exists and refers to finding a different way to achieve all or part of the original Plan A. It's usually a response to trying to keep things going forward.

If you understand that, then be amazed at how today's verse reveals that Jesus' role in saving us *wasn't* a back-up plan that kicked in after people sinned. God didn't create human beings and suddenly say, "Oops, I didn't see that decision coming. I guess I better come up with something now to fix this." Instead, He knew ahead of time all the horrible things people would end up doing and yet decided in advance that we were still worth His love and saving.

Try to recognize how special this is and how special we are to God. If you knew someone was going to physically attack you tomorrow, you'd likely avoid that person today (or at the very least have police with you tomorrow to throw that person in jail). But God is so epic with grace that He not only comes closer to us when we attack Him with our sin but He also takes our place in jail. As Lord, He gives us choices; and as Lord, He also will work within our choices. It's why Jesus coming to earth to die for our sins wasn't "Plan B," but always was, is, and shall be "Plan A."

THERE IS HOPE

Need help loving enemies? Praying for bullies? Forgiving traitors? Even if they haven't yet changed? Jesus does it, and He will help you do it.

Think about different ways your family prepares ahead for things, like stashing napkins in the car for whenever you need one or packing snacks when you travel.

- ***IF*** you had to pick one example of when it felt really good to be prepared in advance for the worst, what would that be?
- ***WHAT IF*** you specifically thanked God for all the ways He's prepared you so far for the hard things you face in life?

13: Timeless Life

***IF** you were invited to a big party by someone famous you didn't know, what would you do?*

***WHAT IF** that person wasn't famous and the party wasn't big?*

READ IT: TITUS 1:2

Once upon a time, there was an orphanage full of kids who never had parents to take care of them. No child knew what would happen to them as they grew up, because the government was only allowed to provide for them up to a certain age. Most of the children sadly assumed that they'd end up homeless adults who wandered the streets in search of their next meal.

All of that changed when a kind, rich man made arrangements with the government for all the kids to come live with him. He had a big mansion with plenty of room, along with miles and miles of land to expand his home if other children also wanted to join the family. The man's only requirement was that each child would have to make a personal choice of their own to either stay in the orphanage or come be a part of his family. Any kids who chose to become his child would gain all the privileges of his home, food, clothing, protection, comforts, and inheritance. They simply needed to make that decision and trust that he would one day come and bring them home.

This story reflects some very real arrangements God's made for us to become a part of His family. He knew before time existed that we would all be orphans and need to be saved, so He made all the arrangements for us to be with Him and all He offers. We can trust that one day He will take us to our heavenly home—a realm where we can experience the joy of knowing and enjoying God personally forever.

THERE IS HOPE

God can make His home anywhere in the universes, but He is most at home in your heart. Face it—He's crazy about you.

Talk about how being a part of our family fills our lives with unique blessings.

- **IF** someone were to ask you what's great about being a part of our family, what would you say?
- **WHAT IF** we were to somehow take care of others who are either orphaned or overlooked in the world?

14: Weekly Recap

***IF** there were just one country and one president in the whole world, how would the world be different?*

***WHAT IF** there were only three countries and three presidents?*

Be careful that no one takes you captive through philosophy and empty deceit based on human tradition, based on the elements of the world, rather than Christ. For the entire fullness of God's nature dwells bodily in Christ, and you have been filled by him, who is the head over every ruler and authority. (Colossians 2:8–10)

CATCH UP

- Who or what made you laugh recently?
- How did life feel easy or hard this past week?

RECAP

- What stood out to you from what we've read together, talked about or attempted to do together over the past week?
- What thoughts or questions do you have from today's Bible verse?

GROW TOGETHER

- What might be the main thing God is trying to tell your family today?
- What if we did something new together or returned to a good habit to live out what we're learning? What might that be?

OPEN UP

- In what ways are you struggling in life or experiencing something hard?
- If we were to confess something to God as a family, what might that be?

PRAY

- Who is Jesus to you today?
- Who would be willing to close out our time with a simple prayer?

HERITAGE

There are a few *H* words that we might think of when it comes to creation. One might be *humanity*, since God made people in His image. Then again, the Lord made a whole bunch of other things before we were created. In the pages that follow, we'll discover more about how all of that is connected.

So perhaps another *H* word could be *history*. It reflects how we like to record and understand the passing of time from our perspective. Notice, though, that *history* could also be pronounced as "His Story." Life doesn't revolve around us; it revolves around God. His perspective is the one that matters most.

That's why the word *heritage* may be a better word to describe why God made us. It's a family-sounding term that describes the values, blessings, and opportunities passed down from someone older to someone younger. Maybe you've felt this when a grandparent explained the sacrifices that were made years before you were born so the life you're now living could even be a possibility. When life isn't perfect, heritage reminds us of the greater gifts and identity given to us to claim from someone who loves us. Before things became backward, they were actually forward.

God began everything and everyone in a good starting place so He could pass down His blessings to us.

15: Preparing the Nursery

***IF** you could create a planet that only you could visit, what would it be like?*

***WHAT IF** you were creating a planet for other people?*

READ IT: GENESIS 1:1

You're pretty special, and someone in your life went to great lengths so you'd know it. Perhaps your parents sang to you when you were a baby inside your mom, or maybe you're adopted and everyone got excited when they learned you'd join the family. Long before you showed your face, someone prepared to meet you!

Granted, not everyone grows up this way. Some people are born into hard homes where they feel overlooked. Even then God can send people to love them on His behalf.

Still, dream for a moment about a family who is excited to greet their new little one. Picture a giddy mom and dad shopping for furniture, like a crib that they'll incorrectly try to assemble multiple times. Imagine them looking at multiple shades of paint colors so they can find the right hue to go up on the walls. They'll spend days upon days tearing down old wallpaper and putting in new carpet. Maybe they'll even "celebrate" by purchasing an outfit they hope to one day put on their little one (not to mention buying diapers in large quantities months in advance). All of this effort is joy filled because of the love they already have for their child.

You are that important to God, and so much more! Creation is our "nursery" that God joyfully prepared for us long before we showed our faces. Picture Him smiling as He thinks about you while making the world. Imagine Him purposefully placing every star in the sky just so you know that as high as the heavens are above the earth so great is His love toward you! That's part of your heritage from Him.

THERE IS HOPE

Take a look around and notice what God has painted, moved, changed, assembled, and hung up just for you to see today!

What are the earliest memories you have of any rooms or toys you grew up with?

- ***IF*** someone prepared a room for you today, what would it look like?
- ***WHAT IF*** someone asked you to change your room to make space for a new baby?

16: Playing in the Sand

***IF** you could design your own beach, what would it be like?*

***WHAT IF** your beach could have a different layout for each day of the week?*

READ IT: GENESIS 1:2

Ever notice how quickly kids on a beach start playing with the sand? It's like that big, formless mass begs us to do something with it, to dig a hole to fill with water or collect sand into a bucket (that we later dump onto someone else). Even grown-ups get into fancy sandcastle competitions. What seems like a land of nothing triggers all kinds of intelligent design in us.

Remember this as you read Genesis 1:2. The previous verse revealed God created the earth, but here we learn that somehow it was formless and empty. Some of the smartest people in history have tried to understand what this means, but maybe it's as simple as being on a beach and enjoying being creative with what's before you.

Still, this whole "formless" planet thing can be pretty hard to understand. We've grown up knowing the earth is like a 3-D circle, but it took us centuries to realize that the earth had this shape (despite the fact that God revealed it centuries earlier through one of His prophets in Isaiah 40:22). So what do we do with a "formless" earth?

Think about the beach. What if God initially made the earth "formless" simply to enjoy standing before the raw materials of what He was about to shape? It could be why He personally hovered over depths of water that were held in place through His will. Instead of being elsewhere and disconnected from it, He was hands-on.

Maybe that's why some of our favorite activities, toys, and video games are ones that let us create. Every time we try to shape something from what it is to what we sense it could be we reflect a heritage God passed down to us. Just imagine what He's about to create in a seemingly "formless" area of your life!

THERE IS HOPE

Not only can God create something out of nothing, but He can create "something better" out of something. Invite Him to form that in you.

Share some of your favorite memories building, cooking, or baking something.

- ***IF*** you could've had a special tool to help you, what would it have been?
- ***WHAT IF*** reading these devotions together as a family is a way God is giving form to what otherwise might be something formless in our lives?

17: Turning the Light On

***IF** you could discover a new kind of animal, mineral, or food, which would you choose?*

***WHAT IF** no one could ever know that you discovered it?*

READ IT: GENESIS 1:3–5

Your favorite treat may have an interesting backstory. Some people think brownies were created when a baker accidentally made a cake the wrong way. Others believe popsicles were invented when a boy left a glass of soda with a stirring stick in it out on a cold night. No one actually knows the full backstory of either treat, but that doesn't stop us from eating them.

Today's passage shares how God created light before He created the sun. We might wonder how that's possible because we're only familiar with how the natural world requires something to give off light we can see, like the sun or a light bulb. But there are light waves our eyes can't see (reminding us that there's always more to something than what we understand of it). This verse further reveals that sometimes light is as much supernatural as natural. Revelation 22:5 mentions this, saying that we won't need a sun or moon in heaven because God Himself will be the light.

If you're wondering how something is possible, remember we're talking about God here! He wanted this truth to be written down so we'd know who He is, what He's capable of, and the heritage He offers us. What happened during creation reflects His character as much as what He created. No one actually knows the full backstory of light, but that doesn't need to stop us from walking in the light.

Think about what this means for your personal life. If God can create light before creating the sun to reveal it, what has He created in your life that you have yet to understand or see? What incredible, shining character and purpose are you capable of if He is the source behind it?

THERE IS HOPE

You are entirely seen and known by God, even in your darkest moments, and He entirely loves you. If you even barely see that, you see Him.

What's an idea God has for our family that hasn't been fully revealed or realized yet?

- **IF** God told you to do one thing tonight, what do you think it would be?
- **WHAT IF** you decided to ask this question every day? What would happen?

18: The Art of Making Science

***IF** you could make words or drawings appear on paper simply by imagining them, would you use it more for fun or as your job?*

***WHAT IF** whenever you looked at a blank piece of paper you could see in advance what someone would write on it?*

READ IT: GENESIS 1:6–10

When an artist begins to paint, he first dips his brush into a small pool of water before dipping it into vibrant colors. All someone observing might see is liquid on a brush, but the artist knows the incredible thing about to happen. With every intentional swipe of his hand, new things are revealed that others can observe and respond to in the moment while still spending a lifetime trying to fully take it all in.

When the world first began, an earth-size pool of water was all that was seen from the surface. As God began intentionally separating this liquid into sections, sky and land formed. People would eventually observe and have emotional responses to these creations while still spending a lifetime trying to fully take them all in. This led to clouds that would move above us and wind that would gently blow fresh air upon our faces. Elements invisible to the human eye but necessary to our lives were formed, like the atmosphere of gases that surround and protect the earth so we aren't burnt up by the sun.

All of this art came together from our Creator God who knew in advance how incredible every aspect of His creation could become. He put such intelligence into it that we've tried to match it with our best intelligence called "science"—one way of understanding how an aspect of life works. Just as a work of art tells you something about an artist or about yourself without telling you everything, science likewise tells you something about God and creation without telling you everything. Nothing natural originally came into existence without His supernatural presence first being behind it. That's why we're alive and breathing air today, which all started centuries and centuries ago through our God who loves us.

THERE IS HOPE

You're always in God's hands and always a masterpiece in the making. He's the painter and knows what the final painting will be. Trust Him.

Talk about who in our family sees life more artistically versus scientifically.

- ***IF*** God let you ask Him about the way He did something or the meaning behind why He did it, which would you rather learn more about?
- ***WHAT IF*** you could help others somehow see both perspectives?

19: Fruit That Makes Fruit

***IF** you could make words or drawings appear on paper simply by imagining them, would you use it more for fun or as your job?*

***WHAT IF** the tree also grew twenty unique fruit every day, and each day the kind of fruit growing on it would change?*

READ IT: GENESIS 1:11–12

God has a great habit of providing what we need way before we'd ever know we'd need it. Before humans were created, He provided fruit that we'd all eventually eat (and all eventually turn into smoothies). He also made grass and flowers before creating the various wildlife that would munch on it. The Lord wanted these plants and fields to stay around a long time, so He gave them seeds that could be planted to make more. Every time you eat fruits and vegetables or toss them into a salad, you're being blessed by this heritage.

Also pay attention to how all of these original fruit, vegetables, and vegetation were made with some age and maturity built into them. They weren't created as seeds, but as full-grown plants that looked like they'd been around a while. Just as God would make the first humans into adults versus infants, He first made the earth and the things upon it in their mature state and gave them the ability to reproduce. They would have appeared old or grown-up to us even on the day they were made. Maybe all those theories about how old or young our planet is really need to take this into account.

The real takeaway here is that God made living things with the ability to create so that life would continue to spread. That applies to what He's doing in us too. Sometimes people will be generally inspired by how we draw, make music, play a sport, fix things, take pictures, or write stories. Other times they'll feel God plant deeper seeds into them out of the "fruit" of our lives. It's His great habit of providing what others need way before they'd ever know they need it.

THERE IS HOPE

Creation doesn't just reveal God's story in the past. Creation furthers God's story into the future.

See if you can guess what each other's favorite fruits are.

- ***IF*** you could create a new kind of fruit, what would it be like and where would it grow?
- ***WHAT IF*** it were possible to merge two of your favorite fruits together permanently? Which fruits would you pick?

20: Look! Up in the Sky!

***IF** every day had an extra hour in it, how would your day be different?*

***WHAT IF** every day had an extra seven hours in it?*

READ IT: GENESIS 1:14–18

You probably have no problem remembering when your birthday is. The same is likely true of how much you look forward to Christmas every December 25. We track special events like these with a calendar so we know when they'll happen, but having a calendar is only possible because God created the sun and the moon. Without these two objects in the sky, we wouldn't know how to count days, weeks, months, or years with any sort of accuracy.

The sun and the moon obviously also provide a form of light for us to see by. The sun directly shines upon us during the day, while the moon indirectly reflects a small percentage of the sun's light to us at night. The stars add to this by giving us something brilliant to look at and wonder about. In fact, long before humans could send satellites with powerful cameras into space to capture the wonders of it all, people generally believed that all stars were alike. God clarified the actual truth about it through one of His spokesmen who said, "One star differs from another star in splendor" (1 Corinthians 15:41).

None of these things were made for us to worship or as the exclusive means to try to figure out all the secrets of the universe (even though some people have tried), but so that through them we'd become aware of God and His care for us. He put everything in exactly the right spot so that we'd have the temperatures and climate needed to sustain life. It's the heritage Romans 1:20 talks about; how His "eternal power and divine nature" are on display through what He made. Think about that the next time you write a date down on the calendar. More specifically, think about Him!

THERE IS HOPE

God is always bigger than the moment you feel stuck in, but He is always in that moment with you. He always is, always was, and always will be.

What are some of your favorite days of the year?

- ***IF*** you weren't able to track when any of those days happened, how would it change your plans or feelings about celebrating them?
- ***WHAT IF*** we had to do all of life in the dark? How would that affect those things you look forward to most?

21: Weekly Recap

***IF** you could rename an animal species, what would you rename it?*

***WHAT IF** you could rename an ocean?*

When I observe your heavens, the work of your fingers, the moon and the stars, which you set in place, what is a human being that you remember him, the son of man that you look after him? (Psalm 8:3–4)

CATCH UP

- Who or what made you laugh recently?
- How did you life feel easy or hard this past week?

RECAP

- What stood out to you from what we've read together, talked about, or attempted to do together over the past week?
- What thoughts or questions do you have from today's Bible verse?

GROW TOGETHER

- What might be the main thing God is trying to tell your family today?
- What if we did something new together or returned to a good habit to live out what we're learning? What might that be?

OPEN UP

- In what ways are you struggling in life or experiencing something hard?
- If we were to confess something to God as a family, what might that be?

PRAY

- Who is Jesus to you today?
- Who would be willing to close out our time with a simple prayer?

22: Swimming and Soaring

***IF** you could create your own island with any unique natural features, what would it be like?*

***WHAT IF** the wildlife on your island could include mythical creatures?*

READ IT: GENESIS 1:20–21

If you've ever owned an aquarium or a bird-cage, you know that there's typically a short period of time when it's in your possession but it's empty. This is usually after you buy it at a store or transport it home after someone gave it to you. It'd be a little odd and quirky to keep the aquarium or birdcage empty for a long time, though. People who came into your home would wonder why you have this particular space set aside for a fish or a bird but you haven't yet put anything into it. (You could mess with them and say, "What? Don't you see Bubba in there?")

For a moment in creation, the world God created was empty of any creatures. He then began making all "kinds" of breathing things on the fifth day of creation. Some of these creatures would live underwater, while others would fly in the air. Just imagine how much imagination and fun the Lord had in speaking each one into existence with a heritage to swim or to soar!

The larger lesson from all of this is yet again God reveals He doesn't create things to be empty or without a purpose. Just as He originally gave form to a "formless" world, He wanted to make sure that same planet didn't sit around without life in it. Pay attention to this value, because the Lord doesn't want you or your family to have certain spaces that you don't invite Him into. He has all "kinds" of life to speak into existence in each of you and is ready to speak the next one into existence right now. What would it look like to invite Him into an area you've kept caged off from Him?

THERE IS HOPE

Some people say, "Just be who you are today." God will help you become who you were created to be. The choice is yours. The power is His.

Dream together about what you sense God wants to do next in our family.

- ***IF*** we knew God's ultimate dream for our family, do you think we'd be encouraged to grow into it or be discouraged because we aren't there yet?
- ***WHAT IF*** God is just as joyful about filling up the empty spots in your life today as He was in making the world?

HERITAGE

23: The First Blessing

IF *you could breathe underwater and withstand any depth of water pressure, what would you do?*

WHAT IF *you could become any type of bird whenever you wanted to?*

READ IT: GENESIS 1:21–22

Life was pretty good for fish and birds during the original days of creation. No people were around trying to lure anything swimming out of the water with hooks attached to rubber worms or shoot anything soaring down with bullets jetting out of rifles. God likewise didn't just create one bird or fish and clone it billions of times. Instead, He gave these creatures the heritage of reproducing and multiplying in great number. It's the first record of Him speaking a specific blessing upon anything He'd created.

Maybe that's why centuries later we've been able to study and categorize around twenty-eight thousand unique species of fish and ten thousand unique species of birds. God gave each creature unique traits and skills to survive and thrive, like how some fish talk by making sounds while others communicate by moving their bodies a certain way as they swim. Birds also converse with each other by making unique noises (and not always with their voices). You'll obviously find a variety of examples in your local aquarium or zoo. If you slow down long enough to take it all in, you can be inspired at the sheer creativity behind all the variety.

This is what happens when God blesses something. Whatever He gets behind goes forward (and keeps multiplying). The Lord knew in that moment of creation that this would be true of fish and birds, and so He concluded that all was good. He could've decided to stop creating here, but thankfully He didn't. He may have spoken the first out-loud blessing, but it wouldn't be His last one. Just imagine the blessing He is capable of speaking and multiplying into you!

THERE IS HOPE

When God declares something good or blessed, get ready to see a whole lot more because He's only getting started.

Recall all the different types of fish and birds you've seen as a family over the years.

- ***IF*** you could have any one of those creatures as a pet in your house or backyard, which one would you pick?
- ***WHAT IF*** all of the varieties of fish and birds in the world are God's way of specifically telling our family something? What might that message be to us?

HERITAGE

24: How About More Animals?

***IF** you were a moose for a day during hunting season, what would you do?*

***WHAT IF** you were a moose for an entire hunting season?*

READ IT: GENESIS 1:24

For some reason people tend to think of God creating things with a real serious look on His face as He speaks in a loud booming voice. What if He actually had a blast getting creative? If so, imagine what God might have said while making some of the various animals that roam or creep along the land:

> *"I'm thinking this breed of dog will look like a small nervous sausage."*
>
> *"I like the flippers and beak on this creature. It just needs a cool waddle. Oooh! I'll also make it black and white so it looks like a walking tuxedo!"*
>
> *"This one will need a long neck. I like that! In fact, I'm going to make something else that crawls that will just be like a long neck. This is so much fun!"*

However God made these land creatures, He obviously had no problem coming up with something new each time. They all maintained some type of connection to all the other animals too. Many would share a similar frame or skeletal structure. Others would live in the same place and share the same resources.

We have our own unique connection to animals who live on land too. Unlike fish or birds, land animals live alongside of us. We are not the same as them, but we do share the same creative Creator. If He was more than excited to invent them, imagine how giddy He was to come up with the idea of you!

THERE IS HOPE

Giraffes. Horses. Dogs. Antelopes. Elephants. Tigers. Squirrels. God thought up all of them and more to teach us something about Him.

Recall a time when you created something as a family, be it something you cooked up or built.

- ***IF*** someone was watching you do this and described the look on your face, what do you think they would say?
- ***WHAT IF*** we had a little more fun creating things together?

25: Good Animals

***IF** you came across a deer that wasn't afraid of you and could talk, what would you do?*

***WHAT IF** the deer asked you to ride it?*

READ IT: GENESIS 1:25

You're either a cat person or a dog person. At least, that's what people commonly think. Maybe you could be both if you catch how their personalities are different. Dogs are playfully social and loyal friends who can't wait to lick you when you get home. Cats, on the other hand, seem to require an appointment before you play with them that they may or may not choose to keep.

Certain animals have a way of becoming special to us unlike many other relationships in our lives. It's why researchers have spent years trying to figure out why we talk with our pets. Even though animals can't specifically understand what we're saying, we seem to find them to be great listeners that we open up to. Some animals are actually called "therapy pets" because of the way they can calm us down when we're feeling rattled by life.

Is this part of what God meant when He looked at all the animals and knew that their existence was somehow "good"? Or was he talking about how in the early days of creation animals got along with each other? Isaiah 11:1–9 talks more about how one day in God's kingdom we'll return back to this, for "the wolf will dwell with the lamb, and the leopard will lie down with the goat" (v. 6). There are other instances in the Bible where animals are shown to be sensitive to spiritual things too (Numbers 22:21–33; Psalm 150:6).

What if that's something you can enjoy now, though? Maybe the friendly "tell-all" friendship we have with the animals is a way the Lord prepares us to talk with Him. You can talk to Him about anything, even when you're feeling rattled by life. He understands you in ways animals don't.

THERE IS HOPE

God enjoys animals and cares about their well-being. When we care for them, we reflect His heart.

Brainstorm what you think would make the perfect pet for your family, even if it means adding some creative features to it.

- ***IF*** we owned a pet that would make our lives better, what would that pet be like?
- ***WHAT IF*** we tried to make that pet's life better too? What would that mean for us? What would that mean for the pet?

26: Personal Space

***IF** one day your dream house magically appeared where your current home is, how would you celebrate?*

***WHAT IF** to live there you had to agree that you would have a dozen dinner guests every night?*

READ IT: GENESIS 2:8

Somewhere in your home there's a couch where the cushion dips from being regularly sat in. Or a well-used bean bag with a hole in it. Or a soft blanket everyone wants because of how it envelops whomever has it.

We all long for personal space that feels like it was made just for us. It could be a space in the garage to enjoy your favorite hobby, a comfortable chair outside where you can be quiet, a backyard park with a beautiful view, or a local café where you enjoy amazing bagels. Such a place can be hard to find, though. Maybe your garage doesn't have extra space, it's too noisy outside, your local park is dirty, or the café is regularly crowded.

What if someone wanted to create a personal space just for you, though? This is what God did for the first man and woman when He made the Garden of Eden for them to eventually live in. It wasn't a mansion or a palace but a special environment custom-made for those first people. Instead of massive paintings on the wall or golden thrones to sit on, they had colorful creatures all around and the natural beauty of the land. Rather than handing them a video-game system or a soccer goal, He created opportunities for them to take care of this new home to feel a sense of ownership.

If God did this for you, you'd have to choose to either embrace it or push back on what He made for you. Maybe things where you live today aren't the way you'd design them, but the Lord has in some way surrounded you with beauty and opportunities that are custom-made just for you. What if the personal space you're looking for is right before your eyes with the very people you're already with?

THERE IS HOPE

If you take the time to acknowledge how God is present in the space you're in, you'll better trust Him with wherever He is taking you next.

What are some of your favorite things about your home or neighborhood?

- ***IF*** you could take anything from where you live now with you if you were to one day move, what would it be?
- ***WHAT IF*** the place where we live isn't just for us but is meant to be shared somehow with others through our hospitality?

27: A Recap and a Response

***IF** you knew a history book was going to remember you for doing something, what would you want to be remembered for?*

***WHAT IF** everybody could tell your life story off the top of their head?*

READ IT: GENESIS 1:1

Your eyes aren't playing tricks on you. We're purposefully revisiting Genesis 1:1 one more time. We need to regularly do this with the Bible, especially when something might have a deeper meaning beyond when you first read it. Like how by now you've learned that the Bible may not answer every "what" or "why" question we wonder about, but it is absolutely clear that God is the "who" to focus on.

So what is the right response to all of that?

Consider a phrase you would hear among people who work in the White House: "I serve at the pleasure of the President." It's their way of saying that they will get behind and do things for the person in charge, even if that means changing their plans or giving up their job if asked. People who take part in this time-honored tradition understand that their personal "wants" aren't greater than the world's deeper "needs." They likewise recognize that how we regard our leaders, good or bad, sets an example others will follow, good or bad.

Such a commitment can be risky toward a flawed human who might do something reckless, but with God we don't have to hold back because He is good, great, and perfect. He may not endorse or affirm your best plans, but He will always be for your best interests (which is what you really want anyway).

This world isn't our world . . . it's God's world. Plenty of things were already happening long before the first humans took their first steps. All of creation was rightly serving at the pleasure of the Creator, and we need to let this recap speak to us. Will your response be to freely serve at the pleasure of your Creator, or will you (like so many others) demand that He serve at your pleasure?

THERE IS HOPE

Having beliefs about God doesn't mean you've responded to God. Discover the difference in Him and uncover the difference in you.

Recognize a time when as a family we returned to an important value, like regularly attending church or serving others in our neighborhood.

- ***IF*** our example then (or today) was to send a message to others, what might it be?
- ***WHAT IF*** we prayed a prayer right now to tell God that we will actually serve at His pleasure as a family?

28: Weekly Recap

IF *someone put you in charge of a news station for a day, what types of stories or headlines would you focus on?*

WHAT IF *all news stations closed down for a day? What would be different in the world if people weren't getting any messages?*

The counsel of the Lord stands forever, the plans of his heart from generation to generation. Happy is the nation whose God is Lord—the people He has chosen to be his own possession! (Psalm 33:11–12)

CATCH UP

- Who or what made you laugh recently?
- How did life feel easy or hard this past week?

RECAP

- What stood out to you from what we've read together, talked about, or attempted to do together over the past week?
- What thoughts or questions do you have from today's Bible verse?

GROW TOGETHER

- What might be the main thing God is trying to tell our family today?
- What if we did something new together or returned to a good habit to live out what we're learning? What might that be?

OPEN UP

- In what ways are you struggling in life or experiencing something hard?
- If we were to confess something to God as a family, what might that be?

PRAY

- What is Jesus to you today?
- Who would be willing to close out our time with a simple prayer?

29: A Complete Me

***IF** once a year you could say the phrase, "Bada Bing, Bada Boom!" and anything you wanted would appear in front of you, how would you use it?*

***WHAT IF** you could use this phrase once a month?*

READ IT: GENESIS 1:26

This is kind of strange to think about, but you don't have to look exactly like your family in order to look like you're a part of your family. Sometimes kids do get a particular physical trait from their parents, like a father's chin or a mother's ears. Family members can also reflect each other's image in personality too. Maybe someone has told you that your sense of humor, love of animals, or hunger for pickles reminds them of someone else you're related to. It's wild how you can represent multiple people even though you are still absolutely unique.

During the incredible moment that God created humanity, we again see that He did this as the Trinity, saying, "Let us make man in our image, according to our likeness" (Genesis 1:26). The Father, Son, and Spirit as one complete identity gave us a complete identity! He made it possible for us to reflect Him and His personality into the world, even though we'd each be doing this through our own unique personalities. We may not automatically feel this now because of how sin has messed with the way we understand ourselves, but thankfully God had a plan for that so we could through Jesus reclaim our original identity (Ephesians 1:4–5; 2 Timothy 1:9).

Being completely human means we come from a complete God who completely carried through on His complete idea to make us complete in Him. You don't have to try to "be real" (think about how silly that sounds). Instead, you can really embrace God really embracing you. He's given you a heritage of so many important things like reflecting His heart, creativity, intelligence, values, and more. When you don't feel like you look like Him at all, He's ready to show you how you're a part of His family.

THERE IS HOPE

God completely made you on purpose, with a complete purpose.

Recognize some of the ways your family members reflect each other in some way.

- ***IF*** there was at least one thing all of our family has in common, be it a physical trait or a similarity in personality, what would it be?
- ***WHAT IF*** we were to sum up in a statement what it means to be a part of our family? For example, "Being a part of the ______ family means . . ."

30: A Relational Me

***IF** you could bring a stuffed animal to life, which one would you bring to life?*

***WHAT IF** that stuffed animal had your exact same personality?*

READ IT: GENESIS 1:27

Who is the best person you know to go on roller coasters with? To get ice cream with? To watch goofy movies with?

Relationships matter. That's probably a no-brainer on some level, but there are some deeper benefits to having others around you. Doctors have studied how being social helps you sleep more deeply, deal with stress, have a stronger immune system, and better survive major illnesses. If you factor in all the great things friends and family offer us, like encouraging us in life or making us laugh until we fall over, being relational is a God-given blessing.

To go even further, being relational also means we're to *be* a blessing. God created a man and a woman in His image, but not every man or woman you encounter may realize this. Some of our friends or family may be stuck in a cycle of putting themselves down or trying to act a certain way for others to love them. Our world only makes things worse by bombarding us with confusing messages about our identity, from, "Don't let anyone tell you who you are," to "Buy these clothes and get this phone if you want people to like you."

Those thoughts are all lies, and we need each other's help to realize it. Being relational is more than just eating fast food together. God's given us the heritage of knowing Him and bringing Him into every connection we have so others can realize how they're also made in His image.

You may not get along with everyone you meet, but by praying and paying attention you can become aware of how the Lord is working in someone's life. Join Him in what He's doing to speak to them. After all, His version of treating people with respect isn't mere tolerance but real transformation.

THERE IS HOPE

Want to change the world? Start by letting the people closest to you know how glad you are that they're in your world.

Discuss what you each think it means to be originally made in the image of God.

- ***IF*** each of us as humans inherits the heritage originally made in the image of God before sin entered the world, what does it mean to develop a respectful attitude toward others?
- ***WHAT IF*** God is just as joyful about filling up the empty spots in your life today as He was in making the world?

31: A Purposeful Me

***IF** you could choose your first job from any of the places in town, where would you want to work?*

***WHAT IF** you were offered your dream job, but without pay?*

READ IT: GENESIS 1:28

Taking care of a rabbit. Running a restaurant. Tutoring younger kids. Being a stay-at-home parent. Driving grandkids to weekly sporting events. Looking out for your brother or sister. Cutting the grass. Getting groceries. Fixing the family car.

What do each one of these very different things have in common? They're all some type of work, whether or not you'd get paid for doing it. Each offers a sense of your larger purpose in some way. Many of them might actually be fun to do!

When God made the first humans, He gave them a job to do too. It was like He said to them, "You've been given a huge heritage from Me. Get to know Me. Get to know each other. Enjoy being a family, and take care of this world I made for you to live in."

The way the Lord worded all of this reminds us of the blessing He gave to the fish and birds. The difference was that we received an upgrade in that we would rule over those creatures and many others. God wants us to know that we are productive beings meant to help life continue.

He's created you with a purpose like this too. Some people think work is a curse, but it's actually a great gift we were given during creation before sin entered into the world so we could know the joy of contributing to life. It's kind of like when someone in your family has a big task or opportunity and the rest of the family enjoys pitching in on it. However this looks for you, be fruitful and multiply.

THERE IS HOPE

Today, faithfulness . . . so tomorrow, fruitfulness.

Specifically celebrate the role each of you play around your home.

- **IF** we each pitched in on each other's chores, what might that look like?
- **WHAT IF** we didn't just try to survive our week but actually chose to thrive instead? What would that look like and what would it require?

32: A Physical Me

***IF** you woke up to discover your legs were made of pretzel dough, what would you do?*

***WHAT IF** you could expand yourself by making your legs grow bigger at will?*

READ IT: GENESIS 1:29

"Don't play with your food." Someone likely told you that the moment you learned as a toddler how to flip your dinner upside down and onto your head. Who could blame you? There's something exciting about piling spaghetti in your hair. At least, when we are young we think there is.

As we get older we can still have a short-sighted relationship with food. Maybe we don't pile noodles on our head, but our culture offers us tasty things to eat that are bad for our bodies. Doesn't it seem odd that many people around the world can barely find anything to eat while others regularly visit buffets that prompt overeating and throwing food away? While some people get sick from too little food, others get sick from too much food.

That information isn't meant to make you feel guilty about your habits but to inspire you to invite God into this area of your life. You don't need to follow a fad diet to begin eating better. It could be as easy as pausing the next time you enter a grocery store and asking Jesus, "What do You think I should buy today?" Be careful not to assume He'd only have you buy tofu. Remember, God is the one who came up with the idea for food!

How fun it must have been for the first humans to discover and taste all the delicious fruit God provided them to eat. What if it could be that much fun for you as you realize God gave you the heritage of amazing things to eat to strengthen your body? When you begin to understand food is a gift to take care of and make sure the rest of the world has access to, you'll begin to see the Giver behind it caring for you.

THERE IS HOPE

God cares as much about your life on earth as He does in heaven. Food is a hands-on way He touches your life with grace that sustains you.

Take a look through your pantry or fridge to be honest about what's in there and why.

- ***IF*** you were to describe your relationship with food as a family with just a few words, what would they be?
- ***WHAT IF*** the next time you went grocery shopping, you and your parents really did pause and ask God to lead how you shopped for your family (and maybe for others)?

33: A Caretaking Me

***IF** buildings were alive, how would that change how you treated them?*

***WHAT IF** cars were alive too?*

READ IT: GENESIS 1:30

There's a special kind of concern we have for things that are alive. We probably don't think twice about the ground we're walking around on, but if we suddenly saw a frog hopping along in front of us it would catch our attention and we'd have to be careful not to step on it. You have to make similar decisions if you randomly come across some deer crossing the street in front of your car or if a bird is making a nest on your porch.

All of these creatures wonder what to do when they see us too. If the animal is fierce and wild, it may come at you to try to scare you away. If the creature is more timid or playful, you might actually be able to watch it up close. Some zoos actually organize overnight parties where you can sleep in groups within aquariums to watch up close how the creatures behave at night.

We didn't always have this kind of guarded relationship with wildlife, though. God's original heritage for people involved taking care of the animal kingdom in a way that the creatures responded to. We ate fruits and vegetables back then instead of burgers and bacon. Things were different until the terror of man entered into animals after the flood and we were given permission by God to eat many of them (Genesis 9:2–3).

Today's passage also hits on how taking care of animals means making sure that the world itself is kept in good shape for them to eat from. The way we treat creatures *and* creation is a spiritual thing. So the next time you're loving on your pet, recycling bottles, planting a garden, or tossing your trash where it belongs (instead of out your car window), count it as an act of worship to the Lord.

THERE IS HOPE

God is interested in people, but He's also interested in all of His creation. Animals are worthy of His attention and deserve our respect.

Who are some people in your life who seem to take good care of animals and/or creation?

- ***IF*** one of the people you mentioned were to tell you how they feel doing what they do, what do you think they'd say?
- ***WHAT IF*** as a family we pitched in even once to help someone take care of animals or creation?

34: A Responsive Me

***IF** you had a book that never ended, how would you know when it was time to take a break?*

***WHAT IF** the pages showed you what was happening in the book, almost like each page was a scene of a movie?*

READ IT: GENESIS 1:31

You know those things in life that take a lot of hard work and creative energy? It might be something at school, at work, or around the house that you really pour yourself into. There's a moment when that project is over or you have time to take a small break and it's easy to just collapse, silence your phone, and take a nap. Who would blame you, right?

There is another option that we have based on what God does in Genesis 1. Five times He's recorded as looking at all He's made and declaring that it was "good." Today's verse shows how He changes His statement after making the first people to note that it's all now "very good." The Lord not only enjoyed what He created as He created it, but He intentionally took the time to say so out loud.

What if we did this with the people and things that matter in our lives? Take being a part of a family, for example. It takes a lot of hard work and creative energy to do life together sometimes. You may not ever feel like you're getting anywhere with things unless you take a moment to pause and simply enjoy the progress you've experienced so far. It might mean regularly pushing back a bit from your table as your family is around it to enjoy how "good" it is to have these people in your life.

We are responsive beings made in the image of a responsive God. He looks at us and all of creation for something worthwhile to appreciate, and then He jumps back into making things even better. Follow His example, starting under your roof.

THERE IS HOPE

Some days God uses your family to grow you; some days God uses you to grow your family. It's usually the same day.

Take a moment to just silently look at and enjoy each other. Don't worry if it feels awkward.

- ***IF*** you did this each day for a week, what would be different at the end of that week?
- ***WHAT IF*** each member of our family was to do this a little more secretly on our own versus everyone doing it at once?

35: Weekly Recap

IF *you were given permission to take as much as you wanted from a store for ten minutes, what would you take?*

WHAT IF *you were given twenty minutes, but first you had to do something embarrassing in front of the manager?*

Praise the Lord from the earth, all sea monsters and ocean depths, lightning and hail, snow and cloud, stormy wind that executes his command, mountains and all hills, fruit trees and all cedars, wild animals and all cattle, creatures that crawl and flying birds, kings of the earth and all peoples. (Psalm 148:7–11)

CATCH UP

- Who or what made you laugh recently?
- How did life feel easy or hard this park week?

RECAP

- What stood out to you from what we've read together, talked about, or attempted to do together over the past week?
- What thoughts or questions do you have from today's Bible verse?

GROW TOGETHER

- What might be the main thing God is trying to tell our family today?
- What if we did something new together or returned to a good habit to live out what we're learning? What might that be?

OPEN UP

- In what ways are you struggling in life or experiencing something hard?
- If we were to confess something to God as a family, what might that be?

PRAY

- Who is Jesus to you today?
- Who would be willing to close our time with a simple prayer?

36: The Rest of the Week

***IF** everyone worked just two days a week, what would you do on your five days off?*

***WHAT IF** everyone worked for one hour daily? What would be different about life on every level?*

READ IT: GENESIS 2:1–3

It's not hard to imagine the first humans enjoying exploring the beautiful world God created. It apparently was a treat for the Lord too! Although He'd already declared everything to be "very good," He set aside a day to delight in and interact with all that had been created. There's something really special about this moment we don't want to miss—God doesn't do things and then leave; He sticks around to enjoy building a relationship with us through what's happened.

The Lord even later blessed the day itself as a holy, sacred "Sabbath" of *restoration* between God and people. This is why regularly taking part in a weekly church service and daily devotions like this are so valuable. We need a life-giving rhythm that puts us around thoughts and community beyond ourselves or else our opinions and schedules will lead us. Maybe we'd never intentionally deny God, but letting ourselves get so busy that we never make time for Him is kind of the same thing.

You may be on fire for God today and in a good routine. If so, protect that even if it means passing on sports, hobbies, work, or activities that would cut back on the time you had to care for your soul. It'll only get worse "next year" with more games to be at, countless tests to study for, unexpected job changes, or new projects at home. By continuing to prioritize time with God and His people now, you'll be stronger to not compromise then.

If you're struggling with this, give yourself permission to cut back on something. When you slow down for a moment to enjoy the Lord, you'll become more aware of Him in other moments. Life isn't meant to be busyness fueled by caffeine, trophies, social media, or the next high five. You're a human being, not a human doing.

THERE IS HOPE

Sabbath: Slow down your pace to make personal space to be transformed by God's grace by seeking Jesus' face.

Talk about any hobby or interest that tends to take over the family's schedule.

- ***IF*** this activity never existed, who would you be as a person?
- ***WHAT IF*** as a family you all took a break from this for an intentional length of time and used the moments you gained to invest into God, each other, and church?

37: Slow-Motion Replay

***IF** an amusement park was made featuring memories from your childhood, what would one of the rides be?*

***WHAT IF** in order to activate the rides every day you had to tell others a short story about that particular memory?*

READ IT: GENESIS 2:5–7

Good coaches know the power of reviewing an athlete's performance by watching a video of it together. Even though that person or team experienced the matchup firsthand, there's plenty they didn't catch because of their perspective. Seeing it from another angle in slow motion helps everyone notice what's important.

Genesis 1 and 2 have a similar connection; the first chapter focuses on the sequence of events that led up to creation while the second one unpacks what it felt like as it all took place. Each perspective needs the other, such as how Genesis 1:11 shows God creating vegetation that doesn't grow until man is created to farm it in 2:5. There's also a special insight into the day the Lord created man from the ground (*adamah* in Hebrew) and breathed into the clump of dust so it'd become a living being.

One perspective we don't get to see is "Adam's" first-person view. There was a moment when he opened his eyes for the first time and saw the face of God staring back at him. Only Adam viewed the expression on the Lord's face, be it a half-cocked smile from all the joy of the moment or a tender gaze with an outstretched hand to make sure Adam wasn't scared.

Perhaps in heaven we'll get the chance to review that "video" too. Maybe we'll get to see some of our own highlights. The real take-away is that no matter what truthful things you know about life, God, or yourself, there is always another perspective to slow down, review, and grow into.

THERE IS HOPE

God created almost everything simply by speaking it into existence. With people, though, He bent down to personally touch us. He still does.

Share an old memory you all share; but let each person tell their version of the story.

- ***IF*** you could review what happened with a video from that day, what else do you think you would notice?
- ***WHAT IF*** you could review yesterday from God's perspective versus your own?

38: Two Trees, but Actually Three

***IF** you had a cup that somehow always had water in it, what would you do with it?*

***WHAT IF** you had a plate that never ran out of food?*

READ IT: GENESIS 2:8–9, 16–17

It's okay. You can ask the question that's probably on your mind or soon will be: *Why did God place two trees in the middle of the Garden in Eden, especially since one of them wasn't to be eaten from?*

To understand why, consider something else for a moment. Imagine calling a radio station and being told by the DJ, "You're free to request any song and I'll play it. Just so you know, though, I only play 'Happy Birthday.'" It'd confuse you since you weren't actually being offered a choice.

The presence of these two trees is about God giving the first two people a choice to be in a trusting relationship with Him. For that to exist, they had to be able to choose something that would be the opposite—even if it meant the choice to reject Him. The tree's presence isn't about this moment alone, but something larger.

You see, there's a third supernatural "tree" that we read about later in the Bible . . . it's the cross of Jesus (Acts 5:30). As we've already studied, Christ is eternal and took part in creation. He always knew one day in our history He would hang and die on the cross for our sins. So while the Tree of Knowledge of Good and Evil brought a curse, the tree of Jesus brought forgiveness.

We're not done with the Tree of Life, though—it shows up again in eternity to bring a blessing. Revelation 22:2 says its leaves are "for healing the nations." In the meantime, the same choice presented to the first people is presented to us: Will we use our freewill to trust God or reject Him? It's a question we've been asking from the very beginning and is a big theme throughout the Bible. The grace He's offering you today is found right here. What will you do with it and with Him?

THERE IS HOPE

Only by the grace of God can we be enabled to one day see the face of God.

Name some decisions you made in the past day that you felt free to make.

- ***IF*** every choice you made about food required written approval, how would you work with that?
- ***WHAT IF*** life didn't have any choices because every decision was made for you?

39: Safety Bar

***IF** you could require everyone in the world to do one thing every year without question, what would it be?*

***WHAT IF** after that, all those people chose on their own to do that same thing every day for a whole year?*

READ IT: GENESIS 2:10–17

Eden was a massive land filled with all kinds of natural wonders. Four rivers marked a major part of the land, each with its own intensity. Adam, being the first man, was placed by God right in the center of it all to take care of it. He was commanded to avoid only one thing: the Tree of Knowledge of Good and Evil.

This wasn't the first command, though. If you remember from Genesis 1, God first commanded people to "be fruitful and multiply." He followed that up with a few other specific instructions about what that meant. This is important to remember because God isn't in the business of making random hard rules to hold us back; He gives us commands to make sure we can fully step into His larger plan for us.

It's kind of like the safety bar that pulls over you when you get on a ride at an amusement park. Someone could get all grouchy and argue that the creator of the ride was just trying to limit his fun with all of the limits. The truth is that God put certain commands in place as safety bars to help you enjoy the ride of life as it was intended to be experienced. If you disrespect it, you will surely die.

Everything God makes is good, including these unique trees that were placed in Eden. If we trust and obey, God's blessings continue to be good to us; if we go our own way, the consequences of our choices will continue to haunt us.

THERE IS HOPE

The greater we know God's heart, the greater we trust Him; the greater we trust God, the greater we know His heart.

What are some rules in life that have spared you from harm?

- ***IF*** God's rules are like the safety bar on a roller coaster, what is one thing He's trying to protect you from through one of His commands?
- ***WHAT IF*** you were in the Garden of Eden? What would you have felt about the two trees?

HERITAGE

40: Duties Before Cooties

***IF** you could own your own dessert shop, what three things would you have on the menu?*

***WHAT IF** you had to do all the cooking and baking yourself without any help or relief?*

READ IT: GENESIS 2:18–20

Ever get the "cooties"? It's an imaginary disease some kids think they get by being around the opposite sex. Boys may shout, "I've got cooties!" if a girl touches them (or vice versa). There does come a point when that changes and you start to consider courting or dating someone you have feelings for. The key is to make sure that person has his or her own rooted relationship with the Lord (as do you) so you can add to each other's spiritual journeys.

God said that it would be good for the man to have someone else in his life, but only after realizing why. Part of Adam's job of taking care of the animals included naming them. He didn't have to get super specific and say, "That's an English Cocker Spaniel." He could simply name the kind of animal, like, "That's a dog." It became an object lesson for Adam about God's plan for males and females to uniquely come together as one and be "helpers" to each other.

Lots of kids, teens, and adults wonder if and when they'll have someone special by their side. Sometimes parents look for any sign of their kids dating so they can point it out as being cute. Kids likewise might rush into dating to feel special. We can get so focused on all this possible pairing up that we don't do the clear things God has given us to do today. Like Adam, God has a heritage to show us in those tasks so that even our waiting becomes purposeful for what's ahead.

Trust God with this in your family. He didn't make the first human couple right away for a reason—we're created to receive all our confidence and security in the Lord first. This way you don't look for another person to "complete" you; instead, a couple is two complete people helping each other follow God.

THERE IS HOPE

"Duties" before "cooties" creates "wisdom" before "kissin'."

Recall when being faithful to what was in front of you prepared you for who or what came later.

- ***IF*** waiting has a purpose, what might be the purpose of waiting in your life right now?
- ***WHAT IF*** you get tired of doing the right or faithful thing while you're waiting?

41: Defining Marriage

***IF** a chicken was thrown at a bride and groom when a couple got married, how would weddings (if not the world) change?*

***WHAT IF** a flock of chickens would instinctively barge in and start flying around whenever a couple got married?*

READ IT: GENESIS 2:21–24

If you've ever been to a wedding you know that it's usually a meaningful, sacred celebration between a bride and groom that reflects them as a couple in some way. You'll see it in the flowers that were picked, the music that plays, the outfits that are worn, and the service that takes place. Some people might call all of this "the bride's special day," but it could easily also be called "the groom's special day." After all, both of them are involved in the marriage being formed before everyone's eyes.

Truth be told, there's a third Person involved in everything, and His role is most important. A bride and groom don't merely make a vow to each other, but together they make a vow with God. He's the only one who can help them faithfully live out their vows anyway. If you think about it, a wedding is actually the Lord's day. Imagine how different the ceremonies and receptions would be if all weddings actually reflected this reality.

We see God's role in how He brought the woman to the man, like how in a wedding a father will walk the bride to the groom. In Genesis, the Lord then made the marriage official by giving her the title of "wife" (and later referring to Adam as her "husband").

All throughout the Bible, God repeatedly affirms marriage as this one-of-a-kind, transparent-yet-unashamed relationship between one man and one woman. Even though some of His own people weren't faithful to this definition (and culture will try to come up with new ways to define marriage), the Lord has revealed what marriage was, is, and always will be. If we want His blessing on such a union, let's honor what He has already blessed instead of insisting it be something else.

THERE IS HOPE

Flawed people don't define marriage. Divorce doesn't define marriage. New laws don't define marriage. God defines marriage.

Talk about what would make the ideal husband or wife.

- ***IF*** every husband or wife had three characteristics, what should they be?
- ***WHAT IF*** Jesus today physically attended every wedding ceremony of a couple who sought His blessing?

42: Weekly Recap

***IF** you were God for a day, what might be a new way you'd express your love to humanity?*

***WHAT IF** today you as a human being found a new way to express your love for humanity?*

I have asked one thing from the LORD; it is what I desire: to dwell in the house of the LORD all the days of my life, gazing on the beauty of the LORD and seeking him in his temple. (Psalm 27:4)

CATCH UP

- Who or what made you laugh recently?
- How did life feel easy or hard this past week?

RECAP

- What stood out to you from what we've read together, talked about, or attempted to do together over the past week?
- What thoughts or questions do you have from today's Bible verse?

GROW TOGETHER

- What might be the main thing God is trying to tell our family today?
- What if we did something new together or returned to a good habit to live out what we're learning? What might that be?

OPEN UP

- In what ways are you struggling in life or experiencing something hard?
- If we were to confess something to God as a family, what might that be?

PRAY

- Who is Jesus to you today?
- Who would be willing to close our time with a simple prayer?

ENEMY

The most important truth you will ever realize in your life is that you have a personal Savior in Jesus Christ. He is real, and He is really fighting for you. He invites you right now to trust in Him to transform your life into what God originally meant it to be.

Another important truth you must realize is that you also have a personal enemy in the devil. He is real, and he is really fighting against you. He invites you right now to trust in yourself instead of God to transform your life into what you think it should be.

It's an unexpected strategy, isn't it? You might expect Satan to invite you to trust in him instead of God. In some cases he might be this bold, but he's smart and realizes it's easier to get people to pursue whatever they think will make them feel happy than it is to follow him. After all, if you knew how real the devil was you just might turn to God for power to resist. If it's just a matter of you taking your eyes off of the Lord, though, the devil knows how to do that to us today just like he did to the first humans. It's why he tends to influence all kinds of creatures (and sometimes people) from the shadows instead of coming out into the light . . . to get us out of the light and into the shadows.

God's people listened to an enemy and became an enemy—to God, each other, and even creation itself.

43: Who?

***IF** you could yell at someone and they would immediately fall down, who are some people you would use that power on and why?*

***WHAT IF** you could yell at anything in the world and make it fall down?*

READ IT: ISAIAH 14:12–15

"Get out of the way and let me do it!" Imagine if one of your family members or friends said this to you while pushing you aside. Regardless of what you were just doing, you'd likely feel awkward about it. Clearly that person feels superior to you in some way, even if he or she isn't.

Hang on to this thought as we take a moment to get to know "who" God's enemy is. Today's Bible passage is spoken through one of God's leaders named Isaiah. He knew things about the supernatural realm because he spent time with the Lord, so he shared some of that knowledge when confronting a corrupt human king who was trying to be a bigger deal than God. Isaiah said the devil had similarly tried to push God aside with a "Get out of the way and let me do it!" attitude.

The phrase *morning star* reveals that the enemy was once a special angel. People have added opinions to this over the years by guessing at what his duties were in heaven or calling him "Lucifer" (because of how this passage was once translated in Latin). The Bible more regularly calls him "Satan" because it means "enemy" or "adversary." That doesn't mean he's God's exact evil opposite but someone powerfully destructive who will end up punished by God in hell. Jesus once spoke about the initial fall, saying, "I watched Satan fall from heaven like lightning" (Luke 10:18).

So Satan isn't the little red guy with horns and a pitchfork you've seen in cartoons. He actually doesn't try to present himself as someone who is evil but as someone who is for your pleasure (even though he's just for his own pleasure). "Therefore, submit to God. Resist the devil, and he will flee from you" (James 4:7).

THERE IS HOPE

The devil is the most powerful force of evil in existence, but compared to God his power is like a drop of water next to an ocean.

Share about a time when you each thought you knew better than someone else but didn't.

- ***IF*** you knew then what you know now, what would you have done differently?
- ***WHAT IF*** you needed to resist someone who was trying to do this to you?

44: What?

***IF** a civilized yeti (otherwise known as an abominable snowman) owned a restaurant, what food would that civilized yeti sell?*

***WHAT IF** the civilized yeti asked you to be his chef and expected you to cook the food in the most delicious way possible?*

READ IT: 1 PETER 5:8

Going to a zoo is usually all about the animals, but have you ever considered the layout of the zoo itself? A team of people specifically designed it and the exhibits so that you can see the creatures while being a safe distance away from any that might harm you. That's not to imply that you can be careless, though. There have been some tragic stories about people who didn't think it was a big deal to cross into restricted areas they shouldn't have and were attacked by ferocious animals.

Today's verse points out that Satan is like a wild animal himself whom we need to keep our distance from. He's compared to a lion who is just waiting to pounce, whether he gets us all in one chomp or devours us bite by bite. We're warned to be serious and alert at all the ways this "devil" might try to attack, which means he isn't just God's enemy but is also our enemy. He's been studying people for centuries and is quite skilled at getting us close to his cage.

Don't miss that Satan does have boundaries. He can't be everywhere like God can, so he picks his prey by prowling around and looking for anyone who is open to attack. If you don't want to be pounced on by him or his minions, develop some boundaries of your own. Don't invite him into your life through sinful things you do, watch, or listen to, even if these things are popular and entertaining. So many of the things that we think aren't a big deal are restricted areas that God doesn't want us crossing into because they set us up for a sneak attack from the enemy. Check out Philippians 4:8 for some tips on what to focus on instead.

THERE IS HOPE

God warns us about evil but also stands against it. Instead of clinging to what He's about to kick over, cling to Him instead.

Identify some things in your home that probably "don't belong" there, like movies, music, books, games, or pictures that tempt someone in the home in some way.

- ***IF*** you were honest, what are some things you're "used to" that are sinful?
- ***WHAT IF*** you determined to help each other get rid of this stuff?

45: When?

***IF** it was possible to completely make one bug species instantly disappear from the earth, which bug would you chose?*

***WHAT IF** you could eliminate five different species of bugs?*

READ IT: EZEKIEL 28:14–17

This is kind of gross, but your home is filled with more bugs than you've seen. There are small ones that only special equipment and effort can find, but the rest are nocturnal and come out at night when there's less chance of being discovered. If you've ever turned on a light and seen bugs crawling around, you know how freaky it can be to see what you hoped to be clean infested with dirty critters.

Relate this to how God created a pure, joyful realm for the angels that became "infested" because of Satan. Ezekiel the prophet shared about this, pointing out that the enemy was originally one of the highest types of angels. We may not know exactly "when" he rejected this blessing, but that it happened near the beginning of time for "he was a murderer from the beginning and does not stand in the truth, because there is no truth in him" (John 8:44).

Maybe Satan rebelled when God made mankind in His image, for angels would be in a higher status over humans only on earth yet in a lower status in the longer scope of eternity (1 Corinthians 6:3; Hebrews 2:6-7). That alone could drive someone full of pride from "bud" to "bug" and get one-third of the angels to turn from agents of Light into creatures of darkness (Revelation 12:3–9). This army has been crawling around on the insides of our lives beyond what we can see. When the light of Jesus lights things up, they quickly start looking for cover.

The real question isn't when the enemy became an enemy, but when you'll become God's ally. Don't be afraid to let Jesus light you up on the inside with His love. As you shine, Satan and his demons will run from the One in you like bugs that run when being exposed for what they are.

THERE IS HOPE

Instead of being stuck cursing the darkness, you can become a light.

When is a time you came across a bug or something else unexpected in the dark?

- ***IF*** someone else had found it, what might have happened instead?
- ***WHAT IF*** you used this analogy to shine God's light into the dark around you?

46: Where?

***IF** dogs and cats would always attack you the moment they saw you, how would it change the way you live?*

***WHAT IF** every animal you encountered attacked you?*

READ IT: 2 CORINTHIANS 4:4; 1 JOHN 4:4; REVELATION 20:10

Monkey bars. Hopscotch. Tetherball. Tag. The swings.

School playgrounds are meant to be fun places where boys and girls can have recreational time while adults stand nearby monitoring things. One sad side effect of this intended blessing is that some kids turn into bullies who trick, intimidate, and overpower others. It's like they're trying to "run the playground" right under the noses of the adults. The kids being bullied might wonder why the teachers don't step in and stop it. Sometimes the adults do, and other times they wait so kids can develop the skills needed to work things out and grow stronger.

We might wonder this about God as we feel the enemy attacking us. God actually *does* step into our situations every day, whether it's in how He uses His authority to limit what the devil can do or by giving us wisdom and power on the inside to take a stand. The Bible calls Satan "the god of this age" (2 Corinthians 4:4) because he does have influence over unbelievers by tricking, intimidating, and overpowering how people think and feel. He even can try to rule and influence culture itself like a bully trying to "run the playground" right under the nose of God.

But Satan doesn't end up as a ruler in hell on a big throne (despite all the pictures or movies that promote this). Satan's rebellion and actions *will* result in God permanently condemning the enemy and his minions into hell for all eternity. While the enemy is roaming earth today, pay attention to "where" he is *going*. So instead of listening to the voice of a bully with limited power, lean into the true Lord, who is greater in you than the one who is in this world.

THERE IS HOPE

When God is lifting you up, expect the enemy to try to drag you down . . . but remember: it's because God is lifting you up!

Talk about some of the situations you've each faced involving a bully of some kind.

- ***IF*** bullies didn't exist, what would be different about us as people?
- ***WHAT IF*** bullies never got caught for what they were doing?

47: Why?

***IF** you were a general in the army but no one else in the army would listen to you, what would you do?*

***WHAT IF** you were a teacher and your class wouldn't listen to you?*

READ IT: ZECHARIAH 3:1–2

We all know someone who is more competitive than we are (and if you don't, maybe it's because you're competitive and want to win the "most competitive" title). Hopefully the competitive people you know are friendly as they scramble to win games and outdo everyone else at school or work. You might even see competition during dinner over who deserves the last tater tot.

Now think about what happens when a competitive person doesn't get what he or she wants. Competition in itself is simply applying effort to outdo others in achieving a goal. It only gets bad when jealousy, pride, and selfishness kick in. Soon it's not about how someone didn't win but that someone doesn't want *anyone* else to win. Does the phrase *sore loser* come to mind?

Consider this when trying to understand "why" the enemy does what he does. A prophet named Zechariah picked up on something through a holy vision that let him peek into the supernatural realm. He saw one of God's chief leaders being accused by Satan before God. The devil hated the whole idea of anyone giving themselves over to the Lord and getting on the winning team, so he did to that man what he does to us: pout, insult, blame, and cause trouble.

Satan knows he can't hurt God in a direct battle because God is infinitely more powerful. Still, he keeps on trying to win when he's losing by attacking the people God loves. Perhaps Satan is so misguided that he still thinks he has a winning chance . . . or maybe as a defeated being he wants to get you feeling defeated too. However you look at it, Satan is the ultimate sore loser.

THERE IS HOPE

When Christ is your Savior, Satan has sore behavior. He'll attack you with lies, but don't fall for them. You'll think he's won when really he's done.

Share about a time when one person's attitude or actions affected others.

- ***IF*** sore losers weren't allowed to play games or do anything competitive, how would the world be different?
- ***WHAT IF*** we're meant to change how another person has made things bad?

48: How?

IF *you were offered one hundred thousand dollars to eat a worm at every meal for a week, would you?*

WHAT IF *you were only offered fifty dollars to do this?*

READ IT: MARK 5:12; LUKE 22:3; LUKE 22:31

Not everyone celebrates Halloween, but those who do celebrate somewhere between "simply dressing up" to "making a home look like a haunted crime scene." Then there are the candy-seeking guests who ring your doorbell to get something sugary as you peer through the dark to see through their costumes and catch who is really under the mask. They might also wonder as they walk around if someone is about to jump out and scare them.

In our lives we'll find the enemy choosing "how" he will attack us, be it by simply "dressing up" or by "making a home look like a haunted crime scene." The Bible gives up his greatest secret—that he actually exists and wants to separate us from God. Satan can also offer only a short thrill when we give in to him, like when we eat cotton candy that feels big in our mouth for a moment and then suddenly shrinks. It seems like Satan would rather distract us with something sugary or cloak himself with invisibility than be directly seen and directly opposed by us.

Another "costume" Satan wears is working through deceived people. He knows that if he revealed his true colors we'd reject him, so instead he uses people we know to start "ringing our doorbell" with sugary lies that they believe.

The Enemy does have power and uses it. Don't miss out on what this means related to the cross of Jesus, though. Christ's death and resurrection prove that even the ultimate evil action can bring about the ultimate good consequence. Thank God for how He will strengthen your faith even when you're feeling under attack.

THERE IS HOPE

You can't stop Satan from ringing the doorbell of your life, but you can send Jesus to go answer the door.

Come up with a simple strategy for how to recognize and call out the lies of people or Satan.

- ***IF*** you knew someone was lying to you, how would you address it?
- ***WHAT IF*** someone sincerely believed in a lie, like a false religion?

49: Weekly Recap

IF *Disney World let you privately live in Cinderella's castle, would you want to?*

WHAT IF *it meant visitors would come through the castle each day and mess with all your stuff?*

A thief comes only to steal and to kill and to destroy. I have come so that they may have life and have it in abundance. (John 10:10)

CATCH UP

- Who or what made you laugh recently?
- How did life feel easy or hard this past week?

RECAP

- What stood out to you from what we've read together, talked about, or attempted to do together over the past week?
- What thoughts or questions do you have from today's Bible verse?

GROW TOGETHER

- What might be the main thing God is trying to tell our family today?
- What if we did something new together or returned to a good habit to live out what we're learning? What might that be?

OPEN UP

- In what ways are you struggling in life or experiencing something hard?
- If we were to confess something to God as a family, what might that be?

PRAY

- Who is Jesus to you today?
- Who would be willing to close our time with a simple prayer?

50: The Tone of a Question

IF *you could change a law and everyone would have to listen to it, which law would you change?*

WHAT IF *your new law had the side effect of eliminating all other laws?*

READ IT: GENESIS 3:1

You know how questions can be used to figure out truth? Did you know they can also be used to distract us from it by criticizing someone or something? Have you ever been asked a question that caused you to second-guess a person or value you trusted, like, "Do your family members *really* have your best interests in mind?" As you think about that bad question now, how might you have responded differently in the moment if you knew listening to it would put you into a funk?

What if the woman had this perspective when the serpent asked her the question he did to cause her to doubt God's goodness? Or what if she and Adam simply remembered how amazing God had already been to them in the past? Can you just imagine them saying to the serpent, "Why would you even try to get us to second-guess someone who loves us so much that He made this glorious, beautiful world for us to live in? *"Hey, God, can You please put this liar in his place?"*

Could this be the way we're to handle things when Satan tries to get us to think that God is holding back on us somehow? How crazy would we have to be to believe lies like that? How easy is it for us to remember all the times God has already blessed us and is trustworthy? What if questions aren't a bad thing in themselves, but the difference is in the tone and reason underneath why we're asking them?

By the way, did you notice this whole chapter is full of questions? Do you think we used them to pursue truth or criticize God? How might understanding the difference help you spot either one together as a family?

THERE IS HOPE

What if the reason Satan is so desperate to get us to second-guess God is because God is that clear to us on how much He loves us?

Can you think of a time you caught someone trying to mislead you or asking you questions just to rattle you?

- **IF** you could redo this conversation, what would you do or say differently?
- **WHAT IF** this person tried to mislead or hassle you again?

51: Finishing God's Sentences

***IF** someone interrupted you every time you spoke, how would that affect your willingness to talk?*

***WHAT IF** sometimes when you tried to say something, you uncontrollably said something else?*

READ IT: GENESIS 3:2–3

It's been said that good friends and close family can finish each other's ________. If you didn't fill that blank in with "sentences," no worries. That's what we typically think, though—that when you know people really well, it's almost like you know what they'll say before they say it. Sometimes we're absolutely right with our guesses, and other times we're absolutely wrong.

This could be why the woman added some extra rules onto what God had originally said in Genesis 2:16–17. She'd spent time with Him and felt like she knew Him. The Lord did say that she and the man weren't to eat from the Tree of the Knowledge of Good and Evil, but He didn't say anything about them touching the fruit. Perhaps she figured, "He probably meant this too."

We also have to be careful when we try to finish God's sentences. It's not that the woman came up with a bad idea, because it actually makes sense not even to touch the fruit if God didn't want her and the man to eat it. But it gave just enough wiggle room for the enemy to realize, *Oh, she really doesn't know what she thinks she knows. I'm going to take advantage of this and try to get her to disobey God.*

It makes a difference to remember who said what between us and God. Mixing up these two things is either called legalism (believing that rules or traditions are the same thing as truth) or heresy (changing God's Word into something that isn't true). We need to pay careful attention to God's words and wisdom instead of trying to add our own opinions and solutions. Otherwise we might end up getting so lost trying to finish God's sentences that we miss what our Creator has clearly said.

THERE IS HOPE

When we don't finish God's sentences, we deepen what it means to hear His voice over our own.

Grade how you do as a family at listening to each other without cutting each other off.

- ***IF*** we were better listeners to each other, what would that look like?
- ***WHAT IF*** instead of waiting for others to finish talking just so we could speak, we took the time to pay attention to what they were saying?

52: Truth Decay

***IF** you could hear only half of what others were saying, how would you get through life?*

***WHAT IF** others only heard half of what you said?*

READ IT: GENESIS 3:4–5

Cookies. Ice cream. Cake. Root beer. Chips. Candy. All of these things are considered "junk food," and yet each one can get your mouth watering just thinking about it. You've been warned not to eat too much of them or you'll get cavities, ruin your health, or spoil your appetite. But they are hard to resist.

Something weird happens when you do eat these items—you actually feel for a moment as if your appetite got larger instead of feeling full. It's because your taste buds are so stimulated that you're tempted to shove more sugar into your mouth. Food companies have become experts at sprinkling in ingredients that get your body to crave something bad for you.

The serpent played a similar trick on the woman when he sprinkled in some half-truths about how she and the man wouldn't die if they disobeyed God. The enemy even claimed that the Lord was somehow holding out on them.

Half-truths are still lies though. Even though the first man and woman wouldn't physically die the moment they ate the fruit, they would experience the death of life as they knew it. In fact, something supernatural happened that affected things we think to be "natural," like death—and eventually, they would experience death as we know it. Just not at the moment they took bites from the fruit.

Just as junk food causes tooth decay, our enemy causes *truth* decay. He wants us to see sin as something good and God as someone bad. The truth is, sin is definitely something bad that our good God wants to spare us from. Don't be confused by half-truths that are full lies, because if you bite down on sin and get addicted to craving it, you'll eventually ruin your spiritual health by spoiling your appetite for truth.

THERE IS HOPE

1. Name the bait: What tempts you and why would you fall for it? 2. Contemplate: What's a better option? 3. Go straight: Follow Jesus.

Talk about how you each feel about rules meant to keep us from harm.

- ***IF*** these rules didn't exist, what kind of danger could you be in?
- ***WHAT IF*** people were generally more trusting of God's commands instead of second-guessing Him?

53: FOMO or JOMO

***IF** it were possible to have anything you want right now, what would it be?*

***WHAT IF** the only way to have that thing meant someone else would have to tragically lose it?*

READ IT: GENESIS 3:6

The term *FOMO* probably sounds like something you'd order in a coffee shop, but it actually stands for the "Fear Of Missing Out." It's a feeling you might get when the latest movie is about to release, a new store just opened in town, or you see a group of friends making plans together without you. It's what causes some people to check their phone or social media every ten minutes to make sure they're keeping up with others. FOMO can even stop you from making important decisions or commitments because you're always afraid there's a better option.

Doesn't that sound exhausting though? The irony of the Fear Of Missing Out is you end up missing out on your own life right in front of you. You might give in to doing something to fit in that appears delightful but is actually bad for you. The first humans fell for this through the lies of the enemy, even though God had obviously given them so much more than they could ever want. The fear of missing out made them distrust God.

One way to combat FOMO is with JOMO—embracing the "Joy Of Missing Out." Instead of focusing on what else you could be doing, celebrate what you *are* doing instead and who you're doing it with. So the next time you're tempted to pout because you didn't get the latest violent video game or see a slasher movie, celebrate that you're protecting your mind. Or if you have to pass on time with your friends because your family is going on a trip, enjoy the adventure with your family. Sometimes the easiest way to avoid temptation from the enemy for something you shouldn't have is to embrace God in the blessings you already have.

THERE IS HOPE

By thanking God for specific blessings each day, you'll find them more ripe than stale—and yourself a little less ripe for temptation.

How many specific ways has God blessed your family?

- **IF** God never gave you anything else but what He's already given you, what would you think of Him?
- **WHAT IF** the only thing God ever gave anyone was Himself and heaven?

54: Letting Sin Happen

***IF** your house were chocolate, how much of it would you eat?*

***WHAT IF** the outside of your house was typical but the inside was made of Jell-O that never got dirty and instantly regenerated any time you ate it?*

READ IT: GENESIS 3:6

There are some things you just don't do, like borrow someone's roll-on deodorant or eat a fast-food French fry off the floor of a mini-van. And it would be incredibly weird if one of your family members came into your kitchen with a sledgehammer and started swinging at the walls. You'd probably be in shock for a moment before trying to get them to stop or explain why they were doing that. Then again, things could get even weirder if you asked for the sledgehammer and started swinging at the walls too.

Today's Bible verse reveals something really weird like that. The man was with the woman the whole time she was tempted by God's enemy to do something that tore their "home" apart, yet the man didn't stop her. He just watched what she was doing and eventually joined in. First Timothy 2:14 says that in this way the man wasn't at all deceived. He literally chose the woman over God; instead of being each other's "helpers," they let a whole lot of hurt happen.

Sometimes we let bad things happen with family or friends when one person's actions dumb down how we respond to things. Maybe we're tired of seeing people always doing the wrong thing so we figure, *At this point, why try to stop them?* Or maybe the popular kid at school wants you to become or do something that will tear you away from the Lord.

God has given you a voice to use to speak up and stop sin from going further. This is true for adults, teens, and kids. Even if everyone else is doing it, be willing to say, "That's enough. We can do better than this. We can follow God together." Instead of tearing down the "home," you'll strengthen it.

THERE IS HOPE

God's enemy can put on a good show of making temptation look good, but one person willing to stand up for truth can reveal it as a lie.

Be honest about any of the ways your family has allowed some bad things to get overlooked.

- ***IF*** I stopped you from doing something that was bad for you, how would you respond?
- ***WHAT IF*** you wanted to tell me something similar about my own life?

55: The Big Cover Up

***IF** every time you ate your favorite food you became invisible for half an hour, how often would you eat that food?*

***WHAT IF** when you ate your favorite food you suddenly felt embarrassed and wanted to hide?*

READ IT: GENESIS 3:7–8

You never see it coming. You simply stand up, sit down, or move like you ordinarily would and suddenly you hear a huge *"RIIIIIIP!"* Yep, you've split your pants, and now you have to figure out what to do about it. Should you ask for help or hide before anyone notices and says, "Feel a breeze?" Not only do you feel exposed physically, but you also feel embarrassed socially.

Before the first man and woman sinned, humans had never experienced anything like this. They were innocent of knowing about nakedness, like how a baby or toddler doesn't think twice about running around without clothes on. But after the man and woman ate from the Tree of Knowledge of Good and Evil, they felt a strange desire to hide from God, each other, and themselves. The man and woman used fig leaves to cover up, as if to say, "Don't look at me." It's like how we can hide behind good deeds or accomplishments, as if to say, "Look at what I did *instead* of looking at me."

Often when we sin, the real thing we're trying to hide from is feeling exposed. We fear how someone seeing us in an embarrassing moment will create a lasting change to our relationship, so we quickly look to cover up. That's what happened when God's people listened to His enemy and became an enemy—to God, each other, and creation itself.

These days the enemy still tries to deceive us into thinking that sin is nothing more than a bad choice, when it's actually a relationship ripper. If we ask God for help, we don't have to hide. But if we insist on trying to hide behind the next thing we find, there's going to be plenty more to be embarrassed about. So come out of hiding.

THERE IS HOPE

There's nothing you've done that God can't forgive. There's nothing you've been forgiven of that God can't help you not do again.

How do you think the man and woman felt about themselves before and after sinning?

- ***IF*** we could walk through the Garden of Eden in our jeans and T-shirts before they sinned, what do you think their reactions would be?
- ***WHAT IF*** we walked around in front of them *after* they sinned? What do you think they would say to us?

56: Weekly Recap

***IF** there was a siren that would go off any time you were tempted to do something wrong, would you want to have one?*

***WHAT IF** life were like a video game where you could restart or respawn if you sinned or made a mistake?*

Satan disguises himself as an angel of light. (2 Corinthians 11:14)

CATCH UP

- Who or what made you laugh recently?
- How did life feel easy or hard this past week?

RECAP

- What stood out to you from what we've read together, talked about, or attempted to do together over the past week?
- What thoughts or questions do you have from today's Bible verse?

GROW TOGETHER

- What might be the main thing God is trying to tell our family today?
- What if we did something new together or returned to a good habit to live out what we're learning? What might that be?

OPEN UP

- In what ways are you struggling in life or experiencing something hard?
- If we were to confess something to God as a family, what might it be?

PRAY

- Who is Jesus to you today?
- Who would like to close our time with a simple prayer?

57: Hide and Seek

***IF** one hundred dollars were hidden somewhere in your house but would disappear in one week if not found, what would you do?*

***WHAT IF** one million dollars were hidden in your house but would disappear in a day?*

READ IT: GENESIS 3:9–10

Behind the lamp. Under a blanket. Inside the back-door curtains. *Say what?*

Playing hide-and-seek with younger kids comes with its own set of rules. They often believe if they can't see you then you can't see them. It's why they'll foolishly hide in obvious places with their feet sticking out. When you "find them," they might even tell you something like, "I'm a statue. You don't see me."

Notice who is doing the hiding in today's Scripture. It isn't God; it's the man and woman. Sometimes in our broken world people assume that God is hiding from us because we can't see Him. Maybe the real reason we don't easily spot Him is because we're hiding beneath something. It could be sin, or it might be things we enjoy doing more than investing in our relationship with Him.

The Lord obviously knew where the man and woman were, just like He always knows where we are. God asking a question like "Where are you?" isn't for His benefit but for ours. Sometimes we need to admit we've been foolishly trying to hide with our shame sticking out.

Thankfully, God is good and seeks us out so we don't live our lives hiding from Him or each other. Even when we freeze up, He says, "I see you." All this is to save us, which is why Jesus Christ came to earth . . . personally entering into our "hiding place" so we can hold His hand and find the way out.

THERE IS HOPE

We don't have to live life hiding or assume God is hiding from us.

Talk about some of your favorite hide-and-seek moments.

- ***IF*** you could find a spot where no one would ever find you, how would that change the game?
- ***WHAT IF*** you knew you never had to "hide out" from your worst choices in life but could be honest with God and your family about everything?

58: Tattling and Blame

***IF** you could shoot steak out of your hands, what would you do with this ability?*

***WHAT IF** when you did this, a cow in the world randomly disappeared?*

READ IT: GENESIS 3:11–13

When you are growing up, it can be confusing when you see something wrong and share it, only to have others say, "Don't be a tattletale." There are times we really do need to let whoever is in charge know that someone else did something wrong so it can be addressed, like when someone in your family is bent over sick after eating a whole slab of chocolate. But some people might think we're just saying things to get others in trouble. That's the big difference between "telling" and "tattling."

It seems like the man and woman struggled with this when God asked them about their sin. The Lord knew what happened, yet He gave them the chance to be honest about it. We often need someone in authority to do this for us when we're embarrassed and start pointing at other people to make ourselves look better in comparison. Is it any wonder why blame is spelled "be-lame"?

In truth, we can all be pretty messed up and regularly try to avoid admitting it. Although it's easy to point a finger at someone or something else and say, "Right there! That person! That situation! There's the problem with the world!" it is more helpful to confront the person staring at you in the mirror.

Thankfully, God has not washed His hands of us. He's always looking to set whatever is upside down right side up again. It involves us allowing Him to wash clean our sinful hands (and our entire sinful lives).

The most powerful sin in your life is the one you won't fully own up to. The enemy tries to get us to avoid it through fear, but God invites us to experience real freedom through truth telling. Why cover up what confession can clear up?

THERE IS HOPE

When we confess the flaws in our character to God, we find a fresh start through the love in His character.

Why do you think God created us to feel regret when we do something wrong?

- ***IF*** you could do whatever you wanted without getting in any trouble, what kind of person would you become?
- ***WHAT IF*** every time we hurt another person we didn't feel sad but somehow became super happy? What kind of world would we eventually create?

59: The Agony of Defeat

***IF** you could create your own sport, what would it be, and how would you get people interested in it?*

***WHAT IF** you knew your team would win every game you played?*

READ IT: GENESIS 3:14–15

It's common for families to cheer for a favorite sports team. You've probably realized this means you inherit a rival team too. There's a certain intensity when these two teams play against each other, be it because of previous battles that got ugly or because both teams are in the same territory of the country. Knowing the history behind it all helps you understand the tension today.

This is true of the intensity between God and Satan that has played out over the centuries. The enemy can't overcome the Lord, so he began attacking God's team through the serpent that tempted the man and woman. God sent a message back to the enemy by humbling the serpent into a creature that would "eat dust" (Genesis 3:14)—a symbol of losing a war (Micah 7:17). The Lord also tossed in a powerful statement about how someone from the man and woman's future family would crush the enemy even further. Jesus Christ lived this out on earth by dying for our sins and rising again in resurrection. He'll crush the enemy again in a final battle, and that will be a team we can enjoy being on (Revelation 12:9; 20:2).

Make no mistake, though—if you choose to be on that winning team, you'll have a rival enemy to deal with in the meantime. He'll attack from the ground up like a snake might nip at someone's heel. The agony of the feet from our perspective is temporary, but the agony of defeat from his perspective is permanent.

THERE IS HOPE

"The God of peace will soon crush Satan under your feet" (Romans 16:20).

What does it specifically mean to be on God's winning team as a family?

- ***IF*** we know God's team ultimately wins, how can we have the confidence that we're on it versus just watching it from the stands? (Check out 1 John 2.)
- ***WHAT IF*** as a family we actively help other people get on the winning team with Jesus? What would that practically look like this week?

60: A Deflated Life

***IF** it were possible to enter into a gigantic balloon and bounce around inside of it, would you want to?*

***WHAT IF** you could shrink down into a regular balloon? Would you want to?*

READ IT: GENESIS 3:16–19

Admit it—you crack up a little bit at the noise a balloon makes when you blow it up and let it go. You probably also feel a little nervous in those moments as the balloon randomly moves around the room in pure chaos, leaving you wondering if it'll smack you in the face or knock something over. This isn't what balloons were made for, but it's what they can end up becoming.

In many ways we're living in a deflated world too. So much of the random chaos around us isn't what life was made for but what it's ended up becoming. Some things may crack us up, and yet we can't deny how tense and confused we can feel in our relationships, work, bodies, families, and more. Even childbirth wasn't originally supposed to be full of pain. Everything God originally created for us to joyfully know Him has been knocked over, all because we listened to our enemy.

There is hope, though. Just like a deflated balloon may fly off and end up in an unintended place, it can be reclaimed and reinflated toward its original purpose. It's no accident that Genesis 3 (in some Bible translations) is the first time we see Adam's actual name used in the Bible (other than the *adamah* word for "ground" in Genesis 2:7). God seems to be reminding the man (and us as we read this) that just as he was brought to life through divine breath, so can we all "be filled with all the fullness of God" (Ephesians 3:19). We may be who we've become, but through Christ we can become who we were made to be.

THERE IS HOPE

In a deflated world where good things exhaust us, "the breath of the Almighty gives me life" (Job 33:4).

Try to think of a time when something that was broken was fixed or restored.

- **IF** it was impossible to fix anything, how different would the world be?
- **WHAT IF** you could fix a relationship between two people? What relationship would you fix?

61: What We Can Do

***IF** you had to get rid of one of the letters in your first name, which one would you eliminate?*

***WHAT IF** you had to change the name of one of your friends?*

READ IT: GENESIS 3:20

Carnivals typically have a wacky building called a "funhouse." It's filled with colorful decorations, slanted rooms, floors that move, and noise-making devices that surprise you as you walk through. You'll also see several curved mirrors that change how you see yourself when you stare at them. Standing in front of these warped reflections confuses how you see who you really are.

We're familiar with this in another way because sin "curved" who we are and how we live. Everything and everyone in the world can reflect something warped about who we are back to us. Our enemy uses these distorted images to mess with how we see ourselves, reminding us of our worst moments so we never reclaim who God originally made us to be.

Thankfully, the Lord speaks truth to us that we can claim into our lives and the lives around us. Adam was onto this when he named his wife "Eve," which literally means "life." Appreciate how special this was, for he gave her this name after they sinned. In the middle of shame and death, Adam reclaimed what God had said—that Eve was originally created to be more than who she was in that moment . . . she was made in the image of God to be a life giver.

Part of our fight against the enemy is helping each other reclaim our "Heritage." We're each in the "naming business" too.* When you've made a big error, you've wished someone would give you a fresh start. So help others in your life quit staring at the funhouse mirror reflection of themselves and see who God originally made them to be. Let it begin today, starting in your own family.

* Thank you to Rick Lawrence for this great observation.

THERE IS HOPE

You can either let your shortcomings, urges, and sins give you a warped image, or you can let God remind you of who He originally made you to be.

Reflect on the story or meaning behind each of your names.

- ***IF*** we were to give one another a new life-giving name to remind each other of something true, what would each of those names be?
- ***WHAT IF*** we called each other these names for the next day?

62: What God Does Do

***IF** hats would gently bite you once whenever you put them on, would you still wear hats?*

***WHAT IF** the hat would continually bite your head gently the whole time you had one on?*

READ IT: GENESIS 3:21–24

If you've ever been to a go-kart track, you know there are certain rules you need to agree to before you can get behind the wheel or ride as a passenger. What you may not be aware of is how this is enforced behind the scenes. Many crews use a "shut-off device" or "kill switch" as needed to remotely cut the power on every vehicle if drivers ignore the rules or an accident occurs. This is great news if you're on the track and see someone heading the wrong way in your direction. It's bad news if you deliberately want to bump everyone.

God used a kind of "kill switch" in the Garden of Eden when He sent Adam and Eve out of it. They were in danger of eating from a second tree that would make them live forever, which would mean they would be stuck in their sin for all of eternity. Adam and Eve were moved out of the Garden of Eden as a form of protection.

God did one other amazing thing, though—He first took the time to clothe them with animal skins instead of leaving them embarrassed by the fig leaves they were wearing. This may have involved sacrificing an animal like a lamb to provide this covering, which connects us to the sacrifice Jesus made on the cross. When we start heading the wrong direction, God shuts it down by being completely righteous and completely tender. He disciplines us while caring for us. He doesn't explain Himself and yet offers Himself. He loves us with the truth and truthfully loves us. He hits the kill-switch on sin by switching us back to life. If you believe, then by all means receive!

THERE IS HOPE

God doesn't just deal with our sin in the moment. He also paves out a plan and puts us on a track for the future.

When in your life have you had the chance to stop something bad from continuing?

- **IF** you hadn't spoken up, what further damage would have happened?
- **WHAT IF** we took a lesson from God in boldly standing against what's wrong while tenderly trying to help transform the person who did it?

63: Weekly Recap

***IF** you had a remote that could make whomever you were pointing at do something, what would you want to make people do?*

***WHAT IF** that remote only had one button that you could reprogram once a day?*

But as it is, Christ has been raised from the dead, the firstfruits of those who have fallen asleep. For since death came through a man, the resurrection of the dead also comes through a man. For just as in Adam all die, so also in Christ all will be made alive. (1 Corinthians 15:20–22)

CATCH UP

- Who or what made you laugh recently?
- How did life feel easy or hard this past week?

RECAP

- What stood out to you from what we've read together, talked about, or attempted to do together over the past week?
- What thoughts or questions do you have from today's Bible verse?

GROW TOGETHER

- What might be the main thing God is trying to tell our family today?
- What if we did something new together or returned to a good habit to live out what we're learning? What might that be?

OPEN UP

- In what ways are you struggling in life or experiencing something hard?
- If we were to confess something to God as a family, what might that be?

PRAY

- Who is Jesus to you today?
- Who would be willing to close our time with a simple prayer?

64: Some Assembly Required

***IF** our family had a yard sale this week, what's one item you'd get rid of?*

***WHAT IF** our family could get something for free from any store?*

READ IT: GENESIS 4:1–2

Three words that regularly cause people to overestimate and underestimate their potential are "some assembly required." It's like something weird happens to our brains when we see this on a package and think, *Yeah, I can totally put that together in five minutes.* Several hours later, we realize that following instructions isn't as easy as we thought. All the jokes or tears of frustration won't automatically fix the wild mess in front of us. That's when we usually invite someone else to help us.

When it comes to family, there is definitely "some assembly required." We can't sit around and expect everything good we want to see in each other or ourselves to form by itself. Like how the story of Cain and Abel begins with what seems to be a sense of hope. Cain's name means "here he is," implying that Adam and Eve thought he might be the one God promised would save them from their sins. Sadly, this wasn't possible, because Cain and Abel were born into the sin that their parents and the enemy brought into the world.

Every human and family has had the same issue since. We can try to do the right things and assemble a nice household, but until we address the sin in each of us, we're overestimating and underestimating our potential. Even following God's instructions will eventually frustrate us if we're doing it in our own power. We're all broken and need God to do something special in us first before He does something special in our families. All the jokes or tears of frustration won't automatically fix the wild mess in front of us. Only by inviting God in do we start making real gains.

THERE IS HOPE

Prioritizing your family doesn't mean you let it become your "god" but that you intentionally make God the priority of your family.

Celebrate something you've accomplished together because you asked for help.

- ***IF*** we asked God for help for our family, what would we request?
- ***WHAT IF*** it takes a lifetime of work for God to put things together in our family the right way?

ENEMY

65: The Sweetest of All Gifts

***IF** every time you were losing at a game you suddenly knew exactly what to do to win, do you think this would be fair? Why or why not?*

***WHAT IF** instead a smarter duplicate of you would take over?*

READ IT: GENESIS 4:3–5

Lemonade stands don't magically appear out of nowhere. For every kid who sits down at a table outside hoping to sell a cold cup of sweet goodness to people passing by, there's a grown-up who provided the pitcher, cups, drink mix, and more to make it possible. It's only fair that this adult should get the first cup of lemonade as a thank-you from the kid. Imagine if instead the kid just brought the parent warm lemonade drops leftover at the end of the day.

Look at the two different offerings Cain and Abel gave God. Abel put the Lord first by giving the best portions from the best animals of his flock. Cain gave something God rejected, which reveals that the Lord looks much deeper into us than what we give Him. Whatever the difference was between the two offerings, God saw Abel's as more favorable, which made Cain crazy with jealousy. Cain could've used this insight to make things right. Instead, he let that jealousy grow in his heart and became more like the enemy.

We might wonder why God doesn't just say "thanks" for whatever we give Him. For example, some people regularly set aside money to generously bless Him though their church while others irregularly toss in whatever they feel like giving. All of it gets used for God's kingdom, but God is more concerned with the heart behind the gift than the gift itself . . . although the gift does reflect the heart.

The next time you feel like God is blessing someone else more than you, don't be so quick to cry out, "Not fair!" Maybe He's just honoring what they did right and it has nothing to do with you. On the other hand, perhaps God is telling you something He wants you to pay attention to. After all, the sweetest gifts involve giving what is "right" versus what is "left."

THERE IS HOPE

Anything you offer God will help you to better know His heart . . . and your own heart.

Take a moment to honor each other by recognizing the motives you've seen in each other.

- **IF** everyone didn't overreact at a person's actions but took the time to understand motives, how would the world change?
- **WHAT IF** we first worked on our own issues before expecting it of others?

66: Or What?

IF you could control how well you heard things, when would you use this ability?

WHAT IF you could control how well others paid attention to things?

READ IT: GENESIS 4:6–7

"Or what?"

That's a two-word question we hide behind when we're thinking about doing something foolish and want to know what the consequences will be. We're most tempted to ask it defensively when someone warns us, "You'd better not do this."

"Or what?" we fire back. It's as if we're saying, "I'm going to do whatever makes me happy unless I'm worried about your threat." Being sassy isn't our only option though.

God told Cain that even though there were some religious habits in his life, a genuine relational gap existed between the two of them. The Lord knew that unless Cain invited Him into that gap now, sin would take over. Isn't it wild that what Cain brought as an offering was actually a bigger deal than he realized? Even today people can create a similar relational gap between them and God by saying, "I get the first and best of my time and stuff. I just fit God in where I can."

A better "or what" when we're tempted to do our own thing is to start worshiping God right then and there. It may not seem like the obvious choice to stop yourself in the middle of something sinful to praise Him, but it gives you a clearer view of who He is and who you can be in Him. When you kneel before God, He stands with you against the enemy, who is trying to get you to give in to your worst temptations. That free gift is available through Jesus Christ, who gave all of who He is for all of who we are . . . because He couldn't stand for an "or what" of us not being together.

THERE IS HOPE

Even when we do something with rotten motives, God can use it to show us how to return back toward a ripe life.

What might be the difference between just doing life around people versus with people?

- **IF** you were to write a handwritten letter of encouragement to someone today, whom would you write the letter to?
- **WHAT IF** you were to write a handwritten letter to God telling Him about the relationship you'd like to have with Him?

67: Stop and Grieve

***IF** people would do whatever you said and would not feel hate or jealousy, what would you do?*

***WHAT IF** they were hateful and jealous after you made them do something?*

READ IT: GENESIS 4:8; 1 JOHN 3:1–12

Where *don't* you like to eat? So many restaurants are easy to avoid for so many depressing reasons. They may be dirtier than you'd prefer or serve up food that is underwhelming. Somehow you know this isn't the way things are supposed to be, even though those restaurants still get customers who blindly grow used to the way things are.

Today's verse is arguably one of the saddest in the Bible, but we may be blind to just how sad it is because we're used to some pretty depressing things in our culture. Not only do we read about one person killing another person, but the concept of "family" itself has become dirty and underwhelming. We actually miss out on how much darkness Cain's actions introduced. Every family has some natural weirdness in it, but the story of Cain and Abel is nothing short of heartbreaking tragedy.

Stop and grieve this for what it is and the pattern it creates, or you'll become a blind customer to it. One sin always leads to another until we let God step in. Adam and Eve's sin led to their kids struggling with sin; Cain holding back in his offering led to him keeping God out of areas of his life. That selective obedience became outright disobedience, and that disobedience led to taking another person's life.

We weren't made for this but were instead made to serve up love to one another. Cain's real enemy wasn't his brother but the sin in his own heart that Satan took advantage of. And when people don't know who their enemy is, they start with the closest people who look like their flawed idea of their enemy.

THERE IS HOPE

Sin is our prison. Consequences are our warden. Shame is our cellmate. God offers us a powerful way out if we trust Him.

Have an honest conversation about any bad habits in your family that may get worse if left unchecked.

- ***IF*** you were to describe our lives together one year from now, what would be similar or different?
- ***WHAT IF*** you were to describe our lives together ten years from now?

68: Anchored to a Cain

***IF** you spoke the opposite of what you meant one day every week, what would you do?*

***WHAT IF** others always spoke to you that way?*

READ IT: GENESIS 4:9–10; JUDE 1:10–11

You probably have some rope in your garage or home. Is it strong enough that you'd use it to go rock climbing or rappelling? Both activities use some of the same equipment to anchor to the cliff, yet each is unique in purpose. Rock climbing is about climbing up a mountain, whereas rappelling involves gradually letting your full weight drop down to the ground from a huge height.

Our choices are equally as versatile in how they either lift things up or drop things down. Cain's response to God is famously the worst version of this, for he chose to sarcastically argue instead of owning what he did wrong. You may remember his parents, Adam and Eve, doing this when they were caught in their sin. We also do this when we try to rationalize our bad choices. If you say that word out loud, though, "rationalize" sounds a whole lot like "rational lies."

Back to climbing or rappelling . . . imagine that you saw a random walking stick at the top of a cliff. Would you tie your rope to this "cane" as your anchor? You'd only be setting yourself up for destruction.

The Bible warns against getting roped up in "the way of Cain" for similar reasons. You can pretend that your argument for why you did something is anchored to something strong when it really isn't anchored at all. God calling us and Cain out on this is actually a good thing. We need the Lord and others who will see what we've hidden and challenge us to live in the truth. Many people fear they'll have to come out of the shadows. The real win comes from letting the full weight of what we've done drop down so we can begin to climb back up, anchored to the Lord Himself.

THERE IS HOPE

Know you're in trouble? Lying to cover it up? Soon you're not just telling a lie, you're living a lie. May the Truth set you free.

Give each other a pass right now to confess anything any of you have lied about or done wrong without any penalty of punishment or discipline.

- ***IF*** we had an "amnesty" night like this every week, what would you think of it? Would you want to use it?
- ***WHAT IF*** whenever you denied a sin, some random person spontaneously became depressed? What would you do?

69: Getting Grounded

***IF** all plant life within fifty feet of you would grow whenever you stayed in the same place for more than an hour, would you enjoy that?*

***WHAT IF** all plant life within fifty feet of you would instantly die whenever you stayed in the same place for more than an hour?*

READ IT: GENESIS 4:11–14

Sending kids to their room used to be a form of punishment. That all changed once kids started filling their rooms with toys, electronics, and the Internet. Now punishment might sound more like, "You're in trouble. Go outside!"

"Getting grounded" means different things to different people. Kids usually think of it as a time out or punishment when they've done something wrong, like when a parent says, "Because of what you did, you're getting grounded from spending time with your friends next week." Adults might define "getting grounded" as becoming more mature or in tune with reality. People who work with electricity have their own spin on the phrase because "getting grounded" means making sure electricity doesn't end up randomly hurting people but instead ends up somewhere safe.

All of those definitions apply to Cain based on what God told him. If you remember that Cain's offerings to God came from the produce he pulled out of the ground, it seems fitting that part of his punishment for killing his brother is that the ground will now resist him. Cain would also be a man who would spend his days wandering across the ground, going from place to place without ever truly feeling settled.

This may sound like a severe punishment, but it's actually full of mercy. God wanted Cain to stop listening to the enemy and start becoming a different man. To help him "get grounded" in a positive way, the Lord removed Cain from anything familiar that would cause him to return back to old habits. For God to move our hearts, He has to remove anything in our routine, actions, or attitude that we would cling to instead. To get grounded, we may have to be grounded.

THERE IS HOPE

You may have to face the consequences of bad choices, but today is a brand-new day. Get grounded (and rooted) in the Lord.

What are some of the different meanings of "getting grounded"?

- ***IF*** we were to each become more like the extraordinary people God created us to be, what kind of changes might that mean to our attitudes or behavior?
- ***WHAT IF*** to get us to that point God needed to remove us from certain things or people? What kind of things might those be?

70: Weekly Recap

IF *you could time travel to any past or future moment in your life, what would you do with that power?*

WHAT IF *you could only observe and couldn't change anything?*

By faith Abel offered to God a better sacrifice than Cain did. By faith he was approved as a righteous man, because God approved his gifts, and even though he is dead, he still speaks through his faith. (Hebrews 11:4)

CATCH UP

- Who or what made you laugh recently?
- How did life feel easy or hard this past week?

RECAP

- What stood out to you from what we've read together, talked about, or attempted to do together over the past week?
- What thoughts or questions do you have from today's Bible verse?

GROW TOGETHER

- What might be the main thing God is trying to tell our family today?
- What if we did something new together or returned to a good habit to live out what we're learning? What might that be?

OPEN UP

- In what ways are you struggling in life or experiencing something hard?
- If we were to confess something to God as a family, what might that be?

PRAY

- Who is Jesus to you today?
- Who would be willing to close our time with a simple prayer?

71: A Beautiful Mystery

***IF** whenever people made a really bad choice they had to get a tattoo explaining what they did, what would you think of that?*

***WHAT IF** the punishment was that they simply had to wear tape over their mouth for an hour?*

READ IT: GENESIS 4:14–15

Take a moment to think about what you don't know. It's tough, isn't it? How can you think about what you don't know when you don't know it? So much of life is this way, for every day is a mystery filled with new things to try to understand.

You may have noticed that this Bible passage is one of those things. Up until this point only four human beings have been mentioned in the Bible, yet Cain was worried that other people were going to kill him. That hints at how Adam and Eve truly were fruitful and multiplied, giving birth to other people. God created the first humans with longer life spans than ours, so those kids had time to grow up and have kids of their own, and so on.

There's also a mystery of what the "mark on Cain" was that God came up with to keep him safe from others. Despite all the guesses people have offered on both of these topics, we don't know what the mark was. It does reveal the mysterious love in how God responds to Cain though. The Lord could have in all righteous justice killed Cain on the spot for what he did. Instead, Cain received mercy in being allowed to live and learn from what happened. God also was graceful in putting the mark on Cain as a declaration of protection.

You'll see these responses from God all throughout the Bible. Justice is when we get what we deserve, mercy is getting less than we deserve, and grace is being blessed with what we could never deserve. Embrace the beautiful mystery of how God is at work in all three, for even when we act like His enemy He begins destroying the real enemy in ways we don't fully understand yet still fully benefit from.

THERE IS HOPE

Healthy faith isn't blind, nor can it be explained in detail. Get to know God in mystery and let your relationship with Him become clearer.

Talk about situations where people do or don't face the consequence for bad choices.

- ***IF*** everyone except you did whatever they wanted and said they could because they were "forgiven," what would you do?
- ***WHAT IF*** no one was ever punished for doing wrong, but they did always have to face the natural consequences of their choices?

72: Moving Day

***IF** you could teleport anywhere right now, where would you go?*

***WHAT IF** when you teleported it was a one-way trip?*

READ IT: GENESIS 4:16

Walking in your home has a familiar feel to it, doesn't it? Whether you have tons of space or very little, it's your space. You and your family understand it in a way no one else does.

Imagine how difficult it would be if you were suddenly told you had to move right now and head to a new land you've never been to before with no guarantee of having another home to live in. Cain experienced this when he moved out into a region that became known as Nod, which literally means a "wandering" place. Even as he began building a life there, he was never truly settled. This is what happens not only when you move out of your familiar home but when you move away from God.

That may sound confusing. After all, God is everywhere and Cain could have reached out to the Lord in this new land. Still, the Lord does make His presence known more clearly in certain places than others based on if people come together in His name. It's why regularly coming together as a church is super important.

There will be moments in your future that involve "moving," like physically moving to change jobs or schools. Or perhaps you'll start moving at a busier pace as your schedule gets busier. It could be that friendships will shift and you'll start moving away from old buddies as you form new connections.

Whenever your next "moving day" is, make a "moving" decision to move toward God in it. You might think you'll get around to Him later after you settle in, but if you don't choose Him at the start, you'll make something else the most important thing. Sometimes you just have to decide to build a worship service in the middle of your chaos. God will meet you there.

THERE IS HOPE

There's no place so empty that you can't find God. Whatever you move into next in life, embrace His presence instead of "moving on."

Recognize together how God has been at work in you in the different seasons of your life.

- ***IF*** you had any favorite ways to connect with God, what would they be?
- ***WHAT IF*** God were to tell us His favorite ways to connect with us?

73: Role Reversal

***IF** you got to make your own city, what would it be like?*

***WHAT IF** for every person who came to the city you'd get twenty dollars?*

READ IT: GENESIS 4:17

Is there anything cuter than puppies? Maybe you're more of a kitten or bunny person. Whichever is your favorite, you're not the first person to want to scoop up that irresistibly sweet and furry animal and bring it home.

Of course, they don't stay this way forever. Puppies turn into dogs, kittens turn into cats, and bunnies turn into rabbits. The responsibilities and chores for them change as well as they get bigger. That only multiplies if they later have pups, kittens, and bunnies of their own.

Cain's story shifted and expanded too. This man who once was a kid became a father. The one who killed his father's son began caring about a son. The wanderer started building a city. What an interesting role reversal, especially since he was in his own way attempting to "be fruitful and multiply." Cain even named the city after his son as a way to honor his own lineage versus using it as a way to honor God. We'll later see how this backfired.

In every family there's a gap between what we want and what we get. Many times it's because that family's foundation is made up of imperfect adults trying to do better and not make the mistakes of their past. That's not a bad motive, but the better one is for God to be the foundation. It's the ultimate role reversal: instead of building our family in our image, we build it in His.

That's meant to be true of anything we do. God is creative and life-giving, yet He only started humanity with two people in this huge world. He wants us to know the joy of being creative in how we give life. Let's make it a goal to do this with and for Him versus with and for ourselves.

THERE IS HOPE

The Bible is full of some pretty bad examples of family, yet underneath it all is an ideal we can commit to and begin taking steps toward.

Share stories about some of your best and not-so-best moments as a family.

- ***IF*** we overlooked some of our faults or mistakes, what would happen to us?
- ***WHAT IF*** we as a family let God define what was bad and good versus defining that for ourselves?

74: Loud, Proud, or Wowed?

***IF** you could force people to love you, would you use that power?*

***WHAT IF** a president had this power?*

READ IT: GENESIS 4:18–19, 23–24

Taking a dog for a walk is something of a risk. Aside from how it might pull away from you in an attempt to chase a squirrel, there's also the matter of the dog randomly choosing to poop in someone else's yard. It's good manners (if not local law) for you to have a bag or scooper on hand to clean up after your pet.

What if instead of this as a dog owner you busted out a bullhorn and started loudly boasting about what your dog had just done? What if someone walked over to give you a bag and you just shouted, "No, I'm good!" and walked away. If this was your regular pattern, people might even get used to you not doing anything about it.

Lamech did something ridiculous in becoming the first person to publicly boast about his sins. He not only murdered someone; he was also the first recorded person to distort marriage into something it isn't by claiming more than one wife. Cain may have tried to hide his own sin, but his great-great-great-grandson Lamech was all about announcing his sins for all to hear.

Declaring something with passion and wearing down the culture around you not to say anything contradicting seems to be how the world works these days. It's like we're all about being "loud and proud" in the name of "being real" instead of being humbled and "wowed" in the name of God. Authentic living embraces how we might be wrong just as much as we defend how we're right. It's the difference between giving up wanting to be seen for how we live so that we can instead see (and live) clearly.

THERE IS HOPE

We can credibly speak up against the Lamechs of the world only after inviting God to first speak into the Lamech inside of us.

Try to remember the last few times you invited someone else to speak into your blind spots.

- ***IF*** we were more of a "wowed" family versus a "loud and proud" family, what would be different?
- ***WHAT IF*** the people who challenged us weren't all "haters"?

ENEMY

75: Creating with Crooked Lines

***IF** suddenly all songs disappeared, and you were the only person who remembered them, what would you do?*

***WHAT IF** you could only share one song with the world?*

READ IT: GENESIS 4:20–22

Someone in your neighborhood works for an airline or drives a taxi because others need to get places and meet up with other uniquely skilled people. Another person down the street sells furniture because people need something to sit on while they're eating food bought from a grocer or watching a movie created by artists. The whole world is made up of random people who are all intentional in each other's lives. It's nothing short of awe-inspiring how God gave us freewill to choose our jobs, yet somehow He brings those random decisions together to form a society.

We see where this started within Lamech's family. Jabal worked with livestock out on the range, which meant he was the first cowboy. That industry included people who would breed animals, get milk, sell fur, and more. Jabal's brother Jubal was an artist and inventor who came up with instruments that added music to the world. Maybe some of the basic sounds we enjoy today were discovered and shaped by him.

Not to be outdone, Jabal and Jubal had a half-brother named Tubal-cain who worked with smelting and forging metals. While this became a sophisticated industry much later, he was the constructor of constructors . . . the forger of forgers.

All of this was happening through the household of a violent man who boasted about his evil deeds. The Lord can do some pretty amazing things even through a messed-up family—not because of who they are, but because of who He is. We do inherit traits from our relatives, but we are ultimately not made in their original image but God's. Create and add to this world accordingly.

THERE IS HOPE

God can "draw straight" using "crooked lines."

Celebrate what each of you are uniquely good at doing or the character you see in one another.

- ***IF*** someone named a sandwich after you, what kind of sandwich would you want it to be?
- ***WHAT IF*** you could name a dessert after one of your family members?

76: The Tip of the Iceberg

***IF** you had an eraser that could permanently get rid of any nonliving thing that you wanted gone, how would you use it?*

***WHAT IF** you had a pencil that would create a real-life version of anything you drew on paper?*

READ IT: GENESIS 4:25–26

Icebergs are floating ice mountains you might see in certain large bodies of water. To be more accurate, you may only see part of an iceberg at first glance. The top part will only show as a certain height while the water hides a much larger mass of ice underneath. We use the phrase "tip of the iceberg" for this reason when we only see a portion of a situation but know there's so much more that has yet to be seen.

What took place in Adam and Eve's family regarding Cain and Abel was like "the tip of the iceberg." They only saw the top portion of what had happened between Cain and Abel. Try to imagine how hard it was on them to learn that one of their kids had killed another, not to mention realizing that Cain wasn't the one who would crush the head of the enemy who had deceived them. Sometimes things happen in our families that make us think all is lost because we only see a portion of things.

Thankfully, with God the "tip of the iceberg" is a different kind of metaphor. We may see a portion of a situation, only to discover what God is doing beneath the surface in our favor. For example, as Adam and Eve had another child, people began to seek God. What looked like it would only be a family tragedy became a glimpse of hope.

Your relatives and household can provide a foundation for life, but they aren't meant to define everything about your life. What you see on the surface doesn't determine what God is doing beneath the surface. Remember, you can never be such a messed-up parent or kid that God can't reach into your life or the lives of your family.

THERE IS HOPE

One generation who "gets it" can revive a previous one who "lost it."

Talk about some of the larger struggles your family has gone through.

- ***IF*** in every struggle we remembered that God was working something larger beneath the surface, how would we handle things differently?
- ***WHAT IF*** we sought His perspective on something together right now?

77: Weekly Recap

***IF** every Tuesday for one hour, a person tried to get in your house, what would you do?*

***WHAT IF** there were twenty people who randomly showed up throughout your week to try to get into your house?*

We know that all things work together for the good of those who love God, who are called according to his purpose. (Romans 8:28)

CATCH UP

- Who or what made you laugh recently?
- How did life feel easy or hard this past week?

RECAP

- What stood out to you from what we've read together, talked about, or attempted to do together over the past week?
- What thoughts or questions do you have from today's Bible verse?

GROW TOGETHER

- What might be the main thing God is trying to tell our family today?
- What if we did something new together or returned to a good habit to live out what we're learning? What might that be?

OPEN UP

- In what ways are you struggling in life or experiencing something hard?
- If we were to confess something to God as a family, what might that be?

PRAY

- Who is Jesus to you today?
- Who would be willing to close our time with a simple prayer?

78: On the Record

***IF** you could eat anything without any consequences, how would you use that ability?*

***WHAT IF** your family could eat anything without any consequences but you couldn't?*

READ IT: GENESIS 5:1–3

Have you come across any interesting headlines lately? The news stories you read are made possible by reporters who look for facts that are worth sharing. Part of their job is getting people to open up and talk about things they might otherwise stay quiet about. To report just one story, the reporters may have to have multiple interactions with multiple people to find someone willing to go "on the record" (share something officially).

The family records in the Bible similarly cover multiple interactions with multiple people to tell a particular story. At first glance you might think these are boring lists full of names that are hard to pronounce. But they're in the Bible for a reason.

For example, Genesis 5 begins by reminding us that mankind was made in the image of God and ends with us learning how a righteous man named Noah came to be born. This isn't to ignore the other people who aren't mentioned but to show that God is up to something in our families that we may only see over time.

Our world is full of the influence and actions of the enemy, and we need reminders like this that God is still in charge and raising up some amazing people right under our noses. Every one of us is originally made in His image, so just imagine what happens when a family goes "on the record" by living it out together. Picture husbands and wives inspiring each other each day, along with kids and parents blessing each other. What do you think would happen if brothers and sisters chose not to get on each other's nerves on purpose but worked it out when it happened on accident? All of this could actually show the image of God to the world.

THERE IS HOPE

Being known for having a happy home is great, but real impact happens when your family is known for becoming more like Jesus.

Have a conversation about what different people are known for in the world.

- ***IF*** ten years from now someone did an Internet search on you, what would you like them to see after typing in your name?
- ***WHAT IF*** you could erase one thing people think of when they think of you?

79: That's a Lot of Birthdays

***IF** a gourmet baker offered to make a cool birthday cake to match your personality, what kind of cake would you like?*

***WHAT IF** a master chef catered any five foods in the world for your birthday?*

READ IT: GENESIS 5:5, 27

Standing on a typical bathroom scale will tell you something, but not everything. A number will represent your total weight, but that number won't explain how much of that weight is you versus the weight of any clothing you're wearing. You won't get a breakdown of how much of your body is and isn't muscle. Then there's the matter of if you're completely standing on the scale or only partially.

The numbers we see in the Bible also tell us something, but not everything. When we read about how long people lived back then, it blows our minds, as we're used to living only a small fraction of that today. Can you imagine celebrating 969 birthdays? Just imagine how big your cake would be to fit all the candles!

One thought is that these large numbers are possible because the atmosphere of the world was different during creation but changed over time due to the effects of sin on the world. Another theory is that the climate was unique due to a massive layer of water around the world that existed until God released it during the big flood. We can also guess at how Adam and Eve's uniquely created bodies before sin extended life for them and their family line, especially since the first humans weren't created with any genetic flaws or disease.

These longer lifespans in the Bible eventually started to decrease after Noah's era, becoming closer to what we know it to be today. But during all of these years when people lived much longer, the world became populated rather uniquely.

We may not have as long on earth to make our contribution, but the time we do have is just as important. It isn't easy with an enemy set against us, but we can still make every day count.

THERE IS HOPE

However long we may or may not live on earth, God invites you to live with Him forever if you receive Jesus as Lord and Savior.

What have been some of your favorite birthday moments?

- ***IF*** you could relive a birthday over again, which one would you pick?
- ***WHAT IF*** you could relive a month of your life over again?

80: Get Onboard

***IF** you could design a train that people would pay money to ride, what would the train be like?*

***WHAT IF** you had to live on that train?*

READ IT: GENESIS 5:21–24; HEBREWS 11:5; JUDE 1:14

Hearing a train whistle inspires different reactions. If you're foolishly walking near railroad tracks, the whistle will let you know the train is about to roar through. But if you're at a train station waiting for your ride to arrive, you'll be relieved to hear the whistle. After all, the real purpose of a train is for people to get onboard so they can go from where they are to where they want to be.

Enoch was something of a "train whistle" in how he walked with God and prophesied to get others on board with the Lord. Living like this will either alarm others or inspire them, for it involves warning them about the danger of the enemy while inviting them to go from where they are to where they could be. The Lord uniquely blessed Enoch for this by letting him into heaven without having to die!

Enoch didn't receive this gift because he lived right his whole life, though. Pay attention to how his faith kicked in after becoming the father of Methuselah. Parenthood can cause adults to circle back to investing into their faith, like God's "train whistle" for us to become a "train whistle." The same thing can happen for kids who realize their influence on siblings or friends.

Getting onboard with God likely won't get us into heaven the same way Enoch did. When God does take us there, there's a greater chance others we know will be there *then* if we help them know the Lord *now*. Wouldn't it be amazing to help people go from where they are to where they could be?

So like a train travels many places, go many places to share Jesus. Perhaps you fear that you *may* come across like an obnoxious train whistle if you bring Him up to others, but saying nothing is worse because it *always* saves no one.

THERE IS HOPE

Great news: There are far more people in need in your community than empty seats in your church. Bring them together.

How has someone else inspired you lately?

- ***IF*** we knew every time something we said deeply affected another person, how might we live or speak differently?
- ***WHAT IF*** you told others more often how much they have impacted you?

ENEMY

81: The Ceiling and the Floor

***IF** it were guaranteed you'd win an Olympic gold medal in any existing sport if you trained hard every day for four years, would you do it?*

***WHAT IF** you could create a new sport that you'd win the gold in?*

READ IT: GENESIS 5:28–29

How loud would it be to live in an apartment and have a rock band living below you? What about if you had a professional dancer living above you? Whichever way, you'd be in for a lot of noise! One person's ceiling is another person's floor.

That's actually one way to understand how a family is meant to work. A parent influences where kids start out in life, for the mom or dad's "ceiling" of character is the child's "floor." As adults feel the weight of that they find motivation to grow to set up the next generation to grow even further. It's the joy of a dad or mom to watch their sons and daughters do better at things than they ever did.

Thankfully, when parents fall short and make a lot of bad noise, the next generation still has a shot of becoming something incredible. For example, the enemy had a hold on Lamech's life, as seen in how he lived and boasted about his sin. Somehow this messed-up guy became the father of Noah, who grew up to become a righteous man. Maybe Noah's secret wasn't that he built his life off of his family but instead chose God Himself to be the foundation.

Take comfort in this, for even the best families are full of flaws. It's great to be born into a home where people love God and each other well, but that will only take you so far in life. You still have to make the choice for the Lord's ceiling to become your floor if you truly hope to be raised up.

THERE IS HOPE

Spiritually speaking, failure doesn't mean "game over." Failure means "game on, knowing God and knowing better."

Look for ways that you as family members have given each other an edge at something.

- ***IF*** you had to pick one area of your life that was most shaped by another family member's knowledge or skills, what would that be?
- ***WHAT IF*** you were able to pass your knowledge and skills to someone else?

82: So, So, So, So, So Bad

***IF** you could change the end of any movie or book, what would you do?*

***WHAT IF** when you didn't like the end of a movie you could change it on the spot?*

READ IT: GENESIS 6:1–6

The phrase "disaster zone" may have been used to describe a room in your house (like your kitchen after making homemade pancakes and omelets), but it actually refers to an area in the world where an overwhelming hazard has put people in danger. Someone in government authority has to declare that it actually is a "disaster zone," though, to release the best resources toward rescue, clean up, and restoration. Situations that will take weeks, months, or years to fix all have to have this starting point.

Whatever happened in Noah's era was its own unique disaster zone, whether intensely evil humans created intensely evil families or the enemy's supernatural minions entered into people to corrupt the bloodline the Messiah would come through. Humanity itself was in danger because of it, for people thought "nothing but evil all the time." Things were so, so, so, so, so bad that the Lord even regretted making people because of all the trouble they created and would have to endure.

God's grief doesn't mean that He's lacking in power or a plan, though. He isn't some random force or power in the sky but is our Father who personally cares for us. It's why He officially declares when things are wrong in order to begin a rescue, clean-up, and restoration endeavor. In this case God even gave humanity 120 years before the flood came, likely as a chance to turn things around. Meanwhile, He would look for His own "best resources" to put into motion as a revolution.

Notice that the Bible doesn't end here. Even when we do the worst of the worst, God doesn't stop reaching out to offer us the best of the best. When we deserve cancelation, He starts working on restoration.

THERE IS HOPE

God demonstrates that justice isn't about getting even but about correcting the broken systems of this world so they no longer exist.

Talk about something in the world or your lives that has become really bad.

- ***IF*** you had to guess, do you think people become used to evil over time?
- ***WHAT IF*** everyone in the world just for today didn't think anything but evil thoughts? What damage would happen in just one day?

83: It Only Feels Like Forever

***IF** you had to eat the same breakfast every day for a year, what would it be?*

***WHAT IF** you also had to eat the same lunch and dinner?*

READ IT: REVELATION 20:10

It's hard to keep track of how many things in life feel like they take forever:

> *"I'm so happy to hear your voice! We haven't talked in forever!"*
>
> *"Let's never eat there again. We had to wait forever for our food!"*
>
> *"You were in the bathroom forever! What, did you fall in?"*

What we mean when we say things like this is "that took such a long time that I thought it would never end." We have to be clear on this or else we'll assume whatever *feels* like "forever" is "forever"—because "forever" actually is real.

Notice this difference when we think of the enemy. If you haven't caught it yet, Satan doesn't have his own book of the Bible written about him, but he tries to nudge his way into God's story like an extra in a movie trying to get the camera to focus on him. There are times when he makes a big scene, like in these last few chapters of Genesis. His wild reign doesn't last forever, though—it only feels like forever. To circle back to Revelation 20:10 again, the real "forever" in Satan's life is how he will face eternal punishment for all the trouble he caused.

Maybe you need to remind yourself of this when you're going through something in life that has the enemy's hands all over it. Feeling constantly under attack or being weighed down by ongoing pain can feel like it's time to say, "I've been going through this forever." Do all you can to avoid speaking this way because the more we remember what "forever" is and isn't, the more we'll keep the right perspective about how all the wrong in this world will one day end.

THERE IS HOPE

Every rock that Satan hurls our way is just another reminder that he is losing ground. Step on those rocks with Jesus into victory.

Commit to help each other as a family to think about life in terms of seasons.

- ***IF*** you could have changed how long it took us to get through something in a previous season, what would that be?
- ***WHAT IF*** we avoided using the word *forever* as a mental trick to help us think more clearly about time and what's happening in the world?

84: Weekly Recap

***IF** you could rid the world of one object, what would it be?*

***WHAT IF** you could make an object to replace it?*

As the days of Noah were, so the coming of the Son of Man will be. (Matthew 24:37)

CATCH UP

- Who or what made you laugh recently?
- How did life feel easy or hard this past week?

RECAP

- What stood out to you from what we've read together, talked about, or attempted to do together over the past week?
- What thoughts or questions do you have from today's Bible verse?

GROW TOGETHER

- What might be the main thing God is trying to tell our family today?
- What if we did something new together or returned to a good habit to live out what we're learning? What might that be?

OPEN UP

- In what ways are you struggling in life or experiencing something hard?
- If we were to confess something to God as a family, what might that be?

PRAY

- Who is Jesus to you today?
- Who would be willing to close our time with a simple prayer?

THERE IS HOPE

REVOLUTION

There's a difference between the way things are and the way things are meant to be. You'll see this in some situations faster than others, like when people in the world do horrible things that affect other people. We also need to pay attention to even some of the "good things" around us though. There's always room to grow in every area of life.

Sometimes when people start to notice these gaps, they react by becoming critical. Others try to be a little more positive by trying to make things better. It's the difference between a rebellion and a revolution—one just pushes back on whatever it finds fault with, but the other tries to bring about something better.

It's why God is in the habit of starting revolutions. He doesn't just sit above the earth and point His finger at all the wrong things we're doing. Instead, He comes alongside of us to show anyone willing to notice how things really can be with His power, wisdom, and presence.

The Lord began His own uprising to turn things around by creating special covenants with His people—covenants that are meant to change the world.

85: Avoiding the Chains

***IF** you could make your own restaurant, what would it serve?*

***WHAT IF** it became so popular that you could make it into a chain of restaurants?*

READ IT: GENESIS 6:8–11

Depending on who you talk with, all stores and restaurants should either be one-of-a-kind local "mom-and-pop" experiences or part of a larger "chain" offering similar experiences worldwide. Some argue that we should avoid chains whenever possible because mass-produced businesses kill small businesses. Others argue that you get better options when something is done at a larger level over and over again.

The same thing plays out at home when you have to decide between cooking from scratch or microwaving a meal. Natural is arguably better than artificial additives, but fast food can save you time that you can spend on other things. With choices like this, it might feel like nothing but a matter of opinion.

How we live is more than mere opinion, though. We *are* held accountable for our choices before God. In Noah's era, virtually everyone had become corrupt by giving into the chains of sin. In contrast, Noah spent his life avoiding these chains by following the Lord. He was by no means a perfect man, but he was a local example of what happens when God is invited to create something from scratch without any artificial additives. His family was a true "mom-and-pop shop" of right living in a wrong world.

Yes, it is possible to live your life in this way and walk with God even when everyone else isn't. Every inspiring leader in history who brought significant change to the world was a regular person who decided to live in a reality deeper than the one a broken world handed them. When it feels like you're the only one who is doing the right thing, remember to keep it up because the world needs you to show them what a practical revolution looks like.

THERE IS HOPE

God hates sin, not because He is mean, but because of the mean things sin does to us. He's your Father. Trust Him. Follow Him.

Share something you each did recently that set you apart from others.

- ***IF*** your actions were inspiring to others, would you want to know about it so you could keep doing it or not know about it so it wouldn't go to your head?
- ***WHAT IF*** you could pick a nickname to be known for?

86: Hero Material

***IF** you were a superhero, what would be your method to knowing where crime was?*

***WHAT IF** you bumped into other superheroes who were using their powers in ways they shouldn't?*

READ IT: GENESIS 6:12–14

Who doesn't love seeing a good hero in action? There's something about someone who recognizes the wrongs in the world and makes things right to rescue others. Whether they're fire fighters and police or everyday people serving those in need, we love watching ordinary people become extraordinary heroes. The world notices such people because the world needs such people.

Perhaps this is why in the absence of real role models we sometimes turn celebrities into "heroes" when they're actually just famous for being famous. It's easy to think of Noah this way, like a "Bible celebrity who rode the ark with all the animals." The truth is Noah was an imperfect person who became an imperfect hero when God used him in the history of redemption. He was a faithful example in his generation, so God asked him to be a faithful leader.

We wouldn't be here today without Noah stepping into this role. As we'll see in a later part of his story, Noah and his family may not have been intentionally evil, but they did have flaws. Still, when God decided it was time for a revolution, He started with someone who had already let that revolution begin in his own heart first.

The world may not always acknowledge someone's hero material like God does. No one other than Noah's family joined him in following the Lord. They likely struggled all those years (like our families might) in doing the right thing when no one else was. Remember the big picture, for humanity is still around because of the faithfulness of this one family. What if God also sees your imperfect family as hero material to do something small or large to perfectly impact the world?

THERE IS HOPE

The world is being shaped right now by ordinary people genuinely following God. Standing for Him, even alone, can make all the difference in the world!

Discuss some real-life heroes from history or even today who inspire you.

- ***IF*** you could become more like your hero, would you want to?
- ***WHAT IF*** others saw you as a hero in their lives?

87: Divine Blueprints

***IF** you could design your own car and have it built for you, but only by using features of existing cars, what features would it have?*

***WHAT IF** you could have a completely customized car in parts and features?*

READ IT: GENESIS 6:14–16

For decades, the Lego Group toy company has been famous for its interlocking bricks that come in a variety of shapes and themes. (It's also famous for causing parents extreme pain when they walk barefoot through toy rooms in the dark.) Earlier generations didn't have much of a selection, as Lego bricks were originally only available in a handful of colors and shapes. These basic-yet-revolutionary concepts are still around, despite the most sophisticated sets being available now. The most creative minds today are still drawing on the original wisdom of the first designers.

People who build ships today also draw on knowledge from the past on what's worked and what hasn't. But Noah didn't have any available information on basic sea travel, not to mention for surviving a worldwide flood. It turns out that the exact ratio of the ark's dimensions was 30 to 5 to 3 (length to breadth to height), which shipbuilders only in the last two centuries discovered is the perfect ratio for anyone trying to build a huge boat for seaworthiness. Even the use of the tar-like pitch to coat the boat inside and out was new technology back then.

Noah wasn't a master shipbuilder who was ahead of his time. He simply knew and trusted the Creator, who had designed everything in the world. God not only knew then what was needed for life to continue, but He still does. The Bible has always contained this ship-building wisdom in stunning detail, and it contains so many more basic-yet-revolutionary concepts we can turn to in the middle of our most sophisticated problems. Imagine what else is right under our noses in the pages of Scripture if only we'd draw on the original wisdom of the first Designer.

THERE IS HOPE

Life isn't about the size of the waves you'll face; it's about who you let build whatever you've placed your life in. Let it be Jesus.

Recognize a few topics where God's wisdom makes more sense than the world's.

- ***IF*** you could get God's instructions on something in life, what would it be?
- ***WHAT IF*** God didn't give us the choice to choose His wisdom but instead made it mandatory?

88: More than a Handshake

***IF** you had to come up with a complicated handshake with someone before asking them for help, how often would you ask for help?*

***WHAT IF** you were obligated to do something equal in return for the other person you asked a favor of?*

READ IT: GENESIS 6:17–18

Do you prefer a high five or a head nod? What about a handshake or a fist bump? There are so many different ways to greet another person, but the simple principle is to find a way to come together. Some friends or groups may take things a step further by coming up with a "secret handshake" only certain people know to show that they're part of something special.

The biblical concept of a covenant, like the one God made with Noah, offers its own version of coming together for something special. When one person had something to offer to another person, the "greater" person would make an offer to the "lesser" person, including what each of them would be responsible for. The person in need could reject the offer, but if the arrangement was agreed upon, both individuals would enter into a special agreement or "covenant." To make things official, there would be something ceremonial, sacrificial, or symbolic involved. This was more than a secret handshake—it was a life commitment. To break a covenant could bring about a penalty of death or severe judgment.

Through Noah, God gave us a glimpse of a covenant He offers all of us. Just as the Lord saved one man and his family through an ark, we're invited to become a part of God's family through one man: Jesus Christ. This revolution is possible because He made a sacrificial death that we symbolize through the cross and celebrate through the ceremony of communion. You can reject this offer or choose to enter into a "more than a handshake" relationship with the Lord. The simple principle is to find a way to come together.

THERE IS HOPE

Jesus proves His devotion to the relationship He offers us by offering His own life.

Chat about some silly agreements you've made compared to more meaningful ones.

- ***IF*** you could've avoided agreeing to something in the past, what would it be?
- ***WHAT IF*** we could enter into a more meaningful covenant with God?

89: Wild Kingdom

***IF** you could combine two animals for a pet, which two would you choose?*

***WHAT IF** combining meant eliminating both original animal species forever?*

READ IT: GENESIS 6:19–20; 7:2–3

Pets have a way of being loyal and friendly when we take care of them. Still, it's not unheard of for a dog or cat to suddenly flip and become wild for a day or longer. Any number of reasons might be behind this, like if someone in the house started playing rough with it or if the animal became sick. It's almost like the look in its eyes and behavior toward us changes as it growls or hisses in our direction, nipping at our hands or dive-bombing for our ankles.

The animals during Noah's era had something wrong with them too. The evil nature of people during that time meant people were more inclined to neglect or abuse the very creatures humanity was told to care for. We can safely assume that over time, the majority of animals became a wild kingdom of chaos that generally couldn't be tamed. All of creation was at odds with itself.

The Lord could have wiped out every creature and started making new animals after the flood. Instead, He looked for who and what was worth redeeming. God made the animals come to Noah so the animal world would be repopulated over time, along with additional "clean animals" that Noah could use after the flood to honor the Lord in worship (Genesis 8:20).

It all comes back to our original Genesis 1–2 calling to oversee creation. When we neglect our God-given responsibilities, it affects everyone and everything under us. So notice who or what you're causing to "growl" in your direction, be it family, friends, or other living creatures. Then embrace being a part of God's rescue plan.

THERE IS HOPE

When God disciplines what deserves being disciplined, He saves what deserves being saved.

Try to think of a time when you were able to save a small thing from a larger thing that broke.

- ***IF*** this symbolized a relationship in your life, what would it symbolize?
- ***WHAT IF*** God wanted us to start over with something we gave up on?

90: Food to Go

***IF** you had a magic plate that never ran out of food, what would you do with it?*

***WHAT IF** you co-owned that plate with a homeless person?*

READ IT: GENESIS 6:21

Do you like cooking competitions? Different cooks try to impress a panel of judges, sometimes with a limited amount of ingredients. The challenge is that every judge has a different sense of what makes a meal worth celebrating. A chef can offer the same plate to everyone, only to have it complimented by one person and criticized by another. It's incredibly hard to balance the right blend of sweet and savory to make everyone happy.

Imagine how hard it was for Noah's family to figure out how to get a large enough supply of every kind of food to be eaten on the ark. Not only did they need to plan for their own meals during that time, but they also needed ingredients to feed all the animals. Plus, they needed to hang on to any seeds to replant the various fruits, vegetables, and grains after the flood. Gathering all this food must have taken a great deal of time, and since food spoils, they'd have to constantly refresh their supply. God at this point hadn't told them exactly when the flood would come, allowing them to own their decisions and consequences within this part of the revolution.

The Lord entrusts us with simple instructions for how we're to live and bring life-giving nourishment to others. You can't achieve the perfect blend of making everyone around you happy with whatever you bring to the table, but know that you're not working with limited ingredients when it comes to God. He's enabled you to bring every kind of spiritual food to others through Him, including those with picky attitudes. Take seriously your opportunity to store spiritual "food" inside of you daily by spending time with Him to keep those ingredients fresh.

THERE IS HOPE

In a world of newsfeeds and trending feeds, claim this: "My food is to do the will of him who sent me and to finish his work" (John 4:34).

Talk about a time when someone around you needed wisdom and you felt ready to give it.

- **IF** the things we learn about God are meant to be shared, what does that mean for us when we're listening to a message or reading the Bible?
- **WHAT IF** when we took notes on things we thought of other people to share them with?

91: Weekly Recap

***IF** instead of boats people used friendly dolphins to cross water, how would you feel about that?*

***WHAT IF** people used tame wolves to get around instead of cars?*

God patiently waited in the days of Noah while the ark was being prepared. In it a few—that is, eight people—were saved through water. (1 Peter 3:20)

CATCH UP

- Who or what made you laugh recently?
- How did life feel easy or hard this past week?

RECAP

- What stood out to you from what we've read together, talked about, or attempted to do together over the past week?
- What thoughts or questions do you have from today's Bible verse?

GROW TOGETHER

- What might be the main thing God is trying to tell our family today?
- What if we did something new together or returned to a good habit to live out what we're learning? What might that be?

OPEN UP

- In what ways are you struggling in life or experiencing something hard?
- If we were to confess something to God as a family, what might that be?

PRAY

- Who is Jesus to you today?
- Who would be willing to close our time with a simple prayer?

92: Make It Happen

***IF** eating ice cream required first exercising for a half hour, how often would you eat ice cream?*

***WHAT IF** to eat ice cream you only had to first exercise for ten minutes?*

READ IT: GENESIS 6:22

There are few things parents dread more than a last-minute school project. But unexpected or last-minute assignments cause your imagination to kick into gear in ways it otherwise wouldn't. Pretty soon you're making something amazingly complicated out of pipe cleaners, shoe boxes, and something fuzzy you found under the couch.

Imagination doesn't always lead to creation though. Our best ideas don't become a reality unless we put some energy behind them. If we just pace around talking about the project more than doing it, nothing gets better. Maybe we don't know where to start (and so we never do), or we hold back because we're not sure we're up for the challenge of seeing things through.

Noah heard everything the Lord wanted him to do and got to work making it happen. Instead of complaining about what it required, he dove in to be faithful to everything God commanded. This added to Noah's spiritual journey too. Obedience isn't just responding to directions but to God Himself.

That's the thing about school projects. For all the frustrations they cause us (even at the last minute), it brings us together to tackle something time-sensitive. Maybe the completed project that arrives at school at 7:00 a.m. doesn't look like it did in your brain at 12:00 a.m., but by all means embrace the swagger of getting *something* done as a family.

God obviously lived this out for us first. He didn't just imagine what people would be like but took the time to create us. When He asks you to do something, He likewise expects you to make it happen so new life can come forth . . . beginning between your heart and His heart.

THERE IS HOPE

Doing what's right isn't just about commands but about connection. That thing that God put on your mind to do? Now is the time.

Recognize some of the good ideas you've followed through on individually or as a family.

- **IF** we only stopped at the "good idea" stage on any of these instead of actually creating them, what would be different today?
- **WHAT IF** we realized that our ideas could benefit other people? How would that change our willingness to follow through on them?

93: Waiting a Little Longer

***IF** you could teleport instantly to any place in your state, how would you use that power?*

***WHAT IF** you could teleport anywhere in the world but you would have to wait two weeks before teleporting again?*

READ IT: GENESIS 7:7–12

More things in life should baffle us than what we let baffle us. Like all the new effort-saving devices we have to spend hours learning how to use. Do we really need a circular robot vacuum cleaner that s-l-o-w-l-y moves around pretending to suck up things while we trip over it? How about inventions we have been waiting for, like a personal jetpack or a teleportation device? If they can make a seedless watermelon, why not a strawberry without leaves on top?

What's especially baffling is waiting on the Lord with all the spiritual advances we have and haven't made. Noah's family and all the animals sat in the ark for a week before the heaviest part of the flood came and lifted the boat. After 120 years of preparation, it was a real test of faith for them to wait that much longer for something they hadn't seen. We can guess why God did this, but 2 Peter 3:9 reveals, "The Lord does not delay his promise, as some understand delay, but is patient with you, not wanting any to perish but all to come to repentance." Waiting in the ark apparently had a larger meaning than simply hanging out to catch a wave.

Through Jesus, claim that deeper perspective and revolution. Noah and his family trusting in God to save them through the ark is similar to us trusting in Christ to save us from our sin. Perhaps it looks foolish to others who think we're inventive enough not to need God in a drizzle of problems, but we know that more water will come. To navigate the storms of life and rise above the flood of sin, you need to trust in Jesus and trust that He'll lift you up in due time.

THERE IS HOPE

God is the slowest person who is always on time. Don't confuse what looks like inactivity for unconcern.

Share about when you've had to wait even longer for something you'd already waited for.

- ***IF*** we eliminated some of this added "waiting," what would we miss out on? For example, what if we didn't stop to pray but just ate food right away?
- ***WHAT IF*** God is using something you're waiting on to prepare you for it?

94: Water You Talking About?

***IF** water parks replaced all their water with milk, would you go to them?*

***WHAT IF** they replaced all their water with Jell-O?*

READ IT: GENESIS 7:11–12, 17–20

What's your favorite way to get drenched? Maybe a massive wave pool that slams you back every ten seconds or a tall water slide that drops you into a watery trench. Perhaps you prefer water-gun fights or a sprinkler under a trampoline. Then again, there's nothing quite like singing and dancing in the rain.

Being drenched can also be quite annoying. Like when you ask for a cup of water in the drive-thru, only to discover that the lid wasn't put on tightly enough. You quickly realize the major damage a "mini" cup can cause as the liquid spreads out.

Noah must have had his fill of water during the flood. This was the first time he'd ever experienced water intensely exploding up from the ground while heavy rain fell from the sky. Such great forces impacting the earth from every direction would've caused shifts on the ocean floors that physically broke the land into the formation of the continents we see today. It's why this event has been historically wrestled over and told in stories by hundreds of different people groups who have all tried to understand what clearly happened.

The broken people we live around will drench us from every direction too. Some will explode up at us with their bad attitudes while others will rain heavy burdens down. There will be many days when you'll have had your fill.

Taking a cue from Noah, recognize that things happen in seasons. It's why "forty days" has become a symbol for a time of preparation. Sometimes we'll enjoy it, like a season of training to achieve a goal. Other times we'll get discouraged and weighed down by the tough stuff poured over us. Whatever happens, let God help you start singing and dancing in the rain.

THERE IS HOPE

God took dry years and years and years to prepare Noah for rainy days and days and days. Remember this as you face whatever is ahead of you.

What fun or challenging memories do you have that involve water?

- ***IF*** water can create so many different emotions as you interact with it, how would you describe your general feeling toward it?
- ***WHAT IF*** we had to describe the season we're in now as a family? Would you say you're having a watery blast or getting soaked with discouragement?

95: Torn Apart

***IF** you could build a dream home anywhere, where would you choose?*

***WHAT IF** the home randomly fell apart one day while you were in it?*

READ IT: GENESIS 7:21–23

If your family has ever moved, then you know the challenge of finding the "perfect place" to live. Some families pursue this by custom designing a home and finding someone to build it for them, but even that takes a long time (not to mention enormous mental and emotional energy). Once everything is done, there's a real sense of accomplishment and joy in being able to move in.

Imagine what it would feel like for a family to get to that point but be forced to tear the house down before moving in. All that time they'd spent making things just right would only deepen the hurt they felt in having to destroy everything. Perhaps they could take some of the materials to build a new home in its place, but even then they would feel very sad.

God felt this way after giving us His best in creating the world, animals, and people, only to have our sin officially state it all needed to be wiped out. He custom "built" knowing that we'd custom "destroy." Imagine the incredible pain He felt from our betrayal. Although He did find something to salvage in Noah's family and the creatures He saved, it wasn't without Him being disappointed.

If you haven't yet noticed this, the Lord has constantly been working all throughout history to redeem us. Jesus Christ knew at the beginning of time that He'd come to earth to have His body torn apart so we could be redeemed. May we never take for granted what hurt the heart of the Lord. "Be miserable and mourn and weep. Let your laughter be turned to mourning and your joy to gloom. Humble yourselves before the Lord, and he will exalt you" (James 4:9–10).

THERE IS HOPE

God grieves, but it doesn't define Him. He doesn't randomly lash out at us like a human being might: He seeks to save us as only He can.

Share about times you've had to start over on something you had spent time on.

- ***IF*** nothing in your life ever needed to be started over, what would you have missed out on learning?
- ***WHAT IF*** everything you made would at some point have to be broken in front of you?

96: Details, Details, Details

***IF** humans could hear the thoughts of animals, what would be different in how we lived or treated them?*

***WHAT IF** animals could hear the thoughts of people?*

READ IT: GENESIS 7:23

How does it feel to be wedged next to other people while sitting in a car or van? The longer the trip, the bigger a deal this becomes. We can get creative by arranging smaller and larger people next to each other, but even then everyone needs a little legroom. One of the needs in life is to stretch out.

People have famously wondered how much space Noah and his family had on the ark with all the animals that were with them. There were more than 1,518,000 cubic feet available that they could be creative with, which is about the size of 569 modern railroad boxcars. When you consider all of the subsections and built-in compartments to maximize space, there would have been ample room for every "kind" of animal that would become the ancestor to that species (i.e. dogs, wolves, coyotes, and more are the same "kind"). It's also likely God sent smaller, younger animals versus larger, older ones to ensure they would have more years to repopulate after the flood.

Taking into account all the varying sizes, ages, and needs, around half of the ark would have been absolutely necessary for just the animals. Sea animals wouldn't need the ark for survival, nor would insects take up much space. If even twenty to thirty percent of the ark was set aside for food, then Noah and his family had more than enough room to stretch out.

All details aside, we have to remember that God's power and wisdom were at work in all of this for something greater. The real miracle wasn't the space made on the ark but that the Lord made space in His heart. When He calls you into a revolution, celebrate . . . and be diligent in the details without getting distracted by them.

THERE IS HOPE

God is massive, but He is also meticulous. You can see Him in the big picture and the details, but you only need to start with one. Get going!

Take note of anything important you each need to do that needs a plan.

- ***IF*** your family could help you with figuring out the details, would that be helpful?
- ***WHAT IF*** your family could help you with keeping the big picture in mind?

97: A Different World

***IF** you found an extinct animal in your yard, what would you do?*

***WHAT IF** you dug up a unique creature that nobody had ever heard of?*

READ IT: GENESIS 7:24–8:5

"Please be careful when opening the overhead compartments, as the continents may have shifted."—Noah, getting sassy on the ark

Traveling to a warm vacation spot probably sounds real appealing if you live somewhere where it gets cold throughout the year. The opposite is true too. If you spend most of your time in hot conditions, you might want something a bit cooler or wet. Our planet has no shortage of variety when it comes to climates. Each has appeal, but they all have unique liabilities for anyone who lives there.

These climates didn't always exist though. The way the earth was described prior to the flood leaves us to think that the way things are now is not how they were then. Did one particular type of climate dominate, like a tropical paradise? Or were the variations in climate something we haven't seen since?

What we can tell is that as God created a massive wind to move the water, the planet was impacted in shape and climate. All the rainforests, ice caps, highlands, dry desserts, volcanoes, and more that we're familiar with today began forming in this process due to the tremendous pressure put forth upon the planet. Some of the marine fossils we've found on high mountains way above sea level give evidence of this process.

Simply put, this flood actually happened and is represented in the world around us today. The Bible may not be a detailed textbook, but it does tell us the most important part of true things that human wisdom is still trying to catch up to. Know that the same Lord who can turn a mess into a masterpiece geographically is right now making a different world inside of you personally.

THERE IS HOPE

When you see life becoming different than you know it, know that God is still with you as you journey into this next new season.

Consider what some of your favorite climates or natural sights are in the world.

- ***IF*** you could live there or visit there, which would you choose?
- ***WHAT IF*** that climate or natural site was found everywhere?

98: Weekly Recap

IF you could control the weather three days out of the year, what days would they be, and how would you change it?

WHAT IF you could control the weather all year?

By faith Noah, after he was warned about what was not yet seen and motivated by godly fear, built an ark to deliver his family. By faith he condemned the world and became an heir of the righteousness that comes by faith. (Hebrews 11:7)

CATCH UP

- Who or what made you laugh recently?
- How did life feel easy or hard this past week?

RECAP

- What stood out to you from what we've read together, talked about, or attempted to do together over the past week?
- What thoughts or questions do you have from today's Bible verse?

GROW TOGETHER

- What might be the main thing God is trying to tell our family today?
- What if we did something new together or returned to a good habit to live out what we're learning? What might that be?

OPEN UP

- In what ways are you struggling in life or experiencing something hard?
- If we were to confess something to God as a family, what might that be?

PRAY

- Who is Jesus to you today?
- Who would be willing to close our time with a simple prayer?

99: Birds of a Feather

***IF** your favorite snack were to suddenly disappear off the earth forever, how would your life be different?*

***WHAT IF** ten of your favorite snacks disappeared forever?*

READ IT: GENESIS 8:6–11

It's hard enough to wait on something you know will happen on an exact day, let alone something with unclear timing. If your family has ever called a repairman, you've likely heard something like, "I'll be there between 10:00 a.m. and 9:00 p.m. on Tuesday, or maybe Thursday." That's obviously an exaggeration, but often it doesn't feel like it is.

Feeling stuck waiting prompts us to look for a way to work through it. We might connect with positive people who encourage us to keep going or end up around negative naysayers who tempt us to feel justified over our frustration. Or we might just pull out our phones and play a game where we shoot birds at things.

We see all of this (minus the phone) in the two birds Noah selected during his waiting period. Ravens are predators of smaller animals, but also literally look for death, as their diet involves feeding on the flesh of decayed animals. As scavengers they find something to nibble on in the worst situation.

Doves, on the other hand, eat berries and grains. They generally look for something that's fruitful and growing. Doves are all about the signs of life.

When we're lost waiting for something, the practical goal is to choose faith over fear. The dove finding and bringing back an olive branch reveals that God will guide us. It was also a symbol that said, "Things are turning around and will become better."

It's no accident that the dove now represents the Holy Spirit. Just as the dove led Noah toward life, so does the Holy Spirit lead us to life in Jesus. The Lord offers you comfort under the shadow of His wing. That's a revolution you don't have to wait for.

THERE IS HOPE

Quit waiting for God to make your life better. Instead, let God make you better for life.

What are some of the different ways you pass the time when you're waiting for something?

- ***IF*** you were auditioning for a talent show, what would you do while waiting?
- ***WHAT IF*** you were more intentional about waiting on something else?

100: The Voice

IF *when people wanted you to do something you heard their voices in your mind, how would that feel?*

WHAT IF *you never had any way to know what people wanted you to do?*

READ IT: GENESIS 8:14–19

Raise your hand if you've ever wondered what God's voice sounds like. Does He always speak booming words with the volume turned up to "11"? Or is He more laidback and cool with whatever we do? People have a habit of making assumptions like this that are more opinion than fact, but it raises a good question—how does a supernatural message "sound" to natural ears?

Try considering all the different ways you can receive a message. For example, if you were driving and came to an intersection, you might see a red sign telling you to stop. You could also get the same message from seeing a red light, a white line on the ground, a police officer personally directing you, a friend who tells you to stop, or . . . you get the picture. We might believe we're owed all these forms of communication at once, but each is a unique method that serves a specific purpose.

Noah waited to hear the voice of God before exiting the ark with his family. Things clearly had changed with the water receding and dry land appearing, but instead of bolting out of his floating home, he made sure it was right to do so. Again, Noah was imperfect and didn't nail every decision. This one was spot-on, though. Listening to God's voice kept Noah inside the ark and led him out of the ark.

God will also "keep" us and "lead" us as we listen to Him. He's constantly sending us messages, be it though the living words of the Bible, the Holy Spirit, godly people, the effects of sin, internal nudges, supernatural visions, divine words, or natural circumstances. Don't demand that you only hear from Him in one form or else you might miss out on the multiple messages He's already offering.

THERE IS HOPE

While you're waiting for God to say something new, you can live out what He's already said in the Bible. Run some green lights!

Have a conversation about what you think God's voice will sound like in heaven.

- ***IF*** God only spoke in a booming voice today, what would be our sense of Him?
- ***WHAT IF*** you only heard God speak through one method your whole life?

101: "Altar" Your Perspective

***IF** your city held a yearly festival in your honor, what would it be like?*

***WHAT IF** the whole state participated?*

READ IT: GENESIS 8:20

Imagine growing up in a family who owned a fireworks store. Think of the access you'd have to colorful rockets, crazy noisemakers, sparkling fountains, zippy spinners, and more. But what if you became an adult and lost touch with how special these things are? How sad would it be if whenever you saw fireworks in the sky you shrugged and said, "Eh, I've seen that. What else you got?"

Some good advice we all need to hear is, "Don't get used to fireworks if your dad sells fireworks." Our heavenly Father is glorious in who He is and what He does. He's literally the Creator of everything good that has ever existed and ever will, and yet our attitude toward Him and His revolution can be, "Eh, I've seen that. What else you got?"

Consider Noah. Most people know he built the ark, but very few people know he also built an altar. Noah didn't get off the boat and kiss the dry land or build a house. Instead, he stumbled off to build an altar, ready to praise God. His devotion deepened as the Lord responded with the same blessing given to Adam and Eve to "be fruitful and multiply on the earth." Instead of demanding something for himself, Noah stopped to burn something pleasing to God . . . like lighting fireworks in His honor.

What things in your life have you gotten so used to that you've forgotten how special they are? When you sit on your couch, it's a gift to be thankful for. When your family enters a room, they are a gift to be thankful for. When you pray to the God who knows your name, He is a gift to be thankful for.

Don't lose your reverence. Fight familiarity. Be grateful for every gift from God that you have. Your Father is lighting off fireworks right now! "Altar" your perspective.

THERE IS HOPE

Worship is about who God is. Praise is about what God has done. Doing both reveals who we are and what we're to do.

Have each person count the letters in their name and thank God for that many things.

- ***IF*** doing something like this is that easy, why is it so easy to forget to do?
- ***WHAT IF*** we built a morning or nighttime habit to do this as a family each night for the next week?

102: Flesh and Blood

***IF** you had to be any animal in a zoo for a year, what animal would you be?*

***WHAT IF** you could choose to know that you're actually a human while you are the animal?*

READ IT: GENESIS 9:2–6

"Gotta get my money's worth!" is apparently the battle cry at every buffet. All the endless food options might tempt you to fill a plate with sixteen carbohydrates, nine kinds of meat, four chocolate desserts, and a single piece of fruit to pretend you're eating healthy. It all comes down to whether you give into your physical urges (even when you know you're crossing a line, and possibly a pants size).

Another "buffet" we struggle with is when we're angry with someone or something and can choose between endless options of how to be nasty. It all comes down to whether you'll give into the emotional urges you feel (even when you know you're crossing a line, and possibly a command from God). He helps us see through these thin moments by drawing an even thicker line.

One of the natural consequences from all the evil that existed before the Flood was that the instincts of animals and people became more hostile. God explained to Noah that we'd crave eating animals in ways we hadn't before, which only made them more inclined to attack us. We'd also be tempted toward violence against each other. To combat this, we were to view flesh and blood with some new limitations: an animal could be eaten as food, but its life still needed to be respected; and people could be punished for murder, but we still needed to see the image of God in them. How do you think we've been doing with all of this?

Life has value that we're inclined to overlook when we're hungry—be it physically hungry for food or emotionally hungry for revenge. This world is not a buffet for us to prey upon whatever we want without consequences. God's revolution means we are to be known for how we respect life . . . including how we handle death.

THERE IS HOPE

A powerful prayer to God . . . in four words: "What did I miss?" In three words: "Change my heart." In two words: "Use me." In one word: "Okay."

Share some of the temptations you each face in acting out in anger.

- ***IF*** there were a rule about expressing anger everyone had to follow, what would it be?
- ***WHAT IF*** we started living out that rule together as a family?

103: Something Colorful

***IF** you could change something about the sky today, what would it be?*

***WHAT IF** that change to the sky stayed that way forever?*

READ IT: GENESIS 9:11–13

Do you tend to look for rainbows after a rain? These colorful phenomena have come to mean different things to different people. A certain cereal with a leprechaun mascot uses rainbows to make you think a bowl of sugary marshmallows is a part of a "balanced breakfast." Others use rainbows to symbolize their opinion that we're to see all ideas or values as acceptable even when they're against God's truths and commands.

What if we paid attention to what the Lord says a rainbow actually represents? He created this natural arc as a reminder of the supernatural promise that He'd never again use a worldwide flood to discipline humanity. There's a certain sense of joy in this, but it's not without a warning. God does have the power to do anything He wants, but He's also good and He limits His wrath to bring about good in our lives. We're not to use that mercy to dive into sin, but we are to dive into Him.

You can personalize that promise, but only if you receive it for what it is versus what you might see it to be. In fact, no two people see a physical rainbow the same way because the angle of sunlight going through the individual colors is different for everyone. And that rainbow only exists because God set such natural laws into motion. Even rainbows found in oily street puddles follow these same rules.

God offers you so many symbols of hope in an otherwise hopeless world. You will face many "storms" in life, but know that something beautiful is on the other side. Let it be something colorful to proclaim that God's revolution is at work in your life.

THERE IS HOPE

*Hope is still hope when storms are still storms;
God is still God when pain is still pain.*

Talk about things you thought meant one thing but mean another, like misheard song lyrics or a movie you had a flawed opinion of before you saw it.

- ***IF*** God wanted one thing about Himself to be clear to you, what would it be?
- ***WHAT IF*** whenever we saw a rainbow we let that remind us to make the good and hopeful things of God clearer in our world?

104: Um . . . Awkward

***IF** whenever you did something embarrassing your closest family and friends took a picture of it, how would you handle it?*

***WHAT IF** everyone in the world saw those pictures of you?*

READ IT: GENESIS 9:20–23

Let's just say it out loud: being a part of a family means things can get awkward. Things can end up funny, like if one of you burps during dinner when guests are over. But a family member can also be destructive and make things inappropriately awkward for everyone else. We may not know the right response in either case.

Noah was described by God as being "blameless" in his generation (Genesis 6:9). That doesn't mean Noah was perfect, for today's reading reveals he was just as capable as anyone of making a bad decision. Sure, he did make good decisions—like building an ark for his whole family instead of a canoe for himself. But here Noah ignored God's stance that we should not get drunk on alcohol. He then passed out naked, which made things even more awkward for his family.

There are lessons here for us, beginning with us realizing if the ways we pursue personal pleasure cause discomfort for our families. Maybe in your home people don't get caught up in wine or beer, but maybe the way you express anger or pursue hobbies creates strain. You may want to ask your family, "Be honest, what is one thing I do for myself that makes things even a little awkward for you?"

Also note how Noah's family members each handled things. One son only wanted to talk about it, while the other two respectfully tried to help. It's easier to gossip about family weirdness than it is to work on it. Some situations may only get better if you invite a counselor to guide you (and will only become more awkward if you don't take this step). The Bible doesn't hold back in revealing the bad decisions of its "heroes," so learn from them as you invite God to work on yours.

THERE IS HOPE

God isn't skipping over the messy parts of your life. Don't skip over the messy parts of the Bible.

Debrief all of this as a family and see what kinds of thoughts or feelings get shared.

- ***IF*** you had a close family member do something that made you feel uncomfortable, would you be willing to let that person know?
- ***WHAT IF*** others told you that you were making them uncomfortable?

105: Weekly Recap

***IF** you could create a new comic strip, what would it be about?*

***WHAT IF** you had to make three new comic strips in addition to the first one?*

[God] didn't spare the ancient world, but protected Noah, a preacher of righteousness, and seven others, when he brought the flood on the world of the ungodly; . . . the Lord knows how to rescue the godly from trials and to keep the unrighteous under punishment until the day of judgment. (2 Peter 2:5, 9)

CATCH UP

- Who or what made you laugh recently?
- How did life feel easy or hard this past week?

RECAP

- What stood out to you from what we've read together, talked about, or attempted to do together over the past week?
- What thoughts or questions do you have from today's Bible verse?

GROW TOGETHER

- What might be the main thing God is trying to tell our family today?
- What if we did something new together or returned to a good habit to live out what we're learning? What might that be?

OPEN UP

- In what ways are you struggling in life or experiencing something hard?
- If we were to confess something to God as a family, what might that be?

PRAY

- Who is Jesus to you today?
- Who would be willing to close our time with a simple prayer?

106: Spread Out

***IF** there were one restaurant that had every type of food from all over the world, what five foods would you order today?*

***WHAT IF** the restaurant only served candy from all over the world?*

READ IT: GENESIS 10:1, 6–12, 21

Where would we be without tacos, ravioli, fried rice, pierogis, gyros, bratwurst, hummus, and other foods that come from unique cultures? What about the way you celebrate different holidays or use certain slang words in your extended family—what different cultures impact those things? Being aware of these foods or traditions helps you note where those tastes and habits came from. We're all a part of a large history created by other people older than we are who formed the cultures we inherited.

It all really took off after the flood. The Indian, Russian, Iranian, Greek, Armenian, German, African, Egyptian, Lebanese, Asian, and Arabian cultures can be directly tracked to this revolution of people finally being fruitful and multiplying. The only sad part is that this occurred not because people were taking part in God's revolution but because of God's discipline after a "powerful" man named Nimrod started a city called Babylon (or "Babel") where people got distracted by power.

We'll read more about that tomorrow, but for now make sure you see one other family line in this passage of names and nations. God's revolution would continue to move forward through the family line of Shem. Two important people who came out of this family are a man named Abraham and our Savior, Jesus Christ. That's the larger history we're a part of, proof that we can enjoy what every nation can bless us with, but also proof of how through God's revolution all nations can be blessed.

So enjoy some Italian Beef (look it up if you don't know what it is). Being cultural in the right ways helps you be spiritual in ancient ways. Spread out!

THERE IS HOPE

All the diversity in the world reveals that we have one Savior who invites every person and people group to personally know and express their love for Him.

Reflect on how our home reflects the culture(s) of our ancestors in any way.

- **IF** there's one thing you like most about the way we do things, what is it?
- **WHAT IF** there was one thing you could make sure every generation after you would do no matter what?

107: The First Selfie

***IF** you could create a new invention and be known for it, what would the invention be?*

***WHAT IF** you weren't known for inventing it?*

READ IT: GENESIS 11:1–4

It's just not easy to talk anymore. Despite all the technology that was created so people would stay connected with others, we use those things less to interact and more to say what we want to say. We've gone from dialogue to monologue.

Look at how our phones became cameras. Any remotely interesting meal you ate suddenly needed to be digitally captured to one day show your great-grandkids. Pretty soon we started taking "selfies" to build a fan base about how awesome our lives appear. These self-portrait photos may be good-natured, but they can also become all we're known for.

The descendants of Noah initially all spoke the same language and took part in God's revolution. Something changed when they decided to use their strengths to focus on themselves instead of God, though. The phrase "Let us make a name for ourselves" (v. 4) means they wanted to overshadow the Lord's name. They started building a tower that was meant to build their confidence higher and higher.

To accomplish this, they used the same material for mortar between the bricks that Noah used to waterproof the ark. Isn't it wild how what God gives us as a gift to advance His revolution with Him can only a generation later become a tool we use to advance ourselves without Him? It's another instance of moving from dialogue to monologue.

Selfies aren't inherently bad any more than towers are inherently bad. What made the Tower of Babel the first "selfie" gone wrong was when we moved God out of the spotlight to put the spotlight on ourselves. So are we just telling our story, or are we expanding God's story throughout the world?

THERE IS HOPE

The more you try to sell yourself, the more you'll become a sellout. Jesus says, "Come to Me." Before you build anything, reset everything.

Take some time to talk about healthy and unhealthy uses of technology.

- ***IF*** technology like phones and computers disappeared, what would be easier in your life, and what would be more difficult?
- ***WHAT IF*** we never shared pictures of ourselves online? What, if anything, would be missing from our lives?

108: For What It's Worth

***IF** you had to witness one bad event in history, which one would you pick?*

***WHAT IF** you could affect that event with your actions during that time?*

READ IT: GENESIS 11:5–7

Think about any board games you've played that use fake money. Ever felt a real sense of feeling rich holding a wad of pretend cash? Imagine trying to go shopping in the real world with it! Some younger kids may struggle with understanding how that kind of paper currency isn't real, prompting a more mature player to explain how this money only has worth in the game.

The things we do for ourselves that try to cut God out of the picture are like pretend board-game money. They may work out for whatever game we're playing in life but have no real weight or worth in eternity. The people who began building the Tower of Babel experienced this without knowing it, for even if they'd built up to twenty-six thousand feet they would've eventually not been able to go any higher due to a lack of oxygen. Try to imagine how silly it was for the people to try to elevate themselves to be on the same level as God just as He moved down to be nearer to them. As He did, He showed them the difference between what is fake and what is real.

People may not build towers these days like they did in Babel, but they build false ideas about God that they think are equal to the Lord. Maybe they get some sort of "value" out of these beliefs while on earth, but those beliefs don't carry any real value before the Lord. We don't need to build fake religions in our search for God, for God offers His real presence in His search for us. Take that in for what it's worth.

THERE IS HOPE

The height of our tallest efforts doesn't impress God, but the depth of our openness before Him widens what our lives are capable of.

Try to come up with a list of things that people may believe in that aren't real.

- ***IF*** someone were really sincere in what they believed, would it make it true?
- ***WHAT IF*** the times God sets us straight are to further His revolution to save us, not to punish us?

109: Do You Habla Français?

***IF** you shared three things about yourself with someone who spoke a foreign language, what would you share?*

***WHAT IF** someone used a foreign language to communicate with you? How would you try to understand them?*

READ IT: GENESIS 11:8–9

Ever watch a movie or video where what you see doesn't match up with what you hear? Maybe it was just a sound glitch, or maybe it was a good old-fashioned karate movie made in Asia. You'll more often experience it when you're watching something that was originally recorded in another language. Voice actors are regularly hired to record a new language over the old one so that more cultures can be reached with the same material. Since the new audio doesn't match up, we tend to stop watching the movie in frustration. Our only other option is to go online to somehow discover the original story.

As God looked at what the people of Babel were up to, He was frustrated they decided to ignore His revolution to be fruitful and multiply across the whole earth. They had become experts at saying the same thing, but what they were saying was destructive. The Lord knew if they felt successful in this anti-revolution, their rebellion would only increase, so He disconnected them from succeeding at the wrong thing so they'd remember what the right thing was. To do this, God introduced new languages to different groups of people and then spread them out across the world. Since the new audio didn't match up, people stopped the project entirely. God intended this for them to somehow discover His original story.

This is an important lesson for us, because God isn't a fan of "unity" unless that unity is around the right things. Revelation 7:9 says what draws people from every nation and language together in heaven is Jesus Christ. That revolution is at work today in how different people and cultures honor Him in what we see and what we hear.

THERE IS HOPE

God speaks all languages—including yours. He is intimately familiar with the slang of your life and fluently whispers into it.

Discuss how language is a powerful tool and a blessing God has given us.

- ***IF*** you suddenly forgot how to speak your language, how would you try to relearn it?
- ***WHAT IF*** everyone else in the world spoke a different language from you?

110: The Merry Old Land of Uz

***IF** someone asked to interview you about your life, what would you say?*

***WHAT IF** that person wrote a book based on your life and what you said?*

READ IT: GENESIS 10:22–23; JOB 1:1

It'll cause your eyes to water, but an intriguing art form called an "autostereogram" lets you see 3-D images in 2-D patterns if you'll stare through a surface image of random zigzags. Not everyone can accomplish this and see the picture-within-the-picture float to the surface, though. It requires changing how you naturally see, be it by crossing your eyes on purpose or letting them become blurry while you focus through them. This may be why the popularity of this art fizzled as people became frustrated with not being able to see what others could.

The land of Uz and the life of Job are equally hard to see past the surface. It's possible one of Noah's great-grandsons founded Uz, but we're not super clear on that. We also don't know exactly when Job lived, though we can put together some clues from the book, like how he lived after the flood (Job 22:16), offered his own sacrifices to God instead of through a priest (Job 1:5), and had tensions with certain people groups (Job 1:15–17). Job's friends couldn't see past the zigzags to recognize how God was at work in Job's life. They couldn't see that Job is yet another example of a righteous man embracing God's revolution while others were focused on themselves.

People who look at you or your family will end up making one of two conclusions. Some will assume you're nothing more than a random zigzag of religion that they'd rather not get to know. Others will stare at you long enough to see Jesus emerging out of your lives. You can't control which conclusion they make, but you can look for Jesus and take part in His revolution yourself.

THERE IS HOPE

One of the greatest things you'll ever see in the Bible is seeing how God is in your life.

Debrief all of this and talk about what you think you are known for as people or a family.

- ***IF*** a single word could sum up your life, which word would it be?
- ***WHAT IF*** you had to pick a single word to describe your family?

111: Pass It On

***IF** someone told you that you'd make a good pastor, what would you say in response?*

***WHAT IF** you knew for sure that if you became one you'd be great at it?*

READ IT: JOB 1:2–5

Among all the newer things in your home might be an old object that was passed down to you. You might own the first dollar one of your relatives made after coming to America from another country, a photograph of a particular ancestor, or a baseball that a grandparent caught at a big game. Perhaps there are secret recipes within your family meant to stay in the family for generations to come. We keep these mementos so that those who came before will bless those who follow and proclaim, "This is where we came from." That is why some relatives pass along photos of family members you've never met—so you know the larger story you're a part of.

Job was up to something along these lines as he regularly made sacrifices to God on behalf of his family. He'd been a great model to them of how to live a righteous life, but we're not exactly sure if Job's kids embraced this. They were a wealthy family by the standards of that day, yet Job regularly asked for forgiveness on behalf of his kids just in case they'd done anything sinful.

Parents today might do something similar by taking their kids to church and praying for God to bless them. It's good and right to take steps like this, but the reasons why need to be passed down carefully as well. Just because one person in the family follows Jesus doesn't make the Lord automatically turn everyone in the family into a Christian.

So remember the sacrifice Jesus made for you. Remember the sweat of your ancestors. Remember why you decided to grow with God. And then . . . pass it on.

THERE IS HOPE

You can get a better crack at a deeper life with God because of the digging that others did with Him before you.

Identify an extended family member or friend you'd like to see become a Christian.

- ***IF*** this person became a Christian, who else would be inspired by it?
- ***WHAT IF*** the things we do to grow in our faith are also meant to bless others? What shouldn't we give up on even if we feel tired of doing it?

112: Weekly Recap

***IF** you could invent a new dance, what would it be like?*

***WHAT IF** everyone loved it and did it daily?*

Instruct those who are rich in the present age not to be arrogant or to set their hope on the uncertainty of wealth, but on God, who richly provides us with all things to enjoy. (1 Timothy 6:17)

CATCH UP

- Who or what made you laugh recently?
- How did life feel easy or hard this past week?

RECAP

- What stood out to you from what we've read together, talked about, or attempted to do together over the past week?
- What thoughts or questions do you have from today's Bible verse?

GROW TOGETHER

- What might be the main thing God is trying to tell our family today?
- What if we did something new together or returned to a good habit to live out what we're learning? What might that be?

OPEN UP

- In what ways are you struggling in life or experiencing something hard?
- If we were to confess something to God as a family, what might that be?

PRAY

- Who is Jesus to you today?
- Who would be willing to close our time with a simple prayer?

113: Being Volunteered

***IF** you were required to volunteer to do some type of community service, what would you volunteer for?*

***WHAT IF** others had the power to make this decision and volunteered you for whatever they wanted you to do?*

READ IT: JOB 1:6–8

Being a part of a family means you get volunteered for things you may not have signed up for. When one person wants guests over, starts a hobby, or signs up for a sport, the rest of the household has to adjust around it. At least 75 percent of parenting, for example, is probably carrying collapsible chairs to local sporting events. The same is true when someone in the home buys a new car or toy that requires everyone else to make space for it. We adapt to what's needed because we value our family.

Taking part in God's family also involves being volunteered for things you may not have directly signed up for. Take, for example, one of the most interesting phrases in the Bible, when God asked Satan, "Have you considered my servant Job?" (v. 8). We might think, *Why would God bring up Job?* Keep in mind that Satan had in arrogance just come to stand before the Lord. Something larger was obviously at stake here in the larger revolution God was up to, for He saw something so special in Job back then that we're still talking about him today (James 5:11).

Whenever volunteers are needed, you may feel a temptation to hide behind other people or hang out in the back of the room in the hope of slipping by unnoticed. You can treat God the same way if you assume that the number one goal of living on earth is to be comfortable and never experience trials. Remember, you take part in a *revolution* in a broken world of sin—it's more like a war where we are active soldiers than a movie where we are a pampered audience. Embrace the difference, and let both the trials and the blessings of your life show others hope in God.

THERE IS HOPE

When we feel God is picking on us, He's actually picking us . . . to take part in a revolution of bringing others into a relationship with Him.

Talk about how you feel about volunteering, being volunteered, or volunteering others.

- ***IF*** your favorite pet was more important to someone else in some way than it was to you, would you volunteer to give it to him or her?
- ***WHAT IF*** you could save lives by volunteering to give your pet to a new home?

114: The Prologue and the Epilogue

***IF** you had a book whose story would literally play out in front of you until you closed the book, what kind of story would you want it to be?*

***WHAT IF** all books were that way?*

READ IT: JOB 1:9–12

All great stories are made of specific parts that when put together help you understand what's going on. For example, a "prologue" at the beginning of a movie or story gives you information about what you're about to see or read. It's like the famous crawl of information at the beginning of Star Wars movies or an episode recap in a TV show. These explanations create insight that help you more naturally understand the story.

Job's prologue seems to be Satan being disgusted with God for blessing this man. The enemy said that Job only lived right because of those blessings but would stop honoring God if everything was stripped away. The Lord then gave permission for Satan to try to prove this, which seems strange from our point of view.

That is, unless we consider the real prologue before this prologue. God's original plan for humanity was that we'd use our freewill to trust Him and not introduce sin into this world. Instead, we listened to the enemy and let evil take over, and so the Lord had to discipline us in the Garden of Eden, through the Flood, at the Tower of Babel, and more. Whatever God is up to with Job is somehow a part of a larger story.

To know more we could turn to the "epilogue" of the story—a summary at the end that helps us understand how all that's happened led to something new. Job's epilogue was amazing, but it isn't just found at the end of his book. He was offered the same revolutionary epilogue we are by trusting in the Lord—that one day the enemy will be permanently dealt with through Jesus and we will permanently enter into heaven. Keep this in mind as you dive more into Job's story . . . and your own.

THERE IS HOPE

Our sin and Satan's attacks do not cancel God's revolution but are used in its larger purposes.

Discuss how life would be different if we knew why everything that happened had to happen.

- ***IF*** you could ask God a question about something you've gone through or seen others go through, what would you ask?
- ***WHAT IF*** God's truthful answer didn't satisfy you?

115: One Bad Thing After Another

***IF** you lost everything you personally owned overnight, what would you do?*

***WHAT IF** your whole family lost everything too?*

READ IT: JOB 1:14–19

"Where's the last place you had it?" That's what people ask when you tell them you just lost something. Only if you knew the "last" place you had something, you'd know exactly where it is!

Losing anything important to you can be devastating. You experience this when you lose all your hard work on a project or discover that your dog actually ate your homework. And then there is that awful, tragic moment when you lose a loved one. No words can fix any of this, even if our well-meaning friends share some.

What happened to Job was an absolutely devastating run of one bad thing after another. He lost everything in his life that could have been his source of happiness—family, wealth, property. Imagine if you had to face all that! You might even feel tempted to question God for allowing it to happen.

Our world tells us that our best option when we grieve is to find a way to manage it. If your dog dies, you're told, "You can always get another one." If we can't stop crying, someone hands a tissue and says, "Calm down."

Know that it's always okay to feel what you feel when you go through a big loss. It's also a great opportunity to trust that God has a much clearer perspective on right and wrong than you do. Just because you don't understand that perspective yet doesn't mean it isn't there.

So let your loved ones keep on giving you well-meant advice. It's their way of saying they love you. And let God keep giving you answers that are bigger than your questions. It's His way of saying He loves you. He won't ever stop perfectly loving us. When everything and everyone runs out, His revolution won't.

THERE IS HOPE

God wants to give us eternal life and help others to be drawn to Him through our lives. Any pain we experience can serve that purpose.

Note the things you've each clung to over the years, like a favorite stuffed animal or a hobby you enjoy.

- **IF** someone suggested that you let go of that object or activity in order to grow as a person, what would you say?
- **WHAT IF** someone who loved you took that thing or experience away from you?

116: Life After the Crash

***IF** you could own a small airplane, a professional racecar, or a speedboat, which would you choose and why?*

***WHAT IF** you had to regularly pay for all the care and storage of the vehicle?*

READ IT: JOB 1:20–22

After a car crash or bike wreck, it's hard to immediately understand what just happened. While wincing in pain, we end up asking, "Am I still alive?" "What just happened?" "Can I move?" "Will anyone save me?"

Job went through all these questions in his own way. Tearing a robe and shaving one's head was a way of recognizing pain out loud; those actions said that you were still alive but confused about what had happened. Job felt naked and helpless like a baby, but he praised God and trusted in Him for help. Job also modeled what it means to experience a loss while still honoring God for blessing him in the first place.

This only seems possible when you remember Job was already worshiping the Lord before all this happened. All those times Job hoped his sacrifices would bless his family ended up strengthening Job, not to mention God's family, for we're astounded by his attitude even centuries later. He shows us that instead of running from our pain or replacing it with another feeling, it's better to face it and process it at a pace slow enough to rest in but active enough to grow in.

Life is going to crash again and again at different levels of intensity. One day a friendship won't be as close as it used to be; your job will suddenly become very difficult; you'll watch big chunks of money go toward unexpected needs; and on and on and on. Again, the first step in a healing process begins with God and specifically seeking Jesus as our healer. We can become "alive" by noting what happened on the cross; we can "move" because Jesus did save us.

THERE IS HOPE

Asking, "What's going on here?" is a valid question, but healing happens by asking, "What am I doing with God based on what's going on here?"

Share a memory of a time when you fell down while using roller skates, a sled, or a skateboard.

- **IF** someone recorded what happened, would you want to see it?
- **WHAT IF** other people who watched your crash could learn something from it that would help them avoid experiencing that kind of crash themselves?

117: And the Hits Just Keep on Coming

IF *once a day a big fuzzy caterpillar the size of a car would randomly bump into you, what would you do?*

WHAT IF *instead an army of small caterpillars bumped into you daily?*

READ IT: JOB 2:4–10

It'll fly a kite, and it'll mess up your hair. Sailors need it, dogs in cars seek it, and people raking their leaves can't stand it. What is it?

Wind. People have been studying the effects of wind on trees as far as back as 300 BC (Aristotle's successor Theophrastus even wrote two books that touched on it). The takeaway is that a rooted tree becomes thicker and stronger when it experiences the tension a thick breeze or storm creates. Trees that don't experience this may grow taller, but they do become weaker over time.

Job was definitely "rooted" in God spiritually, for when his life was blown apart the first time, he swayed with it without falling over. It made Satan so angry that he complained before God again and said that Job would renounce the Lord if more tragedy was allowed. The devil was given permission to prove it, but he was quickly proven wrong again. Job chose the revolution of honoring God whether life was good or bad. He didn't feel the Lord owed him or his wife anything.

When reading this story we wonder about God's will, but there's also the matter of God's war. Perhaps Job went through what he did so we can see how Satan is regularly wrong in what he thinks about us and how he is restrained from doing whatever he wants to us. Remember that when he blows through your life, for such a storm can actually deepen your roots and make you stronger.

It's never easy to understand how pain is serving a higher purpose. Years down the road, when you're thicker and stronger, you may have that perspective when you look back. On this side of things, when you feel nothing but an ache, being rooted in Jesus helps you stand and sway without falling over.

THERE IS HOPE

Every trial we endure with God gives hope and an example to others who think they can't make it through their trials.

Share about how some of your trials have made you stronger.

- ***IF*** you could have avoided going through one particular hard experience, which one would you pick?
- ***WHAT IF*** you were able to control the level of trials the people around you experienced?

118: The Buddy System

***IF** you and a friend were in a circus, what would your act be?*

***WHAT IF** you and your friend were the ringmasters?*

READ IT: JOB 2:11–3:1; 32:1

If army movies have taught us anything, it's that drill sergeants know how to yell and make people do lots of push-ups. Training in the military is about more than making just one person a better soldier, though. Soldiers have to learn how to work as a *unit.* A simple task like running together requires soldiers who can run faster to slow down while others must speed up.

Job needed a *unit* of friends around him as he dealt with the crushing ache inside of him. Three of his friends seemed to offer this "buddy system" by simply sitting with him in support. This fell apart later on as each friend ended up giving Job a lengthy speech about how Job was probably suffering because he'd sinned in some way that he wasn't being honest about.

Job disagreed and responded with his own big speech about how he was a good guy who couldn't figure out why he had to suffer. Only one young man named Elihu, who emerged later, ended up letting Job and his friends know they were all being shortsighted—Job was under the same curse of sin as anyone else and therefore subject to sickness and poverty. God also spoke similar words into Job (Job 42:7–8).

Romans 12:15 says part of God's revolution is choosing to "rejoice with those who rejoice; weep with those who weep." We can reveal Jesus to others in how we give them our attention or speak a kind word. Their pain isn't our chance to give a long sermon full of guesses, but to offer a prayer full of sincere truth.

Invite the Holy Spirit to show you how to be a friend to someone who is hurting and to let God offer Himself plainly through you. That's the real buddy system. And that's the real revolution.

THERE IS HOPE

As you ask God to help you see what He sees and hear what He hears, you will help His people hope for His hope.

Share about when you put the needs of others before your own (or the opposite).

- ***IF*** you knew someone who was really hurting, what would you say to him or her?
- ***WHAT IF*** you were going through a hard time? How would you want other people to treat you or speak into you?

119: Weekly Recap

***IF** you could put a single thought into someone's head, what thought would it be and whom would you pick?*

***WHAT IF** you could put a single thought into everyone's head?*

God is greater than man. Why do you take Him to court for not answering anything a person asks? For God speaks time and again, but a person may not notice it. (Job 33:12–14)

CATCH UP

- Who or what made you laugh recently?
- How did life feel easy or hard this past week?

RECAP

- What stood out to you from what we've read together, talked about, or attempted to do together over the past week?
- What thoughts or questions do you have from today's Bible verse?

GROW TOGETHER

- What might be the main thing God is trying to tell our family today?
- What if we did something new together or returned to a good habit to live out what we're learning? What might that be?

OPEN UP

- In what ways are you struggling in life or experiencing something hard?
- If we were to confess something to God as a family, what might that be?

PRAY

- Who is Jesus to you today?
- Who would be willing to close our time with a simple prayer?

120: A Sweet Restoration

***IF** you could have a dream house without worrying about any of the costs, what would it be like?*

***WHAT IF** you had to invite five homeless people to live with you in the house?*

READ IT: JOB 42:10–17

It's a safe bet that how you feel about splinters is nothing compared to how you feel about getting splinters out. You might have even considered keeping that little piece of wood in your skin forever when someone came at you with tweezers to "help you." That person wasn't trying to cause you hurt but hoped to eliminate the thing that created pain.

We go to great lengths to avoid pain, despite the insight it offers us. For example, if you've ever been stung by a bee, you've walked away realizing not to mess with them but to respect their role in creation. You also may have paid closer attention to where they're active nearby. Pain is an instructor, after all. God will use it to get our attention while waking us up to how broken the world is.

And because of that brokenness, some things are naturally set against us. A bee that stings you acts according to its nature in a fallen world. What God willed into creation doesn't always imply what He specifically wants for you. Sin is that big splinter in our lives that He's always dealing with, even if it means using a method that involves pain.

Job emerged from his pain twice as blessed as before and with a deeper relationship with God. The enemy's attack backfired, revealing God's deeper revolution. At first glance we might think this answers the question, "Why do bad things happen to good people?" The truth is that Jesus Christ is the only "good person" who has ever existed, and He willingly stepped into the bad thing that happened to Him. Jesus experienced a resurrection, and Job experienced a sweet restoration. Just imagine the "honey" God's made for you on the other side of a "sting" in your life.

THERE IS HOPE

"The sufferings of this present time are not worth comparing with the glory that is going to be revealed to us" (Romans 8:18).

Share about a loss you've experienced, be it something you misplaced or a deeper ache.

- ***IF*** anything you lost could appear in front of you now, what would you want?
- ***WHAT IF*** everything you'd ever lost in your life would suddenly appear before you on the last day of your life?

121: Pioneer or Settler?

***IF** you could pick any time in history to live for the rest of your life, what era would you choose?*

***WHAT IF** you lost all of your current memories went you went there?*

READ IT: GENESIS 11:27–32

The first person to ever open a pineapple had to be pretty satisfied with their effort. Whoever discovered that what came out of cows was drinkable probably made a lot of cereal-eating friends happy. Imagine how risky it felt for the first audience member to ever clap to test their expression of enjoyment.

Or how about all those pioneers who came to the United States when it was an open land without any idea of what they'd encounter. Some of those pioneers became settlers who built homes, farms, towns, and more in one place instead of continuing to move around. What was a starting point became a stopping point.

A man named Terah similarly started out as a pioneer but then became a settler. The Bible is full of stories about his son Abram/Abraham, but this is pretty much all we have on Terah. Instead of going all the way to Canaan, he stopped early and settled elsewhere. This may not seem like a big deal, until you realize that Canaan became the promised land of Israel. Terah could've given God's people a better beginning had he only remained a pioneer.

We can also get "Terah-fied" of the opportunities in front of us and stop short. Fear tries to rule when we don't know what will happen, so we stop and plop when God said to go and grow. Being in His revolution doesn't mean that we'll never stay in one place, but it does mean that we are always growing and becoming more like Him.

Settlers see life as a possession, but pioneers see life as an adventure; settlers see God as a sheriff who maintains law and order, but pioneers see God as a scout who tells us where new territory can be claimed. What if life is less about arrival and more about movement?

THERE IS HOPE

When we stop moving, God keeps moving. Where we stop short, He goes farther. His revolution is unstoppable. (Read that again!)

Talk about somewhere new you'd like to visit locally or on a vacation.

- ***IF*** you could name the top reason why you haven't gone there yet, what is it?
- ***WHAT IF*** we picked one of these places and worked toward going there until it actually happened?

122: Move It

***IF** you could be in charge of a friend's schedule for a week, what friend would you pick, and what would you have that person do?*

***WHAT IF** your friend was in charge of your schedule for just a day?*

READ IT: GENESIS 12:1–9

Sometime in the near future your family will all need to be somewhere at a certain time. It will require nothing short of pure hustle as you all get ready to leave, because while everyone seems to be moving in that direction, they will also get distracted. This will become a moment of glory for someone who is willing to step up and rally everyone else to "move it."

God invited Abram into His revolution with a command to move his family to a new land along with a promise that all nations would be blessed through them. Keep in mind that in Abram's era, people worshiped idols they'd made. So having the one true God speaking to him was a new thing. In response to God, the Bible says, "Abram went" (v. 4). Abram without hesitation chose rapid obedience to God instead of arguing back. Although Abram later had moments where his trust in the Lord dipped, this was a great moment we can celebrate and learn from.

You and your family have that same opportunity to respond with rapid obedience to whatever God asks you to do. Don't "get around to it later" or think that someone else will do it for you. Growth is all about you purposefully moving beyond what's familiar and into the unknown.

Choose to be courageous by stepping into these life-changing moments without a guarantee of how everything will turn out. God's revolution is more about putting our faith in Him than in circumstances anyway. Just as He moved you in one way in the past, let Him keep moving you in other ways. By moving, we becoming a movement . . . so move it.

THERE IS HOPE

To reach seriously lost people, do some seriously biblical things. Quit saying, "No, I'm good" and start claiming, "Yes, God's great."

Talk about something you'd be more willing to do if you knew in advance how it would turn out.

- ***IF*** you could ask God one question about it today and get a clear answer, what would you Him?
- ***WHAT IF*** you were no longer allowed to take any kinds of risk in your life? What do you think would be different about the quality of your life?

123: Faith or Fear

***IF** you were not afraid of anything, what smart and not-so-smart things might you end up doing?*

***WHAT IF** you did have one fear—the fear of sharing feelings?*

READ IT: GENESIS 12:10–16

One of the best parts about watching a big sports game is the food everyone brings. That is, as long as you don't get wrapped up with balancing the right amount of chips and dip on your plate. It's an endless battle no one wins.

Watching sports stirs our emotions, especially if we've placed faith in certain players to win the game. Tension grows with every missed shot as we wonder if the worst will happen or if the best is still possible. Maybe certain players have let us down permanently, or perhaps they're just having an off moment.

Abram was in the promised land of Canaan for a short time before tension grew. The fear of the famine chipped away at him until he dipped into fear—and that chip-to-dip ratio created a series of bad decisions. He lived like the absolute worst was all there was instead of trusting that the same God who had led him that far could allow the absolute best to happen. The Lord did get involved and cleared up the situation, but Abram's attempt to get rich created one missed shot after another—and almost caused him to permanently lose his wife.

You and your family will go through seasons of life where you'll be tempted to let fear lead you. Maybe like Abram you'll consider telling lies to succeed at school or work. You'll worry about what will happen if you're honest.

Either fear or faith will guide us. You'll tumble along the way and get it wrong sometimes, but it is possible for any missed shots to be more of an off moment instead of a permanent failure. Remember why you started cheering for God in the first place. It'll help you to better understand how He's cheering for you even now, even if your chip-dip ratio is still not quite right.

THERE IS HOPE

Feeling frozen by fear creates bad choices that snowball, but faith in the Son melts it down so you have a refreshing perspective to drink in.

Talk about a bad decision you learned from and turned into a good decision the next time.

- ***IF*** your brain automatically gave you a single word of advice before you made any decision, what word would you choose?
- ***WHAT IF*** your choices only affected you and no one else? Would it at all change the decisions you make or how you make them?

124: Seeing Stars

***IF** you could create a brand-new method for people to get news, what would that new way be?*

***WHAT IF** for one week every year this was the only method people could use to get their news?*

READ IT: GENESIS 15:1–6

Have you ever tied a piece of string around your finger or placed a stickie note in a certain place to remember something important? Maybe you've seen a man and woman on their wedding day each put rings on to remember that the relationship they share is unlike any other. Visual reminders like these make sure we follow through on small tasks and larger commitments. It's possible that we could get by without them, but they inspire us to be true and to do what matters.

Throughout Abram's life, the Lord talked with him about their special covenant at least seven times. What made this one instance special was how God gave Abram a visual reminder of how the stars themselves reflected how great his family would become. Years had passed since the Lord originally promised Abram and Sarai that they'd have a child. They needed something to look at to remember that although they hadn't yet experienced the promise coming true, they were still right in the center of God's will. It's why Abram was celebrated for believing the Lord. Since Jesus was how God ultimately fulfilled this promise, anyone who is a Christian today was represented in the sky that Abram looked into back then.

We're just as curious to know where we stand with God and if He'll follow through on things that we're still hoping will happen. Think about all the great things He's called you to that you've been tempted to give up on doing because you aren't seeing "life" in it. A core part of His revolution involves you having confidence in Him, who He says you are, and what He says is possible. The relationship you share with Him is unlike any other. You're one of His stars . . . literally.

THERE IS HOPE

As Abram stared at the endless lights in the night sky, one of them represented you. You're living proof that God is trustworthy.

Imagine being able to use the stars to spell out words in the night sky. What would you spell?

- ***IF*** you could have God remind you of one thing each day, what would it be and how would you want Him to remind you?
- ***WHAT IF*** your life is one of the ways God reminds others about Him? What does that mean for us this week?

125: Another Shortcut

***IF** every day you were told on a scale of 1 to 10 how hard that day was going to be, how would you prepare for the harder days?*

***WHAT IF** every easy day you had meant a difficult day for the rest of your family?*

READ IT: GENESIS 16:1–16

It's a little odd how people take the time to say, "It goes without saying." Or how someone introduces another to a crowd by saying, "This person needs no introduction." Between all the big stuff in life and the everyday things that keep us busy, we end up looking for shortcuts, even in how we sum it all up.

Sometimes these shortcuts create new problems and harder burdens, though. For example, a pizza box may instruct you to bake the food at a certain temperature for twenty minutes. If you double the temperature to bake it in just ten minutes, you'll only end up burning the pizza. The same thing happens in life when we try to make things happen faster than they were meant to.

Abram and Sarai had waited all their long lives to have a child. After a decade of waiting on God's specific promise, they decided to hurry things up by having Abram have a child with the maidservant Hagar. As this shortcut played out, Hagar and Sarai became bitter rivals under the same roof. God didn't approve any of this, but He worked within it so that the revolution could continue.

As backward as this situation is, it reminds us that God doesn't want us taking sinful shortcuts based on our feelings. What He's doing and how He's doing it is meant to bless us in the long run. Learn to experience the blessing of enduring by trusting in the Lord versus trying to force His hand. Doing what's right doesn't guarantee that everything will turn out right, but it does mean that we will have the right character and the right relationship with God in His revolution of righting the wrongs in the world. Right?

THERE IS HOPE

God speaks with such authority that we think His promises will happen right away. Trust in Him versus your guess of when He'll do what He said He'd do.

Share some funny memories of when you tried to take a shortcut that failed.

- ***IF*** you could fix a mistake someone else once made, would you ask that person if he or she wanted it fixed or just fix it?
- ***WHAT IF*** God told you He was going to help you make something right that you did wrong?

126: Weekly Recap

***IF** there were no houses and only tents, how would that change how people lived?*

***WHAT IF** you owned the only house and everyone else lived in tents?*

By faith Abraham, when he was called, obeyed and set out for a place that he was going to receive as an inheritance. He went out, even though he did not know where he was going. By faith he stayed as a foreigner in the land of promise, living in tents as did Isaac and Jacob, coheirs of the same promise. (Hebrews 11:8–9)

CATCH UP

- Who or what made you laugh recently?
- How did life feel easy or hard this past week?

RECAP

- What stood out to you from what we've read together, talked about, or attempted to do together over the past week?
- What thoughts or questions do you have from today's Bible verse?

GROW TOGETHER

- What might be the main thing God is trying to tell our family today?
- What if we did something new together or returned to a good habit to live out what we're learning? What might that be?

OPEN UP

- In what ways are you struggling in life or experiencing something hard?
- If we were to confess something to God as a family, what might that be?

PRAY

- Who is Jesus to you today?
- Who would be willing to close our time with a simple prayer?

127: All In

IF you had a button that gave someone else a hundred dollars but caused you to lose ten dollars, how often would you press it?

WHAT IF pushing the button gave a thousand dollars to someone but might cause you a small injury?

READ IT: GENESIS 17:1–16

What would you do if some friends asked you for money to start a new business but they weren't willing to put their own money into it? You'd probably wonder why they weren't personally invested like they wanted you to be. Now compare that to someone else who was all-in themselves and said, "Before I ask you to invest your time, money, or property, let me tell you why I've already invested mine."

Today's Bible passage is an "all in" ask like this that happens more than twenty-five years after God first told Abram and Sarai they'd have a child. Since the baby would be born a year from this point, God wanted Abram's family to demonstrate still being "all in" on the revolution. This meant immediate steps from them that showed their whole household and future family were set apart to the Lord. God also showed He was fully invested by changing the names of Abram and Sarai to "Abraham" and "Sarah," thereby promising them they would be "father of many" and "mother of nations."

That's one of the most beautiful things about a relationship with God—it's a two-way thing! He goes first by showing us how "all in" He is in the ways He pursues us and provides opportunities to respond to Him. He then asks that we go "all in" publicly and privately, too, not because He needs it but because we do. There's no way to make the most of all the wisdom and power He offers you without personally embracing Him, for you can't properly connect with someone you don't properly know. Don't allow any desire to avoid making your own sacrifices cause you to miss out on the blessings provided through His sacrifices. Invest into that relationship up front and watch that investment multiply!

THERE IS HOPE

God became flesh to live on earth to flesh out a way for us to live in heaven.

Talk honestly about who or what gets your three best bursts of energy each day.

- **IF** we tried to figure out what mattered most to you just by looking at how you spend your money or time, what would we say about you?
- **WHAT IF** we saw each of the things God asked us to do as something we "get to do" versus "have to do"?

128: Lunch with God

***IF** you could have a meal with one president from the past, whom would you pick and why?*

***WHAT IF** you could have a meal with someone from any time in the future? Whom would you pick and why?*

READ IT: GENESIS 18:1–15

Eating a meal every day is a gift that not everyone in the world has, let alone eating multiple meals a day. How often are we distracted with "what" is on the menu instead of pausing to be thankful that there's anything on it at all? Someone in your household (if not several people) takes responsibility for making this happen, from earning the money for groceries to planning meals and cooking them. Maybe you're a part of this effort by washing dishes or simply having a good attitude about whatever is served.

We remember another "someone" who is a part of every meal when we pause to pray to God before we eat. Whether in your home, at a restaurant, on a break at work, or sitting in a cafeteria with others, you can pray a personal prayer or a traditional one like, "God is great! God is good! Let us thank Him for our food. Amen." This personal pause expresses a thank-You from your heart to God's heart.

Abraham had the chance to sit down and have a meal with the Lord through the "three men" who appeared before him. It's possible that one of the men was Jesus, since we know that He has always existed and is the member of the Trinity who came to earth as a man. Take note of how Abraham treated Him, for only God deserves our worship, and compare that to how you do or don't regard Him before a meal.

If you're seeking to grow closer to the Lord, seize all those times when you eat to personally connect with Him. Jesus isn't a memory or merely a historical figure bound by time, but is forever alive and actively working in your life. So are the Father and Spirit available to you, for the Three-in-One is offering to be "one" with you.

THERE IS HOPE

Whether you pray traditional prayers or improvise in the moment, you can personally visit with God every day at any time.

Talk about a memorable time you met someone, famous or not.

- ***IF*** you could sit down with anyone in the world from any walk of life (including non-famous people), whom would you want to get to know?
- ***WHAT IF*** there is someone in your life now whom God is asking you to get to know and invest in as a part of His revolution?

129: Five-Second Rule

***IF** every bag of garbage in the world always contained ten dollars, but only you knew about it, how would you use this information?*

***WHAT IF** half of the world knew, and the amount was fifty dollars?*

READ IT: GENESIS 18:1–15

Ever heard of the "five-second rule"? The idea is that if food falls on the floor and you pick it up and eat it, you won't get germs as long as you pick it up within five seconds. Hang on, because research shows that the same amount of germs can get on an item of food in those five seconds as it would if you waited longer. The texture and surface of the food matter most to determine its capacity to grab bacteria.*

The flaw of the "five-second rule" is found in how some people view life. Some believe we can be around sin without it affecting us, but the surface of our lives has a "temptable" texture that grabs hold of sin in varying ways. God saw this in two cities near where Abraham and Sarah lived. The story gets pretty ugly, so discern as a family if it's worth reading the details in Genesis 19. Essentially, everyone in that culture started saying that certain sins weren't sins at all, that people should do whatever they wanted to as long as it made them happy. Sound familiar?

Abraham asked the Lord if the city could be spared if even ten righteous people could be found there. Apparently there weren't, for destruction came. Only Abraham's relative Lot was allowed to leave with his family. Unfortunately, their story got awkward right away because they'd picked up the same broken thinking of Sodom and Gomorrah.

When God is at work in a revolution with humans, He knows we will struggle with temptation. He'll often have to do something dramatic to address the dramatic sin in us or around us. Take note, for He doesn't do this to look for who to blindly eliminate but to look for who to collectively save.

* Studies at the University of Illinois at Urbana-Champaign and even an episode of Mythbusters came to these conclusions.

THERE IS HOPE

You will never influence the world by trying to be like it, but you can by letting God first transform the texture of your heart.

Share about a time when you felt the people around you influenced the way you acted.

- **IF** you could give a friend some advice, which friend would you talk to and what would you say?
- **WHAT IF** we've let some things that God says are wrong start to seem like "not a big deal" in our minds? What might those be?

130: Baby Face

***IF** a childhood dream you forgot came true today, do you think you would remember it? How would you react to it?*

***WHAT IF** a future dream of yours came true? Do you think you would realize now that it was something you'd want in the future?*

READ IT: GENESIS 21:1–7

Babies are awesome! Sure, they cry a lot and need their diaper changed at the most inconvenient times. A baby also has a way of turning us into cute little "goo-goo, gaga" noise-makers too. It's hard to stare into the face of one and not change the tone of your voice or the tone of your attitude. Babies can inspire us without us even realizing it.

Imagine how inspired Sarah felt staring into the face of her baby, Isaac. She'd waited more than twenty-five years since God first promised this child to her! Every moment she had felt like his birth would never happen or that God wasn't trustworthy suddenly was overshadowed by the actual joy she was holding in her actual hands. She may have been older than she wanted to be, but everything about this moment and the promised child before her was just right. The dream was realized.

Among the many things in your life that you're waiting on, know that there will be times when you get to touch and hold a dream as it's realized. This will take place when God says the timing is right, just like how this passage says Isaac was born at "the appointed time" (v. 2). God's revolution takes place in our lives on a personal level while at the same time we are a part of the larger plan of what He's doing in the world.

Isaac wasn't born to Abraham and Sarah because they did everything right but because the Lord does everything right. Perhaps that sounds intimidating, but it is actually comforting. God blesses us not because of who we are but because of who He is. It's hard to stare into His face and not only change the tone of your voice but also the tone of your attitude. God inspires us without us even realizing it.

THERE IS HOPE

The revolution of God takes place just as much in our waiting as it does when something is finally revealed.

What is something significant you hope happens in your life someday?

- ***IF*** one of your good friends also hoped for the same thing, how would you feel about that?
- ***WHAT IF*** to see this dream come true you have to wait twenty-five years?

131: Family Drama

***IF** there were a law that said a family could fight only once a day, what would be different about your home?*

***WHAT IF** families were allowed to fight up to fifteen times a day?*

READ IT: GENESIS 21:8–21; 25:18

He said. She said. We said. Is there anyone in the world who doesn't have family problems? Even the closest families get on each other's nerves from time to time over "who gets what" or "so-and-so gave me a look I didn't like." You may be in an amazing, supportive household that works things out instead of hanging on to hurts or anger, but there are still things that have to be worked out. Love and kindness can change a situation (if not the world).

Unfortunately, the negative stuff in a family can also change a situation (if not the world). Isaac's offspring went on to become the Jews, through whom Christianity began when Jesus came. Ishmael's descendants were a part of what became the Arabic people, out of whom Islam was formed. Every historical violent act or war to gain territory between these people groups are like family members still fighting over "who gets what" or "so-and-so gave me a look I didn't like." This family drama is still in the news today, all tracking back to Abraham's bad decision to have a child with Hagar instead of waiting on God to give Sarah her promised son.

Nothing that happens in your family really stays in your family either. Any big arguments, selfish attitudes, or bullying-gone-too-far under your roof is something each of you carries outside your home. Even small imperfections impact others.

We can get healthier by learning from the wins and losses of families in the Bible. Instead of letting hurt grow into hate, choose to live differently as a family by following God's lead. He has wisdom to give you and your loved ones so that instead of letting your drama be on display as a distraction, people see Him working in your family as a revolution.

THERE IS HOPE

Families can impact the world! Pray right now for your household, extended family, neighbors . . . Pray for a love for the Lord and for each other.

Discuss what "fighting fair" as a family might look like.

- **IF** there were one thing you could change about how things happen in our home, what would you like it to be?
- **WHAT IF** you could guarantee that a few things don't change? What's working that we should keep doing?

132: You Want Me to Do What?

***IF** whenever you experienced something good you would forget a good memory from the past, how would you deal with that?*

***WHAT IF** anyone involved in that memory would forget it too?*

READ IT: GENESIS 21:8–21; 25:18

You've finally bought it! It's that special thing you've searched for and all the stores were out of. You didn't even mind paying $100 more to get it. As you exit the store, you can't help but smile.

All that quickly changes as you notice your car is missing. You fear someone stole it until you're near the spot where you parked and see a sign that says, "No parking. Tow-away zone." Next to a phone number for the towing company you read, "$100 fine." Everyone you might call for help is tight financially, so the only option to get your vehicle back is to return the rare item you bought from the store to get the $100. You believe you'll never see it again. What would you do?

Abraham had a much more difficult problem when the Lord asked him to offer his beloved son, Isaac, to Him. He didn't know the end of this story like we do, but he did know God had promised to produce many descendants through Isaac one day. Abraham doing what God asked without understanding why meant he was willing to live by faith versus sight. No longer would he take shortcuts to serve himself; now he was willing to go on the long journey of serving the Lord.

Know that God isn't asking you to have blind faith but clear faith. When you don't know what He's doing in the story you're in, you can trust Him in what He's doing in the larger story. He'll at times ask you to do things that feel confusing, but if you step forward even in uncertainty you'll be reassured along the way. Note how He sacrifices too: "For God loved the world in this way: He gave His One and Only Son, so that everyone who believes in Him will not perish but have eternal life" (John 3:16).

THERE IS HOPE

Keeping your faith comfortable makes things with God uncomfortable, but getting out of your comfort zone reveals His comfort to you.

When have you been asked to do something positive that you really didn't want to do?

- **IF** whenever you did a certain activity you found you couldn't do it as well as others did, how would you feel about that over time?
- **WHAT IF** you were the person who decided the right way to do everything?

133: Weekly Recap

***IF** every item of clothing you wore had to be one color for the next twelve months, what color would you pick?*

***WHAT IF** wearing these one-colored clothes made an area of your life better for that year? What area of life would you pick?*

Commit your way to the LORD; trust in him, and he will act, making your righteousness shine like the dawn, your justice like the noonday. Be silent before the LORD and wait expectantly for him; do not be agitated by one who prospers in his way, by the person who carries out evil plans. (Psalm 37:5–7)

CATCH UP

- Who or what made you laugh recently?
- How did life feel easy or hard this past week?

RECAP

- What stood out to you from what we've read together, talked about, or attempted to do together over the past week?
- What thoughts or questions do you have from today's Bible verse?

GROW TOGETHER

- What might be the main thing God is trying to tell our family today?
- What if we did something new together or returned to a good habit to live out what we're learning? What might that be?

OPEN UP

- In what ways are you struggling in life or experiencing something hard?
- If we were to confess something to God as a family, what might that be?

PRAY

- Who is Jesus to you today?
- Who would be willing to close our time with a simple prayer?

134: The Game of Love?

***IF** instead of being able to decide whom to marry you had to find your spouse on a game show, would you want to go on the show?*

***WHAT IF** being on that game show guaranteed you a good marriage?*

READ IT: GENESIS 24:1–21, 54–60

Plenty of TV shows let viewers see what happens when random people meet and date. What makes these shows popular is how strange someone might act to win the affection of someone else. Unfortunately, that's also what makes most of these shows kind of horrible to watch. Why would we support turning love into a game on any level?

We might assume that was Abraham's approach to find a wife for Isaac, but what he did was serious business so his son wouldn't marry a foreign woman who worshiped false gods. He sent a servant out who found Rebekah, and she was both attractive and kind. This is what many people might look for in a person to marry, but there is much more to look for—specifically, God's blessing on whom you choose.

The servant came up with a specific test to reveal this, and it was kept a secret from Rebekah. Sometimes people will pretend to be a certain way to get others to like them, and there was no room to play around here. Rebekah proved to be genuine in how she did things in ways that answered the servant's prayer before he even finished praying it. God was clearly a fan of her.

Thankfully, you don't need to look to circumstances to figure out who or what God has given you the thumbs-up on. He's written it down in the Bible, including how the closest relationships in our life need to be stable spiritually (1 Corinthians 15:33; 2 Corinthians 6:14). Growing in your own spiritual journey before you go looking for someone else helps you be a "whole" person instead of looking for another person to "complete you." There's no need to roll the dice on your relationships when it was never meant to be a game.

THERE IS HOPE

As you obey God, your trust in Him grows; as your trust in God grows, you know Him better; as you know God better, you know His will better.

Talk about some of the different ways people try to find love these days.

- **IF** you could pick an age that everyone had to be before they started dating or courting, what age do you think is best?
- **WHAT IF** anyone who dated or courted had to answer any three questions with absolute honesty to the other person? What would those questions be?

135: Will You Stop Touching Me?

***IF** a penguin constantly followed you around, what would you do (if anything) about the penguin?*

***WHAT IF** a small floating whale followed you around instead?*

READ IT: GENESIS 25:19–34

Before we could play movies in minivans or had iThings in cars, kids had to find ways to entertain themselves in the back seat during a long drive. One popular option for siblings (and not-so-popular for parents) was to dangle a single finger an inch away from whomever was nearby and say, "I'm not touching you! I'm not touching you! I'm not touching you!" This would cause the other person to eventually complain, "Will you stop touching me?" The reply, of course, was, "What? I never even touched you!"

Jacob and Esau's struggle was about more than two siblings playfully annoying each other. Esau came out first, which meant he was the firstborn son who would inherit more authority and blessings than his brother. Jacob grabbing Esau's heel was symbolic for how he'd later poke and grab at his brother to get that authority and blessing. Jacob was relentless at trying to get away with taking those things too.

Maybe you've never grabbed the "heel" of one of your family members or hovered your finger over them and said, "I'm not touching you!" What you likely have done (even if only on accident) was grabbed or poked at them about something that hurt or annoyed them just the same. The little things add up; so figure out what in your habits or tone needs to be changed. The best touches are hugs anyway.

What makes a family healthy isn't when we get as close as we can to annoying each other and stop short, but when we do whatever we can to bless each other. Being sarcastic or sassy makes you grow apart instead of growing closer.

THERE IS HOPE

You can't get your family to act perfectly, nor can they get you to act perfectly. So breathe. Forgive. Love. But then grow together.

Take a moment to own how you each may have been a little annoying lately.

- ***IF*** you were doing something that annoyed another person in our family, would you be open to hearing about it without defending yourself?
- ***WHAT IF*** someone in the family was being annoying to you? Would you want to handle that yourself or involve another family member to help the two of you talk about it?

136: Crossing the Line

***IF** you knew someone who regularly stole from others, what would you say to him or her?*

***WHAT IF** that person stole from you too?*

READ IT: GENESIS 27:1–24

There's nothing cute about feeling hurt and mistreated by others whom you expect to be kind to you. These aren't the moments when you feel life's "unfair" because someone took the last slice of pizza or said you couldn't do what you wanted to do. These are larger instances of cruelty when someone attacks you emotionally, mentally, physically, or otherwise. Crossing the line like this can happen in your family, whether it's the oldest hurting the youngest or the other way around. Perhaps the attacker doesn't realize it, or maybe they do but are stuck in habits they don't know how to stop.

The relationship between Jacob and Esau involved this kind of back-and-forth cruelty over the years, especially from Jacob's side. It divided their home just like it can divide yours as sides are taken or hurt feelings are overlooked. Imagine what would've happened if instead of everyone trying to figure it out on their own, they got some counseling to work through their issues and unpack the hurt.

How is God using what happened in the lives of Jacob and Esau to speak into the pain in or around your household? Hopefully you won't experience this often in your family, but maybe you know someone at work, school, church, or in your neighborhood who is being regularly hurt by people closest to him or her. Healing is part of God's revolution, and it isn't by any means simple, but you have the Holy Spirit of God in you to take steps forward. Invite Him to help your family work on things in your home or help an abused person around you.

We all make mistakes and are capable of being cruel without realizing it. Be open to hearing how. There's a difference between being careless and choosing to care less.

THERE IS HOPE

God wants us to speak against injustice, including injustices against us. You have the right to share feelings, be listened to, and have others believe you.

Talk about the difference between ordinary conflict and outright cruelty.

- ***IF*** you ever feel picked on, how do you tend to respond back?
- ***WHAT IF*** right now we shared five sincere things we love about each other as a way to try to build some more encouragement into our home?

137: Your Words

***IF** whenever you wore a shirt whatever was written on it would come true, what words or sentences would you want to wear?*

***WHAT IF** that happened to all the things you owned? How would that affect what you shopped for or how you received gifts?*

READ IT: GENESIS 27:27–45

Which words are "your words"? What do you specifically long to hear said to you because of how it inspires you? Or what phrases or labels anger you? Maybe you've never directly thought about this but you've felt it. Some words, simply put, feel like "your words."

Esau longed to receive his "words" from his dad in the form of a "blessing." This cultural tradition involved a father speaking unique thoughts of love, hope, guidance, and confidence into the firstborn child. It included a meaningful touch along with instructions to follow the Lord so that He would strengthen the blessing.

Rebekah felt Jacob deserved this blessing, though. Perhaps it was because God told her that her oldest son was meant to serve her younger son (Genesis 25:23). Like her father-in-law, Abraham, used to do, she took a bad shortcut through Jacob to force God's hand. Esau's heartache over it all turned into anger that made Jacob flee for his life.

Thankfully, families today can freely declare a blessing into more than one person and on more than one occasion. Parents can speak a revolution into their kids, kids can speak a revolution into their parents, and siblings can speak a revolution into each other. Ephesians 5:19–21 says we make the most of our time by sharing spiritual songs and thankful words with each other that honor Jesus and foster respect between everyone.

So inject some meaningful words into your conversations around the dinner table and sing out to some Christian music while out running errands together. It's really all about pointing your family members to Jesus and sharing who you sense they are (and could be) with Jesus in them. Those are the truest "words" our lives long to hear.

THERE IS HOPE

Homes are less stressed when each person is blessed. Give grace to all flaws by revealing true awe. No one is missed when everyone's kissed.

Share about one of the best gifts of encouragement anyone has ever given you.

- ***IF*** you could share one interesting thing about yourself with the world, what would it be?
- ***WHAT IF*** at least once a week we took a moment to make sure everyone in our family knew something awesome we see in them?

138: Baggage Claim

***IF** all your extended family and friends stayed in your home for a day, would you like that?*

***WHAT IF** everyone stayed in your room the whole time and it was for a week?*

READ IT: GENESIS 28:1–9

If you've traveled on a large airplane you've seen a little game that people play called "How many smaller overstuffed carry-on bags can I bring on the plane to avoid paying fees for checking larger bags?" You'll see multi-pocketed backpacks, collections of shopping bags, larger purses, and more. Airlines allow it to some extent, but there isn't enough room in the overhead bins for every passenger to travel this way. Flight attendants often have to come up with quick solutions that don't leave travelers happy. When we try to avoid one problem, we end up creating new problems.

Isaac, Rebekah, Esau, and Jacob never worked things out as a family after the big deception around the "blessing." Isaac sent Jacob off and told him to get married to a woman who would share his same beliefs, but it was only another way of avoiding the problems they had in their home. Esau's anger grew, so he decided to hurt his dad by doing the exact opposite of the advice Isaac gave Jacob in regard to marriage. When we try to avoid one problem, we end up creating new problems.

Have you ever noticed any area or relationship in your family where life has become about avoiding talking about tough stuff? Families typically do this when they stay busy doing many things instead of sitting down to talk about the important things. It's like instead of owning up to the larger "baggage" you're all carrying around, you try to pack it into smaller carry-ons that create new problems. Remember, God's grace truly is amazing, and He will help you unpack all the stuff you'd rather hide. Give each other the freedom to be honest about it all so that mistakes don't hold you back from taking flight together into God's revolution.

THERE IS HOPE

You aren't doomed to repeat the past if you face each other in the present to reset your future.

Talk about something you've thought you should bring up to your family but haven't yet.

- ***IF*** there is any topic you wished we talked more about, what would it be?
- ***WHAT IF*** you knew we were able to talk about anything we needed to work on without it becoming a bigger deal or you getting in trouble over it?

139: Nowhere Special

***IF** you could call God on the phone, how often would you call Him?*

***WHAT IF** He only answered the phone when you were in trouble?*

READ IT: GENESIS 28:10–22

Ever hear the one about two eggs frying in a pan? The first egg said, "Wow, it's hot in here!" The second egg replied, "Help! It's a talking egg!"

The wildest things can happen to us in the wildest of places. According to today's Bible reading, though, God has no problem working wonders in the middle of nowhere. The phrase "certain place" (v. 11) is important because it references an unimportant place. People used to believe that God would spend time only in uniquely holy areas, similar to how we might think He's more present in a church building than anywhere else. The Lord instead chose to meet with Jacob in a random place off the side of the road. What does that tells us about times when we're at the movies, shopping with friends, or goofing around on the internet?

Also pay attention to how God introduced Himself to Jacob. The Lord didn't claim to be Jacob's God yet, but He did say that He was the God of Abraham and Isaac. Jacob was being invited into the revolution, but he had to decide if he wanted in. He was offered the same promise for the world to be blessed through his family. Jacob considered it, adding that he would in response give the Lord the first tenth of everything he made.

Have you ever been in the middle of some random place or activity yet suddenly felt that something or Someone bigger than you was there? Maybe like Jacob you grew up in a family of faith but realized you had to come to your own decision in following the Lord. While you're out there getting to where you're going, you can take comfort knowing Somebody loves you and is reaching out to you. You're invited to connect with God wherever you are through Jesus Christ.

THERE IS HOPE

When God wants to start a change in your life, He's able to start right where you are.

Share some of the places you've been where you felt close to God.

- ***IF*** God is everywhere, why do you think we look for Him in certain places? Should we maybe have a few places we do look for Him regularly?
- ***WHAT IF*** you knew that by following God today the whole world would be blessed through you, your family, and all of your children?

140: Weekly Recap

***IF** a gym offered you not only physical exercise but also trained you in social skills, would you attend the gym?*

***WHAT IF** you were the manager of that gym?*

Hallelujah! My soul, praise the LORD. I will praise the LORD all my life; I will sing to my God as long as I live. Do not trust in nobles, in a son of man, who cannot save. When his breath leaves him, he returns to the ground; on that day his plans die. Happy is the one . . . , whose hope is in the LORD his God. (Psalm 146:1–5)

CATCH UP

- Who or what made you laugh recently?
- How did life feel easy or hard this past week?

RECAP

- What stood out to you from what we've read together, talked about, or attempted to do together over the past week?
- What thoughts or questions do you have from today's Bible verse?

GROW TOGETHER

- What might be the main thing God is trying to tell our family today?
- What if we did something new together or returned to a good habit to live out what we're learning? What might that be?

OPEN UP

- In what ways are you struggling in life or experiencing something hard?
- If we were to confess something to God as a family, what might that be?

PRAY

- Who is Jesus to you today?
- Who would be willing to close our time with a simple prayer?

141: Bait and Switch

***IF** telling people you loved them required doing one task of that person's choice, how often would you tell people you loved them?*

***WHAT IF** you also had to do something for each of that person's family members?*

READ IT: GENESIS 29:1–6, 16–27

Stores sometimes advertise products they only have a few of for people to buy. Perhaps that's all the manufacturer gave them, but often it's a shady strategy to get you into the store to buy other things. They're hoping you think walking out with "something" is better than not getting anything. This "bait-and-switch" tactic benefits the store more than the customer because they use the popularity of one item to sell something that otherwise wouldn't have been noticed.

Consider this idea in how Jacob was promised one wife by Laban but ended up with another. This bait-and-switch resembled how Jacob stole Esau's birthright and blessing, only now he was on the other end. His love for Rachel helped him endure it, but that doesn't mean he should've had more than one wife. Jacob took his cues from Laban, who talked about tradition and customs more than honoring God. Genesis 30 reveals some of the ugly family stuff that happened because of it, as Jacob got more caught up in building a family than in building a foundation in God.

That's another odd thing about a bait-and-switch—it's easier to spot in other people than it is in how we relate with God. Think about all the times we've promised Him our absolute best if He'd bless us, only to then pull back on that promise. Imagine how that must feel to Him to have it happen from multiple people every second of every day. His love for us helps Him endure it, but our calling is clear: "Present your bodies as a living sacrifice, holy and pleasing to God; this is your true worship. Do not be conformed to this age, but be transformed by the renewing of your mind, so that you may discern what is the good, pleasing, and perfect will of God" (Romans 12:1–2).

THERE IS HOPE

God does the hard work needed to make us His own, regardless of all the things we promise Him and fall short of following through on.

Open up about a time when you felt tricked by someone.

- ***IF*** you had an alarm that went off any time someone was being dishonest with you or trying to trick you, would you want to regularly use it?
- ***WHAT IF*** the Holy Spirit plays a role like that in letting us know when someone isn't being honest with us? How could we begin to figure that out?

142: A Spotty Business Plan

***IF** you had your own manufacturing company, what would the company make and sell?*

***WHAT IF** you somehow made the product better than any other version of that product?*

READ IT: GENESIS 30:29–31:10

You know how sometimes ice cubes randomly spill out of the freezer and hit the floor? What you do about that in that moment is the real you. Think about it.

The same could be said about how you handle money and job opportunities. What do you remember about the first time someone paid you money for work you did for him or her? Chances are you either felt overwhelmed by how much you were given or had a problem with how little you were paid. We generally expect to be treated fairly for our work so we can have money to invest into our most important priorities or desires.

Jacob's job and financial payoff seem a bit odd at first glance. He prepared a unique set of branches that inspired certain males of the flock to seek out and mate with certain females, causing more spotted lambs to be born that Jacob could keep. Only later do we read that God created this plan because Laban wasn't being fair as a boss. The spotty business plan was the Lord's way of making sure Jacob had what he needed for the next leg of the revolution he was about to take part in.

God's wisdom about how we're to work or handle money may appear strange to some people, like a "spotty business plan." The thing to remember is money is never about money but is a way to reveal something more important to the world. If we just use what we're given on ourselves or to show off, we by example tell others to do the same. If we use what God gives us to first bless Him and others, we make sure that whatever is needed for the next leg of the revolution is available.

THERE IS HOPE

God can release the control money has on your life by turning every dollar in your hand into a revolution. Tithing begins this process.

Discuss your family budget, what comes in but also what you spend it on.

- ***IF*** we were to write down everything we spent money on over the next week, what do you think we would learn?
- ***WHAT IF*** we actually did this by keeping a journal that we wrote in together at the end of each night?

143: Idol Thoughts

***IF** whenever you saw someone do something good or bad, you were held responsible for it, how would that change how you lived?*

***WHAT IF** you would be put on trial for the bad things?*

READ IT: GENESIS 31:3, 17–35

It's always sad when a family gets divided over who owns what. There are times that cousins, uncles, and aunts get in on it, like when an older family member dies and everyone wants something from the estate. The tension can linger from one generation to the next without anyone ever really knowing why they're supposed to dislike a certain side of the family or do the things they do.

For reasons we're not clear on, Rachel stole her father's "household gods." These were physical idols made out of expensive metal, as people in that era regularly made things they could touch to try to connect with something larger than themselves. Perhaps this was her way to feel secure in whatever was ahead. She and her sister, Leah, had already tried to prove who the better wife or mother was. Jacob also acted out of fear instead of trusting God to take care of him.

These days hardly anyone intentionally creates something to be an idol like those in ancient cultures did. In fact, the idea of that is so offensive that we may not allow ourselves to honestly consider how we've let things become more important than they should. Some of our habits and hobbies really do steal us away from God, create divisions in our families, and cause us to second-guess how the Lord will take care of us. We end up settling for a version of faith that feels like godliness but denies its power. If you want to understand how deep your faith is, pay attention to what you won't pay attention to, then leave it behind so it doesn't cause problems on the revolutionary journey ahead of you.

THERE IS HOPE

If you open your hands and empty your life before God, whatever made you feel good in the past won't ever compare to the joy He'll offer.

Look at your family calendar together, noting all the events, practices, and appointments.

- ***IF*** someone wanted to know what our most important values were in order, what would this calendar tell them?
- ***WHAT IF*** something we all enjoy doing really does take us away from God, little by little? How could we make sure we were honest about it?

144: Tag Team Wrestling

***IF** you couldn't feel pain or get hurt when wrestling someone, how would that change your willingness to wrestle?*

***WHAT IF** you couldn't feel pain wrestling but could still technically get hurt?*

READ IT: GENESIS 32:1–12, 24–32

Believe it or not, former president Abraham Lincoln was once an amazing wrestler. Historians believe he only lost once in three hundred matches!* On one occasion he openly challenged a crowd of people to see if anyone wanted to take him on. This probably doesn't match up with all the famous pictures we've seen of him wearing his tall hat, but wouldn't it be amazing if he were alive today and wore that as his outfit into the ring? Who do you think he'd partner up with for a tag-team wrestling match? Who would you want to see him wrestle?

It's weird picturing people we have a certain gentle image of being completely fierce in a wrestling match. Jacob had one of these experiences on his way home and had to pass through territory that his brother, Esau, lived in. Jacob wrestled with a "man" whom Jacob later said was God in a face-to-face form. That means this could have been Christ who faced off against Jacob, which probably is a little hard to picture. The wrestling wasn't about body slams, head butts, or clotheslines, though—the Lord was working on Jacob's identity through a real-life, hands-on situation. It was a sort of tag-team match as Jacob wasn't just wrestling against Jesus but also against himself. When God wanted to end the match, He did so with a simple touch that caused Jacob to walk away with a limp and a new revolutionary name: Israel.

God is in the habit of transforming us as we wrestle with Him too. He may "tag team" with circumstances or someone else to get our attention, but it's always about us learning who we really are and can become through Him. We may walk away with a limp like Jacob did, but we'll know that the Lord touched us.

* http://www.history.com/news/10-things-you-may-not-know

THERE IS HOPE

When you think you're winning in a wrestling match against God, He's actually letting you position yourself to be broken so you can then be blessed.

Share about a time you knew the right thing to do but struggled with doing it.

- ***IF*** you could have any kind of help the next time you had to make a tough decision, what kind of help would you want?
- ***WHAT IF*** we talked about what it would mean to "tag team" the problems or decisions we each face together?

145: Oh, Brother

***IF** you had to stand up to someone who picked on you, how would you prepare for that moment?*

***WHAT IF** you had to stand before someone you used to pick on?*

READ IT: GENESIS 33:1–20

One of the greatest tests of pride is when we feel forced to say we're sorry to someone else. It can feel like we're acting, so we don't give much of an award-winning performance. When we're kids we can especially rush through it. Isn't it crazy that one of the most freeing actions known to humanity is to experience forgiveness, yet one of the most painful actions known to humanity is to ask for it?

That's why God opens up doors we didn't think were still able to be opened. As Jacob approached his brother after being apart for twenty years, he saw Esau with an army. It seemed like something vengeful was about to happen until Esau broke the tension by hugging his brother and lovingly asking about his family. God had been working on Esau's heart, and it showed. Jacob was so overwhelmed by the depth of forgiveness that he felt like he'd seen God's face in Esau's face.

Unfortunately, Jacob still acted a bit like his old self in how he promised to meet up with Esau in a certain territory, only to instead go in a different direction. Perhaps Jacob was thankful to have worked things out with his brother but was afraid to stay close in case Esau changed his mind. Jacob additionally pulled back by settling in a land that was just outside of where God wanted him to end up.

When the Lord calls you to work something out with another person, don't go 90 percent of the way in faith and leave the last 10 percent to fear. You'll end up in a place that feels close enough to home that you'll assume "I'm good," but you really aren't where you're supposed to be. Complete freedom requires completely working things out. It'll let you see the face of God in people you once couldn't look in the eye.

THERE IS HOPE

No one is ever too old to be hugged. Make the first move, even if you aren't guaranteed a next move . . . just like God did with you.

Talk about what you think makes an apology sincere and respectful in your home.

- ***IF*** you know someone who hurt you deeply wanted your forgiveness, how would you respond?
- ***WHAT IF*** you could be invisible and spy on that person to learn if they really were sorry for what they did?

146: Mere Mirror

***IF** you could relive a moment in your life, what moment would you relive?*

***WHAT IF** you would forget a random memory if you did?*

READ IT: GENESIS 35:1–15

Do you ever talk with your car? When the "check engine" light comes on, do you shout, "Oh no you didn't!" What do you say when you have to press the button twenty-six times to get the doors to unlock? If only it would just respond to your voice!

And then there are the two types of mirrors to help you see what's behind you. A rear-view mirror helps you see the big picture, and side mirrors show what's happening on the side. Each mirror can help you be a better driver as you travel forward, yet each mirror is also only so big for a reason. You'd get distracted and be more inclined to crash if either was larger. You also can't change anything by just yelling at your mirrors.

Jacob's life was full of distractions and memories of past crashes. The Lord got his attention and reminded him to keep advancing into the land he was intended to be in. Not only did this get Jacob and his family where they needed to be for what was next, but it let him reset old experiences with a new perspective. God again emphasized that the new name of Israel was incredibly important.

We aren't meant to focus on or yell at our past, but we do need to pay attention to it and its impact on everyone (including us). The Holy Spirit will serve us by directing our hearts beyond past failures and successes so that our future revolution is healthier. You're not the same person you were years ago, so don't live like you are. Keep growing by allowing God to guide you—He can use anything to bring value and support those who have responded to His voice.

THERE IS HOPE

Experience by itself doesn't make you wiser, but experience that you evaluate can be a real game changer.

Share about a time when you felt "grown up" or "older" somehow.

- ***IF*** you could give yourself advice five years ago, what would it be?
- ***WHAT IF*** you had heard this advice back then? Would you have followed it?

147: Weekly Recap

***IF** a picture of your family hung in every restaurant in your town, what picture would you choose?*

***WHAT IF** that picture was also in every restaurant in the world?*

Isaac lived 180 years. He took his last breath and died, and was gathered to his people, old and full of days. His sons Esau and Jacob buried him. (Genesis 35:28–29)

CATCH UP

- Who or what made you laugh recently?
- How did life feel easy or hard this past week?

RECAP

- What stood out to you from what we've read together, talked about, or attempted to do together over the past week?
- What thoughts or questions do you have from today's Bible verse?

GROW TOGETHER

- What might be the main thing God is trying to tell our family today?
- What if we did something new together or returned to a good habit to live out what we're learning? What might that be?

OPEN UP

- In what ways are you struggling in life or experiencing something hard?
- If we were to confess something to God as a family, what might that be?

PRAY

- Who is Jesus to you today?
- Who would be willing to close our time with a simple prayer?

148: Having a Ball

IF *every ten seconds in every sport being played an athlete would randomly fall down, how would that impact how often you played or watched sports?*

WHAT IF *the whole team fell down every ten seconds?*

READ IT: GENESIS 37:1–36

Athletes work so hard getting good at what they do that it's wild when they do something foolish, like when two teammates go for the ball at the same time. One player may yell, "I got it!" to let the other know to back off, but the other player may say, "No, I got it!" If neither player submits or sets aside pride, they'll treat each other more like opponents than teammates.

Jacob's kids were equally confused figuring out who was supposed to be "having the ball" in the family. They came from different mothers, since Jacob didn't follow God's plans for marriage, and Joseph seemed favored by Jacob and God. The jealousy tore apart the family and sent Joseph into slavery—definitely a fumble. Thankfully, God can scoop up any ball we drop and create a revolution down the road.

Being a part of a family means you have a front-row seat to the lives of others compared to yours. What you experience beyond that is up to you more than others, though. The difference between being a "brother" or a "bother" is what you "r." Likewise, don't miss being a "sis" 'cuz you "dis" someone's "bliss." Dads and moms? Nurture love to nurture calm.

The Lord is always looking for players who will suit up and step out onto the field. We get to take part in the most epic and fierce competition that has ever existed, but we have to remember it isn't against each other. We're fighting God's enemy, who is crafty at getting the Lord's team to be prideful about who gets to do what. Maybe today you'll get to take the ball and run with it, or perhaps today you're to have a ball letting someone else have a ball. Either way, "same team." Right?

THERE IS HOPE

There will be many days in life when you feel like you collide with God, but never any days when you'll be betrayed by Him.

Share about a time you felt you were competing with someone else in some way.

- ***IF*** it was impossible to do things you were good at unless you were alone, how would that change how often you were around other people?
- ***WHAT IF*** you felt like your friends and the people closest to you liked it when you were bad at something or hated it when you excelled at something?

149: Something More

***IF** light bulbs complimented you when you walked by, would you like that?*

***WHAT IF** light bulbs whispered tempting ideas or thoughts as you walked by?*

READ IT: GENESIS 39:1–23

How would you feel if someone who loves you offered to fly you by airplane to eat dinner anywhere in the world? Clearly that person would be willing to splurge on you! What if they offered to have a limousine pick you up? You'd obviously be pretty excited.

Now imagine if on the way to the restaurant the limousine driver said, "I'm kind of hungry and want to grab a cheap burger. Want one?" It's obviously a silly offer in light of the amazing meal you'll eat that evening, but all the travel you've experienced has caused you to work up an appetite. That cheap burger actually sounds good to a part of you, yet at the same time you want something else even more than that.

Joseph had some "cheap burgers" offered to him. He could've become prideful about his job or given in to the temptation of someone finding him attractive and saying, "I'm tired of waiting for this great vision God gave me to happen. I'll just settle for whatever makes me feel good right now." Instead, Joseph was honest enough with his temptations that he fled from them, as if to say, "What I'm being offered is appealing, but I want something more special and revolutionary than that."

Among all the temptations you'll face, you'll most feel like caving in when you're "hungry" and tired from your journey. The best way to avoid settling for "cheap burgers" is to meet up with God each day to remember what's at stake. He loves you and *is* taking you somewhere that He's paid the price for. Strip yourself of any power temptation has over you by being completely honest with Him about why you're tempted by it. Also be completely honest about the greater thing He's called you to. You don't need something less when you have "something more."

THERE IS HOPE

When God offers "something more" to you, it's because He sees "something more" in you!

Discuss a time when you were tempted with snacks or treats that weren't healthy.

- ***IF*** you didn't know the next time you were going to eat healthy food, how tempted would you be to eat food that had poison in it?
- ***WHAT IF*** when you faced temptations in life now you somehow knew all the greater things God had in mind for your future if you stayed faithful?

150: Rescue?

***IF** everywhere you walked you were surrounded by a floating cage that felt like your own personal jail, how would that affect your social relationships?*

***WHAT IF** you were trapped with a wanted criminal in your cage?*

READ IT: GENESIS 40:1–23

Rescue. Do you long for it in any way? Rescue from a big test at school or a work project at your job that you're behind on. Rescue from upcoming bills or an event on your calendar. Rescue from relationships in your life that have gone bad. Rescue from the piles of laundry in your home or the feelings piling up inside you.

Say this out loud: "Rescue is coming." (For real, say it right now.) This doesn't deny your suffering but claims that there's more to your life than just your suffering.

Joseph longed for rescue over the years while pressing through all his problems. He was hated by his brothers, became a slave to foreigners, was falsely accused of a crime, and was thrown into prison without hope of release. He kept doing what was right despite how life felt wrong, including helping out his fellow prisoners. One of them promised to put in a good word for Joseph if he got out, only he forgot. Do you think Joseph could've genuinely said, "Rescue is coming"? Is it hard for you to say?

In a world where we're constantly let down by others (and sometimes feel that God has let us down), rescue still is possible and happening. It doesn't always look like we think, for rescue requires a willingness to be rescued however and whenever the "rescuer" does it. You can be honest with God about how you feel stuck so a rescue can happen *in* you before it happens *to* you. Perhaps like Joseph you'll also see an opportunity to help others feel rescued. Sometimes when we're waiting for the Lord to do incredible things in us, He's asking us to use our position of pain to tell another person about the incredible things He's going to also do for them.

THERE IS HOPE

Rescue happened in the past at the cross, will happen in the future in heaven, and is available now as you follow the Lord and His wisdom.

Talk about a time when you wanted to be rescued.

- ***IF*** you could be rescued from something this week, whether it was a chore around the house or a deeper thing happening in your life, what would that be?
- ***WHAT IF*** when we're feeling overwhelmed God wants to rescue each of us in a way that doesn't sound like rescue?

151: I Can't, But God . . .

***IF** you could determine what other people dreamed about, what dreams would you give them?*

***WHAT IF** others could determine what you dreamed about?*

READ IT: GENESIS 41:1–16, 28–40

Dreams are like little movies that play in your mind. Each one combines everything you've ever seen or felt with some added imagination beyond your experiences. That means you're the writer, producer, director, and occasional actor in that wild storyline playing out in your head as you sleep. You're also the only audience for the dream, which is why dreams are hard to explain to other people.

The Bible offers another insight in that God has spoken to people through dreams (see Numbers 12:6 and Acts 2:17). That doesn't mean if you're on a dream pirate ship that the talking parrot is the voice of God. What's clear is that God has used dreams to reveal Himself to people. That seems to be the case with the powerful dream Pharaoh had, because he asked everyone for insight on it. That's when the cupbearer who'd been in prison mentioned Joseph.

Notice Joseph's response to Pharaoh's question about if he could help: "I am not able to. . . . It is God who will give Pharaoh a favorable answer." Everything Joseph had gone through over the years forged a revolutionary humility that inspired Pharaoh to make Joseph the second-most powerful man in all of Egypt. All the wrong Joseph had suffered helped him become the right man to oversee what was needed to prepare Egypt for the famine ahead of them.

God will speak wisdom and confidence through you into the lives of others. Sorting through their hopes and dreams (along with any nightmares they fear or are living) is only possible by keeping your eyes on Jesus. To serve them you'll have to risk your own comfort, reputation, and desire for control—and maybe even say, "I can't, but God. . . ."

THERE IS HOPE

If you are bold enough to ask, God is bold enough to respond.

Share about a time when a friend or family member asked for help to figure something out.

- ***IF*** you knew about something big that would happen a year from now to someone you care about, how would that affect your life or that relationship?
- ***WHAT IF*** faith in God is never wasted, even if following Him means you don't get what you want or things turn out harder than you planned?

152: Who's the Man

***IF** you could point at anything electronic to turn it off, how would you use that power?*

***WHAT IF** you were able to completely take over that electronic device and make it do whatever you wanted?*

READ IT: GENESIS 41:53–42:24

Basketball great Larry Bird once said, "I'm just looking around to see who's gonna finish second."* Trash talking like this causes problems instead of solving them. It's a boastful (and sometimes mean) language athletes and politicians use to make themselves feel better than others. This mentality is filled with emotion and competition. It often crosses a line beyond the game or debate, much like how it's hard to forget how someone publicly hurt or shamed you in the past. We can get caught in a cycle of one-upping each other with zingers no matter how much time has gone by.

Joseph had a moment in his life and leadership where he lapsed into this mentality. His brothers showed up looking for food in Egypt, not knowing Joseph was the man in charge. Years after they sold him into slavery, he now had the position and power to decide what would happen to them. All his trash talking came from hurt that he still was weeping over. The story doesn't end here, but this moment is worth pausing over to consider our own temptations.

The highest calling in life isn't to be at the top (something we forget by focusing too much on celebrities and trophies). The highest calling in life is to become a servant who brings life to others by meeting their physical or spiritual needs. You'll have to face what this means for the people in your life, including "that person" who has hurt you in the past. Failing to set others free with forgiveness only makes you a prisoner of hate. When you step out of the pain, you find that the need you're meeting for them begins to meet a need for healing in you.

* Chai, Bryan. "Larry Bird's Best Trash-Talking Story Revealed by NBA Legend." *The Western Journal*, May 1, 2018.

THERE IS HOPE

The faster we get over trying to get to the top, the sooner we can be a part of something truly foundational.

Discuss any area of life where you feel competitive against someone else.

- ***IF*** the competition you feel against this person were to suddenly stop, how would your relationship feel?
- ***WHAT IF*** you started praying for this person to start "winning" in his or her relationship with God? How would that impact how you feel toward him or her?

153: Revolution Remix

***IF** you were able to make every person on earth spend time at any spot on earth when they were eight, where would you send them?*

***WHAT IF** you could make people go to that spot every year?*

READ IT: GENESIS 45:1–28

It's strange how two people can have the same experience yet both leave with different viewpoints. Maybe you've watched a movie with a friend and she liked it but you didn't. Or maybe you've gone through a difficult time with a family member that affects you both in different ways. Or maybe certain life experiences that made you slow down were moments others quickly walked through.

It's also puzzling to consider who God used to take part in His revolution and how each one responded. Every "covenant" He formed with these incredibly imperfect people played out with one letdown after another. You may have found yourself reading about them and wondered, "Why them? I would have handled that so much better." Perhaps you would have, or maybe you would have some dips of your own that would need to be corrected. Hebrews 11 says to be inspired by the *faith* of these various people instead of imitating their *lives*.

Joseph realized his flawed way of dealing with his brothers and corrected it before things got worse. He realized God had bigger plans for him in Egypt, like using his position to make sure his family and future family (who became the Jews) stayed alive. The Lord had also worked this way in the lives and generations before him, from Adam and Noah all the way up through Abraham, Isaac, and Jacob.

We're all going to stumble in our spiritual journey, and it's easy to think that this time we went "too far." As long as we're alive and willing to come to the Lord, He will restore us to Him and His revolution. As you become aware of any temptations in you to lie, steal, gossip, live in fear, or otherwise, invite God to work in you right then and there. This is how the revolution becomes a remix.

THERE IS HOPE

Share your story. We reveal God not just by talking about what He will do in heaven but how He has helped us here on earth.

As a family, brainstorm a list of different people you're grateful for.

- ***IF*** you asked some of these people to share about their flaws, what do you think they would say?
- ***WHAT IF*** what God is doing in the world is more about His strengths than it is about our weaknesses? What would that mean to you personally?

154: Weekly Recap

***IF** your household had no bills and enough food every day, how would the way your family lived life be different?*

***WHAT IF** instead you were each given three items from any store daily?*

[Joseph's] brothers also came to him, bowed down before him, and said, "We are your slaves!" But Joseph said to them, "Don't be afraid. Am I in the place of God? You planned evil against me; God planned it for good to bring about the present result—the survival of many people." (Genesis 50:18–20)

CATCH UP

- Who or what made you laugh recently?
- How did life feel easy or hard this past week?

RECAP

- What stood out to you from what we've read together, talked about, or attempted to do together over the past week?
- What thoughts or questions do you have from today's Bible verse?

GROW TOGETHER

- What might be the main thing God is trying to tell our family today?
- What if we did something new together or returned to a good habit to live out what we're learning? What might that be?

OPEN UP

- In what ways are you struggling in life or experiencing something hard?
- If we were to confess something to God as a family, what might that be?

PRAY

- Who is Jesus to you today?
- Who would be willing to close our time with a simple prayer?

THERE IS HOPE

Ego

Among the many thoughts inside of you that drive how you live and behave, there's a deeper core belief that bundles it all together. It has to do with how you see yourself compared to others—what psychologists might call your "ego." Because it's something you create, it's an identity full of blind spots and false conclusions. That means it's easier to spot how others incorrectly think of themselves than how you think of yourself.

Ego is also a term to describe how someone always wants to be the center of attention or ignores you when you talk. Ironically, your struggle with them doing this has a lot to do with your own ego. Any desire to confront them with how incredibly self-centered they are can blind you to however self-focused you may also be. That's the strange thing about living according to your ego—it doesn't seem like *you're* doing anything wrong but simply want others to give you (and what matters to you) the best attention or acknowledgment.

In the era after God began His revolution, people began living more and more in line with their imagined sense of importance than out of a truer sense of who they were before the Lord. Tribes who worshiped false gods took over the land that God had given to Abraham's descendants, while Egypt gained new pharaohs who built a bigger and bigger kingdom for themselves. In the middle of all this search for power and control, God's people were humiliated into slavery. If they were going to be set free, they would have to deal with their own ego issues in the process.

When humanity as a whole lost sight of how far it had drifted from God, He removed everyone's sense of control by raising up a holy nation of people who descended from His revolutionaries and had His favor.

155: Pharaoh, Pharaoh

***IF** the government charged you 10 cents for every square of toilet paper you used, how would that change your life?*

***WHAT IF** everyone else had to pay you 10 cents for every square of toilet paper they used?*

READ IT: EXODUS 1:6–22

What do you call someone who always has the pharaoh's back? A Cairo-practor. Why did the janitor say while cleaning the pyramids? "Something sphinx."

Ancient Egypt was about more than just sand and pyramids. It was also known for its creative arts, government, religion, and documentation (Egypt was one of the first civilizations to write using ink and papyrus). The Egyptians also valued personal grooming and appearance, expecting each other to bathe daily in the Nile River and dress up in fine clothing. The primary individual who tied all of this together was the pharaoh, who inherited his role from the pharaoh before him. Each ruled all of Egypt as a supreme leader and was thought of like a god.

Of course, a pharaoh wasn't a god. The one during Joseph's era seemed to be more in touch with this than the pharaoh described at the beginning of the book of Exodus. All of the great honor Joseph earned for himself and fellow Israelites in saving Egypt was forgotten or overlooked by this newer, ego-driven leader. He saw the Jews as a threat who could take over the land, so he felt turning them into slaves and killing their sons would demonstrate he was in charge.

It's hard for us to understand why God allows different people to rise up into power, especially when their actions and attitude attack the larger revolution. Remember that God is *always* sovereign and can use the "wrong people" to accomplish the "right things." It's what happened at the Cross when ego-driven leaders crucified Jesus without realizing they were helping accomplish the Lord's greater will. God always gets to determine the outcome of history, no matter what insecure bullies or flawed leaders try to do.

THERE IS HOPE

There's never been nor ever will be a leader greater than God. He can turn anything backward into forward progress. He gets the final say.

Open up about a leader who has inspired you.

- ***IF*** you were to copy one way this person treated others, what would it be?
- ***WHAT IF*** you were ever under the leadership of someone who was intentionally mean and hurtful? What would you do?

156: A Little Help Here?

***IF** you were being chased by a horde of small monsters, how would you escape?*

***WHAT IF** you were being chased by one big, fire-breathing dragon?*

READ IT: EXODUS 2:1–10

There comes a point in life when instead of praying before you eat fries you pray about *if* you should eat fries. One day . . . you're just older. It's like how at some point you stop adding "and a half" to your age without even thinking about it.

But when you're younger so many people in your life watch out for you to make sure you don't get hurt. Parents put up gates so toddlers don't fall down the stairs. Brothers and sisters look out for younger siblings at school. Neighbors and friends of the family keep an eye on each other's kids when everyone is playing outside.

Baby Moses had many different people looking out for him when he was born. His mom secretly defied Pharaoh's command so Moses could live and planned for him to be discovered by Pharaoh's daughter, who would take him into her home as an adopted son. Moses's big sister also helped by making sure their own mother could help the Egyptian woman care for the baby. So not only did Moses live, but his birth mother was also hired to take care of him! Apparently God was looking out for Moses too.

Looking out for others (and being looked out for by others) melts ego issues. It transforms a "me" mentality into a "we" mentality. Someone you know will need your help to work through a tough situation or to speak up when they cross lines they shouldn't have crossed. You'll likewise have to receive their help instead of shaking it off because you're too prideful to let them in or think your perspective on something is better than theirs. Remind your family that it begins in your home—that you are all a team who regularly get to say, "A little help here?"

THERE IS HOPE

When you let God use all of you, even your gaps can help fill others.

Recall a time when you gave help, and then share about a time when you needed help.

- ***IF*** a little kid asked for your immediate help from some bullies, what would you tell him?
- ***WHAT IF*** ten kids asked for your help?

157: Spoiler Alert?

***IF** you could see what someone else looked like (or will look like) at any age, who would you want to see and at what age?*

***WHAT IF** everyone except you could see what you would look like in the future?*

READ IT: EXODUS 2:11–25

SPOILER ALERT! (Still reading? That's totally up to you, but a "spoiler alert" lets you know that something critical to the story is coming up.)

SPOILER ALERT! Moses became a deliverer to the Jews! God used him to free the people out of the horrible situation they were in so the Egyptians would no longer hurt them. We'll explore this more in the next chapter.

That's not the full spoiler alert though. Today's passage shows Moses was already trying to be a "deliverer" on his own terms long before he knew it was his destiny through God. In this instance, Moses acted out of ego, thinking he could fix a problem by murdering someone and getting away with it. It was the wrong way to try to save the person he wanted to help. Moses then set aside his royal life by running into the desert in fear, eventually becoming a shepherd. (SPOILER ALERT: God used this experience to prepare Moses to later shepherd God's people.)

Don't miss this, because you are also capable of rushing into your God-given calling in a not-so-God-given way. The passion inside of you in this chapter of your life may be a "spoiler alert" for a larger destiny God will reveal in your *next* chapter, so be careful not to spoil it by how you pursue it. Maybe like Moses, you're trying to do something good but are causing hurt as you do it, or you might be focusing on helping one person when God knows you're capable of impacting so many more. Instead of living by your urges, seek the Lord to learn why certain things stir you up and what He has yet to reveal to you about those things. Not everything that stirs you will reveal your calling . . . but something will.

THERE IS HOPE

What's happening inside of you is important today, yet it's also part of your character development for a larger role tomorrow.

Talk about a time when you learned something about a movie before you saw it or a book before you read it.

- ***IF*** you had a choice, would you still want advance information about the movie or book?
- ***WHAT IF*** you could know something today about who you'll be ten years from now?

158: Look Again

***IF** your clothes came alive and tried to dress you up in weird combinations, how would you stop them?*

***WHAT IF** you couldn't stop them and they did that every morning?*

READ IT: EXODUS 3:1–6

An "Easter egg" usually refers to a colorful egg kids hunt in the spring. The term also can refer to hidden messages the creator of a movie or video game hides for the fans to find, such as seeing a hidden Mickey Mouse in a Disney movie or accessing special features in a video game. You might initially overlook these features or inside jokes, but when you look again and find them, it's hard to un-see them.

Moses had an "Easter egg" experience while tending his sheep. He'd seen his share of ordinary bushes before, but this one had something extraordinary in it! Once Moses saw it, he couldn't un-see it—not only was the fire not consuming this bush, but an angel of the Lord appeared within it to speak through it.

There's something else for us to "look again" at. Consider how Moses was standing where sheep graze and go to the bathroom, yet the Lord said he was standing on holy ground. Moses didn't give into ego on this; he took his sandals off and stepped forward.

Is there anything that seems ordinary in your life that God is doing something extraordinary in? Maybe you haven't considered how the Lord is at work in a friend's life, an opportunity you've rejected, or a situation you're tired of.

Perhaps He wants to reveal Himself to you through worship songs you'd rather not sing. Or it could be that He's trying to tell you something is "holy ground" that you are grossed out by. Don't let your ego cause you to assume you've seen everything there is to see—look again.

THERE IS HOPE

You walk through multiple moments with God on a daily basis. Many of them are buried in plain sight. Pay attention.

Trade stories of when you each found an "Easter egg" in a movie, TV show, or game.

- ***IF*** our lives were filled with "Easter egg" moments with God, would you be thankful or frustrated that you had to look for them?
- ***WHAT IF*** you were Moses? What would be some of your initial reactions to the burning bush?

159: Instant Messenger

***IF** people couldn't text or email each other for a day. what do you think would happen?*

***WHAT IF** people were only allowed to send a text message or email three times a day?*

READ IT: EXODUS 3:7–22

Years ago, people who wanted to communicate with someone sent a human messenger. Eventually faster methods were developed. Telegraph machines harnessed electricity and radio waves to send messages across a country in a matter of minutes. Today we use phone calls, video chats, emails, texting, and social media. Ever wonder what our next "instant messenger" method might be?

God is fond of using people to share His message. In the book of Exodus, He told Moses He had seen how hard the Israelites had things under the ego of Egypt. Moses himself had also realized it years earlier when he reacted out of anger against the treatment of an Israelite by a harsh Egyptian. The difference was this time Moses needed to carry *God's* message and solution into Egypt instead of his own.

Moses doubted himself, so to ensure Moses could rise up to this opportunity, the Lord shared His name as "I AM WHO I AM." It means many things, like how God doesn't rely on anyone or anything for His authority or inexhaustible power yet will become what we need to help us in all things. It also means that the message Moses was to deliver didn't come from him but from a much higher authority.

Moses was a kind of prophet, but we are evangelists—the next type of "instant messenger" God created. Second Corinthians 3:3 says, "You show that you are Christ's letter, delivered by us, not written with ink but with the Spirit of the living God—not on tablets of stone but on tablets of human hearts." It all comes down to letting God change you in an instant to become that messenger.

THERE IS HOPE

God actually cares about people and is ready to take action. He's looking for people ready to take action with Him. Are you one of them?

Discuss what it's like to have to share awkward messages with others that they need to hear.

- ***IF*** you had to tell your closest friends all the bad things and habits they do that no one else likes, how would your friendships be affected?
- ***WHAT IF*** your closest friends had to share those things with you?

160: But, But, But . . .

***IF** you were offered a chance to win a thousand dollars if you played a professional sport you were not good at, would you?*

***WHAT IF** you were offered ten thousand dollars, but you had to do whatever you were the worst at?*

READ IT: EXODUS 4:1–17

Not every job worth doing sounds fun. It's not exciting to take out the garbage or plunge a toilet, but your home would get pretty stinky if neither happened. It especially gets tricky when we feel like what we're expected to do is beyond what we think we're capable of. We get pretty creative with our excuses when the real problem is we just aren't up for doing something.

Moses gave many reasons why he didn't think he was the right person for what God asked of him. He told God he couldn't speak well and feared no one would take him seriously. Apparently his experience with Egypt in the past made him uncertain about how things would play out in the future. As God stripped away all of his "but, but, but" excuses, Moses said, "Please, Lord, send someone else."

The Lord doesn't easily give up on us in these moments though. What was happening in Egypt had a big stink to it, and someone needed to change things. God saw through what Moses said and asked, "What is that in your hand?" He then made it possible for Moses's staff to do miracles and eventually partnered him with his brother Aaron (whom the Lord had already inspired to seek Moses out).

God may be asking the same question of you and your family today: "What is that in your hand?" Instead of creating excuses why you think you're unqualified to do something incredible, embrace who God says you are and what you're capable of. Your past experiences don't have to hold you back from the significant adventure before you. Whoever you are and whatever you have, offer it all to the Lord and be prepared to get over your "but, but, but."

THERE IS HOPE

God doesn't just offer you heaven. He offers you today—24 hours to find things inside you that you didn't know existed, but He does.

Share a situation you know you could make a difference in but are holding back or making excuses.

- ***IF*** no one but you could make that thing happen, how would it change your willingness to step up?
- ***WHAT IF*** you had to experience danger to help save the life or eternity of another person?

161: Weekly Recap

***IF** you could change your voice to sound like a famous singer or celebrity, whose voice would it be?*

***WHAT IF** that person got your voice at the same time?*

By faith Moses . . . refused to be called the son of Pharaoh's daughter and chose to suffer with the people of God rather than to enjoy the fleeting pleasure of sin. For he considered reproach for the sake of Christ to be greater wealth than the treasures of Egypt, since he was looking ahead to the reward. (Hebrews 11:24–26)

CATCH UP

- Who or what made you laugh recently?
- How did life feel easy or hard this past week?

RECAP

- What stood out to you from what we've read together, talked about, or attempted to do together over the past week?
- What thoughts or questions do you have from today's Bible verse?

GROW TOGETHER

- What might be the main thing God is trying to tell our family today?
- What if we did something new together or returned to a good habit to live out what we're learning? What might that be?

OPEN UP

- In what ways are you struggling in life or experiencing something hard?
- If we were to confess something to God as a family, what might that be?

PRAY

- Who is Jesus to you today?
- Who would be willing to close our time with a simple prayer?

162: Pick a Team

***IF** you could send cookies to any sports team, which would you pick?*

***WHAT IF** those cookies made the team win five games in a row? When would you send them?*

READ IT: EXODUS 4:27–31; 5:1–23

What's your favorite team sport to play? Soccer? Football? Baseball? Basketball? Ultimate Frisbee? Unicycle Hockey (look it up!)?

The last time you played you had to first notice who was on your side. This is much easier if teams wear the same colors or flags. Otherwise you may pass off to the wrong person or let an opponent run by you. Sometimes people play up this confusion against an opposing player by saying, "I'm open! Throw it to me!"

Moses first seemed like a breath of fresh air for the Israelites when the older leaders (elders) saw God was with him. He was like a star player they were ready to pass off to, for he was willing to stand up to Pharaoh and say what the Lord told him to say. When Pharaoh's ego took over and life got harder for God's people, the Israelites complained against Moses. They were happy to wear the "Moses" jersey as long as he was winning. The moment a loss happened, they jumped off the team. Even Moses got so low that he began complaining against God.

Have you ever questioned your team like this when following God's will wasn't easy? Sometimes our loved ones confront us with spiritual decisions we keep putting off, or a church leader dares us to step up when we'd rather sit down. Trying to keep our faith comfortable or doing our best to blend in is just another form of ego; although ego can mean you think too much of yourself, it can also mean that you think too little of God. Pick a team, and stick with it even when the scoreboard says you're down.

THERE IS HOPE

You're on the winning team. If you stick clearly with God even when it isn't easy, it's easier for others to do the same.

Talk about how your family members and friends have helped you go further in life.

- ***IF*** you found out someone signed you up for an activity they felt would help you grow, but you had held back on signing up for, how would you feel?
- ***WHAT IF*** it was time for each of us to do something to share our faith publicly, like baptism or sharing our spiritual story with others?

163: From One Extreme to the Other

***IF** you were put in charge of your favorite company for a day, what would you do?*

***WHAT IF** you were put in charge of it for a month?*

READ IT: EXODUS 6:1–9

If you were to look up the meaning of the word *meltdown*, you might find references to things severely overheating, like a nuclear reactor core. There are other meltdowns, though, like when a kid throws a fit in a store—not because a parent refused to buy the chocolate-coated-sugar-pops from the cereal aisle but because that kid is a tired mess and didn't sleep well the night before. Sometimes we can't hear what is being said because we're beyond tired emotionally or physically.

With the Israelites, it was a matter of both. Centuries of being slaves and recent frustrations with all the extra work affected their ability to understand how they were God's chosen people. They let their exhaustion and discouragement become louder than the truth, much like how our frustrations, fears, and fatigue can keep us from seeing God clearly.

Does that mean that the best thing you can do to hear from God is to take a nap? Maybe, but perhaps the better takeaway is to realize that sometimes you'll feel so overwhelmed by what you feel that you'll lose sight of the truth. The next time you find yourself stuck in an emotional moment, realize that all the sobbing isn't coming from a real situation but from the fact that you are really worn out.

Then again, maybe the best takeaway is to realize that the Lord doesn't stop sharing truth even when we've settled into a funk. In a world that would rather justify itself, be outraged, or throw a tantrum, spending time in His Bible every day renews our thoughts and lives (Romans 12:1–2). The next meltdown in your life might not need to happen if you let the Lord properly fire you up.

THERE IS HOPE

Myth: Reclaiming what's good and true will be easy and comfortable.
Truth: There's far more good and truth to reclaim than evil to fear.

Open up about a time you thought someone was really for you or against you.

- ***IF*** you could hear the thoughts of that person, what do you think you'd hear?
- ***WHAT IF*** most of the hurts we've experienced in life weren't meant to attack us but happened because someone else simply saw life differently?

164: Game On

***IF** it rained grapes instead of water, how would that change how we went out in the rain?*

***WHAT IF** all weather was somehow grape-based?*

READ IT: EXODUS 7:1–25

Certain people seem like they just can't lose. Others just *feel* like they can't lose. Whether you're playing a sport, trying to get a promotion, or hoping to get better grades than a friend, there comes a point when it's "game on" and you find out if things will end up a win or a loss—and not just in terms of a scoreboard or award. A competition doesn't just reveal who does and doesn't walk away with a trophy, but what the character of the person is.

It's why God said He was going to "harden Pharaoh's heart." Maybe that seems strange until you realize how different people respond differently to the same God. For example, putting a pile of clay and a pile of butter under the same sun will cause one to harden and the other to melt. It all comes down to what is presented before that sun.

God knew Pharaoh would bring an ego-driven spirit that would harden before Him, so He told Moses to be prepared for it. Pharaoh may have felt like he couldn't lose, but he stood no chance in a real competition against God. By sending plagues of blood, frogs, gnats, flies, disease, boils, hail, locusts and darkness (as described in Exodus 7–10), Egypt was disciplined and Pharaoh's true nature was revealed.

As you personalize this, consider how God doesn't exist to cater to your desires but to transform you into what He desires. We do have a say in that based on what we bring before Him. It's our "game on" moment that will either reset our desires and deepen our understanding of why we exist or prompt us to harden up against Him if we're led by our ego. What are you bringing before Him?

THERE IS HOPE

God being who He always is makes it possible for us to become who we don't yet realize we were created to be.

Review how being competitive in the past (be it in a sport or in life) revealed things about your character.

- ***IF*** you could relive a particular victory or a loss, what would you do differently?
- ***WHAT IF*** there's a relationship today that's still impacted by how you handled a particular competition in the past?

165: From NO to NOW

***IF** the only way to get someone to listen to you was to stomp your foot, would you talk as often as you regularly do or less?*

***WHAT IF** to ask someone else for permission to do something you had to first slap your face?*

READ IT: EXODUS 11:1–10; 12:1–13, 29–32

Washing the windows. Cleaning the toilet. Pulling weeds. Organizing storage. You know those chores that "somebody" in your house should get around to doing?

How about those larger things God has put on your heart to do? We can pretend we aren't aware of them, but we're actually saying "NO" every time they come to mind. Every once in a while we'll get to a breaking point, like when the pile of dirty laundry creates a funk we can't ignore or a ministry in our church is short on volunteers and can't function. This is when our "NO" becomes a "NOW."

Consider how each time God sent a plague on Egypt, Pharaoh called for Moses to stop the plague. Sometimes Pharaoh would offer a small promise that sounded good, but eventually he'd cave into his ego and change his mind again. The Lord finally sent one last plague that was the worst of all, which is why He warned Pharaoh and the Israelites about it in advance. God's people took steps to prepare for it to "pass over" them through a sacrificial lamb whose blood saved them (sound familiar? Jesus was later called the Lamb of God because of His sacrifice: John 1:29, 36). Meanwhile, Pharaoh did nothing in defiance. That is, until the plague overwhelmed him and in the humility of defeat his "NO" became a "NOW."

You can't (and shouldn't) do everything everyone asks of you, but some things are obvious—especially when they come from God. The Bible is full of these values and commands, but we can pretend like we aren't aware of them . . . which means we're really saying "NO" and pretending it's something else. Let your "NOW" moment happen today. It just may release something incredible that God has promised if only you set your ego down.

THERE IS HOPE

*The Lord sometimes works in not-so-mysterious ways. Whatever right, needed, and obvious thing He's asked you to do can be done **NOW**.*

Brainstorm how you would go about trying to get an important message out to everyone.

- ***IF*** you could make a commercial about anything, what would that commercial be for and what would it be like?
- ***WHAT IF*** a commercial was made about you but you weren't aware of it?

166: This Way or That Way?

***IF** you could add any feature to a GPS or map, what would it be?*

***WHAT IF** adding that feature made you travel slower than others?*

READ IT: EXODUS 13:17–22

Face it—we've kind of lost all our excuses to get and stay lost. That is, if you consider how many drivers have access to a GPS (Global Positioning System). These devices work together with multiple satellites in space so you can learn where you are and how to get where you're going—be it this way or that way.

Of course, you might choose to ignore the step-by-step directions if you think you know a better way to get somewhere. A GPS can adapt to your decisions within reason, but if you keep making the wrong turns you're going to end up in some rough places that you could have avoided. You'll also eventually run out of time.

The Lord doesn't want us to live this way. As the Israelites left Egypt, He made sure they didn't get stuck outside of its borders arguing over which way to go. He miraculously provided a pillar of fire by day and a cloud by night that they were to follow together—"God's Positioning System." Otherwise the loudest egos from the loudest people would have demanded everyone head this way or that way, like down one seemingly good road that was filled with enemies waiting to attack them. Instead, God took them down a different path that led into the wilderness.

The Lord hasn't left us alone in our era to guess at life either. Our two "pillars" are the Holy Spirit and the Bible, for they work together in helping us understand what our position is and if we're getting where we're supposed to go. That doesn't mean we'll know every tiny detail of our lives or that we'll avoid the wilderness, but that we've lost all our excuses to stay lost.

THERE IS HOPE

God isn't just our GPS; He is personally along with us on the ride.

Share about a situation when you felt like you were in the right place at the right time.

- ***IF*** you had showed up just ten minutes later, what would have been different?
- ***WHAT IF*** when we were asked to do something we simply said okay and didn't argue about it?

167: Samples

***IF** you could cross any body of water in one minute, how would you use that ability?*

***WHAT IF** all the animals or fish you passed over would chase you for a full hour afterward?*

READ IT: EXODUS 14:5–31

What do you think about samples? Ice-cream shops might let you taste different flavors until you find the one you want to buy. Food courts or grocery stores will offer you a small piece of food on a stick. Unfortunately, a stranger (or sometimes people you know) can offer you something like a drug or drink that will hurt you. Samples give us a "first exposure" to something, but not a complete exposure.

Pharaoh was a recovering know-it-all after sampling God's power. At the same time, he sampled life without the Israelites around to work for Egypt. He didn't like it at all, so he slipped back into his old ways with a plan to locate and attack God's people.

Meanwhile, the Israelites feared that God was going to abandon them to die. Despite seeing samples of His power during the plagues, they wondered if being slaves in Egypt was better than living on the edge of the unknown. The Lord decided to show another sample of His power by parting the Red Sea and letting His people cross on dry ground. As it closed behind them and crushed Pharaoh's army, you'd think that would have been enough to reset them for good.

God continually offers us samples of His goodness, power, presence, justice, and love. Meanwhile, His enemy and our broken world hand us ideas that aren't healthy, such as how life should be all about us feeling good. Remember, what you're sampling is your "first exposure" and not a complete exposure. Like Moses told the Israelites, let the Lord fight for you. He'll begin by showing you what you've been handed and the larger thing it invites you into—be it life in Him or harmful addictions from ego-centered living.

THERE IS HOPE

Standing still with the Lord helps you figure out where to place your first/next step to run in His power.

Share experiences you've had sampling something.

- ***IF*** you could sample anything before it happened, like seeing in your mind what the first few minutes of it would be like, how would you use that ability?
- ***WHAT IF*** we had no sample of who God is at all?

168: Weekly Recap

***IF** you had to sing a song in front of ten thousand people, what would you sing?*

***WHAT IF** you only had to sing in front of ten people?*

Then the prophetess Miriam, Aaron's sister, took a tambourine in her hand, and all the women came out following her with tambourines and dancing. Miriam sang to them: Sing to the Lord, for he is highly exalted; he has thrown the horse and its rider into the sea. (Exodus 15:20–21)

CATCH UP

- Who or what made you laugh recently?
- How did life feel easy or hard this past week?

RECAP

- What stood out to you from what we've read together, talked about, or attempted to do together over the past week?
- What thoughts or questions do you have from today's Bible verse?

GROW TOGETHER

- What might be the main thing God is trying to tell our family today?
- What if we did something new together or returned to a good habit to live out what we're learning? What might that be?

OPEN UP

- In what ways are you struggling in life or experiencing something hard?
- If we were to confess something to God as a family, what might that be?

PRAY

- Who is Jesus to you today?
- Who would be willing to close our time with a simple prayer?

169: Drink It In

***IF** you could design a drink to be sold locally, what would it be like?*

***WHAT IF** the drink you invented became popular and was sold worldwide?*

READ IT: EXODUS 15:22–27

In the past if you wanted to connect with celebrities you had to find out where they might show up and hope you didn't miss the special appearance. Now you can send a message to famous people online. It's rare that they respond, but it's not unheard of for someone with countless fans to personally reply back to a select few.

You might think God is like this if you believe He's like a celebrity with only so much of Himself to go around. Sometimes we say things like, "I was having a bad day, but then God 'showed up' and everything changed." In doing so we overlook how God is always-present, not to mention all-powerful and all-knowing. He speaks to us when things feel great just as much as He does when life is tough.

The Israelites were just as tempted as we are to overlook the Lord's ongoing presence. As they asked Him to show off His power in providing water, it was as if they thought He'd left them because things seemed desperate. Maybe this is why they grumbled—not because they needed to, but because their perspective of God was small and created emotions that didn't need to be created in the first place. The water they drank was meant to help them drink in God and His love.

Sometimes our "disappointment" with God tracks back to us thinking He's "dissed-an-appointment." Rethink that, because you never have to wait for someone to show up who is *always* with you. Our ego wants us to think we've been overlooked by God when we should be humbled that He's with us so much. Just because the Lord hasn't revealed Himself in a new way doesn't mean He's gone anywhere. Drink it in and be refreshed.

THERE IS HOPE

When we wonder where God is, He wonders how we could miss Him. The Lord is with you right now, ready to refresh you.

Talk about a time you thought you had to do something by yourself until you realized someone was going to help you.

- ***IF*** you did have to do that thing by yourself, what would have been different?
- ***WHAT IF*** instead of saying God "showed up," we recognized He was already there but "revealed Himself" in a certain way?

170: All You Can Eat

***IF** you came home to find your house entirely filled with potatoes, what would you do?*

***WHAT IF** you knew all the potatoes would expire and go bad at midnight but were perfectly fresh until then?*

READ IT: EXODUS 16:1–36

The sign outside of an all-you-can-eat buffet is pretty clear. It plainly communicates that while you are at this restaurant you're able to fill your plate (and stomach) with as much food as you'd like. What this sign doesn't say is that it's an "all-you-can-take buffet." Still, you might occasionally see people putting a few cookies into their pockets (and sometimes more) as they leave.

The Lord miraculously provided something of an all-you-can-eat buffet for the Israelites in the desert. Although there weren't chocolate fountains or gallons of gravy, He offered them all the meat and manna they could eat—as long as they didn't keep any of it beyond their needs that day. It was God's way of helping the people take refuge in Him versus the ego-centered habits they picked up in Egypt.

Some people ignored this command and were surprised the next day when what they had stored was spoiled and infested with maggots. There are consequences to being greedy with God's blessings. The only day He allowed for there to be any type of food storing was when He had the people take a Sabbath day of rest from working.

Like the Israelites, you might hold too tightly to what God has given you today because you fear the future. Maybe like those who stored up food that spoiled, you'll work an unhealthy amount of hours to get a particular grade or win a certain video game and rot your spiritual journey. These habits sound good on the surface, but at their core they tempt you to hang onto something other than God for your security. You're being offered an all-you-can-eat chance to "taste and see that the Lord is good. How happy is the person who takes refuge in him!" (Psalm 34:8).

THERE IS HOPE

Whenever life feels like a "desert," know that God is able to provide what you need from the strangest of places.

Brainstorm what it must be like to have God's ability to do miracles and provide for others.

- ***IF*** you could turn any food into a different food and any drink into a different drink, what would you change?
- ***WHAT IF*** you could turn anything into a food or drink?

171: Listen Up

***IF** you could be an expert on three things, what would you choose?*

***WHAT IF** you learned all the knowledge today but would forget it all in a week?*

READ IT: EXODUS 18:5–27

Think back to when you were in a very large crowd, such as while attending a concert or walking through a busy city. Maybe you were on a cruise ship and liked telling everyone you met, "Looks like we're all in the same boat." Whatever it was, did someone serve as the leader, or did everyone randomly move about doing their own thing? Was there an overall sense of order or chaos?

There is no actual record of the exact number of Israelites who left Egypt, but Exodus 38:26 lists the number of men who could serve in the army as 603,550. That means the total Israelite population, if you include women and children, may have been anywhere from 2 to 3 million people. Not only was Moses responsible for keeping them moving, but he also was the primary leader over the daily needs and disputes they had.

It's probably why he listened to the ideas his father-in-law Jethro suggested. Moses could have brushed Jethro off and said, *"Hey, I'm the leader. God came to me in a burning bush, and since then I've had many two-way conversations with Him. Why should I listen to you?"* Instead of having such a huge ego, Moses humbly heard Jethro out and applied his ideas to make things better.

Everyone you meet has something to teach you and vice versa. But not everyone you meet will embrace this, for some leaders will claim they don't have to listen to anyone. A good leader listens to different ideas in order to pick the best one though. We do this to hear what God is saying, perhaps through an unlikely source. The Lord doesn't speak to puff us up but to mold us into His image and guide us in a life of significant impact. Listen up!

THERE IS HOPE

Neither life nor leadership is about you having all the answers but about asking the right questions to grow with God's wisdom.

Share about a great piece of wisdom you heard and who you heard it from.

- ***IF*** you could put that piece of wisdom onto a billboard people would drive by, what else would you want on that billboard?
- ***WHAT IF*** someone admired something you said and put your wisdom on a billboard with your face on it?

172: Life With(out) Boundaries

***IF** stoplights had other colors, what colors would you pick and what would drivers have to do when they saw them?*

***WHAT IF** you had to pay a quarter every time you stopped at a stoplight?*

READ IT: EXODUS 19:1–13

You know those signs and painted lines you see on a road? Imagine what life would be like if you woke up one day and they were gone. Everyone would suddenly live according to their feelings on where to drive or how fast we could move. There would be tons of accidents that could have been avoided through reasonable limitations. We need boundaries on the road (and in everything else we do or experience) to bring about life, not death.

After three months of journeying away from Egypt, the Israelites were no longer under the boundaries they had during their years as slaves. They probably felt like they deserved some space to start living however they wanted. To guide them, the Lord created a set of circumstances to see His unique, mighty power yet again. Just as the He spoke to specific individuals in the past to establish a covenant, God wanted this entire nation of people to know they were to be set apart from the world and their own egos to spur on His revolution. All the boundaries and rules were meant to prepare them to receive this heritage of spiritual life, not death.

People sometimes wonder why the holiness of God is such a big deal. Without Him being this way and us appropriately responding, we'd start living according to our feelings and cause all kinds of accidents in life that otherwise could have been avoided through reasonable limitations. As Christians we're given the next step of the opportunity the Israelites received, for Jesus enables us to be "a royal priesthood, a holy nation, a people for his possession, so that you may proclaim the praises of the one who called you out of darkness into his marvelous light" (1 Peter 2:9). It's a sign of how to line things up.

THERE IS HOPE

God exposing us to His holiness is also Him exposing us to His grace, for as we feel convicted He starts preparing us to impact others.

When have you felt like you should be especially respectful toward someone (maybe God)?

- ***IF*** you could put yourself back in that moment, what thoughts or feelings would be inside of you?
- ***WHAT IF*** that moment changed you for the rest of your life? Or what if you moved on from that moment as if it never happened?

173: First and Ten

***IF** you could change one thing about how a sport is played, what would it be?*

***WHAT IF** you could only change a sport's uniforms?*

READ IT: EXODUS 20:1–21

Say what you like about football, but it would be more fun to watch if it involved tickling. As it is, you're on a team trying to run or pass the ball into an end zone to score. To get there, you begin with a situation called "first and ten"—your first chance to get the ball at least ten yards from there. If you do this within four standard attempts, you get another "first and ten" to keep going.

What we call the Ten Commandments are God's "first and ten" for humanity. They mark out the initial space God gave us to score in life (known as "The Law"). The Lord eventually gave His people more marks or commands after this (known as "The Law") to show them how to advance even further, but it was summarized here. If they tried to play by their own rules, He held them accountable and appropriately penalized them.

Remember, God tells us these things so we don't have to live in a world full of ego. He wants us to know (1) there is one God, (2) so don't get distracted by false ideas of God or (3) abuse His name. (4) Invest into this relationship by prioritizing it (5) and learning respect through your family. (6) You don't have to let anger lead you, (7) nor lust, (8) nor do you have to take from others. (9) Truth is better than lies (10) and you don't need to be jealous of what others have.

These "first and ten" great ideas from God were His way to show us our need for Jesus—because no one but Christ could keep them all, yet we needed to know them.

The Lord wants you on His team. The wins are clearly marked. Every step forward matters. Through Jesus, keep going!

THERE IS HOPE

Holiness without grace is not holy. Grace without holiness is not gracious. God offers it all. The Law and the Love are fulfilled in Christ.

Discuss how each of the Ten Commandments says something to your family.

- ***IF*** the order of the Ten Commandments matters, what can we learn from that alone? In what ways might one thing make the next thing more possible?
- ***WHAT IF*** a football team only went the first ten yards of a field and then stopped? What if our family only went so far spiritually and then stopped?

174: The Rest of the Details

***IF** you had a job where you only had to work two hours a week to earn a full week of pay, what would you do with the rest of your time?*

***WHAT IF** you had to work twenty different jobs for two hours each week?*

READ IT: EXODUS 23:10–19

One way people strike up a conversation is to ask people, "What's your job?" or "What's school like for you?" These questions help us begin to know them, but it's easy to stop there and sum others up based on what they do. We do this to ourselves if life gets so busy and our schedule determines everything.

The Israelites must have really struggled with this after four centuries of being slaves in Egypt. To reset, God formally told them to set aside a Sabbath day where all work ceased. This wasn't the first time He'd presented it, and yet out of all the Ten Commandments it's the one He spent the most time on (perhaps because it's the one we're most tempted to overlook). The Lord added that they should throw fun and meaningful celebrations. How wild!

Sabbath is all about the "rest" of the details:

- Space with God—we seek out and hear our Lord.
- Space with others—we fully embrace those around us.
- Space with life—we move at a different pace than other days of the week.
- Space with peace—we back away from circumstances so we can better see them.
- Space with purpose—we celebrate being deeply blessed and deeply bless others.

Our own to-do lists can keep us so busy that we end up feeling like slaves to them. Let what God told the Israelites speak to you on this, for His command to set a day aside for Sabbath is a gift. If you start taking small steps in this direction, you'll soon discover how the world really can run on His energy with yours (versus yours alone).

THERE IS HOPE

A regular Sabbath regularly allows us to see ourselves the way God does—full of depth, purpose, beauty, and worth.

Honestly discuss the busyness of your home and what it would mean to upgrade the value of Sabbath.

- ***IF*** Sabbath is a big deal to God, how can we tell if it's a big deal to us?
- ***WHAT IF*** Sabbath is also somehow a daily thing? What would it look like to pause with God throughout each day?

175: Weekly Recap

***IF** you could invent a new sauce that would be as popular as ketchup or ranch dressing, what would it be?*

***WHAT IF** people only used your sauce?*

This Moses, whom they rejected when they said, Who appointed you a ruler and a judge?—this one God sent as a ruler and a deliver through the angel who appeared to him in the bush. This man led them out and performed wonders and signs in the land of Egypt, at the Red Sea, and in the wilderness for forty years. (Acts 7:35–36)

CATCH UP

- Who or what made you laugh recently?
- How did life feel easy or hard this past week?

RECAP

- What stood out to you from what we've read together, talked about, or attempted to do together over the past week?
- What thoughts or questions do you have from today's Bible verse?

GROW TOGETHER

- What might be the main thing God is trying to tell our family today?
- What if we did something new together or returned to a good habit to live out what we're learning? What might that be?

OPEN UP

- In what ways are you struggling in life or experiencing something hard?
- If we were to confess something to God as a family, what might that be?

PRAY

- Who is Jesus to you today?
- Who would be willing to close our time with a simple prayer?

176: Homecoming

***IF** each house were huge and had five families living in it, how would that work for you?*

***WHAT IF** around every house there were fruit and vegetable gardens?*

READ IT: EXODUS 23:20–33; 24:1–7

Homecoming is a celebration that unites people of all ages through their common connection to a school. The "spirit" days leading up to homecoming involve wild-looking activities—at least, that's how it appears to people on the outside who don't get it. There's a big rally, game, dance, parade, and tailgating meal to get everyone pumped up about what they're a part of. Despite how unique life may be for each person, they get on the same page through a common history and common cause. People even work together to find old classmates and grow the guest list.

The Promised Land the Lord offered the Israelites was the "home" coming to them. It was the same land He'd promised Abraham's family (who over time became the Israelites), but other tribes of people had moved onto it over time and claimed it. The covenant ceremony was like their rally to get everyone unified and pumped up about what they were a part of. Despite how unique life had been for each person, they got on the same page through a common history and a common cause.

As Christians, our "Promised Land" is heaven. This homecoming is made possible through Jesus, but it's not merely something in the future. The Spirit-filled days leading up to it involve wild-looking activities—at least, that's how it appears to people on the outside who don't get it—like the transformation of a soul, marriage, family, community, and more to get everyone pumped up about what they're a part of. Despite how unique life may be for you, through Christ you can get on the same page through our common history and our common cause. Let's unite together and grow the guest list!

THERE IS HOPE

You ignite a trail to heaven others can follow by letting the Spirit of God fire you up!

What meaningful event like a homecoming or family reunion have you enjoyed?

- **IF** that event spoke to you in any way, what would that be?
- **WHAT IF** you were asked to plan a big party like this in heaven?

177: God Tech

***IF** every day you would get a box with three random things inside, would you look forward to opening the box or be afraid?*

***WHAT IF** you were guaranteed something good if you opened the box while doing twenty specific things?*

READ IT: EXODUS 25:1–18

Life is pretty fancy today compared to a few decades ago. Take for instance our access to information and communication through technology that's always being upgraded. Some of the devices we use every day still puzzle us because we don't know all the details about how they work or were created. It's why people sign expensive contracts to rent the latest invention so they can keep up with the best available tech.

Take a look at what God invented so the Israelites could best access Him. It began with a contract of sorts where He asked the people to take up an offering of hard-to-come-by items for Him. This meant whatever was created out of that offering wouldn't belong to the people but the Lord. Giving like this takes our ego out of it—when God wants us to be generous He shouldn't have to explain why.

In this instance, God did have more to say and described how they would ultimately construct a large tent-like structure with intentional spaces and materials on the inside for the people to personally communicate with Him. This "tabernacle" on a large scale was represented by a smaller "ark" (not to be confused with the boat Noah built). The ark was like their "mobile device" that they took into battle.

Obviously, technology is a metaphor that doesn't sum it all up. In fact, everything God had the people build only offered a glimpse of what was to come. The real upgrade happened centuries later when Jesus arrived, and then was upgraded again when the Holy Spirit came to live inside of Christians.

Giving up your ego may feel costly, but your generosity will reveal the Lord's generosity. We are the hard-to-come-by offering He's looking for. Build the network.

THERE IS HOPE

Generosity starts with what you have and who you are—not what you don't yet have or who you aren't yet.

Name an invention that lets you connect with other people.

- **IF** you could invent something to change the world for the better but you could never use it yourself, what would it be?
- **WHAT IF** this rule was true of all inventors and their inventions?

178: A Golden Opportunity

***IF** metal was always super hot or super cold to the touch, how would that change how you live?*

***WHAT IF** this super-hot or super-cold metal could shape-shift into whatever the person was thinking?*

READ IT: EXODUS 32:1–6

Certain TV shows only have an audience when nothing else is on. Networks experiment all year, making sure not to put a fluffy pilot show against a proven powerhouse. We know something new won't flip something proven.

That is, unless there's a gap—like how disappointment and jealousy can flip our faith. When life makes us sad or someone else's story seems better than ours, we consider things we'd normally pass on. We all feel rattled from time to time, but what we tune into during those gaps can be nothing more than fluff. Our fast society has lost touch with how to stay faithful while waiting for new content.

Waiting was difficult for the Israelites too. The relationship Moses had with God was amazing but complicated for the people to process. He spoke with the Lord personally, but they didn't—at least, not like he did. Moses was also away for long periods of time, sometimes without an explanation. The Israelites felt disappointment and jealousy over it. They saw Moses not coming down the mountain as their golden opportunity to create something they *could* look at, worship, and control.

Everyone deals with feeling let down differently, especially when it's toward God. Truth be told, any relationship involves someone else who gets to behave in ways we can't predict or direct. Lashing out because of it or being reckless with our insecurities aren't our only options.

The Lord knows all the good we're capable of doing. He also knows how destructive we can become when pride or feeling entitled puts us in a bad mood. Sometimes God may seem more present in someone else's life, but remember that He is always with you . . . always.

THERE IS HOPE

God is faithful to us even when we don't do what He expects of us. Perhaps we can be faithful to Him when He doesn't do what we expect?

When have you had to wait for something that was absolutely worth waiting for?

- **IF** you were to give someone advice on waiting, what would that advice be?
- **WHAT IF** tomorrow you had to wait twice as long for everything than usual?

179: Kitchen Privileges

***IF** you had to store your clothes in a refrigerator, how would it change what you wore?*

***WHAT IF** all your clothing was like dough that had to bake for a half-hour every morning before you could wear it?*

READ IT: EXODUS 33:11–23

Somewhere in your fridge or freezer is a snack you have your eye on. You might've put it behind the leftover asparagus so no one else finds it. But what if someone does?

Have you ever had friends who would randomly eat your favorite foods out of your refrigerator without asking? Is there any home you could go into and make a sandwich without asking first? Having "kitchen privileges" can symbolize the kind of closeness you have with certain people in your life. That's not to say you shouldn't still use good manners and ask for permission before diving into someone's cupboard, but in certain relationships you wouldn't be surprised or offended by it.

Moses seemed to be ready for that stage with the Lord after all the time and shared experiences they had together. Instead of asking for food, Moses wanted to know if he could see God's actual face. This could seem confusing given how Exodus 33:11 describes them as already having a face-to-face relationship. So what's up?

As Exodus 33:11 clarifies on its own, "face to face" is meant to symbolize the "type" of relationship they had—God spoke to Moses "presence-to-presence" instead of through a dream or far-off position. They actually heard each other, like two friends having a real conversation. Moses had "kitchen privileges" that no one else had.

Let's take a cue from Moses. We're often tempted to settle for where things are at in how we see God or only want what He can give us. Moses wanted to use His "kitchen privileges" to deepen the relationship instead of just grabbing a snack of God's goodness. What would a shift like that look like in your life? Maybe it's time to move the leftover asparagus between you and someone else.

THERE IS HOPE

God is everywhere. Sit in His presence, and get to know him "face to face."

Name the friends or family members whom you feel have "kitchen privileges" in your home.

- ***IF*** everyone who came into our home grabbed whatever they wanted without connecting with us personally, how would you feel?
- ***WHAT IF*** you had to choose between not knowing God but still getting His blessings and knowing Him but your only blessing was heaven?

180: Substitute

***IF** you told a random person what you did in detail each day, how do you think he or she would react?*

***WHAT IF** instead you told it to the closest person in your life who would then also share the details of his or her life?*

READ IT: EXODUS 40:1–15; LEVITICUS 9:1–7

The question "Am I a good person?" is hard to answer with honesty, let alone accuracy. Plenty of people in the world are famous for their evil, and so our ego may conclude, "I'm not as bad as they are." Others do more life-giving things than us, so we might believe, "I'm not as good as they are." Just imagine if all the details of your life and theirs were on display though—every thought, word, or action was somehow made public. We'd all find ourselves in need of some forgiveness with God (and maybe each other).

God had set the Israelites free from slavery in Egypt, but they also needed freedom from their sins. Humanity wasn't ready for Jesus to come yet, much like a toddler isn't ready to drive a car but can start riding a tricycle. So the Lord set up a basic "cycle" for His people to recognize sin by turning to Him. It involved two substitutes: (1) a priest set apart to God who made offerings on behalf of the people, and (2) a food or animal offering that was from the best selection and in the best shape. The book of Leviticus details these guidelines, which gave the people a better way to live instead of just doing whatever they pleased.

Centuries later, Jesus Christ became both the Priest and the Offering. He's our "substitute" on the Cross to free us from sin and offer fully-alive living. Although the Israelites made multiple sacrifices, we benefit from God's once-and-for-all sacrifice. It changes the question from, "Am I a good person compared to others?" to "Am I a good person compared to Jesus?" Because of His sacrifice we can even claim a new question—"How am I avoiding sin through God's goodness?"

THERE IS HOPE

You can't break free from sin if you're just anti-sin. Be pro-Christ and He'll take you from feeling stuck in sin into a new freedom from it.

Share about something you've done that required forgiveness.

- **IF** you had to give up one of your favorite things every time you sinned, how do you think that would change what you did when you were tempted?
- **WHAT IF** someone else did this for you by giving up a favorite thing of his or her own?

181: Snack List

***IF** you could make any dessert healthy, which one would it be?*

***WHAT IF** all dessert was healthy, and healthy food was unhealthy?*

READ IT: LEVITICUS 11:1–12

Every parent knows that signing a kid up for a sport means (cue dramatic music) SNACK DUTY for Mom and Dad! It's a burden but also an opportunity. Parents can enjoy finding something tasty to hand out as long as they consider any potential allergies kids may have. Peanuts, milk, gluten, or sugar may be out, but other natural options like raisins, juice boxes, and bananas may be fine. It's all about working within what's best for the team as a whole.

God had a kind of "approved snack list" for His people of "clean" and "unclean" things. It was super-specific, and in looking back we can see some things the Israelites probably didn't see at the time. For example, pigs in the wild would eat just about anything they came across (including trash and dead animals). This was eventually transmitted into anyone who ate the pig. Other violent animals that feasted on dead animals had the same problem and were "unclean." The Israelites didn't have the research we have today on this, but they simply took God at His word. Trusting the Lord in something as common as what we eat paves the way to trust Him in so many other things.

In Mark 7:17–23, Jesus said that these food laws revealed how easy it is for us to become "unclean" on the inside (see Acts 10:9-16; Romans 14:17). In other words, our faith is profoundly affected by the little things we do. Perhaps in Christ setting us free from these laws we feel more liberty while grocery shopping, but there's still something powerful about pausing before we eat something to ask God if we're honoring Him in what we're about to eat. What's on His snack list for you?

THERE IS HOPE

As our Creator, God absolutely has the right to speak into every area of our lives. As His people, we're absolutely blessed that He does.

Talk about a favorite food that would be hard to give up if you found out it was poisonous.

- ***IF*** multiple doctors showed you how eating this food would kill you, what would be your response?
- ***WHAT IF*** you didn't die from eating this food, but it changed your personality into something ugly?

182: Weekly Recap

IF *you were stranded on an island with a luxury shelter, endless food, and endless water, would you be alarmed?*

WHAT IF *you had to choose one of those?*

For if the blood of goats and bulls and the ashes of a young cow, sprinkling those who are defiled, sanctify for the purification of the flesh, how much more will the blood of Christ, who through the eternal Spirit offered himself without blemish to God, cleanse our consciences from dead works so that we can serve the living God? (Hebrews 9:13–14)

CATCH UP

- Who or what made you laugh recently?
- How did life feel easy or hard this past week?

RECAP

- What stood out to you from what we've read together, talked about, or attempted to do together over the past week?
- What thoughts or questions do you have from today's Bible verse?

GROW TOGETHER

- What might be the main thing God is trying to tell our family today?
- What if we did something new together or returned to a good habit to live out what we're learning? What might that be?

OPEN UP

- In what ways are you struggling in life or experiencing something hard?
- If we were to confess something to God as a family, what might that be?

PRAY

- Who is Jesus to you today?
- Who would be willing to close our time with a simple prayer?

183: Grapes and Giants

***IF** you could own any state, which would you own?*

***WHAT IF** you were responsible for keeping the whole state clean?*

READ IT: NUMBERS 13:17–33; 14:1–10

One thing you don't want to do is show up for a big test unprepared. Between study guides and grouping up with others, there are multiple ways to get ready. People with big egos might "wing it" without preparing, but that's not smart. You'll be quite surprised on the big day if you didn't practice and equip yourself in the days in-between.

As the people of Israel approached the Promised Land, Moses sent twelve different men to spy on the land. This alone shows that everyone knew other people were living in the land, and yet when the spies returned everyone started complaining at how hard it would be to claim what God had said was theirs. Despite the tasty-looking grapes that showed them the land was fruitful, the Israelites were more focused on the current residents being bigger than everyone expected them to be. Ten of the spies talked so dramatically that they stirred up countless others to turn back until the Lord stepped in with some hard discipline. When those who are examples complain that what God offers us isn't good enough, it can lead others to abandon God altogether.

That's what happens when we let our fears and weaknesses take over—we lose sight of the Lord along with our courage and strengths. When something is harder than you expected, do you usually complain about the "giant" thing it is and give up, or do you focus on the "grapes" and press on to give your best? Even better, consider the example of Joshua and Caleb who essentially said, "How about we focus on God and let Him lead us?" For that to happen when the big test comes your way, keep studying who He is and preparing with Him in these days in-between.

THERE IS HOPE

No "giant" you face is bigger than God. You don't have to run or be scared when you face one if you arm yourself with this truth today.

Talk about a time when you were caught off guard by a test or project that was harder than you thought.

- **IF** every test you took was impossible to study for, how would you feel about it?
- **WHAT IF** instead of remembering God when things got tough you gave in to your emotions every time?

184: Enough Is Enough

***IF** whenever you got mad a monster appeared that was the same size as your anger, how would that affect the way you dealt with your anger?*

***WHAT IF** it stuck around until you stopped being mad?*

READ IT: NUMBERS 14:26–45

At some point, enough is enough. Certain systems reflect this, like how punching an official in a sport will get you ejected from the entire game. Schools and jobs likewise have a code of conduct regarding how often you can get into trouble before being suspended or fired.

Where it gets blurry is when it comes to relationships. There really isn't a consistent way to gauge how many times we can offend another person before they say, "Enough is enough." We just figure it out as they give us space to make mistakes or let us know when we've crossed a line. Sometimes it's revealed by them losing their temper or withdrawing from the relationship completely.

God works more relationally in this way too. We see it in the way He gave His beloved Israelites lots of slack to grow and make mistakes while leading them through it. Out of that same love, He also let them know when they had crossed a huge line. Because of the ego of some Israelite leaders (who should've known better by now), all the Israelites had to wander the desert until that whole generation of adults died (except for Joshua and Caleb) and their kids grew up to claim the Promised Land. What could have been a journey of days became a journey of years.

There are some things God will let us stumble through in life. Other times we'll experience His direct discipline. It'll get confusing, especially when others seem to get away with things we don't (or vice versa). Just remember that God isn't a system. His grace and holiness are unique in every person's life in ways we can't understand but can absolutely trust. Whatever we face in life, God is enough to help us face it . . . and "enough is enough."

THERE IS HOPE

If you only do what you can do in your own power, you aren't powerful enough. With God, you have enough power for all things.

Share about what pushes you to where you feel like "enough is enough" with a person.

- ***IF*** you had to sum it up, would you say you act more emotionally or logically in these moments when you are pushed too far?
- ***WHAT IF*** someone said you had crossed a line with him or her but you didn't think you had?

185: A Rock and a Hard Place

***IF** you owned a rock that would give you a cup of any particular liquid when you tapped it, what liquid would it be?*

***WHAT IF** anything could come out of the rock?*

READ IT: NUMBERS 20:1–13

It's a big deal when someone we look up to does something wrong. Leaders impact us in what they say and in how they live, and they will disappoint us. Only Jesus is perfect in ways we expect out of others, but that doesn't mean leaders shouldn't be responsible for their actions and attitudes.

The Bible is filled with high praise for Moses and the leadership he generally offered to the Lord and His people. Numbers 12:3 says, "Moses was a very humble man, more so than any man on the face of the earth." Unfortunately, he also had some anger issues that influenced his interactions with others. In this instance it got in the way of him being obedient to the Lord. God had to hold him accountable for this, which meant Moses wouldn't enter into the Promised Land.

How do you feel about that? We might think God should be a big softie and let Moses into the Promised Land anyway. The Lord certainly had the right to make that decision, and that's actually the point—only God has the right and ability to accurately determine what needs to happen in a bad moment so the future can best become what it's intended to be. As Numbers 20:12 points out, Moses rejected God's holiness and plan by doing things as he saw fit . . . an ego issue that he doesn't get a pass on simply by being Moses. He put himself into his own hard place.

What if instead of using this lesson to talk about the flaws in others we used it to pray for them and ourselves? Compliment good character in people when you see it, including when they own their mistakes and grow from them. Grow into that kind of living too. It's not about perfection; it's about direction rooted in affection.

THERE IS HOPE

God is bigger than any mistake you or anyone else can make. He'll walk with you through the consequences into a new perspective.

Talk through what you look for in a leader and if it's reasonable or not.

- ***IF*** leaders do bad things yet still somehow look like they succeed in life, what does that tell us about the world we're in?
- ***WHAT IF*** we welcomed God's leadership into our lives to teach us how He wants a leader to live?

186: Curses . . . Foiled Again

***IF** you had to eliminate one color in the world, which would you pick?*

***WHAT IF** you could still see that color in only five things on earth? What would they be?*

READ IT: NUMBERS 22:1–35

You know those over-the-top villains in cartoons? When their plans flop they say things like, "Curses . . . foiled again" as they twist their evil-looking mustaches. Creepy.

Certain people in life will be like over-the-top villains who go out of their way to make your life miserable. They'll try to get others to dislike you because of something you did or believe. Or perhaps that person's own flaws and insecurities will be the reason you're getting attacked.

A king named Balak struggled with the Israelites moving into territory he thought was his. He hired a unique man named Balaam to curse God's people in the name of God (think about how weird that sounds). The Lord told Balaam not to play a part in any of this, but when Balaam kept Balak's men around to entertain better offers, God told Balaam to go with them (without Balaam knowing that this was to have his attempt at curses foiled).

That all became revealed by a donkey that God spoke through. Creepy. But this animal had more respect for the Lord and His angel than Balaam, and Balaam seemed to get on board with it by speaking blessings instead of curses at God's people. Unfortunately, Balaam later found a way to take money from Balak by distracting God's people another way.

What makes this story shocking isn't that a donkey talks but that a man who clearly hears from God ignores what God clearly says. Take note of how you're tempted to do this or curse at another person for some kind of gain, like getting involved in something that pushes the Lord out of your life or being quiet while others speak against Christianity so you can gain some "cool points" with them. How would God get your attention (perhaps through an uncommon, if not creepy way)? Twirl your mustache on that.

THERE IS HOPE

No amount of opinion toward you or money spent against you can top the blessing of God when it's on you.

Discuss some of the everyday temptations like money, trophies, or popularity that can distract us from God.

- ***IF*** you gave in to these temptations, what would your life and faith be like?
- ***WHAT IF*** you didn't give in to these temptations—what would your life and faith be like?

187: Royally Important

***IF** your family had to get rid of its last name, how would you introduce yourself to people so they would remember you?*

***WHAT IF** you created a symbol to represent your family and could use it to talk about your family?*

READ IT: DEUTERONOMY 6:1–5

During the Middle Ages, knights, royalty, and nobles creatively claimed and shared their "royally important" family history through a picture called a coat of arms. They'd display it on shields, banners, and homes so others knew who they were and what they stood for. A typical coat of arms included a motto (a phrase about what the family was known for), a crest (a symbol representing a family achievement), a field (meaningful colors and symbols), and supporters (two drawn animals or people that held the crest up).

God's people have historically had a similar relationship with Deuteronomy 6. Moses shared these royally important words with the Israelites so they wouldn't just hear God's commands but also act on them. That's the motto in verse 4, known in Jewish circles as the "Shema." To this day, Jewish people encase a scroll with lines from this passage into a small box that's hung on the entrance to their homes (like a coat of arms). They kiss it or touch it with respect as they pass by.

What in your family is "royally important"? Consider what your daily routines, weekend habits, and spending reveal about what you prioritize. Imagine what neighbors who don't know you well might say if they had to sum you up from perception alone. Maybe none of what you get caught up in feels like it's outright evil, but that doesn't mean it's not distracting you from something more meaningful and lasting.

What if instead of looking like everyone else or living out of our ego, people knew us for our heritage and revolution? God thinks *you* are royally important. The way we live will either keep us busy and sidetrack us from that truth, or help us pay attention and respond to that deep love.

THERE IS HOPE

Recognizing and claiming the total uniqueness of God helps us recognize and claim our total uniqueness as His people.

Brainstorm some of the things that make God unlike anyone or anything else.

- ***IF*** we were radically honest, what would we say we spend most of our time or attention on?
- ***WHAT IF*** we were to make a coat-of-arms about our journey with God, what would be on it?

188: One Size Fits All

***IF** you had to give an outfit to one of your friends, who would get it and what would you give that person?*

***WHAT IF** you found out that all your clothes once belonged to a random person?*

READ IT: DEUTERONOMY 6:6–25

Do you own any hand-me-down clothing? Maybe shirts or shoes that belonged to someone else who shared them with you. Older siblings commonly pass outfits down to someone younger in the family, but it's not unheard of for kids to pass things "up" to their parents. Sometimes friends of the family drop off items for your household. It all comes down to if what's being offered fits right away or has to be grown into.

God designed faith to be passed from one person to another too. This can happen in every direction, from every person, and from every age. The striking difference is that the Lord isn't a hand-me-down that you only grow into when you get bigger or somehow outgrow as you get older. He is the "One"—a one-size-fits-all God for you (and everyone you know) today!

This is what's behind the powerful words Moses shared with the Israelites. Instead of rolling our eyes at people who are older or younger than we are, we should invest in them spiritually (whether they're our family or others we care about). To "talk" about our faith together means that each person plays a role in the conversation. We inspire each other by our examples, so when a dad lives for Christ, a mom pursues being a godly woman, or a kid has a pure heart for Jesus it becomes easier for others to see the benefit of it.

Every person, regardless of age, has something to offer another person, regardless of age. As it's offered, we have to each receive the hand-me-down instead of living by our egos. God is our "One" God and willing to clothe us with Himself. This has been handed down to us over the centuries for us to claim. Now it's our time and our turn to pass that great heritage along.

THERE IS HOPE

The more relationship we have with each other in the middle of life means the more life we have with each other in the middle of those relationships.

Check in with each other about how everyone feels about other generations.

- ***IF*** everyone could relate to each other no matter what age, how would things change in our world or your family?
- ***WHAT IF*** people couldn't understand people of their same age?

189: Weekly Recap

IF *you could jump into any TV show for an hour, where would you go and what would you do?*

WHAT IF *you were able to bring things or people back and forth?*

For those who live according to the flesh have their minds set on the things of the flesh, but those who live according to the Spirit have their minds set on the things of the Spirit. (Romans 8:5)

CATCH UP

- Who or what made you laugh recently?
- How did life feel easy or hard this past week?

RECAP

- What stood out to you from what we've read together, talked about, or attempted to do together over the past week?
- What thoughts or questions do you have from today's Bible verse?

GROW TOGETHER

- What might be the main thing God is trying to tell our family today?
- What if we did something new together or returned to a good habit to live out what we're learning? What might that be?

OPEN UP

- In what ways are you struggling in life or experiencing something hard?
- If we were to confess something to God as a family, what might that be?

PRAY

- Who is Jesus to you today?
- Who would be willing to close our time with a simple prayer?

190: God Nod

***IF** you were suddenly the best in the world at any three sports, what would you choose?*

***WHAT IF** for this to happen you had to be the worst in the world at all other sports?*

READ IT: DEUTERONOMY 9:1–6

You've seen a "God nod," right? Like when watching an awards show or sporting event and someone gives a little shout out that says whatever triumph just happened was all because of the Lord. It's a great sentiment but often confusing if the person giving the God nod doesn't really seem to live for God. We might feel we're more qualified to do that.

Maybe that's why God reminded His people that we each fall short of His glory and holiness even on our best days. The Israelites weren't blessed because they were "more good" than the people around them, but because God is good. The revolution of covenants He made with specific people now included the entire nation of Israel because of His grace. Through Jesus, it all became available to anyone who would choose to receive it by making Him Savior and Lord.

It's easy to roll your eyes at someone who clearly lives for themselves giving a God nod on a stage. Instead, perhaps thank the Lord that His grace was extended to *you* in the first place (and then extend it to the people you roll your eyes at). There will be times when God will ask you to stand against the evil in this world or the people who do it, but His larger goal is something genuinely transformational.

That's why the Lord wants us to recognize our sin—not so that we feel guilty beyond hope or superior that we're forgiven, but to remember He's our source for life. Trust Him with and through your weaknesses. The best "God nod" is the one you do inside of you by owning your need for Him. Praising God can come from the most unlikely of sources, including you . . . and including "them."

THERE IS HOPE

Ego says, "I'm better than they are." Shame says, "I'm not good enough." Grace says, "God's better than all of us yet can do good in any of us."

Imagine what it would be like if reporters and photographers followed you around.

- ***IF*** a reporter wrote a story about something in your life you were proud of, what would that be?
- ***WHAT IF*** a reporter captured things about your life that you didn't want others to see? How might this relate to how God sees us yet loves us anyway?

191: Spiritual Scam

***IF** you could change what everyone thought about something, what would it be?*

***WHAT IF** you could change three things everyone thought?*

READ IT: DEUTERONOMY 18:9–22

It sounds like good news. You receive a random email from someone who appears official informing you about an unknown relative wanting to give you money. Meanwhile, a different email explains that you've won a huge cash prize in a contest you didn't enter. All you have to do is give them your bank information so they can send you what's promised.

These are actually scams where someone tells a lie to get personal information and bank access from you. Other fake emails like this may appear to come from a real company you're familiar with. The liars behind this believe that if what's being offered sounds real to you that you'll fall for their lie.

God warns us about similar spiritual things. Some official-sounding people we encounter will claim to know the future or talk with dead people. The danger is these "psychics" or "ghost hunters" are (often unknowingly) goofing around with Satan despite claiming that what they're doing is helpful or entertaining. That's a huge ego at work, for just as Satan will pretend to be an angel of light, "his servants also disguise themselves as servants of righteousness" (2 Corinthians 11:15).

Don't mess around with this stuff. God is passionate to help us know that there is both life and death available through the supernatural. Certain people, books, movies, and events may say the dark stuff is entertainment, but it's a spiritual scam. So lean into the other thing God said about how one day a unique "prophet" would step forth to lead everyone with authority. He was talking about Jesus Christ, who instead of getting us to focus on the dead or the stars died to give us Life and reveal the Maker of the stars. It *is* Good News.

THERE IS HOPE

Although there are many false things you can fall for, hope in Jesus Christ is not one of them.

Name some specific things that promote false ideas of the supernatural (be it in real life or fiction) that focus on some sort of "power" other than God.

- ***IF*** you had to guess, what are all the reasons why people watch spooky movies or read books that make the occult look like fun?
- ***WHAT IF*** someone we knew was getting mixed up with all of this?

192: The Little Guy

***IF** each day for an hour everyone in the world felt stuffed like they'd overeaten, but you felt massive hunger, what would you do?*

***WHAT IF** you were the only person in the world who felt stuffed for that hour each day?*

READ IT: LEVITICUS 23:9–14, 22; DEUTERONOMY 24:19–22

Someone invented the word *leftovers* to describe an amazing thing—food that's still around after we've eaten a meal. When you consider how many people in the world wonder if they'll even eat a meal each day, the idea that we have more than enough to spare is an often overlooked blessing. And as with any blessing, it's also a responsibility.

This was important for God's people to know as they prepared to claim territory in the Promised Land. Whomever was blessed to grow and manage food needed to look out for the "little guy"—foreigners, orphans, widows, and more who otherwise wouldn't have anything to eat. The poor could harvest anything on the edges of a field or gather leftovers in the main area after it had been worked.

The Lord also told everyone to give Him the "first" and best part of their harvest or livestock. In this way they'd remember that they were blessed and meant to be a blessing to others. It was a brilliant plan that ensured everyone was cared for as they each worked hard while putting God and His values first over ego.

Food is a pathway to honor God and care for others. Every time you pray before a meal it's not about asking Him to "bless" that meal but thanking Him for what He's blessed you with. We also do this by looking out for others who are in need or overwhelmed by life, perhaps by making them a meal "just because" so they know someone cares for them. Through your investment, they'll begin to realize God cares for them. The key is to not make the "little guy" feel small, but to look out for him or her so that there's more dignity than humiliation, more food than hunger, more teamwork than ego.

THERE IS HOPE

Your heavenly Father doesn't just love everyone equally. He loves everyone uniquely . . . including you and the person in need around you.

Talk about someone whom your family could bless with a meal or two.

- ***IF*** we could do this in a way that wasn't about us feeling good but about simply blessing them, what would be the best way to go about it?
- ***WHAT IF*** we challenged ourselves to do this once a week for the next month?

193: Follow the Leader

***IF** you were hired to run a big company but showed up to find out someone else had been given the job, how would you react?*

***WHAT IF** you worked the job for a whole year and really enjoyed it but knew at the end of the year someone would take your job?*

READ IT: DEUTERONOMY 31:1–15

There's no way to keep track of all the games we play growing up. Each is fun in its own way, like how "Simon Says" or "Red Light, Green Light" gives everyone a chance to lead and follow. You may be in charge of things in one round, but then in the next turn someone else is the leader.

Moses probably thought early on that he'd lead the Israelites over the borders of the Promised Land himself. He later learned that a new generation would enter under new leadership. Part of this was because of some issues in his character while leading the people, but it also had to do with how God uses many people to take part in His revolution. We each take turns doing things during our season of life or responsibility while investing into others who will take things further, much like how Moses did that in Joshua's life.

It all makes sense on paper, but our egos can tempt us to still believe we "deserve" to always be the leader. It goes back to our inclination to be pleasure-seekers who want to experience another high, be it through achievements, relationships or whatever next experience will make us feel more satisfaction. Maybe we'd never say this about ourselves, but it's fun to be first—which if taken too far is like saying it doesn't matter who God wants to be the leader.

First Thessalonians 5:11 offers that we should "encourage one another and build each other up as you are already doing." One way to grow into this is to cheer on whomever and whatever God is cheering on. By celebrating the opportunities others are given instead of envying them, we learn how to follow the true leader—God Himself.

THERE IS HOPE

Just as the sequel to a story reveals more than the story before it, the next person God raises up can further the impact of the first.

Share about what it feels like to hand off something important to another person.

- ***IF*** you never handed things off in life, what would eventually happen?
- ***WHAT IF*** something you're a leader or follower in now is preparing you for something else? What might that be?

194: The Last Day

***IF** you could live forever and never age physically past twenty-five, would you want to?*

***WHAT IF** you could never die from age or sickness but only if someone wounded you?*

READ IT: DEUTERONOMY 32:48–52; 34:1–12

This is sadly serious . . . at some point in your life you will be at a funeral. Death is an unpredictable yet constant part of life. Perhaps you've had uncomfortable feelings as people you cared about got sick and you knew their time on earth was coming to an end. It probably also messed with you spiritually. Death has a way of causing us to wrestle with the deepest aches and questions.

In that sense, death can also make us more aware of what it means to live and take God up on His offer to spend eternity with Him. Imagine how unique it must have felt for Moses to know in advance the day he was going to die. There's not much written about his emotions on this, which is rather interesting if you remember how often his feelings were described in other situations. It would seem that what was more important to Moses was trusting the Lord with whatever needed to happen. It was the people who needed to mourn, for they truly grieved over losing him.

You are right to be sad when someone dies. You can also be absolutely at peace as you face death when your day comes if you have invited Jesus to be your Savior and Lord. Our old bodies will remain behind like an old cocoon that a butterfly has emerged out of, yet our soul (who we really are on the inside) is able to live on to be with Christ in a new body in heaven. Make sure everyone you know receives Him so that they can live on too. Our last day is not our last moment.

THERE IS HOPE

Sometimes God changes a situation. More often He changes what created a situation. "The last enemy to be abolished is death" (1 Corinthians 15:26).

Chat about any questions or thoughts you have about what happens after death.

- ***IF*** part of being a Christian means that after we die we are in the presence of God, what do you think your first thoughts or feelings would then be?
- ***WHAT IF*** you shared an invitation to Jesus and heaven with someone you know who hasn't yet clearly made this decision?

195: The First Day

***IF** one of your friends grew up to be president, who would you want it to be?*

***WHAT IF** you could be vice president?*

READ IT: JOSHUA 1:1–11

The first day of school. Moving to a new neighborhood. Giving a speech. Walking into a dark room full of tiny building blocks. Working on a friendship that went bad.

Each thing requires courage. You won't take a step in any of these unknown experiences until you determine to take that step. Before real change can happen in life, real change needs to happen in your heart.

Moses's last day on earth became Joshua's first day as the new leader. As the Israelites camped on the safe side of the Jordan River, they eventually finished their mourning for Moses and wondered what was next. This was Joshua's opportunity to step up and say something important.

Instead, Joshua waited until the Lord spoke to him before he did anything. It's the difference between being called versus being driven. He'd spent years as Moses's right-hand man, be it serving as an aide or leading troops into battle. Throughout that time he learned the value of trusting in the Lord when compared to the hard consequences of living according to ego. So instead of being anxious about taking over Moses's job, Joshua chose to be courageous and inspire others to do the same as they prepared to enter into the Promised Land.

Notice that God told the people that wherever they took a step within the 300,000 square miles of the Promised Land, that land would become theirs. Sadly, over time the Israelites only claimed around ten percent—a small portion of this land. As you consider some of the things that could happen if you don't put courage into practice, also consider the things that won't happen if we aren't courageous. God doesn't want us to miss out on something huge He is ready to do through us!

THERE IS HOPE

It is in God's heart to fight for you, which makes it possible for your heart to fight for God.

Talk about how your family is brave, along with how it could be more courageous.

- ***IF*** you were Joshua, what would it specifically look like for you to be courageous?
- ***WHAT IF*** God has a huge opportunity for us—will we be faithful and courageous to claim all of it, or part of it?

196: Weekly Recap

***IF** robots were available to help people with one task, what do you think that task should be?*

***WHAT IF** only you had a robot like that?*

Moses was faithful as a servant in all God's household, as a testimony to what would be said in the future. But Christ was faithful as a Son over his household. And we are that household if we hold on to our confidence and the hope in which we boast. (Hebrews 3:5–6)

CATCH UP

- Who or what made you laugh recently?
- How did life feel easy or hard this past week?

RECAP

- What stood out to you from what we've read together, talked about, or attempted to do together over the past week?
- What thoughts or questions do you have from today's Bible verse?

GROW TOGETHER

- What might be the main thing God is trying to tell our family today?
- What if we did something new together or returned to a good habit to live out what we're learning? What might that be?

OPEN UP

- In what ways are you struggling in life or experiencing something hard?
- If we were to confess something to God as a family, what might that be?

PRAY

- Who is Jesus to you today?
- Who would be willing to close our time with a simple prayer?

197: Studying for the Test

***IF** a meteor was going to hit the earth a year from now but you were the only one who knew about it, what would you do with that information?*

***WHAT IF** the meteor was going to hit the earth in three days?*

READ IT: JOSHUA 2:1–24

Does this sound familiar? You start your day and discover that a big project or test you knew about slipped your mind. Not only are you not prepared for what you're about to face, but it's totally on you for forgetting.

Or does this sound more familiar? You're aware of the various big things in your life coming up so you schedule time to prepare for it all. It means giving up doing whatever your ego says sounds better, but you study and train hard anyway.

Consider how the spies who scouted out the Promised Land this second time weren't like their ancestors. It wasn't about deciding *if* they would go in, but working ahead to gather as much information and wisdom about *how* to enter—like studying for a test they knew was coming. This "due diligence" involved taking reasonable steps to honor the opportunity before them.

Rahab also prepared to change her life by following the one true God. She had a shady past and told lies in the present, but she heard of God and wanted her future transformed by Him. As it turned out, she later married a Jew and is found in the family line of Jesus Himself—whose scarlet blood saves us all (Matthew 1:5).

When you're putting your life on the line for something, it only makes sense to strengthen your faith through faithfulness. Perhaps the space you'll claim is a relationship you want to be better, someone you care about becoming a Christian, or a huge turnaround in your own life. Whatever it is, the hard work you put into knowing more about it will help you better claim it. Studying for the test begins by claiming the morning so that you can claim the day.

THERE IS HOPE

Even the best planning can't predict the unexpected. Instead, let God prepare who you will be in that moment.

Share about a time when preparation made an incredible difference in what happened.

- **IF** there is one thing you don't like about preparing for something, what would that be?
- **WHAT IF** you could get help from us to prepare for something big coming up in your life?

198: Snapshots

***IF** a stranger showed you several photos of you that you'd never seen before, how would you respond?*

***WHAT IF** instead you walked into your room and discovered these photos on a table?*

READ IT: JOSHUA 3:14–17; 4:1–14

As lovely as all the family photos in your home might be, why are they there? Is it to remember a laid-back vacation or think about someone who is no longer with you? Perhaps the photo captured a rare moment when everyone set down their ego to look in the same direction together.

How memorable do you think it was for the Israelites to cross the Jordan River together? The twelve stones they gathered were their version of a family photo. But this wasn't a laid-back vacation—they stepped into a thick flood of dangerous rapids to then enter into a territory full of people ready to attack them. None of that would hold them back or stop them from celebrating, for it was a rare moment when everyone set down their ego to look in the same direction together.

They weren't alone, though. God was with them and did something public and powerful so they'd think beyond how Moses was no longer with them. Just as God parted the Red Sea under Moses's leadership, He parted the Jordan River under Joshua's leadership. What made this miracle unique (because God is creative in how He does miracles) is that this time the people needed to first get their feet wet before the waters separated and dry ground appeared. The Lord sent a clear message that His blessings were available as long as His people were faithful.

Your "Jordan River" could be an illness, difficulty at school, relationship tension, or a new opportunity. God may want to see if you'll get your feet wet before He offers you a solution. One way to take that step is by remembering how the Lord has been faithful to you and others in the past. These snapshots of His story offer perspective and meaning for the snapshot we're in today.

THERE IS HOPE

Every time we remember God's blessings in the past we become more likely to spot Him at work in our future.

Look at some of the photos in your home and talk about the memories that come to mind.

- ***IF*** these photos weren't hanging up, what effect would it have on us?
- ***WHAT IF*** there was a particular object that symbolized the season of life we're in right now? What would that object be?

199: Marching Orders

***IF** a tiny marching band marched through your house playing the same song all day, what song would you want them to play?*

***WHAT IF** instead a full-sized marching band circled your house?*

READ IT: JOSHUA 5:13–15; 6:1–7

Sometimes instructions don't seem to make sense. You may have heard that if a car begins to slide on ice, the driver should "turn into the slide." It sounds like horrible advice that would make things worse, but what it actually does is give the tires the traction or grip they need for the driver to regain control.

Imagine how Joshua felt getting instructions from an angel that the people should walk around Jericho for several days. These "marching orders" seemed odd, but they gave the people the "traction" or "grip" they needed with God. For Him to fight for them, they'd have to live by faith, not their ego. It's why the priests were to blow their ram's horns (a special trumpet used in celebrations) to proclaim with each blast that the victory was already won before it could be seen.

As odd as these instructions were, the confusion likely grew as the people realized how tough Jericho would be to conquer in a traditional battle. It had a double set of walls that made it hard for the average army to overtake. This was no average army, though—God was leading His people.

When the Lord gives us marching orders for life, we may want to resist them if they feel odd. For example, He tells us to forgive people who have hurt us, be generous rather than keep more, and practice self-control with our bodies in a world that says to do whatever gives us pleasure. Like the angel who appeared before Joshua, these commands don't take sides but are of God. It's up to us to decide if we'll wisely follow Him even if something appears foolish, or foolishly demand that He do everything for us as we do nothing. Meanwhile, the Promised Land awaits us.

THERE IS HOPE

However thick the walls in your life are, God can bring them down . . . as long as you don't put up a thick wall between you and Him.

Share about when you didn't understand the point of something a boss, coach, or teacher asked of you.

- ***IF*** you waited to understand everything perfectly before doing it, how much would you actually do in life?
- ***WHAT IF*** there was a way to trust God with the unknown? What would you suggest?

200: Fight for Your Home

***IF** you had to pick between helping your local firefighters or helping your local donut shop, which would you choose?*

***WHAT IF** you could have the help of someone else around your home once a week? What kind of help would you want?*

READ IT: JOSHUA 10:1–15

One of the hardest ways to get something done is to "try" to do it. Meaning, if we've attempted something hard we're quick to quit and say, "I tried, but it didn't work." Giving *some* effort can become our excuse for not giving *continued* effort. It'll take something special to keep us pressing on, like knowing that if we quit, our family or home is affected by it.

God's people were similarly tempted to give up as they moved into the Promised Land, but they pressed on to fight for their home. Although others had moved into that land and believed it was theirs, the Lord was committed to His promise that it belonged to the descendants of Abraham. Sometimes God allows people who want nothing to do with Him to oversee things that are meant for His kingdom—so they'll care for it without knowing its greater purpose (which they would resist).

In this particular battle, God's people honored a commitment with the Gibeonites who once claimed part of the land but then submitted to Israel. The Israelites marched all night and then jumped right into battle, trusting God to support them—including Joshua ordering the sun itself to stand still so they could finish the fight. God honored that faith by giving them the daylight they needed until the end.

Claiming any victory in life requires pushing past quitting points and claiming God's support. For every moment in your life when you're tempted to give up with the excuse that you "tried," remember that you're fighting for your family and home . . . including your heavenly family and home. God wants to see lost people found and His kingdom on earth as it is in heaven. Don't give up fighting for the people in your life who are far from Him.

THERE IS HOPE

If God can cause the sun to stand still for Joshua, what is He ready to do for you and with you as you give your best?

Brainstorm a list of things that are worth speaking up for as a family.

- ***IF*** God were to look over our list, what do you think He would cheer on?
- ***WHAT IF*** He was to add one thing and subtract one thing from our list?

201: Beyond the Bleeding

***IF** bandages dissolved within five minutes of using them, how would that change how you used them?*

***WHAT IF** the bandage would not dissolve if you painfully ripped it off and then put it back on within five minutes?*

READ IT: DEUTERONOMY 19:1–7; JOSHUA 20:1–6

Bleeding is always shocking. It doesn't matter if it's from a little paper cut or a more critical wound—anytime we see blood, it's a reminder of how precious life is. What we do next determines whether the wound will have the final say or we will, by treating it.

It can be just as shocking to see how much war and bloodshed are in the Bible. There are times when the Lord allows battles to take place in our broken world, even going so far as to anoint His people to physically fight against others for a season. These are worst-case scenarios, when people have had the chance to turn away from their corrupt ways but instead chose to stand against God and His people. Sometimes we're given an explanation for the battle, and other times we aren't.

What we can't afford to miss is what God does beyond the bleeding. He'd rather provide healing and protection, as revealed in His creating cities of refuge for anyone who accidentally killed another person. This shows that the Lord is most interested in treating a wound instead of letting it have the final say. The Bible ultimately teaches that life is sacred.

That's why the blood of Jesus shows that He was willing to make the ultimate sacrifice to give life to the world. Although the wound of our sin has caused a lot of bleeding in this world, the Lord has the final say. Heaven is the ultimate city of refuge, for it isn't merely for our accidental sins but also for the ones we've done on purpose. How amazing is it that God is willing to look beyond the bleeding to offer us life and forgiveness?

THERE IS HOPE

Our refuge isn't in a place, but in a Person—Jesus Christ.

Talk about some of the ways our world does and doesn't value life.

- ***IF*** life matters to God, what does that tell us about the kind of involvement He wants us to have in organizations that take care of orphans and others?
- ***WHAT IF*** you could snap your fingers and immediately change one thing the world gets wrong about the value of life?

202: Recruiting Season

***IF** you could enter a demanding relay race that would push you beyond what you can easily run, but your team members would each be given $1,000, would you race?*

***WHAT IF** only you received the money?*

READ IT: JOSHUA 23:1–8; 24:14–15

Coaches routinely visit and watch high school athletes to determine whether they want those players on their college teams. Good athletes usually receive offers from many schools, so at some point each player must pick one school through a declaration of "intent." The player's family may have a lot to say, but it is the athlete who must personally decide whether or not to bind with the college. The athlete offers skills, and the school offers an education; the athlete will play for that team, and the team will share its playbook, protection, and advantages. The recruit and the coach basically begin a relationship with each other that benefits everyone involved.

As Joshua realized his life was ending, he urged the Israelites to declare which team they would serve—would they serve the Lord, or whatever else they wanted to believe in? Joshua hoped they'd understand that God was the only wise decision, but each person had to personally decide to either bind with God or live according to his or her own ego and desires.

Have you made a declaration of intent when it comes to your life or family? Maybe you're doing well at work and at school, everyone is getting along at home, and there's a smile on your face today. Is your success built on the Lord, or on temporary values, such as "Don't do a bad job" or "Give your best"?

For whatever reason, God lets teammates like us know His playbook, experience His protection, and have advantages in life. We basically begin a relationship with Him that benefits others . . . we're being recruited for the greatest team ever. Choose for this day whom you will serve. If you don't decide to be a world-changer, you'll end up being someone who is ultimately changed by the world.

THERE IS HOPE

If you determine Whose you are, you suddenly know who you are.

Talk about what it means for each member of your family to make this decision.

- ***IF*** you were to describe to someone what it means to serve the Lord, what would you say?
- ***WHAT IF*** you applied those same standards to your own service to Him?

203: Weekly Recap

***IF** everyone heard cartoon sound effects whenever you got into a fight or were play fighting, how would that affect you?*

***WHAT IF** your body also reacted as if you were in a cartoon?*

Now every house is built by someone, but the one who built everything is God. Moses was faithful as a servant in all God's household, as a testimony to what would be said in the future. But Christ was faithful as a Son over his household. And we are that household if we hold on to our confidence and the hope in which we boast. (Hebrews 3:4–6)

CATCH UP

- Who or what made you laugh recently?
- In what ways did life feel easy or hard this past week?

RECAP

- What stood out to you from what we've read together, talked about, or attempted to do together over the past week?
- What thoughts or questions do you have from today's Bible passage?

GROW TOGETHER

- What might be the main thing God is trying to tell our family today?
- What if we did something new together or returned to a good habit to live out what we're learning? What might that be?

OPEN UP

- In what ways are you struggling in life or experiencing something hard?
- If we were to confess something to God as a family, what might that be?

PRAY

- Who is Jesus to you today?
- Who would be willing to close our time with a simple prayer?

204: Looking After Things

***IF** you could create your own independent state where you could do anything you wanted, what would it be like and what would you do?*

***WHAT IF** everyone in that state did what you said without question?*

READ IT: JUDGES 2:6–23

At some point in life, kids are given an adult responsibility they can handle. A parent who has to run errands might ask an older kid to watch his or her siblings. If both parents go away on a date or a trip together, they may entrust their teenagers to stay home and take care of their younger brothers and sisters. By "looking after things," kids grow up a bit, but they still aren't alone. Many families have another adult available to ensure things happen as they're supposed to, like a relative or neighbor who can jump in as a temporary leader in case things go bad.

As Joshua's life and godly leadership ended, a new era began for the people of Israel. Rather than raise up a new human leader, God wanted them to follow Him and claim all the Promised Land before them. Sadly, instead, like irresponsible kids, they again let ego take over and did evil. As Judges 2:10 reveals, an entire generation grew up not knowing the Lord or anything about Him.

So, God raised up leaders called "judges" to make sure things happened as they were supposed to. These ordinary people, although they certainly had flaws of their own, jumped in as temporary leaders because things had gotten so bad. Their leadership into battle and reminders about the authority of God offered the Israelites a nudge to grow up a bit and take responsibility.

When it comes to your home, workplace, school, or neighborhood, God wants you to be "looking after things." He hasn't left you alone to figure out how but offers you His church and His Holy Spirit to journey with you so you'll influence others who may be off track. The Lord really believes that one person in one generation who follows Him can impact the next generation to follow Him. Will this become a reality in your life? You be the judge.

THERE IS HOPE

Some things that aren't your fault are still your responsibility to help fix. Some things that are your fault can be fixed as others help.

Share an experience when you were placed in charge of something important.

- ***IF*** you acknowledged one thing from that experience that you might not have managed in the right way, what would that be?
- ***WHAT IF*** God told you that you could be in charge of anything for Him? What would you say?

205: First Impressions

***IF** after every meal you had to eat one bite of something extra (the same bite after every meal), what would it be?*

***WHAT IF** you had to eat a whole meal's worth of that extra food?*

READ IT: JUDGES 4:1–10

This may be uncomfortable to visualize but imagine walking outside one day and hearing gunshots. After quickly looking around, you see a neighbor holding a gun she's just used to shoot something down the street. What would be your first impression? Would you feel afraid?

Now picture yourself looking down the street and realizing that your neighbor shot a wild animal that was about to attack a small child. Suddenly the larger story is before you, especially as you remember your neighbor has a gun because she's a police officer. She may not have been wearing her uniform, but she stepped up to protect and serve.

Deborah wasn't your typical girl-next-door either. As a judge, she protected and served God's people. The "wild animal" in their neighborhood was a military commander named Sisera, whose army of soldiers in chariots prepared to attack the Israelites. Deborah told an Israelite leader named Barak that the Lord would give him victory over Sisera, but Barak insisted that Deborah go with him as assurance. It was as if he felt that her relationship with God was more important than his own. His lapse in faith moved God to instead let a woman named Jael have the final victory over Sisera.

We can be just as quick to make conclusions about life and what we're capable of based on what we first hear or see. It's our ego taking over as we end up believing our first impression of something rather than considering God or the larger story at play. The Lord invites you to see what He is doing as you face down the "wild animals" before you. Instead of giving in to fear or thinking someone else should do what He's asked you to do, push past the confusion and step into the greater good He's doing.

THERE IS HOPE

You can either trust in or second-guess God's plans, but either way God has plans. He's doing something, and you're invited into it!

Share about when you felt inspired to do something but held back until you felt more comfortable.

- ***IF*** we always held back until we felt comfortable, how would life be different?
- ***WHAT IF*** you could redo something today that you held back on before because of your first impression of it?

206: Priming the Pump

***IF** you had to choose one person in your life who from now on would always doubt what you said, whom would you pick?*

***WHAT IF** you always doubted yourself?*

READ IT: JUDGES 6:11–23; 7:1–8

When it comes to everyday miracles, have you thanked God lately for indoor plumbing? Before it was invented, people got their water supply from outdoor water pumps that required you to pour a small amount of water in first to shift the air inside so that water would have pressure to flow out. "Priming the pump" like this isn't necessary today, as we just flip a handle at our modern sinks and water pours out.

Gideon spent his workdays at the bottom of a well so he could hide from the Midianites. Ironically, the angel of the Lord who greeted him didn't call him a coward but a "mighty warrior." It was as if God were priming the pump for Gideon to realize what he was capable of. Gideon wanted to make sure this was all genuine, so he asked some pump-priming questions back. We see this again later, when God asks Gideon to shrink down his army, prompting Gideon to do another series of tests to figure out who should stick around.

Our spiritual journey regularly needs some pump priming too. We may want our faith to always feel like a steady stream that pours forth whenever we need it, but life is full of unexpected things that cause us to wonder if our faith is full or empty. Having someone speak a bold word of encouragement into us can make a real difference, but so can asking God questions to get to know Him better (versus simply pushing against Him out of our ego). It all comes down to if we're pouring something into our faith to get things going or letting our restlessness and uncertainty shut things down. It's incredibly powerful to wonder as you wander, but be careful not to wander as you wonder.

THERE IS HOPE

There's more to you than you know. There's more to God than you know. The real you and God Himself are waiting for you in your questions.

Who has inspired you to see God or yourself in a way you otherwise wouldn't have?

- ***IF*** you could say something to another person that would inspire him or her, who would it be and what would you say?
- ***WHAT IF*** everything about who you are, what you're capable of, and what you're weak at were written in a book that could be read by anyone?

207: Set Apart

***IF** hairstyles gave us different superpowers, would you have a silly hairstyle to get the power you wanted?*

***WHAT IF** getting any kind of haircut canceled out your powers for a week?*

READ IT: JUDGES 13:1–24

You know those things in your home that only come out for special occasions? Like certain dishes during holidays, fancy towels for guests, or clothing during formal events? They've each been set apart for a special purpose instead of for everyday use. In fact, some families set their things apart so much that they never get used at all. Others do the opposite and use these items so often that they get worn down and aren't ever at their best for special occasions.

People can also be "set apart" to the Lord for a special purpose in their lives. Samson was such a person, despite how imperfectly he ultimately lived it out. His parents couldn't naturally have children until an angel shared God's supernatural blessing that Samson would be born to save Israel from its enemies. The angel then told Samson's mom to avoid alcohol while pregnant, along with other food that would make her ritually unclean. Samson likewise wasn't to drink any wine or alcohol or cut His hair. All of this was so incredible that his dad, Manoah, prepared a sacrifice to the angel, but the angel refused to eat it, saying that such things were to be set apart only for God.

It's a simple principle—to get what you want later, set yourself apart for it now. If you play a sport and an important game is coming up, you don't stay up late every night but instead eat healthy, work out, and stick to your routine. When you have a big job interview, you learn about the company ahead of time.

So what does this look like in your life and spiritual journey? What is so worthy that you'll set aside your ego today to make sure that thing is all it's meant to be for the long haul?

THERE IS HOPE

God doesn't commit to us in pencil, but in "permanent marker": in stone, in flesh, and in blood.

Talk about some things in life that are worth waiting for despite what our world says.

- ***IF*** you could help people remember things they once said they wouldn't do but ended up doing anyway, what kinds of things would you want to help them remember?
- ***WHAT IF*** you could make a vow with three friends? What would it be, and which friends would you make it with?

208: Cute Doesn't Cut It

***IF** things that did not look dangerous really were, how would you change your life?*

***WHAT IF** things that did look dangerous were really not?*

READ IT: JUDGES 16:1–30

Some good advice for any kid wanting to pet a cute animal is, "Check with your family and the owner of the animal first." Simply because an animal is cute doesn't mean it won't harm you. Sometimes it takes getting scratched to learn that "cute" doesn't mean "comrade." It's a lesson we should keep in mind (but tend to forget about in the moment).

Samson struggled with this as he continually gave in to temptation. He may have been publicly known for off-the-charts strength and battle skills, but his affection for women who didn't follow God overpowered him in private. Despite his vow to God to be set apart, he pursued whatever brought his ego satisfaction. By the time Delilah came along, he'd developed a routine of honoring God in big things but not everyday things—which isn't really honoring God at all.

That was the real loss of Samson's strength—he may have gotten a haircut and lost his physical strength, but his real weakness was in cutting God out of his life. Samson traded God for Delilah because she was attractive . . . but "cute" doesn't mean "comrade." Keep that in mind.

It took Samson getting blinded to see he needed to surrender to God again.

When he did, the Lord turned tragedy into triumph. Jesus does that when we turn to Him in the same way—not when we make a loud vow *to* Him or do big things *for* Him, but when we do life *with* Him. It'll cost us our ego as we stop making ourselves the center of everything, but the payoff is true life as Christ takes His rightful place in our hearts.

THERE IS HOPE

When the consequences of your sin catch up to you, God is still willing to catch you and redeem your story with His own.

Samson was known not only for his strength but also for his weak character that he was blind to. What's the takeaway for you?

- ***IF*** you had to have one overemphasized muscle that was in perfect shape, which muscle would you pick? Why?
- ***WHAT IF*** there's a specific analogy here for your spiritual journey? What is it?

209: Meanwhile

***IF** little kids took care of their older siblings, what would happen in most homes?*

***WHAT IF** little kids took care of their parents?*

READ IT: RUTH 1:1–18; 2:1–16

Other people can be a real encouragement, like when your family pitches in on a big chore. The opposite is also true, however, if someone gets upset and you're affected by it despite not doing anything wrong. The choices others make can be a blessing or a burden to us.

Ruth lived during the era of Judges, when God's people were fickle in how they treated Him. That meant she was affected by their ego-driven issues, including the conditions that made it hard to find food. As a foreign widow who decided to stay with her Jewish mother-in-law (Naomi), Ruth had just one option: to make the most of the law that said poor people could pick from the edges of the fields. In one field she met a landowner named Boaz who was inspired by her character and blessed her for the good she'd done. Over time, Boaz courted Ruth and they were married (and became a part of Jesus' family line).*

We get to read this story with the happy ending, but Ruth had to live in the middle of it without knowing what God was ultimately up to. That's the essential idea of the word *meanwhile*—none of us know in detail what the future holds, but "meanwhile" have to live the life before us. Ruth's story also shows that the Lord isn't just mindful of the bigger things happening but also cares about the everyday lives of His people.

What's your "meanwhile"? Are you dealing with the blessing or sting of someone else's choices? Is what's happening in the world warping your world? You may think God has bigger things to work on, but don't give up. Even when we don't understand the situation, the Lord completely understands us and what we need.

* Matthew 1 shows five women in Jesus' genealogy: Tamar, Rahab, Ruth, Bathsheba, and Mary.

THERE IS HOPE

While life can work out to be mean, God works in the "meanwhile."

Discuss who or what in today's verses particularly inspired you.

- ***IF*** you could have given Ruth any advice or encouragement, what would it have been?
- ***WHAT IF*** Ruth could give you some advice or encouragement? What do you think she would tell you?

210: Weekly Recap

***IF** you had a tiny hammer that could be used once a day to stop chaos, yelling, and any kind of tension around the world, how would you use it?*

***WHAT IF** you couldn't talk for an hour after using the hammer?*

For God loved the world in this way: He gave His one and only Son, so that everyone who believes in him will not perish but have eternal life. For God did not send his son into the world to condemn the world, to save the world through him. (John 3:16–17)

CATCH UP

- Who or what made you laugh recently?
- In what ways did life feel easy or hard this past week?

RECAP

- What stood out to you from what we've read together, talked about, or attempted to do together over the past week?
- What thoughts or questions do you have from today's Bible passage?

GROW TOGETHER

- What might be the main thing God is trying to tell our family today?
- What if we did something new together or returned to a good habit to live out what we're learning? What might that be?

OPEN UP

- In what ways are you struggling in life or experiencing something hard?
- If we were to confess something to God as a family, what might that be?

PRAY

- Who is Jesus to you today?
- Who would be willing to close out our time with a simple prayer?

THERE IS HOPE

IDENTITY

Amnesia is a disorder that causes people to experience some loss of memory, perhaps to the point that they forget who they are. If you've ever watched a movie in which this is a part of the story, you've seen that the person who lost his or her memory must ask others what they know about the lost identity. Strangely, we have a way of doing that with people even when we haven't lost our memory—we tend to try to figure out who we are by asking others to tell us.

After the era of Judges, Israel began losing its sense of identity. Rather than letting Israel's various tribes become more detached from each other, the people felt that their best solution was to have a human king, like other nations did. He could tell them who they were (and perhaps they could tell the king what they wanted from him). God wasn't a fan of this idea yet decided to let the people own their decision with all of its consequences. Over time, the very confusion and fighting Israel had wanted to avoid ended up being exactly what it experienced. Other nations also noticed how divided God's people had become, and they invaded the land and put the Israelites into captivity.

This is what happens when people begin living more and more in line with their imagined sense of importance than out of a truer sense of who they are before the Lord. We build things for ourselves, like little kingdoms that we can manage as little kings who feel a sense of power and comfort. The more we do this over and over, the more we lose sight of how far we've drifted from God (if we don't forget about Him altogether).

God's people strangely tried to find their uniqueness by looking like everyone else, so the Lord allowed many of their shortsighted decisions to play out while He spoke wisdom into them to bring them back to their true, intended selves.

211: Here I Am

***IF** we could show up to school or work at whatever time we liked (and still receive the same credit or pay), how would that affect things?*

***WHAT IF** you were the teacher or boss and had to manage all of that?*

READ IT: 1 SAMUEL 3:1–21

Getting a new teacher or boss means the person above you doesn't yet know you. To make introductions, it's common for the person in authority to read everyone's names off a roster to figure out who is who. As your name is called, you might say, "Present" or "Here I am" to begin the connection.

God calls out your name too—not as a stranger who has to get to know you, but as Someone who already knows who you are and are called to be. Notice how He personally reached out to Samuel, who as a boy served under the godly leadership of Eli the priest. Samuel's parents struggled to have kids, so to honor God they dedicated their son back to the Lord. Samuel was raised in a great, faith-filled environment where he learned about God and served Him.

Don't miss this, because despite growing up doing religious things and being around people who loved the Lord, Samuel still needed to *personally* respond to God. He had knowledge about matters of faith but didn't know how to recognize the Lord's voice. Eli helped him understand what was happening so Samuel could then take part in the introduction and begin a relationship with God, offering that he was a "servant" who was ready to listen and take action.

As God calls out to you by name, respond with a fully present "Here I am." He'll use different methods to get your attention, sometimes speaking one important word at a time until you recognize His voice. As you obey God in His commands that you're clear on, your trust in Him grows; as your trust in God grows, you know Him better; as you know God better, you know His will better; and as you know His will better, you'll know His voice better.

THERE IS HOPE

God doesn't just call out to you once, but every day. As you respond with a willing life, He'll turn you into a person of impact.

Share some fun memories of when you felt awkward meeting someone for the first time.

- ***IF*** you could meet anyone in the world, who would you choose and how would you prepare for that moment?
- ***WHAT IF*** you knew that God was going to speak to you in the next hour? How would you prepare for that moment?

212: King Me

***IF** each ecosystem had a "king" creature that was twice the size of an average person, what would you do?*

***WHAT IF** these "king" creatures were thirty times bigger than the average person?*

READ IT: 1 SAMUEL 8:1–22

It's been said that Elvis Presley was the "king" of rock and roll. Others claim James Brown was the "king" of soul, Michael Jackson was the "king" of pop, and Michael Jordan was the "king" of basketball. Perhaps you'd disagree, or maybe you simply consider a "king" to be someone who wears a golden crown and sits on a big throne. Kings in general (whether the cultural kind or the royal kind) are looked to by others for leadership, wisdom, and advancement. Unfortunately, following human kings is a flawed idea—they'll let you down either in their character or in their eventual death, and you'll crave a new leader.

Wouldn't it make sense, then, for us to look to God to be our King? It's always been His plan for His people to find their identity in Him versus someone who's here today but then gone tomorrow. The Israelites instead insisted on having a human leader who would be their champion and decision maker, just like all the other kingdoms had. Despite God using the prophet Samuel to caution them against this, the Lord ultimately decided to let the people have what they demanded as a way to reveal over time how their priorities were misguided.

God loves and leads His people to be different from the world instead of blending into it. He knows it's in our sinful nature to want to follow a flawed leader we can see and touch rather than become a community that's uniquely led by Him. Yet again, though, God can use what He doesn't choose to seed our greatest need. He established a human line of kings in Israel—like King Saul, King David, and King Solomon (despite knowing they were imperfect)—to prepare the way for the greatest King in all history—Jesus Christ.

THERE IS HOPE

"From [David's] descendants, as he promised, God brought to Israel the Savior, Jesus." (Acts 13:23)

Share about someone who insisted on things being a certain way despite it being a bad idea.

- ***IF*** you were to describe yourself more as a listener or a talker when you're about to make a decision, which would you say you are more like?
- ***WHAT IF*** a bad decision you made in the past is still influencing you today? What would it look like to invite God to do something redeeming with it?

213: First Pick

***IF** your country had no president or ruler for a year, what would be different and what would you do during that period?*

***WHAT IF** this was the case all around the world, in every country, and lasted forever?*

READ IT: 1 SAMUEL 9:1–2, 15–17; 10:1–27

It's tense being in a group of people who are each being picked by captains for a team. We may dread being picked last, also assuming that being picked first is ideal. What if being the first person selected has its own identity issues, though?

The Israelites initially found Saul to be a great choice as their first human king. He was tall and easily spotted in a crowd, which seemed to meet their demand to have someone they could see who would lead them. This ironically came up during Samuel's search for a king when Saul was easily spotted trying to hide among the supplies. Whatever demands God's people had put on Saul, he seemed more awkward about being king than confident rising up to it.

A "first pick" often isn't what we hope it'll be. We may elect a politician we think will fix the world, hire a person to increase our company's profits, or hand a video-game controller off to a friend so he or she can beat a level we can't. Those "leaders" may get some things right, but they'll ultimately fall short.

It's possible for anything to become our "first pick" in how we turn to it to lead us. The most common temptation is to let our feelings, routines, and fears get in the way of putting God first in all things. We feel it in all the backward situations it creates and the identity issues that weigh us down instead of lift us up. Eventually we see it in our culture as people look to everything but the Lord for leadership. Invite Him to start the change in you by turning to Him each day as your "first pick." You really can find life in simply pausing with Him for wisdom, perspective, and power.

THERE IS HOPE

Jesus is God's "first pick," but we're the "next pick." He calls us onto His team to reach lost, broken, and distracted people around us.

Remember a time when you had a role in putting a team together or selecting a leader.

- ***IF*** you had to be a leader or a follower, which would you pick, and why?
- ***WHAT IF*** to be a good leader you have to first be a good follower, and to be a good follower you have to first be a good leader?

214: Everyday Importance

***IF** you were elected president, what would you do your first month in office?*

***WHAT IF** you were president and it was your last month in office?*

READ IT: 1 SAMUEL 11:1–15; 12:1–15

It's commonly said that you only get one chance to make a first impression. You do have multiple chances to make a *lasting* impression though. The way you live life in the everyday moments says more about you than whatever you do on your first day.

We can gain insight by watching what happened after Saul became king. Despite being clearly recognized as Israel's human leader, he didn't start actually leading but instead slipped away, back to his home, to work in the fields. God was ready to give him his first victory for the people, but the Israelites living in the city of Jabesh first had to go find him. Saul would go on to struggle with his identity all throughout his years as king.

Meanwhile, Samuel as an older man and faithful prophet invited the people to hold him accountable for how he'd spent his time while serving. Through this the Lord declared that if the Israelites were faithful, they'd be blessed back. Once again, God invested himself into the everyday lives of His people despite them often bordering on turning away.

Many people spend their lives pursuing big opportunities to shine when the eyes of other people are on them. What you do during the "smaller" moments of life, when people *aren't* looking your way, is what matters most. One common definition of integrity teaches that who you are when no one is looking is who you really are. It seems that God's definition of integrity goes deeper as we own the everyday importance of how we spend our time. Just as He was ready to offer Saul a victory, His eyes still today "roam throughout the earth to show himself strong for those who are wholeheartedly devoted to him" (2 Chronicles 16:9).

THERE IS HOPE

Making every day important turns meaningless moments into a meaningful movement.

Share how you felt in the past when you began or ended something important.

- ***IF*** all the important things you've done were an example to others, what might they learn from you?
- ***WHAT IF*** fifteen years from now, you could be the best in the world at something that you currently dislike doing? What would you decide to do?

215: Identity Theft

***IF** you had a loyal dog that could run at the speed of sound, what would you do with it?*

***WHAT IF** the dog could also fly and had the strength of a bulldozer?*

READ IT: 1 SAMUEL 13:1–23

Imagine working really hard to complete something only to have another person take credit for it. Even weirder, imagine you taking credit for something someone else had done. It can happen when we're afraid of losing a job, getting a bad grade, or being stuck without hope. We may feel as though time is slipping away and that our only option is to overstep our identity or steal someone else's.

King Saul struggled with this fear and claimed what wasn't his to claim. He blew a victory horn after his son Jonathan had won a huge battle, making everyone assume Saul himself was behind the win. He repeated this type of behavior when the Israelites realized they needed God's blessing through Samuel to face the Philistine army. As time ticked away and Samuel hadn't yet shown up, Saul again let his insecurities take over as he made the offering that Samuel alone was meant to make. Samuel arrived moments later, revealing that if Saul had waited just a little longer, things could've been different.

What would cause you to quit waiting on God and take matters into your own hands? Perhaps you've been eager for something to happen for a long time and the season you're in has become the most difficult part of it all. Many times a quick response isn't the best response, especially if being nervous and stressed out is what's keeping you from being still.

Fear is a lousy leader. It prompts us to tell ourselves stories that aren't true because we believe they might be. It'll eventually drive us to create a sense of security at any cost, even if it means nudging someone else out of the way. In doing so we end up inviting God to discipline us instead of bless us. "What could have been" is its own form of identity theft.

THERE IS HOPE

Fear causes us to try to be someone we're not. Faith invites our Creator to reveal the identity He originally intended for us.

Share a memory of when you let fear lead you to do something you otherwise wouldn't have done.

- ***IF*** there is one fear or phobia you're most afraid of, what is it?
- ***WHAT IF*** you never doubted yourself or what God could do in you?

216: A Cheap Shot

***IF** a family member or friend crossed a line to try to get out of trouble, how would it change your relationship with that person?*

***WHAT IF** someone who deeply hurt you tried to make up for it by buying you things?*

READ IT: 1 SAMUEL 15:10–23

How weird would the world be if people could do whatever they wanted to each other as long as they paid a dollar afterward? Picture random strangers slapping you in the face but you not being allowed to react if they presented you with money. In a sense, this type of "cheap shot" is what happens when we do whatever we want without considering how it affects God, assuming that if we do something religious, He won't mind.

This was King Saul's struggle as He lived life on his own terms and set up monuments to himself yet tried to balance out his disobedience through some spiritual moments with God. His "cheap shot" at worship was empty and caused him to lose the Lord's favor as king. God had told the people from the beginning that things like this would happen if they sought their identity under a human leader. The Lord clearly had some very real emotions about it. We sometimes forget that although He's sovereign and eternal, God feels every moment we bless Him or slap Him.

"Religion" is anchored to the idea of us doing whatever we can to reach out to God or earn His blessing. We may do this to try to prove something to Him or to cover up our sins with what we consider to be good deeds. Perhaps we hope that the right amount of religion will cause God to put up with us more.

Christianity is anchored to the idea of God doing what we couldn't to reach out to us. He does this to prove His love and undo our sinful nature through the ultimate "good deed" of Jesus dying on the cross. Perhaps He hopes that the right amount of understanding will cause us to put Him first in all things more often.

THERE IS HOPE

Sacrifice without obedience is throwing blank, crumpled-up pieces of paper at God; sacrifice with obedience is handing Him a love letter.

Discuss what you think the difference between obedience and sacrifice looks like in your home.

- ***IF*** we did things for each other but never spent time building our relationship with one another, how would our home feel?
- ***WHAT IF*** we were to sum up our relationship with God? Would you say we lean more toward religious habits or that we follow Him throughout each day?

217: Weekly Recap

***IF** whenever you played a video game, whatever you were doing in the game would happen in another dimension, how often would you play video games?*

***WHAT IF** the events in the video game happened in this world?*

As for man, his days are like grass—he blooms like a flower of the field; when the wind passes over it, it vanishes, and its place is no longer known. But from eternity to eternity the Lord's faithful love is toward those who fear him, and his righteousness toward the grandchildren of those who keep his covenant. (Psalm 103:15–18)

CATCH UP

- Who or what made you laugh recently?
- In what ways did life feel easy or hard this past week?

RECAP

- What stood out to you from what we've read together, talked about, or attempted to do together over the past week?
- What thoughts or questions do you have from today's Bible passage?

GROW TOGETHER

- What thoughts or questions do you have from today's Bible passage?
- What if we did something new together or returned to a good habit to live out what we're learning? What might that be?

OPEN UP

- In what ways are you struggling in life or experiencing something hard?
- If we were to confess something to God as a family, what might that be?

PRAY

- Who is Jesus to you today?
- Who would be willing to close our time with a simple prayer?

218: Out of the Ordinary

***IF** your friends acted like adults when they were kids and like kids when they were adults, what would your friendships with them be like?*

***WHAT IF** you lived like that? What would change about you as you grew up?*

READ IT: 1 SAMUEL 16:1–23

It's surprising to watch someone you've known for years suddenly become well-known, like if a teenager is cheered on by a whole school for being great at a sport, or a coworker receives a big promotion. You may wonder if you'll still connect as easily with that person as you did before things changed. How we see the out-of-the-ordinary identity of others is as powerful as how we see our own identities.

David was someone who started out simple yet became famous. As the youngest in his family, he took care of sheep and ran errands for his dad until the Lord sent Samuel to anoint him as king. David may not have looked like the obvious choice on the outside, but he had the right character on the inside (Acts 13:22). From the ordinary life of this ordinary kid, God's people eventually gained extraordinary leadership and extraordinary hope.

The first glimpse was when David didn't claim the throne right away but humbly served under King Saul as a musician and armor-bearer. This opportunity let him see what being a king was all about years before he needed to live that out. It revealed that David really was chasing after the heart of God.

Feel like your life is ordinary? God hasn't forgotten you, nor is He wasting your time. Like David and Samuel, we may have to see past what we think about ourselves or others to claim what God says is possible: victory when defeat seems unavoidable; forgiveness when revenge seems justified; freedom when sin seems abundant. There is much more happening around us and in us than what we're naturally aware of. How we see the out-of-the-ordinary identity of others (starting with God) can be as powerful as how we see our own identities.

THERE IS HOPE

God doesn't always take us from the ordinary to the extraordinary in a straight line, but He is taking us there. Follow Jesus.

Talk about someone you've watched step up into an important role over time.

- ***IF*** you could give this person one piece of advice that he or she had to listen to, what would it be?
- ***WHAT IF*** you could be either rich or famous? Which would you pick and why?

219: A Real Head-Turner

***IF** you could be twice the size you are now, would you want to be?*

***WHAT IF** every year on your birthday you could choose the height you would be for that whole year?*

READ IT: 1 SAMUEL 17:1–30

Ever notice the strange relationship our culture has with fear? Between hopping on death-defying roller coasters and buying tickets for gory movies, people claim to hate being afraid all while seeking it. Fear is basically a false head-turner. We wonder *"What if?"* more often than we claim *what is*.

Goliath came across as an expert in getting people to be afraid. As a giant in full battle gear, he issued a bold dare to Israel as if the real contest was to get them to quit before the battle started. By the time David showed up to the field while running food out to his brothers, all hope seemed lost. Everyone felt like a victim, unable to do anything.

David wouldn't give up, though. He lived out a "what is" faith among people who shared "what if" fears. When criticized for it, he simply "turned from those beside him to others in front of him" to find out more about the situation. David was smart enough to realize that if he didn't turn his head to find the truth, he'd end up letting fear turn his head away from the truth.

God's enemy, Satan, also comes across as an expert in getting people to be afraid. The fears we believe from him about life or our identity can make us feel like powerless victims too. To get rid of false head-turners, you need a *real* head-turner, and this is why God invites you to focus on Him. When a giant fear is all you focus on, it'll always be bigger than you; however, when you put that "giant" next to God, you realize all the *what ifs* don't compare to *what is*. The healing and freedom you long for begins by claiming in Christ that you can be more than a victim . . . you can be a victor!

THERE IS HOPE

Your faith loses focus when truth is out of focus. To see what you need to see, look at what God already sees.

Share about some of the things you fear, whether small things you hope don't happen or large things that keep you up at night.

- ***IF*** you weren't afraid of failing, would that be a good thing or a bad thing?
- ***WHAT IF*** you could help someone else completely conquer a fear or phobia?

220: Solid as a Rock

***IF** you had the ability to cause earthquakes of any magnitude, how would you be tempted to use your power?*

***WHAT IF** a bad guy also had that power?*

READ IT: 1 SAMUEL 17:31–51

Earth is commonly described as the "big rock" we live on, but it's actually made up of several layers of ingredients that include rocks, minerals, and more. It doesn't stop there, because each layer contains its own layers of ingredients. That's the nature of rocks, for whatever seems solid and strong required several things getting packed together over time.

This back story would apply to the five rocks David picked up in preparation for his battle with Goliath, but those stones weren't the only rocks in that battle. David was something of a "rock" himself by being formed by God and by his own experiences over the years that taught him how to have faith and fight. It enabled him to see this as more than a battle against a big, bad guy, but as a way to honor God.

Being "solid as a rock" also came in handy when King Saul tried putting armor on David that didn't fit him. Perhaps Saul meant well, but David had the confidence to know that his identity and purpose weren't in trying to be like someone else but by being who God had called him to be. It's a good reminder for us when others attempt to put their values or methods on us.

Take a lesson from David, who went into his battle as solid as a rock because he'd been formed by *the* "Rock"—God Himself. Just as the Lord used David's past to prepare him for his "giant" moment, He can use your past to get you ready for whatever is ahead of you. So instead of trying to muster up courage by yourself, let the Lord pack all of your layers together to form you into something solid. What He does inside of you is always more powerful than whatever is happening around you.

THERE IS HOPE

Whatever evil you stand against now will prepare you to stand up even more firmly against it in the future.

Celebrate a time you had the courage to face a major problem, person, or fear.

- ***IF*** you had to guess, what's different about the courage of Christians who don't spend time each day with God versus those who do?
- ***WHAT IF*** every time you drank water, you got a refreshing amount of courage? How many cups would you drink each day?

221: (Dis)Honor

***IF** you could choose any person to be your best friend, who would you pick?*

***WHAT IF** you could choose four more people to be your best friends?*

READ IT: 1 SAMUEL 18:1–16; 19:1–3

How would people describe you? Perhaps with something positive, about how you make others laugh, enjoy books, or work hard? Or something negative, like how they don't trust you around their pizza because you'll eat it when they aren't looking? Every person would answer differently—not just because of how each one sees you, but because of how each one sees himself or herself.

This is seen in one of the Bible's greatest examples of friendship. Jonathan, the son of King Saul, was arguably entitled to royal treatment by common people. Instead of using his position to place himself above David, he shared his royal clothing and equipment to honor David as an equal. Jonathan was a man of honor, and that inspired him to see David as someone to honor and support.

At the same time, a sad tension took place between David and Saul. Every time David brought success and honor to the kingdom, Saul became jealous and tried to harm David. Saul was a man of insecurities, and that made him see David as someone to dishonor and reject.

None of that stopped David from choosing to honor both men. Again, David wasn't perfect and made some big errors later in life, but at this moment in time he was rock-solid with God. On one specific occasion when he could've killed Saul, he said, "I will never lift my hand against him, since he is the LORD's anointed" (1 Samuel 24:6).

It takes great faith to see your identity beyond how others see you. It's also incredibly tempting to honor only our "Jonathans" while dishonoring our "Sauls." Take a cue from David—you can't fully honor people if you refuse to honor God . . . nor can you fully honor God if you refuse to honor people.

THERE IS HOPE

Being dishonored creates an opportunity for you to reveal what honor truly is.

Talk about a time when someone honored you.

- ***IF*** you had to sum up that experience with a particular feeling or word, what would you pick?
- ***WHAT IF*** the honor you give someone today would inspire others to honor the people around them?

222: A Different Kind of King

***IF** whenever you embarrassed yourself, someone's illness would heal, how often would you try to embarrass yourself?*

***WHAT IF** greatly embarrassing yourself also helped your life or healed you too?*

READ IT: 2 SAMUEL 5:1–5; 6:12–23

You're driving down the road with your family, and everyone is laughing together. Or you're by yourself and loudly singing along to your favorite song. As you casually look around, you realize that other drivers have been watching you this whole time. Either you smile back in joy and keep cranking away, or you sink down in embarrassment. Getting caught worshiping God inspires those same two responses.

After years living under the awkwardness of King Saul, Israel got a new human king in David. A sign that he was a healthier leader was how David turned the first big parade he took part in into a worship service. Despite his wife (Saul's daughter) telling him he was acting like a fool, David had no issue being even more undignified for the Lord.

When was the last time you and your family enjoyed God out loud together without worrying about how it looked? As David was willing to look foolish in his genuine love for the Lord, we can let others see the genuine smile and joy in our hearts versus sinking in embarrassment. There is nothing you need to be ashamed of when it comes to your faith or identity in Christ. There's so much to thank God for, so why not be the biggest out-loud fan of what He's doing in your life?

Sing out a new song, even if you can't sing. Let there be a spring in your step, even if you feel you can't dance. Bring a generous offering to your church, even if you feel poor. Bless a neighbor or someone you're at odds with by giving him or her a random gift or dessert, even if awkwardness is still there. Let nothing get in the way of enjoying out loud how you have a relationship with a different kind of King.

THERE IS HOPE

If we spent half the time we fear being embarrassed for our faith enjoying it instead, we'd hardly ever feel embarrassed for our faith.

Name something you can freely talk about with others whether they're into it or not.

- ***IF*** you had to pick one person you would least want to be embarrassed in front of, be it for your faith or something else, who would it be?
- ***WHAT IF*** that person's sense of God could genuinely change if he or she saw you freely and joyfully speak about Him?

223: A Not-So-Different Kind of King

***IF** you owned a device that could change any conversation (for better or for worse) with just a push of a button, how would you use it?*

***WHAT IF** everyone owned a device like that?*

READ IT: 2 SAMUEL 11:1–13; 12:1–15; PSALM 51

We all put our pants on like everybody else—by getting our pinky toe caught in the knee while hopping around. Recovering from failure is a skill we all need, like when you fall off a bike. Observing what went wrong helps you do things differently next time.

We probably don't spend nearly as much time thinking about how to recover from success, though. After an accomplishment, haven't we all been tempted to "cut loose"? Maybe we feel we deserve a break after being "good."

That was David's struggle long before he started spying on women from his rooftop. As a successful king, he (like other kings in his day) didn't think it was a big deal to have multiple wives despite God's clear command against it (Deuteronomy 17:17). Such gray decisions paved the way for dark issues between his kids (another tough read in 2 Samuel 13). David also stopped leading his troops into battle and instead stayed back to relax. He seemed to get away with it because of his famous past.

That is, until God sent Nathan the prophet to call David out for being a not-so-different-kind-of-king. David's secret plan to trick Bathsheba's husband had ended in murder. Nathan's confrontation helped recover David's true identity. David even wrote a song (Psalm 51) as a public confession that everyone could read.

This is what being a man or woman "after" God's heart means. You will stumble, and at times keep stumbling. Don't get stuck in that cycle. Turn every failure into an invitation for God to lift you up, and every success into a moment to kneel down before the Lord. And remember to listen to godly people—King David dipped when he was alone but was redeemed in community.

THERE IS HOPE

The problem with "getting away with something" is that you never really do. Let your mistakes take you where God can remake you.

Reflect on what it would be like to have our worst blunder or sin pointed out by someone else.

- ***IF*** you were offered lots of money for being on a TV show that recorded every good and not-so-good thing you did for a month, would you accept the offer?
- ***WHAT IF*** you always got away with every bad or sinful thing you did? What kind of person do you think you would become over time?

224: Weekly Recap

***IF** any fire you looked at instantly became ice, what would that mean for you?*

***WHAT IF** you could instantly defrost ice with a simple touch?*

God, create a clean heart for me and renew a steadfast spirit within me. Do not banish me from your presence or take your Holy Spirit from me. Restore the joy of your salvation to me, and sustain me by giving me a willing spirit. Then I will teach the rebellious your ways, and sinners will return to you. (Psalm 51:10–13)

CATCH UP

- Who or what made you laugh recently?
- In what ways did life feel easy or hard this past week?

RECAP

- What stood out to you from what we've read together, talked about, or attempted to do together over the past week?
- What thoughts or questions do you have from today's Bible passage?

GROW TOGETHER

- What might be the main thing God is trying to tell our family today?
- What if we did something new together or returned to a good habit to live out what we're learning? What might that be?

OPEN UP

- In what ways are you struggling in life or experiencing something hard?
- If we were to confess something to God as a family, what might that be?

PRAY

- Who is Jesus to you today?
- Who would be willing to close our time with a simple prayer?

225: Extended Family

***IF** your main family vehicle could do one special super-trick, what would it be?*

***WHAT IF** for that vehicle to do that trick, you'd have to give up control of it for ten seconds while the vehicle was moving?*

READ IT: 1 SAMUEL 16:1–23

Right now, close your eyes and describe a dollar bill in detail. Don't just settle for saying, "It's green," but be incredibly specific. If you're up for it, draw the front and back of one.

Needless to say, you're going to overlook some things regardless of how many times you've been around a dollar bill. The same can be true with family as you become so familiar with your loved ones that you lose touch with the details of who they are or are becoming. What's happening in their lives that you're losing touch with?

David's relationship with his son Absalom was like that. It tracked back to a tragic situation in their extended family that David didn't speak into, perhaps because he felt he'd lost the right to lead his family after the big public sin in his own life. It led Absalom to act out in anger that became ongoing disrespect, eventually leading him to woo people into an army against his dad. David yet again chose to be passive and leave the palace, weeping as his son took over, versus confronting his son. He kept on weeping in the end when Absalom was killed after his hair got caught in a tree (2 Samuel 18:9).

Waiting around for things to get better like David did isn't any more a solution to your problems than protesting like Absalom. Every family must commit to put character and ideas into action or else we'll pretend problems don't exist that are ripping apart life around us. Speaking truth and confronting lies in your home mean paying attention to your loved ones (and yourself) so you don't become so "familiar" that you lose touch with what's really happening. No matter your age, role, or background, speak into your extended family to help get the wrong things retracted.

THERE IS HOPE

You don't have to worry about establishing yourself as a perfect leader. That's Jesus' job. Simply let Him lead through you.

Talk about something positive or negative happening in your family that you may have all overlooked.

- ***IF*** we needed to celebrate one thing together, what would it be?
- ***WHAT IF*** we worked on something together today that for whatever reason we keep putting off addressing?

226: Wit and Wisdom

***IF** you were picked for a day to drive a large robot and fight other bots in a competition for fun, would you be interested?*

***WHAT IF** you were given this as a well-paid job to do once a week?*

READ IT: 1 KINGS 1:11–31; 3:1–15

Who invented the crazy idea of whacking a big stick at a piñata while wearing a blindfold? Or how about "pin the tail on the donkey," where you blindly walk around with a sharp pin to tack somewhere? If you're going to do either activity, you'll need guidance or you will trip and suffer pain (or cause others pain).

It's a reminder of how God will guide us so that we don't live blindly. His initial offer to Solomon to bless him with whatever he wanted was generously open-ended. Imagine all the things that would go through your mind if you were in Solomon's place! Do you think he wondered if he could wish for more wishes?

God isn't a genie though. This was a unique opportunity for Solomon to think ahead. He ultimately chose the gift of wisdom and was blessed with more. Second Chronicles 9:22–23 says, "King Solomon surpassed all the kings of the world in riches and wisdom. All the kings of the world wanted an audience with Solomon to hear the wisdom God had put in his heart."

But having wisdom didn't overpower Solomon's free will to make choices. He started well but got distracted like his dad in having multiple wives and women around to make him happy. This led to idol worship through these relationships too. It's ridiculous that he didn't use his wisdom here. It was like someone who was healed from lifelong blindness choosing to wear a blindfold daily.

God is willing to give you wisdom without taking away your free will. To help you find the right balance and identity, Proverbs 9:10 offers, "The fear of the Lord is the beginning of wisdom." He'll remove your blindfold so you don't have to live by your wits. You just have to use His wisdom and power to stop putting it back on.

THERE IS HOPE

As you see God correctly, you become able to see more of life correctly.

Try to remember and share about one of the biggest and boldest prayers you've ever prayed.

- ***IF*** you were Solomon, what would you have said to God's offer?
- ***WHAT IF*** God made you that same offer, only it was to bless someone else with anything you requested of Him?

227: Master Builder

***IF** you could run an ice-cream stand with an unlimited budget, how would you design it?*

***WHAT IF** the ice cream and toppings always replenished themselves automatically?*

READ IT: 1 KINGS 8:1–23; 9:1–9

Does this routine sound familiar? *Wake up. Go to the bathroom. Say hi to family. Go concentrate on doing something. Come back. Eat. Clean. Go to bed. Wake up. Go to the bathroom. Say hi to family. Go concentrate on doing something. Come back. Eat. Clean. Go to bed. Wake up. Go to the bathroom . . .*

Having a daily pattern gets stuff done and helps life function. Over time, though, you'll realize that you were made for more than your routine. You might look for a special project or discover purpose in the mundane. Perhaps both.

Solomon took on the project of building a special space for people to honor the Lord. This "temple" was like the big tent the Israelites traveled with under Moses, only it would be built to last. Solomon went all out in finding the best materials and dedicating it to the Lord with a special ceremony and prayer.

God appreciated this special project, but He didn't want Solomon to overlook the larger opportunity. The Lord still wanted a faithful relationship with His people and said that it started with Solomon. In other words, "Thanks for all the religious things you just did, but nothing you built matters unless you let Me build into you each day."

You're a child of God, made for a greater meaning and purpose than just getting through your day. He wants to do life with you in the big things and the little things, beginning by you realizing your identity is in Him. Personally invite Him into each moment of your day, and you'll eventually start seeing relationships, money, goals, schedule, and desires with more substance and perspective. It took Solomon six years to build the temple, but God is the real "Master Builder"—He can build something into you today that lasts forever.

THERE IS HOPE

It's better to let God build your life than ask Him to fix it. He'll do both, but one will spare you incredible regret.

Celebrate some of the things you've each done that took a long time to accomplish.

- ***IF*** that whole process either took less time or more time, what would have been different about how everything turned out?
- ***WHAT IF*** what God is building in you goes faster or slower than you want?

228: Love and Romance

***IF** you knew as a child what your first date would one day be like, how would that change how you went into that date?*

***WHAT IF** it were possible to travel through time to find people to date?*

READ IT: SONG OF SONGS 2:1–15

"BLECH!" That's the right thing to say after opening up a fridge and finding all the food inside is moldy. You wouldn't want to just close the door and do nothing about it, or stand by and watch others grab that food to eat. You have a God-given voice to say something so nobody gets sick.

The same thing applies to love and romance. Song of Songs 2:15 says, "Catch the foxes for us—the little foxes that ruin the vineyards—for our vineyards are in bloom." God invites us to care about how people know and experience love, including catching anything that can ruin what He's trying to teach them about it. It may seem as if we should mind our own business, but saying something *is* part of our identity as Christians.

That's the beautiful thing about Song of Songs, for it's an out-loud celebration of a courtship that leads a couple from attraction and romance into marriage and sex. As the couple expresses pure affection for each other, a chorus of people respond. It shows how others learn about God's brilliant design for relationships as we live it out. There's no reason to hold back from declaring how God knows what He's talking about.

So what are those "little foxes" worth "catching"? They could be popular songs, TV shows, movies, and more. We may need to point out that they are wrong in how they redefine what God meant to be beautiful and life-giving. Maybe the "little foxes" are people trying to find their identity in someone other than Christ—only He can complete them so they have complete relationships in life. Our world needs courageous voices like yours to speak into their lives. If you don't want the people you care about ending up with moldy relationships, point out the mold.

THERE IS HOPE

The best way to redefine the world's definition of love is to be defined by how God loves you.

Discuss the different ways that dating and marriage are different.

- ***IF*** you knew from the moment you were born whom you were going to marry, what would be different about your life?
- ***WHAT IF*** you knew you would be single throughout your life?

229: Sex and Marriage

***IF** you were asked to plan a stranger's honeymoon, how would you plan it?*

***WHAT IF** you were planning your best friend's honeymoon?*

READ IT: SONG OF SONGS 8:4–7

Between birthdays and Christmas, not opening gifts until the proper time takes patience and trust. It's not just about leaving the wrapping paper alone, for your mind can obsess over what the gift might be—as if you've started opening the present up mentally. What you do or don't do during this time ultimately affects your relationship with the giver.

The analogy couldn't be clearer in keeping the gift of sex intact for marriage. When a husband and wife physically come together, a spiritual bond is formed. This is why God created sex for marriage and celebrates when it happens the right way. The problem is we live in a world that is so curious about that gift that it becomes obsessed, constantly thinking about it and opening it before its time.

Today's Scripture states, "Do not stir up or awaken love until the appropriate time." A fire in your fireplace warms your house, but that same fire just a few feet out of context on the floor will burn your house down. God created sex to be a very good thing that warms a marriage versus burning up our identity as we fixate on it. What happens in our minds alone in this area can create some long-term damage to how we view ourselves and others.

What if your family could safely talk about this topic, perhaps by using a good book as a support?* That isn't to say conversation won't feel awkward at times, but together you can claim growth instead of shame. The healthiest decisions are made in the light and not the dark, so give each other the space to seek God's heart on it. It's not a one-time talk but an ongoing conversation—one that you can invite the Holy Spirit to lead you through into life.

* We recommend *Preparing Your Son for Every Man's Battle* by Stephen Arterburn and *Preparing Your Daughter for Every Woman's Battle* by Shannon Ethridge.

THERE IS HOPE

God has a grand blueprint for your love life. He is building a "mansion" for you; don't build a "shack" on your own instead.

Share in your own words what you sense God's dream is for each person in the area of love and sex.

- ***IF*** someone told you that you were "worth the wait," would you believe it?
- ***WHAT IF*** we set up a time right now to talk about this topic again, whether it's one-on-one or as a family?

230: Saltwater, Sin, and Wisdom

***IF** you knew you were going to be chased once a week by a friendly slime monster that wanted to sit on you for an hour, how would you prepare for it?*

***WHAT IF** the slime monster couldn't stay alive without you?*

READ IT: PSALM 1; PROVERBS 1:29–33; ECCLESIASTES 4:13

Two men were stranded on an island in the middle of the ocean. Plenty of fish and fruit were available for food, and every three days, rain came down to fill containers for drinking water. Even though the men got thirsty and frustrated by the "world" they lived in, they always had enough.

That is, until one man became especially thirsty between rains. He saw the ocean around and thought it would keep him from dying of thirst, so he filled his container with saltwater, thinking himself to be clever. "I can drink as much as I want," he concluded.

Do you see the flaw? The thing with saltwater is, after you drink it your body tries to get rid of the salt by going to the bathroom, but since there's so much salt in you from it, your body gets rid of more water than what you drank to dispose of the salt. That comes from places like your heart, lungs, muscles, and more . . . which only makes you thirstier and needing more water than before. So as the man foolishly drank to quench his thirst, he did the opposite of what he intended and died drinking the wrong water. The other man lived on because of his faith in the rain that eventually did come.

The "books of wisdom"—Psalms, Proverbs, Song of Solomon, and Ecclesiastes—reveal that life can be like that. God offers refreshing truth, yet we're surrounded by "saltwater-like" options we could drink in instead. If we give in to the world or Satan's temptations, we'll end up thirstier and die spiritually. Sin is not just a religious concept—it's a real, tragic thing we can choose that creates tragic consequences to our identity and the identity of others. How clever do you think you are drinking "saltwater"?

THERE IS HOPE

When Satan tells you the Father can't be trusted, he's trying to "adopt" you himself. Trust you heavenly Father to care for you.

Confess some of the temptations around you, whether or not you actively feel like giving in to them.

- ***IF*** you could interview three people in the world to get their wisdom on these temptations, who would you want to talk with?
- ***WHAT IF*** we prayed for each other right now concerning each of these areas?

231: Weekly Recap

***IF** everything tasted like your favorite food, how would your diet change?*

***WHAT IF** everything tasted like metal?*

There is an occasion for everything, and a time for every activity under heaven: a time to give birth and a time to die; a time to plant and a time to uproot; a time to kill and a time to heal; a time to tear down and a time to build; . . . a time to be silent and a time to speak; a time to love and a time to hate; a time for war and a time for peace. (Ecclesiastes 3:1–3, 7–8)

CATCH UP

- Who or what made you laugh recently?
- In what ways did life feel easy or hard this past week?

RECAP

- What stood out to you from what we've read together, talked about, or attempted to do together over the past week?
- What thoughts or questions do you have from today's Bible passage?

GROW TOGETHER

- What might be the main thing God is trying to tell our family today?
- What if we did something new together or returned to a good habit to live out what we're learning? What might that be?

OPEN UP

- In what ways are you struggling in life or experiencing something hard?
- If we were to confess something to God as a family, what might that be?

PRAY

- Who is Jesus to you today?
- Who would be willing to close our time with a simple prayer?

232: Divide and Conquer

***IF** all your toys and all your neighbor's toys came alive and went to war against each other, what would you do?*

***WHAT IF** it happened to your entire neighborhood and everyone's toys came alive?*

READ IT: 2 CHRONICLES 10:1–18; 12:1–8

A parenting truth: Letting the kids stay up late means the youngest one still wakes up at 6 a.m.

You've probably noticed that if just one person in your family acts foolishly, then the frustrations other family members have in them come out. This principle has also launched major wars as the actions of one person released a reaction in others. Soon those who had nothing to do with that fight felt trapped in the chaos that was created.

After Solomon's death, his son Rehoboam took over and foolishly made life harder for everyone. This one man's attitude and actions released frustrations in the Israelites, who then split into two kingdoms. The ten northern tribes continued to be known as Israel and eventually had nineteen kings, who all turned the people away from God. The two southern tribes became the kingdom of Judah. Only eight of its twenty rulers loved God.

This was a confusing time for God's people. To remind them of their identity, He sent prophets to explain how things could get better if they returned to Him. As they refused, God allowed them to feel the full weight of the wars they got caught up in. All of this happened more than 600 years, and it all tracked back to one man's foolishness unleashing foolishness in others.

Thankfully, the principle can work the other way. If one person genuinely loves God out loud, it can inspire others to set down their frustrations and pick up a life-giving identity in Him. Some people did this during the "divide and conquer" era, and your family can do it in this generation. You really can make a difference. Determining which difference your household makes is up to you.

THERE IS HOPE

You don't have to live feeling divided or conquered. Jesus entered into the divide of your sin and conquered it.

Think about some ways our family can genuinely appreciate God in full view of other people.

- ***IF*** other people saw God as we do, how might they better respond to Him?
- ***WHAT IF*** they saw us turning to God not only on our best days but also on our worst days?

233: From Starting Line to Finish Line

***IF** whenever you didn't move and speak, no one in the world would fight, how often would you freeze in place?*

***WHAT IF** you also gained a hundred bucks for every hour standing still?*

READ IT: 2 CHRONICLES 14:2–7; 15:1–7; 16:1–6

Picture yourself preparing to run a race. You ready yourself, the signal is given, and everyone starts moving. You find and keep a good pace at running well. Others around you start cheering you on, and it feels really good, especially since this is a long marathon of many miles. As time passes and you finally see the finish line ahead, you (for some strange reason) sit down and say, "That's good enough."

King Asa started out well with a great passion for God. He tore down all the pillars and altars people used to worship false religions and commanded everyone to obey the Lord. When he faced the threat of attack, he deliberately trusted God and invested in his spiritual journey. Then, he strangely "sat down" after thirty-five years of being on track. When he faced a conflict with a king who worshiped a false god, Asa bribed him with money that was meant for God's temple. Asa began well and hung in there well, but he didn't end well.

Every day you have a choice to either keep running your spiritual race or to "sit down." Some days will be harder than others, especially if you feel tired or hurt from giving your best. One of the biggest reasons we give in to temptation is that we feel we deserve a break or that God won't mind because of all the good we've done.

As always, the key isn't in trying harder but in remembering you aren't alone. God is continually looking at each of us so that He might strengthen us. That doesn't mean He'll run your race without you, but that He'll run it through you in truth, wisdom, community, power, victory, and more. From the starting line to the finish line, "run in such a way to win the prize" (1 Corinthians 9:24).

THERE IS HOPE

When you can't yet see the finish line, remember what you clearly knew at the starting line.

Brainstorm what it would be like to be farther along on your spiritual journey in the years to come.

- ***IF*** you were to describe the kind of person and Christ-follower you want to be five years from now, how would you sum yourself up?
- ***WHAT IF*** you could give your future self advice that you would have to listen to? What would you say and how old would you be?

234: Spread the Word

***IF** you could heal anyone by touching them and saying the medical term for their illness, how would you use that power?*

***WHAT IF** every time you used that power you forgot the medical term and had to research it?*

READ IT: 2 CHRONICLES 17:1–11

Which is it? White lights or colored lights at Christmas? Staying up at midnight on New Year's Eve or going to bed before the countdown?

When two or more people celebrate a holiday together, they aren't all celebrating the exact same thing in the exact same way. We each have different memories and values that we put into such moments. It's even possible to begin celebrating the celebration more than what the celebration is intended to celebrate.

Asa's son Jehoshaphat as Judah's king didn't want anyone making up ideas about God or getting mixed up with the corruption in the northern kingdom of Israel. He also didn't want them just going through the motions of traditions, so to strengthen and deepen things, he spread the words of God to all the people. This wasn't an easy task, yet Jehoshaphat knew that if the people truly knew God better and found their identity in Him, they could face down any threat before them.

Knowing God's truth is powerful in our lives too. We suddenly can see through lies and deception, recognize what others don't, avoid arguments that critics try to start, spot danger we otherwise would've missed, and discover what it means to love others. We can also take a cue from Jehoshaphat in making sure we spread God's words around so others can benefit from coming to know the Lord too!

So, begin memorizing some Bible verses together as a family. This way you'll always have God's words with you to face down temptation with truth and have something deeper to live by. You'll also be able to share with others who have questions, need comfort, or are struggling. Start with Romans 6:23 and 10:13. Spread the Word!

THERE IS HOPE

First, own how culture has affected your spiritual journey. Then, own how your spiritual journey can affect culture.

Share some memories about your favorite teachers or mentors.

- ***IF*** you had to be a schoolteacher, what would you want to teach?
- ***WHAT IF*** you could teach your friends three things from the Bible? What would those three things be?

235: Better than I Deserve

***IF** people said thank you by placing a cookie on each other's noses, what would happen?*

***WHAT IF** everyone had an unlimited bag of cookies supplied to them by the government so they could always say thank you?*

READ IT: 1 KINGS 16:29–30; 17:1–24

It's a question we regularly ask without always thinking about what we're asking. *"How are you doing?"* We use it as a quick greeting or to start a conversation.

So how are you doing? And do you have a way to truly answer this question? Think about how you'd begin to describe the depths of your feelings for your family or friends (whether everything is great or you're in a season of tension). Can you sum up what it means to have access to what you have access to, like how every gift someone gave you over the years was meant to bless *you*? What would you say that could adequately sum up your thankfulness for how Jesus is your loving Savior?

"Better than I deserve." Maybe that's the best answer. Maybe it's the only answer.

Life may be difficult, like it was during the time Elijah served as God's prophet. As he disciplined the northern kingdom of Israel and its leader Ahab for the evil happening, Elijah also reminded random people that God still noticed and loved them. There's the woman in 1 Kings 17 whom God uniquely considered—especially after she considered Him. Not only did she receive food during a famine, but her son was raised back to life!

Sometimes people ask why a good God lets bad things happen. We need to first ask why a righteous God would let sinners into heaven. We deserve nothing from Him—yet He calls us to Him anyway. We truly are doing "better than we deserve," so remain faithful even if you're discouraged. Your identity isn't defined by the moment you're in or the corruption around you, but by your God who loves you, considers you, and hasn't given up on you.

THERE IS HOPE

"You are my hiding place; you protect me from trouble. You surround me with joyful shouts of deliverance." (Psalm 32:7)

Ask each other, "How are you doing?" and reply to one another with some detailed answers.

- **IF** everyone was a girl for a day, what might be different in the world for those twenty-four hours?
- **WHAT IF** everyone was a guy for a day?

236: Breakthroughs and Breakdowns

***IF** you could only make right turns in a car, what route would you take from home to the grocery store?*

***WHAT IF** you could only turn left? What route would you take to get ice cream?*

READ IT: 2 CHRONICLES 21:5–7; 22:1–4, 10–12; 23:1–3, 16–17

Think about your first day being a car owner. Depending on where you are in life, that day is either behind you or ahead of you. There's something special about all of the excitement and emotions associated with being able to get behind the wheel and go wherever you'd like. It feels like a personal breakthrough.

That is, until the day you have your first breakdown. It could be that something mechanical on the car stops working, or you slide into another object and end up in an accident. It's easy to get permanently discouraged by circumstantial problems.

Elijah knew the power of a breakthrough and a breakdown. In one moment, he stood before several false prophets who couldn't stand up against the truth of who God is. In another moment, Elijah ran in fear for his life. Many people of faith go through these quick changes in perspective despite God being with them every step of the way. It may be why the Lord wanted to remind Elijah that He was with him not only in power but also in a whisper.

Life will be incredibly difficult at times. You may be going through a season right now where you've had a deep loss, are experiencing health issues, face the possibility of a relationship changing, feel mistreated in some way, or have bills you can't pay. Like Elijah, you may feel that God may have been faithful in the past but you aren't sure if He'll be there for you again. Instead of running away, run to Him, for He is our only hope of peace in an overwhelming world. He actually has a great purpose for you that may only be revealed if you slow down to listen for His whisper.

THERE IS HOPE

The best way to feel God's hand at work is not to run away from wherever He's placing you. He'll move you in or out as needed.

Open up about some times when you really felt overwhelmed by a particular situation in life.

- ***IF*** life ever gets too tough for you to figure out, would you be willing to share it with us somehow?
- ***WHAT IF*** I felt you were overwhelmed but you didn't want to talk about it right away. What would be the best way to help you open up?

237: Apples and Oranges

***IF** everyone in the world was overwhelmingly attractive, what do you think would be different about life in general?*

***WHAT IF** everyone could demand once a week that someone else swap clothes with them?*

READ IT: 2 KINGS 2:1–15

It's kind of hard not to compare yourself to others. Siblings wonder how they measure up against each other. Students evaluate who at school is smarter, stronger, or better-looking. Employees weigh their pay and benefits against coworkers'. We're constantly wondering if we're "good" based on how "great" others appear to be.

Elisha felt this as he compared himself to Elijah. Both were prophets, but Elijah had been around longer and famously urged kings and commoners to turn away from sin and return back to God. Imagine being Elisha and having Elijah above you as your example and coach. Instead of shrinking back out of intimidation, though, Elisha boldly asked that God give him twice the opportunities and impact to carry things further. The people ended up recognizing that the Lord was indeed with Elisha.

Considering two things that are different from each other is called comparing "apples and oranges." Both items share similarities, but their core differences are so unique that we shouldn't compare them in the first place. It's the kind of thing to remember when you consider your strengths and weaknesses against someone else's. Others will excel in some things we don't just as we'll excel in some things others don't. In some cases, it may just be (like Elijah) that another person was doing something first and for that reason alone has a longer list of achievements than you.

The great prophets of old were ordinary people like us whom God chose to reveal Himself through. He has a unique purpose for you too, one that will play out differently in your generation. Be bold and ask God for a "double share" understanding and capability to do that work well.

THERE IS HOPE

Apples and oranges were both made to be fruitful and multiply so that many people can be fed.

Talk about some areas of life in which you sometimes feel stuck comparing yourself to others.

- ***IF*** you never got better in those areas, what would be true of your worth?
- ***WHAT IF*** you could be really incredible at only one thing? What would it be?

238: Weekly Recap

***IF** a tree appeared in your yard and its trunk and branches formed a huge system of platforms, paths, and slides, what would you do?*

***WHAT IF** that tree changed its shape daily?*

Don't envy the evil or desire to be with them, for their hearts plan violence, and their words stir up trouble. A house is built by wisdom, and it is established by understanding; by knowledge the rooms are filled with every precious and beautiful treasure. A wise warrior is better than a strong one. (Proverbs 24:1–5)

CATCH UP

- Who or what made you laugh recently?
- In what ways did life feel easy or hard this past week?

RECAP

- What stood out to you from what we've read together, talked about, or attempted to do together over the past week?
- What thoughts or questions do you have from today's Bible passage?

GROW TOGETHER

- What might be the main thing God is trying to tell our family today?
- What if we did something new together or returned to a good habit to live out what we're learning? What might that be?

OPEN UP

- In what ways are you struggling in life or experiencing something hard?
- If we were to confess something to God as a family, what might that be?

PRAY

- Who is Jesus to you today?
- Who would be willing to close our time with a simple prayer?

239: Setting Things Right

***IF** you found out that a spy had been protecting you your whole life from bad guys who were regularly trying to get you, how would you feel?*

***WHAT IF** the spy stopped protecting you today?*

READ IT: 2 CHRONICLES 21:5–7; 22:1–4, 10–12; 23:1–3, 16–17

Every once in a while, you'll notice a police officer or sheriff driving through your neighborhood. You're meant to be comforted by this, knowing that someone is looking out for you in a dangerous world. Much of life involves people around you doing little things to bless you, like not taking seconds at dinner because you want thirds, or not yelling back as you mouth off and rant. Perhaps someone has taken on a financial burden so you don't have to, or courageously says what you need to hear while everyone tells you what you want to hear. Every time someone is kind and considerate, he or she is setting things right in some way.

After enduring multiple corrupt kings and leaders, a priest named Jehoiada stepped up to start setting things right in his era. By taking down the evil leadership of Queen Athaliah, he helped seven-year-old Joash become the rightful king. Joash went on to become an outstanding king who for most of his life honored the Lord in how he reigned and (for a season) brought the people back to their true identity in God.

It's easy to recognize the impact of people in the spotlight who (like the ancient kings) are considered leaders because of their position. Don't overlook the greater lesson though. Without everyday people like Jehoiada who step up in everyday moments to look out for others, so much of our lives would be different. Whether or not you'd consider yourself the kind of person who feels comfortable in an official leadership role, you *are* a leader who is influencing someone in some way. Use that opportunity to begin setting things right around you without ever doubting the difference it can make on others beyond your circle . . . if not the world itself.

THERE IS HOPE

Life isn't just time you waste until you go to heaven. Make a difference. Set things right. Life is a mission—not an intermission.

Remember some times you've helped a situation get better by speaking up or taking action.

- ***IF*** the greatest thing you can do for others is introduce them to Jesus, then what are some things worth speaking up about or taking action on?
- ***WHAT IF*** you could let someone know God loves him? Who would you pick?

240: Resist or Restore

***IF** you could go into an arcade that had all the games in the world, what game would you most want to play?*

***WHAT IF** you had to donate blood to the Red Cross first, before you played that game?*

READ IT: JONAH 1:1–7; 3:1–5; 4:1

Some people are known for evil. We might call them "bad guys," "bullies," "troublemakers," or "terrorists" based on their harmful choices. If several of them got together somewhere, you'd probably avoid that place.

But God is always able to work a miracle in anyone's life. That's hard for us to remember when we face "bad guys." Jonah as a prophet struggled with this as God called him to reach out to the people of Nineveh, who boasted about their cruel violence. These non-Jews stood against Israel and the Lord Himself, so Jonah ran instead of toward such an obvious enemy.

There will be days when you'll feel like resisting God when He's asked you to restore someone or something. You may be driven by pride, judgment, or fear—especially if God's asking you to connect with someone you've pulled away from. As Jonah discovered, this thinking doesn't make things better. It wasn't until he decided to head into what he was uncomfortable doing that a whole city full of people miraculously turned to God. And yet, in the end Jonah then became angry about their transformation, for he didn't think they deserved it.

The moment we think someone doesn't "deserve" God's forgiveness is the moment we lose touch with His forgiveness. You might try to ignore or run from opportunities, but the Lord will keep tapping on your heart about it—not to annoy you, but so you claim the joy of releasing others into their intended identity in Christ. He wants the friends, family, neighbors, classmates, coworkers, and strangers around you to know Him. Instead of resisting, choose to restore. May the opposition around you never overtake the obedience inside you.

THERE IS HOPE

All the people you don't feel you have any love for? God does. He also has enough love to share with you so you eventually love them too.

Take turns sharing about something you sense God has clearly asked you to do, big or small.

- **IF** you put off doing what God's clearly asked you to do, what do you think over time would change about who you are or how you see God?
- **WHAT IF** when God demands more of you it's because He sees more in you?

241: Just Browsing

***IF** a toy store let you play with all its toys for eight hours, which toy store would it be and what would you do?*

***WHAT IF** a clothing store of your choice gave you fifteen minutes to take as many outfits for yourself as you wanted?*

READ IT: ISAIAH 6:1–8; 7:13–14; 9:2–7

People who work in stores regularly ask customers questions like, "Are you looking for anything in particular?" A typical reply they hear is, "I'm just browsing" or "I'll know it when I see it." Customers may just want to walk around unbothered or perhaps don't know how to share what they're actually looking for. Meanwhile, the store *is* full of treasures to discover if they tap into the help being offered. Maybe the customer can even find something that inspires others to come in the store.

Have you ever felt this way trying to discover your identity? Life seems to ask, "Are you looking for anything in particular?" Whether we reply, "I'm just browsing" or "I'll know it when I see it," God offers so much treasure to discover if you take the time to tap into His help. Maybe you can even find something that inspires others to come to God.

Isaiah the prophet personally experienced this when God helped him see the supernatural realm that's always around us. It's no accident that Isaiah then began sharing truth that had both a present-day and a future sense to it—what he told others in his generation had something for them to learn then, yet those same words also revealed how Jesus Christ would one day come to earth.

Every day, you're given an opportunity by God to discover a treasure He's placed before you. Some embrace this while others casually walk around, "browsing" their lives away and refusing any help so they can "see it" on their own. The more you open up to personally experiencing God, the more you become someone who can share what you've found with others. Just as Isaiah's life revealed incredible things about Jesus, so can yours.

THERE IS HOPE

When you discover something God has to say about your life today, you discover something God has to say about your future.

Brainstorm some of the ways God tries to help us not have to walk around life without His help.

- ***IF*** you could tell others your age one thing about this, what would it be?
- ***WHAT IF*** you had a moment like Isaiah did before God?

242: A Bunch of Nobodies

***IF** you always knew who would be at your door or calling you right before it happened, how would you use that?*

***WHAT IF** you could make people answer their door or phone whenever you wanted?*

READ IT: AMOS 1:1–2; MICAH 1:1–2; HOSEA 1:1–3

Modern technology has a way of making us feel like "somebody." When you call someone, your name is announced on their phone. A picture of you on social media allows strangers to "like" it. Video-game systems note your presence by always scanning and listening for you. It's a virtual challenge to be a "nobody" these days.

Then again, we still might feel like a "nobody." Technology leaves us more "seen" than "known." Any "like" from the past doesn't guarantee another in the future. Every moment we feel noticed quickly goes away, leaving us regularly checking to see if someone has yet again acknowledged us.

Consider the people in the Bible who are called "minor prophets." That word *minor* makes them sound less important than the others, but it's only about a difference in the amount of information we have on them. At first glance they may seem like a bunch of nobodies: Amos was a shepherd and fruit picker; Micah came from the country; Hosea was a husband to an unfaithful wife; all we know of Joel is that he was the son of someone named Pethuel; and all we know about Obadiah is that his name was Obadiah. The limited information goes on for Nahum, Jonah, Habakkuk, Zephaniah, Haggai, Zechariah, Joel, and Malachi. Yet although we "just" have bits of their stories, their impact in sharing God's story wasn't "just" anything.

Remember this when you question your own identity or impact. God does incredible things through anyone open to Him, including you. Through prayer, study, and church, you can regularly check your soul and life to see how Someone significant has yet again reached out to you. Let Him work through you too.

THERE IS HOPE

A perceived nobody can help everybody personally know the one Somebody who can transform anybody.

Share about a time when you felt one of your family members did something significant.

- ***IF*** you were on a talk show, what would you want the interviewer to ask you to talk about?
- ***WHAT IF*** you could interview two people and ask them about anything?

243: An Overdue Book

***IF** you found some random instructions for a device that could make you smarter but not the device itself, would you spend any time looking for the device?*

***WHAT IF** you found the device but it didn't have any instructions?*

READ IT: 2 CHRONICLES 34:1–21, 27–33

So what do you think is the longest amount of time that's passed before someone returned an overdue library book they borrowed? Twenty years? Forty years?

Guess higher. For example, *The Adventures of Pinocchio* was returned to an England library after being overdue sixty-three years. Other books have been returned after having been gone for way longer than that, but this one came in during an eight-day period when all fees were waived. Had it not, the fine could have been around $5,000.*

Every book has worth, especially if that book contains the words of God. King Josiah realized this after the "Book of the Law" was discovered. He was already taking steps to tear down the places where people practiced false religions, but he could only go so far—it's one thing to transform things and another thing to transform people. The discovery of the Scriptures (likely the book of Deuteronomy) let people clearly respond to God's words versus stories they'd heard about Him.

The Bible can be like an overdue book in our lives. We perhaps aren't timely with it, keeping it in a pile we'll eventually get to. We overlook how special it is and how it's meant to be shared with others. Then one day, we open it up and are astonished by what we discover. Maybe you wouldn't rip your clothing, like Josiah did when God's words penetrated him, but it's right to feel spiritually ripped up in realizing that you or your family have drifted away from truth. It's understanding what our identity has become in comparison to what it's meant to be. So, don't just read the Bible . . . let the Bible read you.

* Ben Endley, "Library Book Copy of Pinocchio Overdue by 63 YEARS Is Returned During Amnesty Sparing Borrower Fine of £4,000," *DailyMail.com*, updated February 19, 2014.

THERE IS HOPE

There's no need to rely on random stories about God when we have access to the one and only book of truth about God.

Share about something valuable you once lost and compare that to what it might be like if the Bible disappeared.

- **IF** you found a toy, movie, or game that used to bring you the most unique joy, what would you do with it?
- **WHAT IF** you could not remember it when you saw it?

244: Doubt, Feelings, and Faith

***IF** you suspected that your friend had been replaced by someone who looked exactly like him or her, what would you do?*

***WHAT IF** you were right and your friend was returned to you . . . only now your friend didn't remember you?*

READ IT: JEREMIAH 1:4–10; 17:5–10

Should you eat a piece of fuzzy fruit? Or use a bathroom stall that only has minimal toilet paper in it? Should you walk your dog down a dark street?

What was the last thing you doubted? Don't feel you have to go super deep on this, because we question things all the time. Doubt involves being honest about how we don't know everything. It only becomes a bad thing when it takes over your life instead of helping you grow into a stronger, sounder sense of truth and faith.

And then there are your feelings—which, if left unchecked, can also be a bad thing. As God points out through Jeremiah, our "heart is more deceitful than anything else, and incurable—who can understand it?" Being led by our emotions is the opposite of doubt in that we act sure based on how we feel.

So consider the calling of Jeremiah as an example of how doubt and feelings can submit to God through faith. Here's an ordinary guy (likely a teenager) who heard from the Lord that he was to become a prophet. Jeremiah's two-sentence reply confessed his mental and emotional confusion, but then he let God have the next word. That's the key for us too—when you doubt or feel overwhelmed by your feelings, share it with the Lord and then let Him share something back.

God has a one-of-a-kind purpose for your life that your doubts and fears will try to reject. Rather than settling into being overly cautious or reckless, embrace the holy ache of letting Him show you your true identity. The message He'll share with the world will grow stronger as you let Him first share that message with you.

THERE IS HOPE

When you doubt your identity, trust in God's identity.

Talk about the differences (as you understand them) between a thought, a feeling, and the voice of God.

- **IF** something you strongly think or feel doesn't line up with what the Bible says, what is the wise thing to do with that?
- **WHAT IF** we each took a moment to share something we're sure of?

245: Weekly Recap

IF *you could become any kind of aquatic creature, what would you pick?*

WHAT IF *becoming that aquatic creature meant you'd be all alone and could never communicate with any other aquatic creatures or humans?*

"The Israelites and their ancestors have transgressed against me to this day. The descendants are obstinate and hardhearted. I am sending you to them, and you must say to them, 'This is what the Lord God says.' Whether they listen or refuse to listen—for they are a rebellious house—they will know that a prophet has been among them." (Ezekiel 2:3–5)

CATCH UP

- Who or what made you laugh recently?
- In what ways did life feel easy or hard this past week?

RECAP

- What stood out to you from what we've read together, talked about, or attempted to do together over the past week?
- What thoughts or questions do you have from today's Bible passage?

GROW TOGETHER

- What might be the main thing God is trying to tell our family today?
- What if we did something new together or returned to a good habit to live out what we're learning? What might that be?

OPEN UP

- In what ways are you struggling in life or experiencing something hard?
- If we were to confess something to God as a family, what might that be?

PRAY

- Who is Jesus to you today?
- Who would be willing to close our time with a simple prayer?

246: Soul Food

***IF** you momentarily grew a foot taller when you stood up for yourself, how often would you do it?*

***WHAT IF** when you gave in to fear or chose not to speak up, you shrank a foot for a few moments?*

READ IT: DANIEL 1:1–21

Doctors regularly instruct patients not to eat or drink anything right before a major surgery. It's called "fasting." You fast because you don't want anything to distract the body from what needs to happen medically. This same principle is behind spiritual fasting, where we give up something we regularly do (like a meal or a favorite activity) to spend that time with God.

If the Israelites would've done more of this, they might not have ended up in captivity. God had to get their attention by allowing the foreign nation of Babylon to capture the people. To make things even more uncomfortable, the Babylonians customarily recruited any potential young leaders by offering them tasty food and influential positions. Imagine how this probably sounded to the ones who were selected and offered a way out of living on the streets.

Keep that in mind to appreciate how challenging Daniel's "fasting" might have been. He determined not to "defile" himself with the pleasures he was offered but only to eat food that honored God. His bold example and rooted identity inspired his friends to join in. The Lord blessed them all, as they ended up in bigger positions of authority without having to lower their standards or hide their faith.

Life will regularly offer us quick temptations that slowly harm us. Just consider how people regularly sacrifice their health to gain money, but then have to sacrifice money to regain their health. Jesus hit on this further in Mark 8:36 by warning us to not end up feeling that we've gained the whole world while giving up our souls to do it. The question we need to ask isn't how close to sin we can get without crossing a line, but why we'd even want to run toward that line to begin with.

THERE IS HOPE

Don't worry about being spectacular. Be fully faithful, and spectacular will happen along the way in its own, best way.

Think of someone you know who seems to honor God in unique ways.

- ***IF*** you could sum up how this person inspires others, what would you say?
- ***WHAT IF*** something you gave up would inspire another person to grab hold of a relationship with God?

247: Chocolate Faith

***IF** you had to spend ten seconds with either a lion or an alligator, which would you pick?*

***WHAT IF** you had to spend ten minutes with a lion or an alligator?*

READ IT: DANIEL 3:8–15; 6:1–28

You've had homemade chocolate milk, right? The kind where you drop chocolate syrup or powder into white milk? You have to stir things up to experience the flavor.

What if that white milk represents your life and the chocolate dropping into it represents you inviting Jesus to be your Savior? You could correctly claim that He's "in your life" despite how everything looks like it did before. What's obviously missing is that you haven't intentionally stirred your life into His. It's as if your relationship with God has sunk out of sight.

Daniel and his friends regularly had their faith stirred. At times it happened to them, like when they were threatened for not worshiping a statue. Other times it happened through them, like when they chose to pray every day no matter what. The pressures they felt were a larger version of what we feel when we consider hiding our faith at school, at work, or among others. Maybe being thrown into a furnace or a lion's den isn't something you regularly face, but some type of judgment or rejection is.

What might Daniel say if he were to share some wisdom with you? Here's a guy who let the Lord use chaos to stir up the flavor of his faith—a guy who didn't stand up to make noise but lived his faith out loud. He walked in his true identity by honoring God in full view of people who criticized him for it.

The heat and roar you face may look less like a furnace or lion and more like insults and betrayal. As it does, you can let your spiritual journey sink, or swirl yourself into God through habits that blend things into a richer faith. Remember: people will never know about the flavor of Jesus if we look and "taste" like the world. Is it time to stir things up?

THERE IS HOPE

God takes us places we wouldn't go if it were up to us. But being challenged is how we become champions.

Share about a time you felt God was with you despite you feeling overwhelmed.

- ***IF*** you discovered that going into battle with a particular army meant you would never be hurt, would you join that army?
- ***WHAT IF*** part of being a Christian means we experience more hurt in life than we want but still end up winning in other ways?

248: Report Cards

***IF** your grades were printed in candy wrappers for people to read, what would you do?*

***WHAT IF** only your best grades were printed in the wrappers?*

READ IT: EZRA 1:1–4; 3:10–13; 7:8–10

Report card time! Whether you've ever dreaded or looked forward to one, you know the letters used to grade you don't tell the whole story. You may have gotten an A in a class that you never had to study for or received a C in a course where you studied all the time. A strong grade doesn't in itself show that you worked hard any more than a weak grade declares you didn't grow. There's always more going on behind the grade than the grade itself.

God's people struggled with this when foreign leaders released them from exile. As everyone went back home to begin rebuilding their culture, it appeared as though things would finally head in a good direction as they built a new temple to worship God together. Only, this "A" to the younger generation felt like a "D" to the older leaders, who remembered what the original temple was like. It's why Ezra sought to fix everyone on God versus the way things "were" or "are"—there's always more going on behind the grade than the grade itself.

Life is filled with people who will disagree with you. Even Christian friends can debate whether a certain worship style or way of doing things is more meaningful than another. Sometimes someone's perspective will be wrong and need to be confronted because it doesn't line up with the Bible, and other times the disagreement will merely be a matter of opinion. Either instance is an opportunity to find out why someone may have graded something an A that you see as a B, C, D or F. Like Ezra, guide others to look for God and His standards to discover your identity together in Him versus in your argument.

THERE IS HOPE

Disagreements over things that matter don't need to divide us but can become a way to figure out what matters most.

List some things Christians disagree about that are more preferences than truth.

- ***IF*** you never got to hear or sing your favorite songs in church anymore, how would you respond?
- ***WHAT IF*** the way someone taught you the Bible was either too relaxed or too structured for how you like it?

249: Right Here, Right Now

***IF** something became big when you pointed at it and said "Poink!", what would you enlarge?*

***WHAT IF** you could only say, "Poink!" three times a day?*

READ IT: ESTHER 2:1–20; 3:5–6; 4:13–14; 5:1–2

Obeying the people above you is a choice that over time can become a natural response. When someone in authority tells you to do something, the first response should be, "I will" or "Yes." Any questions you have can wait until after that so you first demonstrate respect right here, right now. That doesn't mean it isn't hard to do this, whether we need to obey our coach, boss, teacher, or family. We may know how good their intentions are, but personal issues or insecurities can get in the way. Maybe we demand to know why, or perhaps someone in authority let us down.

Examine the relationship between Esther and her older cousin, Mordecai, on this. As the king of Persia searched for a new queen, Esther became the top candidate by following Mordecai's advice. She may have thought this was only to save her life, yet through it she did something greater when the lives of the Jewish people were at risk. Mordecai challenged her as the new queen to say something to the king—something that put her at the risk of death if he became offended. Esther did speak up to honor God and her people for such a time as this, eventually saving them.

Our lives have purpose, as do the lives of the people above us. Good authority figures don't just want us to obey them but also to trust them. This all begins with how we view God Himself.

Wherever you are in life, you've been chosen to make a difference "right here, right now." Whatever God is asking of you, start saying, "I will" or "Yes" right away. Let the questions come after that, but begin with immediate obedience—for such a time as this.

THERE IS HOPE

Extraordinary movements of God begin with ordinary acts of our obedience.

Discuss how it can be difficult to know when to speak up, remain quiet, or follow the advice of others.

- ***IF*** whenever you did what someone told you to do, you got in trouble with someone else, how would that affect how you listen to people?
- ***WHAT IF*** the punishment didn't happen for a year, but it was big?

250: Measure Twice, Cut One

***IF** you could restore any building in history back to its original condition, which one would you pick?*

***WHAT IF** you then had to stay at the restored building for a year?*

READ IT: NEHEMIAH 1:1–11; 2:1–6, 11–18

What was the last thing you measured? We're constantly trying to sum things up, like how tall, wide, heavy, cold, or warm an object is. Or we engage in "fuzzier" measuring, like explaining how "fun" or how "boring" someone is. Every measurement tracks back to what you're comparing against.

Nehemiah had a comfortable life as a drink taster for the king of Persia. When most of the other Jews left to rebuild their culture, he stayed behind for reasons we don't know—perhaps to honor his job. As Nehemiah heard about the horrible condition of the city walls, though, he became broken and sought God's favor in being a part of making things better. The king released him for a season to go begin this work, with plenty of resources to do so.

When Nehemiah arrived, he did something unexpected. Before telling anyone about how he was going to lead the charge in fixing things, he first took the time to study the condition of the walls himself. Knowing the details helped him to better guide the people to work in the most productive way possible.

People who work with wood say it's better to "measure twice, cut once" than "measure once" and have to "cut twice." In other words, you're better double-checking for accuracy before wasting time and material. This applies to any areas of your life where you'd rather not do a real detailed look at the way things are, such as a situation that makes you feel frustrated, or a part of your character you're embarrassed by. Like Nehemiah, study the condition of things for what they are so you can ensure that a real, lasting repair is able to happen.

THERE IS HOPE

Being broken creates the pathway to fixing things. We can give without loving, but we cannot love without giving.

Open up about something you would really like to see made right in the world.

- ***IF*** you had a magic hammer that could fix anything or anyone you waved it over, who or what would you fix?
- ***WHAT IF*** you still had to work hard to fix that thing, but in the end it was guaranteed to be completely fixed?

251: Good Enough?

IF *parents never asked their kids to clean, what do you think would be different around the average house?*

WHAT IF *there were never any accountability to clean up anything?*

READ IT: MALACHI 1:6–10; 2:13–16; 3:7–12

There you are, in front of your favorite food or dessert that someone made with love just for you. Yet for some odd reason, before you bite into it, you decide to dump dirt on it. Ridiculous, right? Even weirder would be if you actually believed this combination tasted good.

In the time of Malachi, God shared that He was tired of our dirty piles we kept dumping on Him. People back then struggled with the same temptations we do in only giving what feels convenient and calling that a sacrifice of worship. The Lord wanted to be clear that He saw through this and didn't like us thinking so little of His identity or our own.

It's like asking if something is "good enough"—if you have to ask, it probably isn't good enough. We'll act moral and hope our actions make God think, *I guess that person is good enough.* Or we'll become leaders in church and think He'll say, "Good enough." What God instead wants is a real relationship with us. Any connection needs to begin with honesty about our need for Him rather than the lame game of "good enough." True worship is giving all of who you are for all of who God is, recognizing that He gave all of who He is for all of who you are.

Malachi ends by speaking about the day the Messiah will come and set things right. Take that into account, because the pathway toward things getting better always begins with Jesus. We can't come to the Lord and tell Him how good of a person we are based on what we've done, but we *can* come before Him to be received based on what Christ has done. Let whatever you honor Him with honor His sacrifice versus offering Him only what's convenient and comfortable for you.

THERE IS HOPE

Our sacrifices to God don't get Him to love us, but they do reveal what we think of Him.

Share about the power of accountability by naming an area of life that you'd like others to challenge you in.

- **IF** you could say anything to anybody and he or she would have to pay attention, who would you pick and what would you say?
- **WHAT IF** what you said really did change that person's life?

252: Weekly Recap

***IF** every broken thing became truly beautiful with your care, how would that change the way you treated things?*

***WHAT IF** the worse something was treated, the worse it would become, eventually eliminating the beautiful thing?*

I cried out to him with my mouth, and praise was on my tongue. If I had been aware of malice in my heart, the Lord would not have listened. However, God has listened; he has paid attention to the sound of my prayer. Blessed be God! He has not turned away my prayer or turned his faithful love from me. (Psalm 66:17–20)

CATCH UP

- Who or what made you laugh recently?
- In what ways did life feel easy or hard this past week?

RECAP

- What stood out to you from what we've read together, talked about, or attempted to do together over the past week?
- What thoughts or questions do you have from today's Bible passage?

GROW TOGETHER

- What might be the main thing God is trying to tell our family today?
- What if we did something new together or returned to a good habit to live out what we're learning? What might that be?

OPEN UP

- In what ways are you struggling in life or experiencing something hard?
- If we were to confess something to God as a family, what might that be?

PRAY

- Who is Jesus to you today?
- Who would be willing to close our time with a simple prayer?

THERE IS HOPE

SHHH

We're kind of spoiled.

We live on the other side of Jesus Christ having come to earth in the first century. It's easy for us to open the Bible and read how He was born, grew up, and lived among us. We also can recognize why He willingly died and was resurrected so that we might have the forgiveness of sins, real transformation, new purpose, and eternal hope.

We also can see as we read through the Scriptures that there is both an Old Testament and a New Testament. Most Bibles separate the two with a blank page, perhaps to give us something to visually separate the two. Again, we're kind of spoiled having access to all of this . . . we know there are two huge parts to the Story.

But pay attention to all that's "written" on that blank page. It's not there in any type of invisible ink, but we know about it by studying history. That blank page represents four hundred years of waiting for God to say or do something new, like a great big "Shhh" that affected everyone—especially His people. This is why by the time we open up the book of Matthew in the New Testament, it feels as though we're in an entirely different world . . . because that's exactly what it was like.

So, what happened between the last thing the Lord said through the prophet Malachi and the introduction we get in the New Testament to Rome being in power? How did God's people handle not having anything new said to them all throughout that time? Can you imagine living through that time?

For that matter, how do you handle the times in your life when God seems silent?

For years, the Lord didn't reveal Himself in any way that was recorded but instead let His previous words be more than enough while creating the right timing for His arrival.

253: To Be Continued

***IF** you could watch a sneak peek of an upcoming TV episode or movie, which would you pick?*

***WHAT IF** everyone except for you could see the next episode long before you did?*

READ IT: MALACHI 1:6–10; 2:13–16; 3:7–12

"To be continued." These three words at the end of a TV show or movie can drive you crazy. You may have to wait hours, days, weeks, months, or years in confusion over the cliffhanger you just witnessed.

One upside to a "to be continued" moment is you're more apt to consider the story. It causes you to review the parts you have access to, study information devoted to the plot, sit down with strangers to speculate about it, or develop personal theories about what will happen next.

After the book of Malachi, God's people experienced a big cliffhanger. The kingdom was split in two, multiple leaders selfishly rejected God, and the Israelites' general identity was in question. Meanwhile, a group of faithful God-followers hung on to a promise that the Messiah would come. He'd be preceded by someone like Elijah, who would prepare the way for Him to arrive. That promise in itself and all the Scriptures God gave His people to study were more than enough to hold them over.

This is recognized in Galatians 4:4–5, where we read that "when the time came to completion," Jesus came to earth to save us. The Lord knows when it's time for the "to be continued" to *be* continued. As we'll discover, He used the four hundred years after the Old Testament to set the stage for what needed to happen in the New Testament—all to impact the most people (including us).

The next time you encounter a cliffhanger in life, remember that the story isn't over. Study what you do have access to. Wrestle over it with others. Perhaps the waiting is driving you crazy, but you are not alone, and God has not stopped working.

THERE IS HOPE

People can comfort one another without words. Why is it hard to understand that God is reaching out, even now?

Talk about a cliffhanger you've experienced in life when you had to wait for something to resolve.

- ***IF*** you could have changed one thing about that, what would it have been?
- ***WHAT IF*** that situation was meant to prepare you for something ahead of you?

254: A Sideline Insight

***IF** you were in a major football game but your coach never let you play, how would you feel?*

***WHAT IF** you were the only person who played in that game against the other team?*

READ IT: DANIEL 2:1–49

On any sports team there's a general reason why certain players are on the field versus the bench. Usually it comes down to whoever can offer what's most needed in that moment versus later in the game. Some players use their time on the sidelines to rest or amuse themselves, while others stand close to the field to stay engaged until called in. It helps to have an assistant coach who keeps you prepared and aware of what's coming up.

The prophet Daniel offered such coaching two centuries before the "Shhh" era, when the Jews were sidelined in captivity. Through a dream the king of Babylon had about a large statue, God told Daniel how the four different sections of the statue represented kingdoms that would destroy each other until God established His kingdom through Jesus. History proved this to be true in what followed through the Babylonian, Persian, Greek, and Roman empires. This incredibly specific "sideline" perspective can be helpful in understanding the four hundred years of silence.

What if our sidelines can be just as useful? Perhaps you *won't* get invited to a party, *may* have to deal with a breakup, *will* get skipped over for a promotion, or feel that life *hasn't* changed for the better for years. Yet feeling "benched" by life doesn't mean you're out of the game.

God sees the field *and* the roster, knowing who or what is needed for every play while also knowing when someone needs to sit out (even if he or she doesn't want to). Suit up, pay attention to your Coach, and take good notes on the game. Whether you're on the field today or can give some wisdom to your fellow players who are about to be out there, your sideline insights really do matter.

THERE IS HOPE

What God does on the field while you're on the sidelines is just as important as what eventually happens through you on the field. Be ready.

Share about a time you didn't get picked to do something you wanted to do.

- **IF** you were always picked all the time, how would that affect other people?
- **WHAT IF** your time on the "sidelines" is meant to give you perspective?

255: It's All Greek to Me

***IF** your favorite book or movie was in a foreign language, do you think you'd know about it?*

***WHAT IF** all books and movies were in a foreign language?*

READ IT: DANIEL 11:1–4

Have you ever enjoyed a song sung in a foreign language? How about a movie or TV show? If you can translate even a little, you'll feel a sense of power, for language unlocks and assigns meaning. People who can speak more than one language arguably have a larger perception of the world.

If the world had a common language that people used to talk or write to one another, it seems like that would be the perfect situation for Jesus to come to earth so His message could be shared all over. Strangely enough, that's what life in the first century was like. The common language of the day was Greek, and the New Testament Gospels were passed around in that language.

It all came to be when Alexander the Great conquered the known world for Greece. He was a leader Daniel prophesied about (two hundred years earlier) who for thirteen years imposed Greek values and language upon every culture. Alexander literally shaped the thinking, literature, athletics, and atmosphere of things. When he died, his empire was divided among his four generals. Eventually the Roman Empire took over and capitalized on the Greek language.

God's people didn't know that this would all end up useful. At the time it was devastating to have their heritage and culture taken over by someone else. The Lord seemed silent to them, for they didn't know He was using these circumstances to prepare and position things for greater purposes in their lives.

God is using your circumstances to prepare and position things in your life too. You may look around confused by it all and think, *It's all Greek to me!* Just keep in mind that when the language of life changes, God is creating a new way for you to understand Him.

THERE IS HOPE

God doesn't generically oversee the universe. He works in every moment in every person's life according to what He knows is needed.

Chat about the power of words in the world, to your family or to you personally.

- ***IF*** you knew a special word that could stop a conversation, would you use it?
- ***WHAT IF*** after it stopped you were the only one who could restart it?

256: Falling for Lies

***IF** you bought something expensive and found out it was fake, what would you do?*

***WHAT IF** you found out this fake item was made by someone you knew?*

READ IT: DANIEL 11:21–35

The name Antiochus Epiphanes doesn't get brought up much these days. He was an Arab leader who in 167 BC tried to eliminate the Jewish faith by killing 80,000 Jews and enslaving many others. As Daniel had prophesied hundreds of years earlier, this man used an army to stop the Jews from worshiping in the temple so they'd instead use a pagan altar. He imposed the death penalty on any Jew who circumcised a baby boy, celebrated Sabbath, had a copy of the Scriptures, or wouldn't sacrifice a pig. The actions of this one man are a glimpse of the Antichrist, who will one day demand that all people worship him (Revelation 13).

Antiochus Epiphanes didn't last forever, though. During his reign people lived in terror of him, but then one day it ended, and another false leader rose up. Eventually a Roman named Caesar tried to be the next big name—and now we only use that name when describing a crouton-heavy salad, ordering cheap pizza, or naming dogs.

We have a habit of letting the wrong people come to power but don't seem to learn from our mistakes. The political "knight in shining armor" you're waiting to rescue you may actually be a court jester ready to use you for a laugh. An attractive person eager to make you feel good by agreeing with your perspective can quickly become an ugly stumbling block in your life. Your new BFF may set off some TNT if he or she suddenly becomes the MVP instead of you.

When life feels dark, it's hard to tell the difference between what's gray versus what's colorful. But when we fix our eyes on Jesus, His light reveals the way things truly are. Keep hearing what you need to hear and seeing what you need to see by following the only true leader: Christ.

THERE IS HOPE

God is never silent. When the loudmouths get louder, He gets clearer.

Brainstorm a mini checklist of what makes a leader worth following versus avoiding.

- **IF** you had a friend who always settled for following the wrong kind of leaders, what would you do?
- **WHAT IF** that happened to everyone unless you physically stood nearby them?

257: Making Stuff Up

***IF** you met someone who never suspected that other people might be lying, how would you interact with that person?*

***WHAT IF** you met someone who always suspected that everything was a lie?*

READ IT: ISAIAH 29:13–14; MARK 12:13; 12:18

Despite all the social media, we don't know everything about our favorite celebrities. Sometimes famous people keep parts of their lives hidden or suddenly quit whatever made them famous. It prompts many people to make stuff up about what happened.

Parts of God's life feel hidden to us too. At times He seems to stop doing what He's famous for doing. It prompts many people to make stuff up about what happened, if not more.

During the four hundred years of silence, two major groups of Jewish authorities emerged to make sense out of what was happening. The Pharisees wanted to ensure that the people could find favor with God by doing all the things that Moses taught. Another group, the Sadducees, rejected anything supernatural to instead become extreme thinkers. Both groups missed something big in all the little ideas they created. It just confused the Jewish people as a whole.

Before you criticize, try to relate. The reason people start making stuff up about God is because knowing Him truly is the most important thing in life. Feeling confused about what He's up to can easily make any of us unsettled about who He is or where we stand with Him. It may help to recognize that the Bible spans thousands of years and sometimes skips over certain eras of time without telling us every detail.

Not seeing God's hand at work doesn't mean He isn't at work. Nor does it mean you need to construct something, call it "God," and wave it around for Him. Our relationship with the Lord, like any relationship, needs faith and trust. You don't need to start making stuff up about Him or you when He's super clear about how much He loves you.

THERE IS HOPE

Just because God doesn't tell you everything doesn't mean He hasn't told you enough.

Open up about some of the things you're tempted to believe when God doesn't act the way you expect Him to.

- ***IF*** you could ask God to perform a miracle He hasn't done, what would it be?
- ***WHAT IF*** God doing that miracle meant He wouldn't do another miracle He was planning?

258: Waiting Room

***IF** your house had a waiting room, how would you use it?*

***WHAT IF** every home and building in the world had a waiting room?*

READ IT: LUKE 2:1; 1 CORINTHIANS 13:9–13

How do you feel about waiting rooms? What about the ones that are stocked with free food and a remote control to a big-screen TV? Others have people who warmly greet you as you walk in. Hospitality like this makes the waiting pass by more comfortably.

It also stands out because our culture has trained us to expect that we can have whatever we want right now. Whether we're waiting for a pizza or something huge in life, being patient without having something to nibble on in the meantime feels harder than ever. It's as if we each have a little clock counting down inside of us, determining how long we'll last.

God is always actively helping us feel at home in Him. As Rome sought to rule the known world, the Lord utilized the flaws of people craving power to prepare everyone for the arrival of our Savior Jesus. Israel itself had become a land bridge between the continents that Rome controlled, causing world travelers to regularly pass through the area where Christ would be born.

Examples like this help us understand the Bible's great promise that faith, hope, and love aren't going anywhere despite our hard experiences. There are so many examples in the Scriptures and around us of people who felt their dreams had died but they found a reason to press on. Maybe that's why it's so sad when people give up and we think, *Why would you quit with so much possibility before you?*

Honestly, waiting on God is kind of weird because although you hope to see Him do something "next," He's already with you now. You are never alone, so enjoy His warm hospitality. The best way to pass the time as you wait for a new blessing is noting all the ways the Lord has *already* blessed you.

THERE IS HOPE

Patience lets you discover treasure hidden in the ground you're already standing on.

Think of some things that are better when patience is involved.

- ***IF*** everyone except for your family didn't prepare or cook food but just ate it all raw, how would you deal with that?
- ***WHAT IF*** nobody ever complimented you for the food you gave them unless it was raw and unprepared?

259: Weekly Recap

***IF** every person you touched would go limp and be unconscious for an hour, how would you live differently?*

***WHAT IF** whenever you touched something mechanical, it would shut down?*

I waited patiently for the Lord, and he turned to me and heard my cry for help. He brought me up from a desolate pit, out of the muddy clay, and set my feet on a rock, making my steps secure. He put a new song in my mouth, a hymn of praise to our God. (Psalm 40:1–3)

CATCH UP

- Who or what made you laugh recently?
- In what ways did life feel easy or hard this past week?

RECAP

- What stood out to you from what we've read together, talked about, or attempted to do together over the past week?
- What thoughts or questions do you have from today's Bible passage?

GROW TOGETHER

- What might be the main thing God is trying to tell our family today?
- What if we did something new together or returned to a good habit to live out what we're learning? What might that be?

OPEN UP

- In what ways are you struggling in life or experiencing something hard?
- If we were to confess something to God as a family, what might that be?

PRAY

- Who is Jesus to you today?
- Who would be willing to close our time with a simple prayer?

THERE IS HOPE

HERO

Finally, after centuries of waiting . . . the hero emerged.

Or . . . what if He was always with us the whole time?

You might think that Jesus Christ has four books in the Bible written about Him. He does, but He's also a part of every other book of the Bible too. Being a part of the Trinity means He was involved in everything the Father and Spirit said or did. It just so happens that Jesus' unique role involves the time He lived among humanity for thirty-three years in the first century. The four Gospels—Matthew, Mark, Luke, and John—tell the true details of this life from different angles while always reflecting back on how Christ was spoken about all throughout history before this point.

That means the voice and presence of Jesus are just as much in all of the commands of the Old Testament as they are in all of the grace spoken about in the New Testament. When people say, "Jesus never said anything about ________," they may be overlooking how often the older Scriptures do show God clearly speaking on that topic. A key reason to remember this is because Jesus isn't the "upgrade" or "cooler version" of God but has always been and always will be Lord. Despite all the different churches and denominations in the world that try to say something unique about Him or the Christian faith, the truth is that there is only one form of Christianity, and Jesus lived it.

He now invites us to step into it with Him, knowing that we can't do it without Him. Jesus didn't intend to merely be a really good teacher on how to live a moral life, although the things He does tell us explain the way the world really is meant to work. Christ came to become our one and only hero. He led the perfect life we couldn't ever live to pluck us out of the sinful life we shouldn't ever live.

Jesus Christ came to earth to live among us, inspire us with truth, reveal His kingdom, save us from sin, and unleash us into a fully alive life.

260: The Words Before the Words

***IF** you could only speak one sentence out loud each day, how do you think you'd use that sentence?*

***WHAT IF** you couldn't communicate in any other way other than one daily sentence?*

READ IT: LUKE 1:1–21

It happens just about every day, doesn't it? You have a misunderstanding with someone, feel confused, or generally feel as if life is asking more out of you than you can give. Usually a larger perspective is required or else you'll only approach things based on what you know. To see everything you need to see, a little background goes a long way.

The Holy Spirit made this clear through a guy named Luke whom God inspired to write about Jesus. As a first-century doctor, Luke was committed to research. His book almost feels like an investigative news report in how he detailed everything that happened before and after Jesus came. Luke's initial words basically said, "To see everything you need to see, a little background goes a long way."

This plays out in the trials you face. Trying to do everything today the way you did it yesterday will eventually stop working. By getting new perspective—the words before the words—you can be more thoughtful in how you work through things.

Luke did something unique to teach us about this. In the original Greek language in which he wrote, the first four verses are one long sentence written with fancy words smart scholars would use. For the rest of the book, though, Luke spoke God's truth in the common language of the people. Since God inspired all of this, the Lord basically told us that what was shared about our Hero, Jesus, had all the credibility a smart doctor would look for but is available to everyone.

If God goes to such great lengths so everyone can understand who He is, are you willing to learn a truth today about what you're sorting out personally? To see everything you need to see, a little background goes a long way.

THERE IS HOPE

Just as a generation twenty centuries ago saw what Jesus did in His life, today's generation sees what He's doing in our lives.

When have you been able to better understand something after someone explained it to you?

- **IF** you were to write a book to explain something to others, what would it be about?
- **WHAT IF** no one ever read your book except your family and friends, but it changed *their* lives forever?

261: The Miracle Before the Miracle

***IF** one of your family members turned into a goose for a month, what would you do?*

***WHAT IF** you turned into a goose for a month?*

READ IT: LUKE 1:5–25

You push a button, and life is easier. That's the way we believe everything should work, right? You push a button to open your garage so everyone can enter your house. Or you're sitting on a couch and push a button to access your favorite TV show.

And yet it doesn't always play out that way. Your garage door can start to open and then suddenly shut down. The batteries in your TV remote may be drained, and you feel frustrated because now you have to get up after you just got comfortable.

We do this with God sometimes, believing that if we push His buttons, He's supposed to make life easier. We reason, "If someone does good things, then good things should happen to them." Yet that isn't always accurate either. Although the Lord always enjoys us trusting and following Him, we can't manipulate Him with our actions.

Still, blessings happen. Zechariah seemed to do the right things, yet he and his wife, Elizabeth, couldn't have children. They may have felt shut down, drained, and frustrated after years of trying. That is, until an angel of God said they finally would have a child, a child who would be the miracle before *the* Miracle of Jesus. Zechariah questioned this great gift, so the angel said if he wasn't going to cheer this blessing on out loud, then he'd watch it happen without being able to speak. And yes, Elizabeth did finally become pregnant just as God promised.

We may wonder whether God will reward our obedience with a miracle or "overlook" us. But God doesn't overlook anything. You may not have the life you want, but you are offered an eternity you don't deserve. God's unfailing love *is* the miracle before the miracle.

THERE IS HOPE

God may not do everything we ask Him to do, but He also doesn't give up on everything we give up on.

What is something you've been praying for a long time that you're tempted to give up on?

- ***IF*** an angel appeared and told you it would happen, what would you say?
- ***WHAT IF*** God didn't give you what you wanted, but something different?

262: The Visit Before the Visit

***IF** you one day found your room flooded with Jell-O what would you do?*

***WHAT IF** you could choose a food that your room would be flooded with?*

READ IT: LUKE 1:26–38

What's the deal with how protective we can get of our bedrooms? Family members can get mean shouting "GET OUT!" at each other for entering in without knocking (and sometimes even if someone does knock). Maybe it has to do with how life is filled with responsibilities that don't leave us alone, and we all want a little space to personally relax. Kids, teenagers, and adults alike can look forward to shutting the door, retreating, and feeling safe.

We walk around life with a kind of invisible boundary around us too. What we'll do, who we'll allow close to us, and how much we'll sacrifice all relate to what we feel we can do and still have some "me" space. That is, assuming we won't ever change.

Mary gives us something to think about, as she had some comfortable plans like marrying Joseph and forming a future with him. Like any Jewish girl in her era, she may have even wondered if she'd have a child who might be the Hero/Messiah prophesied to be born one day. Kind of ironic when you think about it.

But then an angel paid her a visit and she learned she would become pregnant supernaturally. Not only did God change what she thought about the size and boundaries of her life, but she also got a new "roommate" of Christ inside of her for nine months. Rather than shouting, "GET OUT!" at God, she opened up the door of her heart to Him.

Being a Christian isn't about God fitting into what we expect of Him or us merely knowing the truth and being done with it. We ultimately aim to follow the Lord with an open life. Like Mary, the key is not to shut Him out but to let Him into every space of our lives—including new spaces we've never even considered.

THERE IS HOPE

Jesus broke through heaven to invite us into His circle. Letting Him work in you and your circle invites others into heaven.

What might it mean to have God expand the circle of your life?

- ***IF*** you knew you couldn't fail at what God asked you to do, would you do it?
- ***WHAT IF*** doing what God asked you to do meant your life would significantly change (in tough ways and great ways) for the next two years?

263: The Testimony Before the Testimony

***IF** a stranger said you had incredible potential at a career you've never considered, would you choose that career?*

***WHAT IF** that person said you would be great at something you knew you absolutely didn't want to do as a career?*

READ IT: LUKE 1:39–56

Every day, all over the world, people visit courthouses. It could be for happy events, like adoptions or weddings. It may be for sad situations like trials. Whatever the circumstance, there is a process.

A typical courtroom has a judge who makes sure everything happens properly and that decisions are made wisely. Sometimes a jury, a group of everyday people, are present, and they speak. There's also a secretary who takes notes, and a bailiff, an officer who keeps order. Then there's the person who gives a "testimony"—telling the truth, the whole truth, and nothing but the truth. Sometimes that person has a lawyer who helps share that testimony in the clearest way.

The baby in Elizabeth had a special purpose in life as he grew up to years later share a testimony about Jesus that basically said, "This man is the Hero we've been waiting for. It's the truth, the whole truth, and nothing but the truth." The angel was like a lawyer making sure it was clear, while Mary, Elizabeth, and the rest of the family participated like an observant jury. God was the Judge who made sure this all happened properly and that decisions were made wisely, while those who wrote down the testimony for us to read were the secretaries.

To top it off, the baby inside of Elizabeth started moving around when he heard Mary's voice! Somehow, he knew that Jesus was inside of Mary and was the Hero of the world. He gave this "testimony" before the testimony!

God has a message like that to give to you and through you today. Maybe life isn't complete, but something is being formed right now. Let Jesus show you the hope that will one day be fully birthed. Anytime you hear Him, give a testimony about it!

THERE IS HOPE

Telling God's story is how you discover your story.

What is one of your favorite moments in a movie? How about a true story you've heard someone share?

- ***IF*** you were to create an inspirational quote based on that, what would it be?
- ***WHAT IF*** something great God did in your past is a glimpse of your future?

264: The Baby Before the Baby

***IF** you had to choose one flower to replace grass, what would you pick?*

***WHAT IF** you could replace the bark on a tree with carpet?*

READ IT: LUKE 1:57–80

A "weed" is typically defined as a wild plant that chokes the growth of other things. For some strange reason, dandelions have been regarded as weeds. It could be because they randomly pop up all over and frustrate how neat and tidy we want our yards to look.

It turns out that dandelions are actually one of the most powerful, nutritious foods on the planet. They're packed with vitamins and minerals proven to help with bone health, liver disorders, diabetes, urinary disorders, skin care, weight loss, jaundice, gall bladder disorders, anemia, high blood pressure, digestive disorders, and cancer!*

Zechariah and Elizabeth's son, John, would be this blessing for the world and Jesus. John said random things that got in the way of how neat and tidy the religious leaders of his day wanted things to look. We get a glimpse of it in how his very birth started out, along with noting that he grew up in the wilderness—not the most desirable area to live in, but one that allowed him to bloom into a life-giving prophet.

Think about all the times that you've regarded yourself or others as "weeds." Obviously, there are people you need to be careful around because of how they sprout up alongside of you only to steal life versus give it. They may say that you're worthless or tell you that you should just wither away. Lies. All lies.

On the other hand, people can also bring great life and health as random pop-ups we can't ignore. Knowing who is who requires letting God tell us the true worth of another person. May we never hold back what the Lord is trying to mean as a blessing . . . even if the people it comes through seem wild and they upset how tidy we want our lives to look.

* Thank you to our good friend Linnea Wolf for this insight on dandelions.

THERE IS HOPE

People see Jesus in us not when we look right, but when we live right.

Imagine someone paid you to make a thirty-second commercial to tell the world anything.

- ***IF*** you knew the whole world would see your ad, what would it be like?
- ***WHAT IF*** only world leaders would see your ad? Would you change it? Why?

265: The Evidence Before the Evidence

***IF** a detective offered to help you look for something, find someone, or figure something out, how would you use this offer?*

***WHAT IF** this person could time travel? What would you want to found out?*

READ IT: MATTHEW 1:18–25

What are the odds that one day you'll be president? Put some numbers to it, like how some people say, "There's a 1 in 700,000 chance you'll be struck by lightning" or "There's a 1 in 180,000,000,000,000 chance a meteor will hit your home." It's hard to figure out, isn't it?

What's even harder is figuring out the odds of Jesus fulfilling the more than sixty specific biblical prophecies in the Bible about the Messiah. To simplify this, consider how rare it would be if He were to just fulfill the eight most important prophecies—around 1 in 10,000,000,000,000,000,000,000,000,000 (or 10 octillion).*

But Jesus didn't just fulfill eight prophecies—He fulfilled all of them. That's like tossing a pebble into one of the massive Great Lakes, mixing it in, and asking someone who was blind to find it. We can't take for granted how special our Hero is.

Joseph really struggled with the odds of Mary's story being true. All he knew was that the woman he was engaged to was pregnant and he wasn't the father. He could've made a big scene out of this but chose instead to be gracious and quietly end their engagement. Only after the Lord spoke to Him and revealed the big picture did he step in and step up to become an incredible human father to Jesus.

When God says something is true, the odds are 1 out of 1. Think deeper, though— will we be the "1" who steps in and steps up into that "1" thing? Some people say "seeing is believing," but "believing is seeing"—the evidence before the evidence. Like Joseph, be gracious in the way you respond to it and whom you share it with when God says it's true.

* *Science Speaks: Scientific Proof of the Accuracy of Prophecy and the Bible* by Dr. Peter W. Stoner and Robert C. Newman (Moody Press, 1976).

THERE IS HOPE

Wisdom is the ability to see reality for what it is or what it could be despite your personal experience. (Read that again.)

What is something you didn't believe when you heard, but later you realized it was proven true?

- ***IF*** we knew everything and didn't need to trust each other, how would relationships in general be different between people?
- ***WHAT IF*** you could get others to believe something they currently won't?

266: Weekly Recap

***IF** there were no type of police force anywhere in the world, how would you and the world change??*

***WHAT IF** there were no heroes of any kind who stepped up to stand against evil??*

The one who commits sin is of the devil, for the devil has sinned from the beginning. The Son of God was revealed for this purpose: to destroy the devil's works. Everyone who has been born of God does not sin, because his seed remains in him; he is not able to sin, because he has been born of God. (1 John 3:8–9)

CATCH UP

- Who or what made you laugh recently?
- In what ways did life feel easy or hard this past week?

RECAP

- What stood out to you from what we've read together, talked about, or attempted to do together over the past week?
- What thoughts or questions do you have from today's Bible passage?

GROW TOGETHER

- What might be the main thing God is trying to tell our family today?
- What if we did something new together or returned to a good habit to live out what we're learning? What might that be?

OPEN UP

- In what ways are you struggling in life or experiencing something hard?
- If we were to confess something to God as a family, what might that be?

PRAY

- Who is Jesus to you today?
- Who would be willing to close our time with a simple prayer?

267: Origin Story

***IF** we celebrated our birthdays every month, what would be different about birthdays?*

***WHAT IF** we only celebrated our birthdays every five years?*

READ IT: JOHN 1:1–18

Where does a hero's story really begin? It's not always obvious. Batman's origin story wasn't revealed until six issues after he debuted. Other comic books include something up front that tells how it all started—for instance, the hero was bitten by a radioactive spider, or the hero grew up with powers that showed up early in life. It helps you see the hero not only as someone who does something, but as *someone*, period.

So where does Jesus' hero story really begin? He always existed as a person of the Trinity but then intentionally came to earth by being born through Mary and living among people. This is referred to as the "Incarnation"—God personally coming to earth, to personally invest in us. It helps us see Him as more than someone who will do something; we see Him as *someone*.

Jesus becoming incarnate doesn't mean He's just like us, though. It's popular for people to make Him seem super laid-back and okay with everything, but He's truly holy and can't be redefined. The more we try to make Jesus into something else, the less He gets to show us who He really is.

Wonder where your story really begins? Jesus coming near answers that question. If a powerful person lives in a tower and never lets anyone up there, it says something about the kind of value that person places on others. But if that powerful person shows up where you live and offers to serve you, then you'll understand how valued you are. This is why our Hero became a human—to heroically love and lead. Instead of just waving His arm to do things from heaven, He wants to interact with us now and forevermore.

THERE IS HOPE

God is in the habit of being with people. He's not just a historical figure, but today's Hero.

What do you think it was like for Jesus to leave heaven to come to earth? What would you compare it to?

- ***IF*** you had to leave your family to live somewhere else away from them for the next thirty-three years, what would that feel like?
- ***WHAT IF*** one of your family members had to leave you like that?

268: Legacy

***IF** you could see a family member's future and send them a message, what would you say?*

***WHAT IF** you learned that he or she was the worst person in your family tree?*

READ IT: MATTHEW 1:1–17

What might it be like to have all of history remember you? Isaac Newton described gravity and the laws of motion. Joan of Arc as a teenager led the French army to key victories during the Hundred Years' War. Neil Armstrong walked on the moon. Mother Teresa of Calcutta served the poor.

Now go further with that. Imagine being one of the people God talks favorably about in the Bible! Or having someone from your family tree specifically mentioned. What if you could tell others, "I'd like to introduce you to a relative. Turn to page 742." What a legacy that would be!

What if you could go even further and show how one of your relatives was in the family tree of Jesus? Matthew 1 offers that by tracking things back to Abraham (and another list like it in Luke 3 tracks things back to Adam). This genealogy is our spiritual family tree and arguably a literal bloodline (since we all descend from Adam). It isn't a complete inventory of every person before Jesus came, but it highlights how some pretty flawed people were included in God's heroic story.

Trying to be remembered on purpose for something positive is called living a legacy. After all, people aren't remembered for what they *planned* to do but for what they did and who they were. Thankfully, God can do something incredible that is greater than our best days and redeems our worst days. Given all the great and scandalous people in Jesus' family tree, that's a hopeful takeaway for us.

You are like no one else in this world. Make a memorable impact on others as a part of the family of God. Don't worry if you or your household are a little loony; the Lord invites flawed people into awesome things.

THERE IS HOPE

The scandalous people in Jesus' genealogy aren't just part of His story—they're the point of His story.

What do you like about your family, from its traditions and foods to its people and interests?

- ***IF*** you could add someone into your family tree, who (or what kind of person) would you add?
- ***WHAT IF*** Jesus were to grow up in your home? What would that be like?

269: All Wrapped Up

***IF** you had a tool that would wrap anything in wrapping paper, how would you use it?*

***WHAT IF** you could choose nine other people to have a tool like that?*

READ IT: LUKE 2:1–7

Superman's back-story is well-known across the world, but do you know about his cape? This red, flowing fabric was originally the blanket he was wrapped up in as a baby after being sent to earth in a rocket. His adoptive parents, the Kents, were alone when they found him all wrapped up in it, but they hung on to the material and later added it to his costume as he made his entrance into the world.

We're familiar with this concept. How many times have you put a blanket or towel on as you ran around the house to feel heroic? It seems like something a typical kid might do, but don't count adults out—some grown-ups still like dressing up like their favorite heroes during Halloween or at conventions. You may even find a few who still own a blanket they had as a baby or kid.

The Bible reveals that Mary wrapped Jesus in strips of cloth when He was born. It was less like the heroic cape He deserved and more like temporary rags she had on hand, but she and Joseph were alone in helping this special baby into this world. Perhaps Mary felt she was gift-wrapping God's gift to the world with the best she had.

What would you use to wrap Christ up in if He were born today? Maybe you have a soft, flowing blanket that He could keep with Him His whole life. Perhaps you'd grab the best pile of random cloth you could find. Yes, He absolutely deserves our best— but He's all wrapped in you. It doesn't matter if giving your best looks more like strips of yourself than you looking all put together. He'll turn it into something heroic through the "up, up, and away" life He invites us into.

THERE IS HOPE

Give God your best, and He'll take care of the rest.

Do you think Jesus should have worn a superhero uniform? Why or why not?

- ***IF*** Jesus had worn a costume, how might others have thought of Him?
- ***WHAT IF*** Him not wearing a costume tells us something about His character?

270: Sidekicks

***IF** you were a superhero and could design your own sidekick, what would that sidekick be like in terms of powers or abilities?*

***WHAT IF** you were a sidekick and could pick any famous superhero to work with?*

READ IT: LUKE 2:8–20

Batman and Robin. Captain America and Bucky. Wonder Woman and Wonder Girl. Who the hero is says something about the side-kick, but who the sidekick is says something about the hero.

God invited shepherds to be among the first eyewitnesses of baby Jesus. These often-smelly outdoorsmen weren't typically invited anywhere. They worked in the fields with animals and held a lowly status as the most common of commoners. So, if these were the sidekicks, what does that say about the Hero?

Jesus was born in a place where animals lived, which means His first breath was likely filled with the smell of animal stink. Inviting the shepherds to be present said that this wasn't a one-time thing. Christ would all throughout His ministry invest in people no one else would to show He was able to face the odor of our sin without pushing us away.

Maybe another reason the shepherds were invited was because they were the only ones who would actually come. Most people avoid anything God invites them into that "smells" awkward. Isn't that what makes a sidekick special, though? Not only does the sidekick take part in the glory of the hero, but he or she also goes through the same tough stuff to help good defeat evil.

Our Hero didn't need backup and was completely able to fulfill His mission without any human help. The fact that He chose to be born as a helpless baby and invite others to seek Him shows that He's a hero who raises sidekicks up on purpose for a purpose. Like the shepherds who told everyone about it (implying they crossed social lines they typi-cally wouldn't cross), we're each invited to join Him in this way by telling everyone about our Hero.

THERE IS HOPE

Jesus takes people kicked to the side and turns them into sidekicks.

What do you think the place Jesus was born in smelled like? Would you have wanted to stay there long?

- **IF** this is where Christ was born, what does it tell you about Him?
- **WHAT IF** Jesus is working in a person or place in your life you'd rather avoid?

271: Secret Identity

***IF** you could be incredible at one sport but first had to spend a year taking care of the equipment, which sport would you pick?*

***WHAT IF** you were only the best at that sport unofficially, never getting fame for it?*

READ IT: LUKE 2:8–20

Some of the greatest superheroes didn't pick the best ways to hide their secret identity. Superman wore eyeglasses and slouched as Clark Kent. The Green Arrow took off his green hat and mask to be Oliver Queen (who had the same unique beard as Green Arrow). Wonder Woman spun around and looked like . . . well . . . Wonder Woman in a dress. If the idea of a secret identity is to keep it secret, they could have all tried a little harder.

Jesus, on the other hand, spent His supernatural life on Earth naturally overlooked by others. He slowly revealed Himself during His adult years, but two older people who were paying attention recognized how special He was even as a baby. Anna never left the temple, ever in search of the coming Messiah, and Simeon had been told by God that he'd personally see the Hero of the world with his own eyes. One day—after all their faithfulness—they saw Christ and knew it was Him.

Why would God choose such a humble arrival instead of making Himself known with fireworks? Perhaps it was to address the temptation in us to impress others. How refreshing it is to realize that Jesus would rather be fully present than fully impressive. He showed us what our hearts are truly aching for—to look for the Lord and realize He's right in front of us and in plain sight.

Remember this as you feel the urge to hide behind one more trophy, promotion, compliment, or high five. The humility of Jesus can set us at ease in who God is making us to be versus in who we're trying to prove we are. Him becoming less than He's capable of was to inspire us toward more of the good we're capable of.

THERE IS HOPE

Instead of just solving our problems for us from afar, our Hero solves our problems with us up close.

Chat about how tempting it is to want to be famous or thought of as being good at something.

- ***IF*** you could break any world record, which one would you pick?
- ***WHAT IF*** you could have either the ability to break every world record or train others to break those records? Which would you pick?

272: Archenemy?

***IF** you had to say the worst-case scenario and the best-case scenario you can think of, what would you say?*

***WHAT IF** both scenarios came true?*

READ IT: MATTHEW 2:1–23

Some competitors are easy to spot. McDonald's and Burger King have been rivals for years. So have Pepsi and Coca-Cola. Each company wants the same people to focus the same attention on only one place—their place.

God's true archenemy is obviously the devil, but certain people throughout history have represented Satan's interests. King Herod was one of them in how he reacted after hearing the Magi describe Jesus as the true "king of the Jews." Since two kings can't rule the same kingdom, Herod felt that Jesus was coming for him. Herod wanted the same people to focus the same attention in only one place—his place. Refusing to give up easily, he chose to steal, kill, and destroy.

This piece of the Christmas story is missing from the typical Christmas play. Among all the roles actors play, you'll find Mary, Joseph, the shepherds, the animals, and so on. Seldom does King Herod get included, though. Truth be told, he's the first person in history who really did start a "war on Christmas."

In life we'll meet people who seem like our archenemies. It may be those who have what we want, who put us down, who spread rumors about us, or who just live differently than we do. We can even see something of an archenemy in ourselves at times. We may feel that our only option to stop the "Herod" before us is to become like him.

Instead, remember what the Magi did. As they visited Jesus when He was a toddler, they immediately fell to their knees to worship Him. While Herod was focused on getting rid of Jesus to hold on to what he thought he owned, the Magi were focused on giving up what they owned because of what they thought of Jesus. How will you choose to respond to Jesus today?

THERE IS HOPE

Want to give Jesus the very best gift? Let Him have all of you, just as you are. Then He'll give you two gifts: grace and growth.

When has someone in your life felt like a rival or archenemy?

- ***IF*** you could get two people you know to work things out versus fighting, who would you pick?
- ***WHAT IF*** you could get two countries to stop fighting?

273: Weekly Recap

***IF** you were randomly given a giant light bulb that did not need electricity, how would you use it?*

***WHAT IF** once a day a random stranger handed you a potato?*

What was from the beginning, what we have heard, what we have seen with our eyes, what we have observed and have touched with our hands, concerning the word of life—that life was revealed, and we have seen it and we testify and declare to you the eternal life that was with the Father and was revealed to us. (1 John 1:1–2)

CATCH UP

- Who or what made you laugh recently?
- In what ways did life feel easy or hard this past week?

RECAP

- What stood out to you from what we've read together, talked about, or attempted to do together over the past week?
- What thoughts or questions do you have from today's Bible passage?

GROW TOGETHER

- What might be the main thing God is trying to tell our family today?
- What if we did something new together or returned to a good habit to live out what we're learning? What might that be?

OPEN UP

- In what ways are you struggling in life or experiencing something hard?
- If we were to confess something to God as a family, what might that be?

PRAY

- Who is Jesus to you today?
- Who would be willing to close our time with a simple prayer?

274: Super Kid

***IF** you could see the whole life and history of anyone, who would you pick?*

***WHAT IF** you could see the full, unexplained past of a fictional character in a movie, TV show, or book?*

READ IT: LUKE 2:40–52

A little secret—kids ask questions adults don't know how to answer. It works both ways, though—parents ask kids questions they don't know how to answer. We have that in common. That, and an adoration for eating ice cream whenever possible.

We also emulate our birth families physically, perhaps by having our "father's jaw" or our "mother's eyes." Your hair color, skin tone, and height reflect your family heritage. Maybe even your taste buds are inherited.

So, if we're all a genetic mix of our parents, how did that work for Jesus? Did He have "Mary's smile" or "God-the-Father's smile?" It's a fun question that we can't answer—especially since Jesus wasn't recognized by the very people He came to save. As the brightest thinkers in His day debated about when the Messiah would come, the boy walking by their window was that very Hero.

What they did notice was that Jesus was a super kid of Scripture. We might think, *That's because He was God.* But as Luke 2:52 points out, Jesus "increased in wisdom." In other words, He *chose to learn* things as He grew up. The one who taught the earth to spin *chose to learn* how to walk. The one in union with the Father *chose to learn* prayers. The one who knew all things decided not to be born with great knowledge but *chose to learn* about the very Scripture He created.

Being a kid is difficult. Growing into becoming a teenager and then an adult isn't any easier. Jesus could've skipped over all the awkward, uncomfortable parts. Instead, He chose to grow up and become strong, "filled with wisdom, and God's grace was on him."

What does this tell us about God? What does it tell us about you and me? What does this tell us about God's love for you and me?

THERE IS HOPE

Jesus' family went through everyday tensions, real feelings, and confusing moments as other families do.

What's a subject or skill you wish you'd been born knowing everything about?

- ***IF*** Jesus chose to learn instead of show up on earth knowing everything, what do you think that was like for Him?
- ***WHAT IF*** to learn something new in life you had to forget something else?

275: Super Ready

***IF** you were to use one word to describe the outdoors, what word would you pick?*

***WHAT IF** everyone could only think about the outdoors according to your one word?*

READ IT: MATTHEW 3:1–12

How do you define "going camping"? An air-conditioned trailer at a luxury resort, right? Or maybe you'd say it requires tents and sleeping bags over dirt. Whichever you prefer, each type of camping requires preparation since it's different from the life you normally live.

John the Baptist was more of a "roughing it" kind of guy who lived in the wilderness. Some people choose this life to get close to nature or be someplace quiet in the country. John took part in something larger, for God said in Isaiah 40:3–5 and Malachi 3:1 that the person who would get people ready for the Messiah would live out in the desert. Although John could've lived in whatever comfortable life his family had created, he instead lived simply, humbly, and openly before the Lord. He basically lived out his message.

In this way, John was "super ready" for God and showed what it looks like to live that way. He ministered near the Jordan River, which was the same water that had parted for the Israelites centuries earlier so they could step into it and cross into the Promised Land. It was yet another way to make sure everyone knew that if they wanted the blessings the Hero would bring, then they'd need to "get their feet wet."

People try to define Christianity in different ways. One family may think of it as a life of nothing but denial while another family may think of it as a life full of nothing but comforts. Whichever camp you fall into, you need to take steps out of your definition and into God's definition. Whether that's just one step into the great landscape of the Lord or a whole leap into it is a choice He gives you. One way or another, repent and get super ready for Jesus to do something "in-tents."

THERE IS HOPE

You can't make a movement of God happen, but you can prepare for one. Your steps today create momentum for tomorrow's steps.

What do you think it would be like to have a conversation with John the Baptist?

- ***IF*** John were just a regular guy who happened to take a few important things seriously, would you want to hang out with Him?
- ***WHAT IF*** John were intense all the time? How about if he were more joyful all the time? Would either be okay? Should we be one way more than another?

276: Super Model

***IF** you had a friend who couldn't do anything without you showing him or her how to do it, how would you handle that?*

***WHAT IF** you had another friend who couldn't do anything even if you did show him or her how to do it?*

READ IT: MATTHEW 3:13–17; JOHN 1:29–34

Our relationship with water isn't shallow. God created a non-salty form of it so we can stay alive by drinking it, yet He also made saltwater to uniquely serve ocean life. We use water to clean our food, wash ourselves, rinse dishes, nurture lawns, brush our teeth, and pump waste out of our homes. We also use it to fuel sprinklers, wet slides, and fill balloons to throw. Well, well . . . water is all about life.

Bottle this up by looking at why Jesus chose to be baptized. Colossians 2 and Romans 6 tell us that baptism is a step of obedience and identification we take after giving our lives to Christ. Before Jesus' death and resurrection, baptism was what people did to prepare their hearts for God to reign over them. He was already living this way and without sin yet wanted to be baptized publicly anyway as an example for us. So instead of being "stage models," like the Pharisees, who tried to look good on the outside, our Hero did something on the outside to show what good surrender looks like on the inside. This "super model" still serves as our example today.

John the Baptist was humbled and confused. Can you imagine having the greatest athlete ask you to lace up his or her shoes before a game (or, perhaps even weirder, for you to play in his or her position)? John did glimpse what was happening, though, as the Spirit descended on Jesus and the Trinity was fully present with one another.

Later on in His ministry, Jesus referred to himself as "living water" (John 4:13–14; 7:37–39). He wanted to clarify that only by knowing Him can we find eternal life. The next time you're around water—be it to refresh you, clean you, or make you laugh—think of Jesus. And if you haven't yet been baptized as a believer, what are you waiting for?

THERE IS HOPE

Water can be wild and unpredictable—yet also cleansing, still, calming, and purifying. So, if Jesus is described as "living water" . . . amen?

What might it look like to let your life be like a cannonball jump into Jesus?

- ***IF*** you fully dove into your relationship with the Lord this week, how might it splash some people? Do you think they'd find it fun or annoying?
- ***WHAT IF*** other people did find our fun in Jesus annoying? Should that change how we feel about diving in?

277: Supernatural

***IF** you saw the yummiest dessert in the world next to a note saying, "Do not touch," would you eat it? (Be honest.)*

***WHAT IF** when you saw that dessert you heard a whisper in your ear saying, "Eat it"?*

READ IT: LUKE 4:1–15

Sugarcoated cereal. Are you a fan of it, or does your family debate buying it? It really is all about the coating.

It's also insight into how temptation works. After the incredible baptism of Jesus, He didn't go off that high point right into ministry. Matthew 4:1 says He was "led up by the Spirit into the wilderness to be tempted by the devil." God's enemy then dared Jesus with the sugary side of evil: in a world full of starvation, Jesus could've turned stones into bread every day; in a world looking for a leader, Jesus could've presented Himself with powers that wowed everyone; in a world filled with war, Jesus could've showed how big His angelic army is. These were the very things that others demanded of Christ throughout His ministry.

How did Jesus avoid the supernaturally sweet taste of these temptations? He allowed the Holy Spirit to lead Him and fought every sugarcoated lie with truth. This one-two punch also allowed Jesus to start His ministry "in the power of the Spirit." Avoiding temptation isn't about saying no to the wrong thing through our willpower but about saying yes to God through His power.

What good-looking thing in your life isn't good for you? Maybe it's a hobby that feels innocent but steals your time. Perhaps it's an attitude you feel justified about holding on to, or virtual entertainment you look forward to so much that it takes your eyes off real things. It could be hidden in a relationship with something or someone that is drawing you away from the Lord. Just as Jesus prepared in forty days for what He'd be tempted by for three years, ask God to use today's temptations to prepare you for tomorrow's victory.

THERE IS HOPE

The war around you can never be stronger than the worship service inside of you . . . if there is a worship service inside of you.

How do you usually handle some of the different temptations you face?

- ***IF*** someone you look up to did something surprisingly out of character, how would you react?
- ***WHAT IF*** a fictional character you looked up to in a TV show started making decisions that really offended you? Would you keep watching the show?

278: Super Vision

IF *a theme song played whenever you walked into a room, what song would you want it to be?*

WHAT IF *everyone had music that played whenever they ran?*

READ IT: LUKE 4:16–30

What would be the ideal first job? Maybe manual labor, like landscaping a yard, harvesting on a farm, or swinging a hammer on a worksite? Perhaps driving for a delivery service or standing behind a counter? Countless opportunities like this produce character as you start at the bottom and work your way up. Some supervision can help us see plain things we might miss.

Jesus was thirty when He began His public ministry. He'd just come out stronger than ever from a character-producing time of testing in the desert, but now he had to face the testing of people. And it wasn't easy. That's true for us too. Sometimes when you're charged up, another person is ready to take you down.

For Jesus it happened when He was in a church-like setting. It's sad that criticism can happen among God's people, but Jesus faced it and still regularly gathered with others like this because it was the right thing to do. The usual order of service involved prayer, praise, and Scripture readings. Then someone with "super vision" (like a rabbi or teacher) helped others see plain things they might miss so they could spot bigger things they hoped to see. Jesus was that person in Nazareth that day, which meant He taught in the same hometown where people knew Him from His "first job" as the carpenter's son. Sadly, they wouldn't see past how they were used to seeing Him and blinded themselves to Jesus as our Hero.

Ever notice how some people who say they want to serve God only want to do so as His boss? Don't be like the people in Jesus' hometown who missed out on miracles by limiting their faith. If you want some super vision for life, open up to His supervision.

THERE IS HOPE

When you seek vision, you don't always gain God.
When you seek God, you always gain vision.

What would be hard for someone who knew you years ago to learn about you today?

- ***IF*** you were to run into a friend you hadn't seen in five years, what are some things you could reasonably expect to be different about him or her?
- ***WHAT IF*** Jesus surprised you today with something new about Him that was hard for you to believe?

279: Super Friends

***IF** you could recruit three superheroes to come into real life, who would you pick?*

***WHAT IF** the main villains to these superheroes eventually showed up too?*

READ IT: JOHN 1:35–51; MARK 1:16–38

They're called "team ups." Comic-book history is filled with these stories of heroes coming together to take on a larger-than-life mission together. Sometimes they end up becoming a group, like the Justice League or the Avengers. It usually comes down to at least one hero challenging the others to step up and fight an important foe. If you were the one giving the speech or recruiting other super friends, you'd likely make sure you had the best of the best of the best.

Our Hero Jesus had a different way of recruiting His first disciples, though. Instead of picking the most religious people in that era or finding people who already got along with each other, Christ formed His group of twelve out of common people who otherwise wouldn't have hung out with each other. Those who agreed discovered an inspiring purpose for their lives.

That's why Simon Peter quickly left behind his moneymaking fishing business in a culture where money was hard to come by. Jesus offered to take what this guy was good at to show him something more important He'd be great at. Our Hero invites all misfits, outcasts, and commoners into this great, uncommon purpose.

God doesn't just reach out to "the best of the best of the best" in our world, but He sees the best of the best in all of us. There's no truer purpose for your life than the one He offers you. Like the disciples, you may have bumped into Him more than once, but there comes a point when you hear Him calling, "Follow Me." Notice He didn't just say "Believe in me"—He invites us to walk with Him as His super friends. And if Jesus invites us to follow Him, then following in His footsteps means we're able to invite others to follow Him too.

THERE IS HOPE

We're right where we need to be to hear Jesus calling out to us. All we have to do is listen, say yes, and follow Him.

What do you think it was like for Jesus to call the disciples to follow Him?

- ***IF*** you could comfort family members of the disciples who left to follow Jesus, what would you say?
- ***WHAT IF*** someone in our family left for three years to do something they felt God calling them to do?

280: Weekly Recap

***IF** everything smelled like bacon, what would your typical day be like?*

***WHAT IF** everything you ate tasted like bacon?*

The stone that the builders rejected has become the cornerstone. This came from the LORD; it is wondrous in our sight. This is the day the LORD has made; let us rejoice and be glad in it. (Psalm 118:22–24)

CATCH UP

- Who or what made you laugh recently?
- In what ways did life feel easy or hard this past week?

RECAP

- What stood out to you from what we've read together, talked about, or attempted to do together over the past week?
- What thoughts or questions do you have from today's Bible passage?

GROW TOGETHER

- What might be the main thing God is trying to tell our family today?
- What if we did something new together or returned to a good habit to live out what we're learning? What might that be?

OPEN UP

- In what ways are you struggling in life or experiencing something hard?
- If we were to confess something to God as a family, what might that be?

PRAY

- Who is Jesus to you today?
- Who would be willing to close our time with a simple prayer?

281: Let's Get This Party Started

***IF** you were a rock star, how would you start your concert?*

***WHAT IF** whatever you did at the beginning of your concert was all you did?*

READ IT: JOHN 2:1–12

Musicians have to be strategic about how they put their concerts together. It's not just about the right opening song or yelling, "Let's get this party started!" The whole night has to flow well so that everyone joins in and stays engaged. A wise musician will use whatever happens up front to lead into all that's to come.

People expect this when they go to wedding receptions too. A good host doesn't just greet guests at the door but makes sure that they're taken care of all night. The host's family typically helps with this too.

A wedding banquet in the first century was a big deal, often lasting for days. It was an embarrassing social mistake for the host to run out of food or drinks. Jesus' mother noticed that very thing at this particular wedding banquet and urged her Son to perform a miracle to fix things.

Some consider what Jesus did next to be the "opening act" to His ministry. Instead of just quietly saying a word or waving His hand to make more drinks for the party, He went public and involved others. In fact, the jars that He had the servants fill were what people used to wash their hands. He didn't tell the servants to first clean the jars up but instead took what we might think of as dirty water and turned it into something drinkable.

Isn't this what Jesus does with our lives? Our Hero doesn't ask us to get clean first before we come to Him but encourages us to come as we are to then be made into something new. If this was His opening "song," He definitely used it to get everyone to join in and stay engaged. What if we help Him in getting the whole world to jam to this melody? Let's get this party started!

THERE IS HOPE

Jesus walked around on dirty streets among dirty people. When His followers do the same thing, the world becomes cleaner.

How would you feel if Jesus wanted to give you a drink of juice or punch that He had made out of dirty bath water?

- ***IF*** God can do this with water, what do you think He can do with people?
- ***WHAT IF*** someone you think of as dirty is one step away from becoming clean with Jesus? What might that step be? How can we help?

282: You Wouldn't Like Me When I'm Angry

***IF** you could invent a new craze that everyone took part in, what would it be?*

***WHAT IF** you could stop a craze that's popular right now (or might become popular)?*

READ IT: JOHN 2:13–25

Remember being a toddler and getting in trouble when you ran into the street? Your safety was so important that someone gave you a memorable consequence for disobeying. As you got older and rode your bike, you were told to ride on the sidewalk. Again, this was to keep you safe, and there was a consequence if you disobeyed.

This scenario repeated itself throughout the years, although the consequences have probably changed from when you were a toddler.

We can understand the Bible and God's discipline this way too. Humanity started out historically thinking like babies, then toddlers, and eventually like older kids. By the time Jesus came, humanity was like an older teen or young adult, and things could be more relational between us and God. That didn't excuse us from consequences, though. Sometimes God still has to raise His voice.

For example, Jesus cleansed the temple at the beginning and end of His ministry. These events resembled Leviticus 14:33–53, which describes a house with a visible mildew contamination. A priest would send everyone out so the house could be made clean by removing the contaminated stones. If the house was later found to still have disease, then the priest would declare the whole house's destruction. This is what happened on Jesus' second visit to the temple when the people didn't respond to the opportunity He had given them to change (Matthew 21:12–13; Mark 11:12–17; Luke 19:45–46).

Our Hero offers grace *because* we otherwise couldn't stand before His holiness. He is willing to get angry when a situation demands it, but it isn't His preference. Whether He's blessing our obedience or disciplining our disobedience is largely up to us.

THERE IS HOPE

God's discipline isn't meant to "pay us back" but to bring us back. Not to randomly harm us, but to intentionally keep us from harm.

What is something you had to be told more than once because you didn't pay attention the first time?

- ***IF*** we're like this with people, how might we be like this with God?
- ***WHAT IF*** God put you in charge of disciplining people who disobeyed Him?

283: In Brightest Day, in Blackest Night

***IF** a sound went off in your head whenever someone you knew had a baby, do you think you would like or dislike it?*

***WHAT IF** you heard a sound when someone you knew became a Christian?*

READ IT: JOHN 3:1–21

Where is it? That special place where you go to quickly be alone and let your guard down? Your room, with the door closed? The side of your bed? A hammock or chair in your backyard? You know you've crossed over into adulthood when you seek out peace and privacy in a public bathroom stall.

Nicodemus knew something about responsibility and life in the spotlight. He was looked up to as a religious leader who felt the pressure to say and do all the right things. Still, there was something about Jesus that he didn't yet understand but wanted to. Since going to talk with this Miracle-Maker was risky, Nicodemus chose to instead make this visit at night.

Thankfully, our Hero seemed okay with this. Jesus loves it when we approach Him without a filter but will still receive us if we have our guard up as we seek Him. It's just that He'll at some point dare us to drop the act to enjoy Him in the light. It's something He shared with Nicodemus during their chat.

And what a chat that was! Jesus challenged Nicodemus to think about life with the Lord as being born again—not physically, but spiritually. As a caterpillar enters a cocoon and emerges a butterfly, we each can become a new creation through Jesus . . . not a more moral or religious version of ourselves, but the person God originally created us to be.

You can come to Jesus in the brightest day. He'll also talk with you in the blackest night. Like Nicodemus, you may feel religious or have studied the Bible your whole life yet still find there's much you don't understand. Know that if you come to Him with your questions, He won't judge you but will receive you. In fact, He'll invite you to keep stepping in His direction to feel His embrace.

THERE IS HOPE

Your spiritual transformation can develop the world instead of the world developing you.

In what ways do you think a spiritual birth might be like or unlike a physical birth?

- ***IF*** there's one thing you want to see in someone who is a Christian, what is it?
- ***WHAT IF*** you had a set of glasses that let you see who was a Christian?

284: The Man Without Fear

***IF** we discovered that apple cider, not water, was essential to all life, what would be different about your day or week?*

***WHAT IF** apple cider became the only drink we could drink?*

READ IT: JOHN 4:1–42

Some things seem culturally "off-limits" to chat about. It's been said you should never bring up religion or politics (despite both topics being important to everyone everywhere). We're also not supposed to ask about someone's weight, income, insecurities, or mistakes. When you're younger and don't think about any of this, you blurt out whatever is on your mind. As you get older, you're taught to shut down tense moments by saying, "New topic" or "Let's agree to disagree."

Jesus was a man without fear in conversations. He knew our temptation to hide behind safe chit-chat instead of truly talking, so He brought up important things that others avoided. Instead of agreeing to disagree, He basically said, "Let's talk about what matters, whether we like it or not."

Notice how He did this with the woman at the well. First, he sat down with her—something a typical Jew wouldn't do based on her beliefs and lifestyle. Asking her for water was also an "unclean" practice, but He used it to engage her heart. Every time she tried to change the subject, Jesus brought her back to talking about real life until she realized He was the Hero she was hoping for.

As Christians, we may talk more about our beliefs or our church than about our pain, blind spots, and struggles. Jesus wants to bring up the things we'd rather stuff down—not to embarrass us but to free us. Like the woman at the well, you see God in new ways if you let Him crack open the parts of you that you've spent time covering up. As you feel exposed, He'll offer you the same grace He did to the woman at the well. And maybe like her, you'll be so inspired that you'll lead everyone around you to Jesus . . . because you've let yourself be led by Jesus.

THERE IS HOPE

Jesus could have come to earth to take a stand against sinful people. Instead, He sat down next to them to lift them up.

What do you think it means for Jesus to reach out to sinful people like us without crossing the line of sin?

- ***IF*** Jesus won't allow anyone to run away from their potential, what kind of conversations do you think He'd want to have with our family members?
- ***WHAT IF*** feeling spiritually "fed" only comes by doing the will of God?

285: Great Power = Great Responsibility

***IF** your face could only smile,*
how would you express other emotions?

***WHAT IF** everyone's only facial expression was a smile?*

READ IT: JOHN 4:46–54; MARK 2:1–12

Your favorite team is making a big play, and so you pray, *"God, please!"* You get ready to open mail that will change your life, and quickly hope, *"God, please!"* You're in the middle of traffic, trying to get someone to the hospital, and cry out, *"God, please!"*

These moments make you wonder how prayer works. You may think something untrue, like *God is too busy to bother with me,* or *God has to do what I ask because I'm a Christian.* Does prayer work this way? Do we ever turn it into a silly thing or insult God based on what we ask?

Pay close attention to the official who asked Jesus to heal his son. Despite being a man of power and wealth, he humbled himself and begged the Lord for a breakthrough. Jesus said it would happen, so the man trusted as he headed home that his son was healed. The same is seen in the group who tore open a roof, believing that Jesus could change everything for their paralyzed friend.

God wants a *relationship* with us. Just as you wouldn't want a friend only coming around to ask you for money, He doesn't only want us coming to Him to ask for stuff. BUT that doesn't mean He doesn't want to hear what you need or want. You can always turn to Him, even about the smallest or silliest of things, knowing that He cares about you.

Just remember that Jesus said the greater miracle is Him saving us from sin. Anything you pray about connects you to this truth because prayer connects you to Jesus. Whether or not God says "Yes," "No," or "Not yet" to what you ask is based on a deeper wisdom He's working off of. With Jesus' great power comes great responsibility. So, put *everything* before Him and get to know *Him* as you do.

THERE IS HOPE

When we pray, we at least for a moment put our eyes on God versus our difficulties. That in itself is an answer to the prayer.

How amazing is it that God can hear everyone's prayers all the time?

- ***IF*** you had to guess, how many conversations can you focus on at once?
- ***WHAT IF*** prayer changes us so God can then bring change through us?

286: Shazam!

***IF** whenever you touched a liquid it turned green, what would you do?*

***WHAT IF** you could also change the taste of the liquid through your thoughts?*

READ IT: LUKE 5:27–29; MARK 2:15–17

What do you say when great things surprise you? Probably "WOW!" or "AWESOME!" An older expression that was popular is "SHAZAM!" In the comic books it was also a special word that a young boy said to summon a lightning bolt that changed him into a superhero.

We don't know what each of the disciples said when Jesus invited them to follow Him. We do know that Matthew was willing to leave behind his money-making business as a tax collector. Doing that job meant taking money from others. It didn't afford you many friends, so perhaps the only people Matthew knew were others society had rejected.

That didn't stop Matthew from throwing a party together with lightning speed to introduce those friends to Jesus, though. This angered the religious leaders who saw it, but it gave Jesus the chance to reveal His heart for lost people. Matthew simply provided the space for Jesus to be the Hero He is and say what He came to say so more people could receive Him as Savior.

Each of the young men who followed Jesus became a kind of adult hero who served others. We may not know everything about their "SHAZAM!" moments, but they each had one. They also made sure what Jesus did in them kept going.

Some churches today throw parties like Matthew did to get believers and nonbelievers around each other. It usually involves something relaxing, like dinner or a movie, but the idea is that Jesus is introduced by naturally sharing stories and a relationship with each other. Maybe you'd be up for something like this or will do something else entirely, but one way or another, let's bolt with lightning speed to introduce everyone we know to Jesus. *SHAZAM!*

THERE IS HOPE

You don't need to know how to say everything significant about Jesus in order to say something significant about Jesus.

What do you think would be a fun way to get Christians and non-Christians together with a purpose?

- **IF** we were to host a fun night for something like this, whom would we invite?
- **WHAT IF** we were like Matthew and invited people right away?

287: Weekly Recap

IF *you had five times more garbage to dispose of each week than normal, what would need to change around your house?*

WHAT IF *a monster came to take a bite out of your house if you didn't take your garbage out every day?*

[In my visions] one like a son of man was coming with the clouds of heaven. . . . He was given dominion, and glory, and a kingdom; so that those of every people, nation, and language should serve him. His dominion is an everlasting dominion that will not pass away, and his kingdom is one that will not be destroyed. (Daniel 7:13–14)

CATCH UP

- Who or what made you laugh recently?
- In what ways did life feel easy or hard this past week?

RECAP

- What stood out to you from what we've read together, talked about, or attempted to do together over the past week?
- What thoughts or questions do you have from today's Bible passage?

GROW TOGETHER

- What might be the main thing God is trying to tell our family today?
- What if we did something new together or returned to a good habit to live out what we're learning? What might that be?

OPEN UP

- In what ways are you struggling in life or experiencing something hard?
- If we were to confess something to God as a family, what might that be?

PRAY

- Who is Jesus to you today?
- Who would be willing to close our time with a simple prayer?

THERE IS HOPE

OPPORTUNITY

It'll be hard to remember this, but it'll change your life if you let it change how you speak and think: the word *normal* is one of the most misused words in the world.

It ranks right up there with *love*, *hate*, and *always*. We use these words to try to make a point about something that otherwise wouldn't stand on its own. You may say, "I *love* cheeseburgers" or "I *hate* cats" when you have no intention of marrying that sandwich or attacking every feline with vengeance. A family member may claim, "You *always* use up all the toilet paper in the bathroom!" when what he or she means is, "Can you quit leaving everyone else just four squares on the roll?"

So, when it comes to "normal," it helps to remember that the world hasn't been *normal* for quite some time. You know this when you wake up and feel that you're made for something more significant than your to-do list. It's bouncing around inside of you every time you consider walking away from negative people or are drawn toward positive people. It's why you weep hot tears at funerals, slam the laptop shut when headlines overwhelm you, and sleeplessly stare at the ceiling all night because a relationship has gone sour. This world is not normal, and we all know it.

What if we were given an opportunity to join God in changing this, though?

"Normal" can't be voted on, nor can it be eliminated despite all the voting we do to try to take abnormal things and call them "normal." Every time ordinary people embrace this extraordinary truth, we realize the opportunity for things to get better.

One day the ultimate "normal" person came to show us what "normal" is. He did this not just by critiquing the way things are or telling us to be cocky. We're not right because we're Christians, but because Jesus is right and He makes it possible for us to get right with God through Him. In the same way that He lived among us and taught us truth, so can our living with Him inspire others. In doing so we reclaim "normal" in how we think, feel, live, serve, and connect. This is an opportunity for uncommon living in a common world.

Jesus didn't just tell us what to do but made it possible for us to seize the true life through Him and the Holy Spirit.

288: Fair? I See. Sad. You See.

***IF** you could change your skin color whenever you wanted (but it would stay that way for a day), what would you do with this ability?*

***WHAT IF** someone told you that you could only use this ability on Sundays?*

READ IT: MARK 2:18–28; JOHN 5:16–23

Every school year, kids wonder if their teachers will be easy or strict. Adults have the same fear at work with new supervisors.

People in the first century were nervous about their religious leaders too. The Pharisees ended up focused on the rules they invented more than God's Law itself. The Sadducees were rich men who only accepted the first five books of Hebrew Scripture (the ones Moses wrote) but denied the spiritual world and the resurrection of the dead. These two groups together comprised the Sanhedrin, which was like a Jewish Supreme Court. There were also Zealots, who used military force to change things, and scribes, who were passionate about reading and writing the Law. They focused on what was "fair" as they saw it or made people sad through extra rules that should have never been made in the first place.

Jesus made these religious leaders nervous! Any question they threw at Christ made them look silly when He was done answering it. As they focused on the blind spots in others, He showed them their own.

Jesus isn't just some "cool" teacher who lets us do whatever we want, though. Sin is a big deal, and something needs to be done about it. Where the Pharisees and Sadducees went wrong was in thinking that life could be fixed by getting people to take on more holy habits or memorize certain thoughts. Jesus did the exact opposite by taking the burden of our sin on Himself so we'd have an opportunity for forgiveness and transformation. The Lord does enjoy it when we do good deeds for the right reasons, but *"the sacrifice pleasing to God is a broken spirit [or] . . . a broken and humbled heart" (Psalm 51:17).*

THERE IS HOPE

You don't become good to get grace; you get grace to become good.

What if the way the Pharisees see life is like not being able to see any color in the world?

- ***IF*** everything became zebra colored in your home, how would it feel there?
- ***WHAT IF*** the whole world were zebra colored except for your house?

289: Passed but Not Crushed

***IF** you knew that tomorrow you would only have the things you thanked God for today, how would that change the way you prayed today?*

***WHAT IF** this were the case every day? Do you think you'd genuinely become more thankful or tired of being thankful?*

READ IT: MATTHEW 5:1–12

A "car crusher" is a massive rectangle-shaped machine big enough to fit a car or van into it. Scrapyards use them to powerfully squeeze thousands of pounds of pressure onto that vehicle to flatten it into a slab of metal. Just imagine the power that takes!

Now picture that car crusher plate pressing down just enough to stop and hold a single, ordinary egg in place. Instead of all that power squashing that delicate shell and its insides, it keeps the egg from rolling off and breaking apart. If that egg could talk, what do you think it would say?

You already know the answer if you've ever felt God use His power to hold you in place during a tough spot in life. That's why the "Beatitudes" of Matthew 5 explain that it's a blessing to feel heartbroken or stressed, because we can only get to know this side of the Lord as He keeps us from rolling off track and breaking apart. We also experience it when we are "humble" to others—which means we have the power to somehow crush someone (as a car crusher can crush an egg) but instead look for a way to gently hold that person up with meekness.

Jesus isn't asking you to just think about things more positively, but to really get to know Him when things get tough. Anytime you feel that you're about to crack is an opportunity to rest in Christ instead of your circumstances. You can see any attack you're experiencing through His eyes and realize that the way you're being treated feels wrong because it is wrong—but doesn't need to be dished out in revenge. The Beatitudes are an invitation and opportunity back to the way things are supposed to be . . . especially when life feels anything but that in the moment.

THERE IS HOPE

We are afflicted in every way but not crushed . . . persecuted but not abandoned . . . struck down but not destroyed. (2 Corinthians 4:8–9)

How are you really doing? Is there anything tough or challenging worth sharing?

- ***IF*** there is one thing you end up thinking about a lot, what might it be?
- ***WHAT IF*** you could change something that's happening in the world?

290: Stick and Shine

***IF** you had a sombrero that always had tortilla chips in it when you wore it, what would you do with that sombrero?*

***WHAT IF** the sombrero also lit up and played music when you wore it?*

READ IT: MATTHEW 5:13–16

Quick! Think of all the uses you can for salt. Ready? Set? Go! (If you feel stumped, salt adds flavor to what we eat, creates thirst, helps heal injuries, preserves food from getting rotten, and melts ice.)

Now do the same thing again by thinking of all the uses you can for light. Go! (Stuck? Light helps plants live, giving animals who live off of those plants the ability to survive. It also develops Vitamin D to grow strong bones, enables us to see objects, brings out depth in colors, affects temperature, maintains our sense of time, alerts us to things, and kills bacteria.)

Put all of that together, and you'll realize a big opportunity. Jesus didn't tell us to become "salt" and "light" but plainly said we *are*. In Christ, we "stick" like salt to add flavor to the world, create a thirst for Jesus, help heal hurts, keep truth from getting rotten, and melt the icy hearts of others. We "shine" by lighting the way that helps the right things live (which helps others live), giving faith a backbone, seeing life clearly, bringing out depth in people, adding warmth, giving perspective on time, alerting others to important things, and killing the spread of sin.

The choice is ours. The world will keep trying to make people a little more bitter and darker each day. Jesus can give them "salt" and "light" through us so they don't keep struggling with the same rotten or dying things currently tempting them. Go through the lists of what salt and light do to specifically invite the Lord to raise that up in you and your family. The flavor and sight the world is looking for are found in Christ, but He wants to be found in you. What an opportunity!

THERE IS HOPE

It's easy to be sugar or shade. It's transformational to be salt and light. There's no need to shove or shout. Just stick and shine.

What do you think Jesus meant about how salt and light can become useless or hidden?

- ***IF*** regular table salt were to disappear, what food would you no longer eat?
- ***WHAT IF*** all forms of light also disappeared and we lived in the dark? What would that be like? How does that show the importance of Christianity?

291: Most of the Least

IF *you could enlarge any picture or painting to make it gigantic, what would you pick?*

WHAT IF *whatever you enlarged had to be a picture you were in?*

READ IT: MATTHEW 5:17–37

"At least I didn't ______."

When have you said something like that? It may have been more like, *"It's not like I ______"* or *"Just because I did that doesn't mean ______."* We say things like this to try to make something bad sound better.

That only makes things worse, though. Look at how angry people can be online or in person. It's like we're little mob bosses ordering "hits" on people or businesses we don't like. We say things like, *"No one shop there!"* or *"Everyone snub this person!"* We then try to excuse it by saying, *"It's not like I said to punch that person,"* or *"At least I didn't say everything bad I could've said."*

Jesus dares us to live better. He explained that everything in the Old Testament was only the beginning of knowing God's heart for us. Christ didn't come to get rid of any of it but to reveal the larger value. We'd be more likely to live "at least," but He shows us how to live "at most."

So, He pointed out some real-life examples, like how words and hate are as bad as murder in how they kill relationships and attack people. He explained that lust was like adultery in how focusing on a fantasy version of a person keeps you from fully enjoying a real relationship. He called us to be faithful to our commitments, be it marriage, family, or doing what we said we'd do.

It's as if Jesus were enlarging a photograph to show what couldn't be seen in its smaller size. As detailed as the Old Testament is, it offered a tiny snapshot of God, life, and truth. Jesus Himself is the human-sized photo (and heaven will be another God-sized enlargement). What He said back then is possible now, but only if we make the most of the least.

THERE IS HOPE

God doesn't change, but your understanding of Him does. The more of Him you know, the more your life can grow!

Take turns sharing something about God that you are each personally thankful for.

- **IF** there is one thing all our answers have in common, what is it?
- **WHAT IF** we asked each other a question to get to know something we may not have ever known about each other?

292: Another Kind of Love

***IF** a random person followed you whenever you were outside your house and was critical of whatever you did, what would you do?*

***WHAT IF** this also happened to your entire family each day?*

READ IT: MATTHEW 5:38–48

Hate is a dumb idea that tries to disguise itself by looking smart. Consider how the weapons of war have adapted over the years. First, there was a fist. Then a rock. Soon we swung a club, then a mace, and then a sword.

Next up, we fired an arrow. It gave us the idea for a single bullet, which gave us the idea for many bullets fired at one time. Missiles came along, eventually becoming bombs. Then chemical warfare emerged. Apparently, this is more civilized.

Hopefully you see through all of that, and yet hate may be hiding out somewhere in your life. One way to figure out where is to ask God, "Who or what do I often wish wasn't around?" We have a habit of putting distance between whoever or whatever that is, but we have another opportunity.

Jesus showed us a better way by loving us when we acted like enemies toward Him. As we do to others what Christ has done for us, we show how Christianity is incredibly unique in reaching out to others who push us away, with grace and love from the heart of God. Jesus doesn't mean for us to be doormats for uncaring people to walk over, but to help something incredible happen by walking with them.

When you are frustrated, something violent doesn't need to happen, because something violent already did. Christ died on the cross not only to pay the penalty for all your sin but also for the person who wronged you. So instead of punishing that person, let the punishment Jesus took on Himself matter. Also remember that the Story continues, for just as there was a resurrection for our Hero, so can something come alive again in your relationship with another person.

THERE IS HOPE

Loving your enemies isn't saying that what they did or still do is right. It's saying that God is right about what He says about loving your enemies.

When in life or in a story have you seen the forgiveness or attitude of one person turn an enemy into a friend?

- ***IF*** a cartoon character most represented how you usually express anger, who would that cartoon character be?
- ***WHAT IF*** we committed to memorizing Matthew 5:44 over the next week?

293: Secret Service

***IF** you could have an award named after you, what field would it be in?*

***WHAT IF** you could rename an existing award after someone you know?*

READ IT: MATTHEW 6:1–4; 6:16–18

Those people in dark coats and sunglasses who hang out around the president? They're not just sharp dressers who like looking cool. They're Secret Service agents who protect the first family from danger. You won't always notice them, especially since some hide out in plain sight by dressing like regular people. For years the Secret Service headquarters was also hidden as a common-looking building.

It's rare to learn the name of a Secret Service agent. Agents do their best to make sure the work of the president gets done without spotlighting themselves. That has to be a challenge in the culture we live in, where people are more inclined to only do something if they feel there's something in it for them.

Jesus said some interesting things about how this value plays out in our giving. He didn't say, "If you give . . ." or "If you . . . fast," but "when" we do either, we're to do it so the work of God gets done. When we're regularly giving our finances to the church or giving up a meal to spend that time with God, we do it to grow and not for show.

Ironically, the Lord somehow uses our humble obedience to model to others what this looks like. We don't need to slam-dunk our offering into a collection plate to show others how to do it, but our regular giving keeps a church financially healthy in ways that others notice. The same is true when we are quiet about fasting but later share what we got out of it.

This opportunity keeps our hearts in check, but it also lets our lights shine. Like the Secret Service, our focus ends up being on our Leader versus on ourselves. He'll keep you moving if you keep responding to Him everywhere and anywhere.

THERE IS HOPE

Tithing and fasting help you put God first in manageable ways while prepping your heart to seek Him first in unmanageable moments.

Share about a time you wanted people to notice a good deed you did.

- ***IF*** no one would have said anything, how would that have affected you doing that same good deed again?
- ***WHAT IF*** you were never thanked for any of the good things you did?

294: Weekly Recap

***IF** you had an extra eye anywhere on your body, what would you use it for?*

***WHAT IF** others couldn't see the eye but you saw through it just fine?*

Hallelujah! Praise God in his sanctuary. Praise him in his mighty expanse. Praise him for his powerful acts; praise him for his abundant greatness. Praise him with trumpet blast; praise him with harp and lyre. Praise him with tambourine and dance; praise him with strings and flute. Praise him with resounding cymbals; praise him with clashing cymbals. Let everything that breathes praise the Lord. Hallelujah! (Psalm 150:1–6)

CATCH UP

- Who or what made you laugh recently?
- In what ways did life feel easy or hard this past week?

RECAP

- What stood out to you from what we've read together, talked about, or attempted to do together over the past week?
- What thoughts or questions do you have from today's Bible passage?

GROW TOGETHER

- What might be the main thing God is trying to tell our family today?
- What if we did something new together or returned to a good habit to live out what we're learning? What might that be?

OPEN UP

- In what ways are you struggling in life or experiencing something hard?
- If we were to confess something to God as a family, what might that be?

PRAY

- Who is Jesus to you today?
- Who would be willing to close our time with a simple prayer?

295: How to Pray: Personalize

***IF** your head suddenly got all soft and fuzzy like a cotton ball, what would you do?*

***WHAT IF** over a year this began spreading to the rest of your body, making all of you soft and fuzzy?*

READ IT: MATTHEW 6:5–9; 1 JOHN 3:1–3

"Hi!" "What's up?" "Aloha, y'all" "Whatcha doing?" We use different greetings depending on who we're talking to. Family, friends, or other familiar people likely get casual greetings, while others you don't know as well or who have a position of authority over you get something formal. The way you begin a conversation sets up everything else.

Prayer is having a conversation with God, which means the way we begin our prayer also sets up everything else after that moment. Jesus basically said, "Begin by remembering that you're talking with a Father who loves you." It answers the question, "Why does God want me to pray when He already knows what I'm going to ask?" By remembering that you are taking part in a relationship with someone who loves to do life with you, your prayers can become a natural chat with the Lord.

There is also power in that simple pause, as it can help you think about how you're addressing a God who is capable of incredible things! His power set the universe in motion, landscaped the earth, scattered stars, invented atoms and molecules, ignited the sun, and created human life. Are your prayers as big as He is? Or are they filled with the word *just*—asking Him to "just" do the bare minimum?

Prayer is an opportunity to share your heart with God and let Him share His heart with you. Maybe change a quick "Dear God" to "Lord, You are good and powerful in my life today." The more we personalize our prayers, the more we remember the Person of God.

THERE IS HOPE

For us, prayer is often more about the ask and less about the ongoing relationship. With God, it's often the other way around.

What do you appreciate most about God these days?

- ***IF*** you started out your prayers a little differently, what could you say?
- ***WHAT IF*** the beginning of a prayer isn't just a chance to tell God what you think of Him but also to remember what He thinks of you?

296: How to Pray: Remember

***IF** you could attach your home to any building, what would you attach it to?*

***WHAT IF** someone attached his or her home to yours?*

READ IT: MATTHEW 6:10; JOHN 10:27–30

"What's happening?" That's the question we're always asking on some level. Maybe it's what we wondered as babies while being birthed. What we thought to be "life" ended up being way bigger than we could ever imagine.

What if, while you were inside of your mom, your dad had somehow been able to show up as another baby next to you? It would obviously have made things more cramped (especially for your mom), but let's say this special baby spoke in a way that you understood. He explained about how there was a huge world outside that was bigger than the only space you knew, claiming that what happened out there directly impacted what happened inside your space.

He'd then say, "Sometimes when you feel tapping or hear a muffled voice singing songs your way, it's your father telling you how much he loves you and wants you to know him. He's touching your life even now. In fact, the father and I are 'one'—I'm here with you now, and one day we'll be together in a new way. It starts now."

That's one way to understand what it meant for Jesus to walk the earth and talk about the Father's love. He said His kingdom isn't just something we wait for, but it's something we can take part in even now as we connect with Him. He's likewise given us authority to share about it with others.

The kingdom of heaven isn't just bigger, though. It's also brighter and full of things we didn't know existed. What we call miracles here happen every day in God's kingdom. Remember that; it will change how you view what's happening and what could be happening. It'll impact how you pray and what you pray for.

THERE IS HOPE

Christianity isn't an encounter with concepts, but a pathway to a Person: not a realm of religion, but a King who brings us into a kingdom.

What are some things about life or heaven that you feel you know a lot about versus other things you don't?

- **IF** you could be any person or creature in the world for a day, who or what would you be? What do you think would change about how you view life?
- **WHAT IF** you could be an angel for a day? How would you see life after that?

297: How to Pray: Ask

IF you could send one type of food to any part of the world to feed an entire people group, what food would you send and where?

WHAT IF you were not allowed to get food yourself or ask for it but could only eat if others chose to hand it to you?

READ IT: MATTHEW 6:11–13; 7:7–11

Why does literally every noise sound like a car door when you're waiting for food to be delivered? Your neighbor opens his grill. *"Was that a car?"* A cat scratches the door. *"Was that a car?"* Someone flushes the toilet. *"That was definitely a car."*

When we want something, we talk about it. Think about how you let your family know what you'd like for your birthday. You can drop hints, like, "What a beautiful sunset. I wish I could take a picture of it." Or you can be more obvious by making every other word a clue, like, "What *camera* a *camera* beautiful *camera* sunset *camera*." A more traditional option would be to create a wish list you pass out to anyone who's interested.

Is any of this appropriate, though? It's worth asking, especially since some people don't always want to be told what to get us. You might also feel awkward being gracious with odd presents by saying, "It's the thought that counts" (and it is). Still, it's nice to get something you might actually like.

What if a wish list was meant to do more than get us stuff? Jesus spoke of asking God for our "daily bread" in our prayers. He didn't say to pray for a week's worth, but for what we need today. It's His way of using the moments you turn to Him for something as a way to have a daily relationship with you.

You don't need to drop hints when it comes to God (especially because He knows everything). Trust that every noise He hears from you is a delivery He's waiting for. He loves you and wants you to ask Him about ordinary things and extraordinary things, be it the food you need, strength against temptation, help to forgive someone who's hurt you, or anything else on your heart.

THERE IS HOPE

There are no unanswered prayers. God may not give you what you want, but He always answers. Pray boldly.

When was the last time you asked someone for something important?

- **IF** there were one thing you wished people didn't ask you for or about, what would that be?
- **WHAT IF** God shared His wish list with you? What might be on it?

298: How to Pray: Yield

***IF** your best friend randomly threw whipped cream at your face, what would you say?*

***WHAT IF** you randomly threw whipped cream at others but didn't know why you did?*

READ IT: MATTHEW 6:11–13; 7:7–11

Some things just go together. What would life be like with peanut butter but without jelly? Or chips without salsa? Bacon without eggs? Spaghetti without meatballs? Cookies without milk?

Obviously, these are not the most important things in the world. If they never were put together, we'd get through life just fine. Well, except for if peanut butter and jelly had never paired up. C'mon . . . *it's peanut butter and jelly!*

Jesus said that two big things meant to pair up are being forgiven and forgiving others. Not only are they absolutely incredible together, but they "prove" each other. If you're unwilling to forgive someone who's hurt you (or aren't willing to become willing) then you're not in touch with how God has forgiven you. Likewise, the more you become willing to forgive others, the more you can personally appreciate God's forgiveness. You can't separate the two.

Not fighting the Lord on this (or anything else) is called "yielding." In battle, that word describes one person submitting to the other after being outmatched. With God, we yield by trusting that His way of doing things is genius and good for our lives despite how hard that truth may be. We can also yield in advance, like Christians who pray the Lord's Prayer and end it by saying, "For Yours is the kingdom and the power and the glory forever. Amen."

In teaching us how to pray, Jesus was pointing out that we need to practice with others what we ask for from Him by forgiving others, probably because that leads to yielding in other ways. He's asking that you realize how much He's done for you so you can approach others humbled instead of self-justified. Yielding and forgiving can change the world and your family at the same time. Some things just go together.

THERE IS HOPE

Prayer helps us get to know God and ourselves. He tells us what we're capable of. Yield with a yes!

In what ways is forgiveness one of God's most genius ideas? How does yielding to Him help?

- ***IF*** from now on your best friend would always forgive and forget everything you did, how would you treat him or her?
- ***WHAT IF*** everyone forgave and forgot everything out of respect for what God does for us? How would the world be different?

299: A Tale of Three Dollars

***IF** you had an endless supply of money, what would be the first three things you'd spend it on?*

***WHAT IF** you could only buy three things daily?*

READ IT: MATTHEW 6:19–34

Once upon a time, there were three different dollars that belonged to three different people. Each person saw life differently, not to mention the value of money.

The first person spent his dollar as soon as he got it. He felt an urge to buy the first thing that caught his attention, which was a package of bubble gum. He chewed it right away, blew some bubbles, popped them, and then tossed the container away.

The second person was more careful than the first person and felt it was a better idea to save his dollar. He hid it in a shoebox in the back of a closet, tucking it underneath a pile of blankets. "It'll be safe there," he said.

The third person was also unique in how he treated a dollar. He prayed and said, "God, this is Yours. Thanks for giving it to me to manage. I'm immediately giving You the first 10 percent without question. How would You like me to use the rest?" After personalizing, remembering, asking, and yielding like this, he felt led to go for a walk with a friend who was feeling sad. Along the way, they came across some kids selling lemonade, and he spent the remaining money there. It was a great investment all around.

Which of the three people represents how you tend to spend money that comes your way? What God gives you can be quickly spent, cautiously saved, or generously invested. All three have their place, but it seems like the third way can lead to the other two (while the other two don't always lead to the third). Money will either be how you find a sense of security or become a tool to invest in others and God's kingdom. As Jesus said, we can't serve both. One will always win out.

THERE IS HOPE

It's not money that's evil, but the "love of money" (1 Timothy 6:10). Money is a way to fuel what is important to you and to God.

What is usually the first thing you do when you get money that you've earned or as a gift?

- ***IF*** you were given $1,000 but had to give half to a charity, which would you pick and how would you feel about it?
- ***WHAT IF*** someone you know asked to borrow $100 from you?

300: This Doesn't Look Right

***IF** every gift you received was broken, would you still look forward to gifts?*

***WHAT IF** the doors of your house randomly moved to different places every day? How would that affect you?*

READ IT: MATTHEW 7:1–6, 13–28

Your favorite fast-food restaurant offers different food you can get in no time at all. You're always taking a risk though. Sometimes what you end up getting doesn't match the pictures on the menu. Your bun may come upside down, toppings could be missing, or the whole thing might appear as if someone sat on the food.

It's okay to evaluate the food you see and say, "This doesn't look right." You wouldn't do this by standing up and pointing fingers but by approaching the counter with respect to make the servers aware of the error. In doing so you stand a better chance of seeing things restored to how they were meant to be.

The same is true in life and faith. When someone or something doesn't look healthy or is passing off something flawed as "fine," we can either ignore it or address it. Jesus said the challenge is not to attack the person but instead to address the problem. We can get that wrong just as much as if we ignored things and let whatever is wrong continue.

A common way to say this is that we "hate the sin but love the sinner." For example, if one of your family members fell into a hole, you wouldn't want to hate that family member but you could hate the hole together. As you helped him or her out, you could then work together to fill up the hole so others won't fall in.

Jesus isn't saying that we aren't to evaluate what's wrong. He's saying, "Before you hate someone else's sin, deal with your own sin before God. Once He starts working on you, then go and, with Him, try to restore someone else." When the foundation of our lives is Jesus, others find a place to rest.

THERE IS HOPE

If we do nothing for fear of being judgmental, we make a judgment. If we help someone see a blind spot, we make a breakthrough.

What do you want in a friend when it comes to having that person speak hard truth or encouragement into you?

- ***IF*** I needed to hear one thing from you today, what would it be?
- ***WHAT IF*** you knew people wouldn't be offended if you told them something they needed to hear?

301: Weekly Recap

***IF** you could control the land, wind, and water for ten minutes a day, what would you do with this power?*

***WHAT IF** you could control all this for two hours?*

He got up, rebuked the wind, and said to the sea, "Silence! Be still!" The wind ceased, and there was a great calm. Then he said to them, "Why are you fearful? Do you still have no faith?" And they were terrified and asked one another, "Who then is this? Even the wind and the sea obey him!" (Mark 4:39–41)

CATCH UP

- Who or what made you laugh recently?
- How did life feel easy or hard this past week?

RECAP

- What stood out to you from what we've read together, talked about, or attempted to do together over the past week?
- What thoughts or questions do you have from today's Bible verse?

GROW TOGETHER

- What might be the main thing God is trying to tell our family today?
- What if we did something new together or returned to a good habit to live out what we're learning? What might that be?

OPEN UP

- In what ways are you struggling in life or experiencing something hard?
- If we were to confess something to God as a family, what might that be?

PRAY

- Who is Jesus to you today?
- Who would be willing to close our time with a simple prayer?

302: Add-Ons That Subtract

IF *no one ever worried about fitting in, how would relationships or life be different?*

WHAT IF *everyone worried about fitting in every moment of the day?*

READ IT: JOHN 5:1–15; LUKE 6:1–11

Imagine going with a friend to watch a movie. After sitting down, what if your friend said, "Actually, first we have to do twenty jumping jacks. That makes us more tired so we aren't as tempted to get up in the movie. Cool?" Your friend wouldn't be asking you to do anything evil, but the suggestion is an unnecessary add-on that could keep you from simply enjoying the movie.

The Pharisees, in their attempt to preserve traditions, ended up adding extra rules onto God's pure words. For example, Exodus 20 simply says to keep the Sabbath holy by not working on it. The Pharisees wanted to define in goofy detail what "work" meant, so they said handling food, drinks, ink, or paper of a certain weight counted as "work." They likewise developed rules about how far people could walk on the Sabbath, or if they could lift their children up. Basically, the Pharisees took what was a simple command to bless Israel with rest and created thirty-nine categories (and several sub-categories) about "work" that stressed everyone out.

This is why these religious leaders were upset that Jesus healed a sick man on the Sabbath. All their "add-ons" subtracted from them seeing the miracle before them. We do it too when we create traditions or preferences that we assume are just as important as truth. We can also do the opposite in ignoring some of the clear things God has said.

The Pharisees were know-it-alls who missed it all. It turns out that the blind man saw better than they did spiritually because he was willing to let Jesus change him. If you're willing to get to know Jesus and the purity of God's words for what they are, you're less likely to be confused or distracted too.

THERE IS HOPE

Others can point us to God, but they can never take His place. Use their wisdom for what it is while seeing through what it isn't.

What do you think were some big differences between the Pharisees and Jesus?

- ***IF*** you had a teacher or boss like the Pharisees, how would it feel?
- ***WHAT IF*** someone said you can do whatever you want as a Christian, as if there weren't any values or commands from God?

303: Water and Rest

***IF** people drank lava instead of water (but the lava didn't burn us), how would we get the lava?*

***WHAT IF** lava flowed in the ocean, lakes, rivers, and so on?*

READ IT: MATTHEW 11:28–30; JOHN 7:37–39

A standard marathon is a demanding race that wears your body out over 26.2 miles. Even the strongest athletes need regular water stops of refreshing cold drinks from people along the race route who shout out what they're offering. It's up to the runner to decide who they'll accept help from and whether they'll keep moving as they grab a drink or pause before continuing. A water stop can also sadly become a quitting point for runners who think, *I can't go on.*

The Pharisees told people the only way to succeed in life was to be more religious. When a rabbi offered a way of thinking like this it was called a "yoke" (which was the same word used to describe a piece of wood that hooked two animals together so they could plow a field). The yoke of the Pharisees meant carrying added burdens, but Jesus said His yoke was gentle and freeing. Think of the difference between a person on the sidelines of a race yelling at a tired runner, "You're doing it wrong!" versus another person who says, "Come to me. I have refreshing fuel for you. I'll help you out."

So what does that look like? What Jesus simply offers is Himself. He doesn't tell us "Follow these seven self-help steps" or "Say *'Om'* while you meditate" but offers, *"Come to Me . . . all of you."* He won't take your race away from you but will take away the burden of your sin and give you wisdom to wisely step forward. Your time with Him is meant to be a launching point instead of a quitting point. Some people call Christianity a religion, but it's actually an opportunity for a personal relationship with God that feels like water and rest so we can "run with endurance the race that lies before us, keeping our eyes on Jesus" (Hebrews 12:1–2).

THERE IS HOPE

Life is a run. Press on each day.
Jesus is rest along the way.

How do you like to relax?

- ***IF*** you were to describe one thought that seems to go through your brain most nights before you fall asleep, what would it be?
- ***WHAT IF*** you could physically feel a hug from Jesus right now?

304: This Is Real

***IF** you could see gravity, what do you think it would look like?*

***WHAT IF** you could see all invisible things including the spiritual world?*

READ IT: MATTHEW 12:22–45

Pretend a neighbor friend asks, "Want to go for a bike ride?" You agree, but then your neighbor runs out of his garage riding a tennis racquet. "Ready to go?" he asks, absolutely convinced that this is real bike riding.

For centuries Satan has been getting us to believe his racket of false ideas about life and God. His demons also attack people using fear or deception, mystical beliefs, horror movies, psychics, hypnotists, and more to get us intrigued in the wrong things. Jesus made it clear that nothing can share the same space as Him—either we'll completely receive Him and completely eliminate all the other stuff, or we'll hang onto the other stuff and ultimately reject Him.

Satan's other strategy involves getting us to demand that God prove Himself regularly. basis. Imagine if a friend insisted that we prove our friendship every day! God chooses to inspire people relationally instead of through hocus pocus. Only a few times in the Bible did big miracles happen daily. Jesus doesn't want us chasing miracles but embracing Him.

Yet God also knows that we crave proof, so Jesus did perform miracles. He just didn't comply with every request to do so. Remember this when others give you a hard time about something and say, "Prove it!"—you may not need to prove everything simply because someone demands it.

The fact that God came to earth was the biggest miracle of all. Every miracle He did wasn't to show something that wasn't in this world but to reveal the way the world will one day be. In God's kingdom, there is no sickness, disease, spiritual competition, or hunger. Anything Jesus does is an opportunity for Him to say, "That kingdom I keep telling you about? This is real."

THERE IS HOPE

Evil doesn't win against Jesus. Critics don't win against Jesus. Nothing wins against Jesus. Whose team are you on? JESUS'.

What is a miracle that happens every day that you probably don't think of as a miracle?

- ***IF*** you could see one of Jesus' miracles, which one would you want to see?
- ***WHAT IF*** Jesus asked you to pick a miracle for Him to do for you personally?

305: Simply Incredible Stories

***IF** there were no such thing as TV, videos, or movies, how would that affect how you spend your free time or understand the world?*

***WHAT IF** there were no such thing as apps or texting on mobile devices?*

READ IT: LUKE 8:1–15

There's something special about seeing someone you know on stage. If you've been to a play, game, or ceremony that a friend or family member had a part in, you naturally paid attention to them more than others. Having a personal relationship with someone better tunes you in to what they say or do.

In Jesus' ministry, He used *parables* as a teaching tool. These simple yet amazing stories helped people learn about God's kingdom by comparing it to something they were familiar with. For example, by talking about the ordinary act of planting seeds Jesus helped everyone learn more about what spiritual growth and transformation can look like.

Not everyone was able to understand the parables, though. Those who turned away from having a personal relationship with Jesus probably felt they were dropped into an elementary school play without any connection to the kids on stage. This was one of the points of a particular story Jesus told. Just as a good seed won't penetrate or take root in hard soil, so the wisest wisdom spoken to a closed mind naturally sounds like nonsense.

Every parable had something unexpected that kept people wondering about its meaning. Jesus seemed okay with that, though. He didn't want them to just hear a truth and move on, but to keep thinking about it as a way to turn to Him.

Life is full of ordinary moments packed with extraordinary meaning, and we might skip over them if we're not careful. Jesus told some simply incredible stories to help us realize what we're missing, just as He walked among us to help us realize His love for us. Having a personal relationship with the Lord will better tune you in to what He says or does.

THERE IS HOPE

Jesus uses what we know to point us to what we don't yet know. So, what do you know?

Share what your favorite children's book is and why.

- ***IF*** everyone who was important to you had their own books written about them, what might people learn about you through those stories?
- ***WHAT IF*** there was a children's book that summed up your life? What would you hope that book would be like or describe about you?

306: Meaningful Sacrifice

***IF** you could turn any food to a different food or any drink into a different drink, what would you transform?*

***WHAT IF** you could turn anything into a food or drink?*

READ IT: MATTHEW 14:1–21

Would you rather sit in a recliner or go for a motorcycle ride? Go for a walk or go rock climbing? Order from a familiar restaurant or have someone bring you strange new food from a place you've never eaten before?

We crave safety, yet at the same time we're driven to take risks. It's contagious too. When people make meaningful sacrifices with each other, trust grows. Maybe you've seen or experienced a "trust fall" where one person willingly falls backward to be caught by others who care about that person.

John the Baptist lived a life of meaningful sacrifice for God. His death was sadly brutal, as it seems like his life was in the hands of a group of people who *didn't* care about him. In reality, his life was always in God's hands. The Lord welcomed John into eternity because the end of his life on earth wasn't the end of his story.

We get a picture of this as Jesus, right after John's death, took a small amount of food and miraculously multiplied it to feed thousands of people. Maybe it's not by accident that these two events are connected. As Jesus later said, "Unless a grain of wheat falls to the ground and dies, it remains by itself. But if it dies, it produces a large crop" (John 12:24).

Being a Christian doesn't mean life on earth will be comfortable. After all, Jesus was the ultimate "good person" yet had the ultimate evil done to Him. Yet here we are today blessed from His meaningful sacrifice. You have the daily opportunity to put your life in His hands and know that He's there for you. Give Him whatever you have and watch Him multiply the impact of your life to impact more people than you can count.

THERE IS HOPE

Suffering can cease to be suffering if it finds meaning. In that moment, suffering becomes sacrifice.

Who in the last week has made a meaningful sacrifice for you?

- ***IF*** you counted up all the sacrifices someone made for you yesterday, how many would that be total?
- ***WHAT IF*** you believed that your life really will impact thousands of people?

307: Sink or Swim?

***IF** you could fall from any height and not get hurt, how would you live differently?*

***WHAT IF** anyone you were touching during a fall also wouldn't get hurt?*

READ IT: MATTHEW 14:22–36

It's happening all the time. It never stops, even if you miss it. You are constantly talking to yourself. If you disagree, guess what? You just talked with yourself to consider if it was true!

This "little voice inside your head" combines with your feelings and experiences into what's commonly called "intuition." It kicks in when you're considering a decision and feel an urge in a particular direction without knowing why. This may seem helpful, but all intuition is flawed because it's based on human experience, ideas, hurts, and more.

You see, we either live by fear or faith. Fear is a made-up story we tell ourselves is true, while faith is a story based on truth. If we fear ending up alone, we complain now as if we've already ended up alone; if we fear losing a position, we panic now as if we've already lost it; if we fear failure, we get depressed now as if we've already failed. The only way to get rid of untrue stories in your head is to embrace a true one in faith.

Eleven of the twelve disciples had the intuition that they were going to die, and so fear took over for them. The only one who had faith was Peter. We can focus on how he eventually sank, or on how he had the trust to get out of the boat. He did end up with more steps walking on water than the other disciples did.

So it seems we have a third option other than "sink or swim." We can "step" by following Jesus across whatever waves we face. Life can be frightening, so invite Jesus to lead you beyond the emotions and reset your intuition. There's always a third possibility when He's involved.

THERE IS HOPE

No matter how deep you feel you're sinking, God is speaking. His whispers can lead you through the world's loudest screams and shouts.

When did a risk you took in the past turn out well for you?

- ***IF*** you knew someone afraid to take a risk, what advice would you offer?
- ***WHAT IF*** you weren't ever afraid of what Jesus asked you to do?

308: Weekly Recap

***IF** you found a large diamond out in the street, what would you do?*

***WHAT IF** you found an old abandoned diamond mine?*

When Jesus came to the region of Caesarea Philippi, he asked his disciples, "Who do people say that the Son of Man is?" And they said, "Some say John the Baptist; others, Elijah; still others, Jeremiah or one of the prophets.""But you," he asked them, "who do you say that I am?"Simon Peter answered, "You are the Messiah, the Son of the living God." (Matthew 16:13–16)

CATCH UP

- Who or what made you laugh recently?
- How did life feel easy or hard this past week?

RECAP

- What stood out to you from what we've read together, talked about, or attempted to do together over the past week?
- What thoughts or questions do you have from today's Bible verse?

GROW TOGETHER

- What might be the main thing God is trying to tell our family today?
- What if we did something new together or returned to a good habit to live out what we're learning? What might that be?

OPEN UP

- In what ways are you struggling in life or experiencing something hard?
- If we were to confess something to God as a family, what might that be?

PRAY

- Who is Jesus to you today?
- Who would be willing to close our time with a simple prayer?

309: The Stranger We All Know

***IF** cats had to live in fishbowls with water like fish, what do you think would happen?*

***WHAT IF** the homes we lived in all were like fishbowls where people could look at us anytime they wanted to?*

READ IT: MATTHEW 17:1–13

People can always do or say something that surprises you no matter how long you've been friends. Maybe one day you learned a story about them that you never knew. Or perhaps you finally heard them pronounce "nuclear" and "coupon" and thought, *Really?*

Jesus regularly surprised people who thought they knew Him too. Sometimes it was because of what He said or did, but usually it came down to who He was with them. The shock and wonder inspired some people to know Him (and eternal life) personally, while others walked off in frustration.

The Transfiguration was one of these surprising moments for three of His disciples. Jesus became so bright in appearance that He was difficult to look at (like staring at the sun). It revealed who He is on the inside, like Superman busting through in full power under Clark Kent's disguise. It was like this miracle was a window that showed Jesus' divinity before anyone else was allowed to see it.

So in one moment, Jesus seemed like a stranger to His disciples because they didn't know what to do in the presence of a Jesus beyond their understanding. Peter ended up saying something like, "This is awesome! How about we just keep things like this and live here?" It turns out that this is a fitting response; it shows us how incredible and exciting it'll be in heaven to be around Christ.

Jesus displaying His full glory should blow our minds—not just because of who He is but who we are in light of Him. Colossians 2:9–10 says, "For the entire fullness of God's nature dwells bodily in Christ, and you have been filled by him." With Jesus fully in you, so much wonder has yet to be fully revealed in your life!

THERE IS HOPE

Jesus is absolutely a friend to us and will show Himself in ordinary ways. Don't ever forget how "more than ordinary" He is, though.

When has something a friend or family member did stood out to you, surprised you, or inspired you?

- ***IF*** you were constantly surprised by others every day, how would it feel?
- ***WHAT IF*** your relationship with Jesus was filled with big surprises every day?

310: Do-Overs

***IF** your watch let you travel back in time to redo any moment you set it to, how would you use it?*

***WHAT IF** everyone had a watch like this?*

READ IT: MATTHEW 18:1–3, 15–35

Around your home, there's probably a right way to do certain things depending on who you talk to. One person may believe hot dogs should be stored in a freezer while others want them in the fridge. You'll hear differences about how the lawn should be mowed based on who's doing it. Sometimes the littlest things can divide us.

Jesus said that the littlest things can also unite us. In today's verse He's talking about "do-overs." When games or life don't go as kids plan, they just start over with the same people and situation to reclaim whatever moment went sideways.

When we feel offended by someone who has sinned against us or get divided on small things, we remember that people are more important than pride (despite how we may make pride more important than people). Kids get it, though—it's better to jump back into an adventure together than lose a friend over a weird moment.

A do-over says that what's happened doesn't define the relationship from this point forward. Anger is allowed, but in our anger we don't sin. Instead, Jesus helps us to look at another person and not let what they did wrong be the first thing we think of. Some things don't need to matter. Every human being needs do-overs, and we have the opportunity to help each other claim them.

THERE IS HOPE

Like getting do-overs? Give them. Give them quickly and often. Others need to see what they look like so they know how to pass one your way.

How did Jesus tell us to confront people who sin? What are the steps?

- ***IF*** you didn't feel like doing these steps, what would change (if anything) between you and that person?
- ***WHAT IF*** you followed these steps whether or not they always "worked"?

311: Do You See What I See?

***IF** you could change what a holiday was known for, what would you change?*

***WHAT IF** you could make your own holiday that people would celebrate worldwide?*

READ IT: JOHN 7:53–8:11

Some days a whole lot of people may roll their eyes at you, or someone in authority will make your life hard. It's as if they can't see any other option.

Jesus experienced this from certain officials who tried to make Him look bad. They once found two people caught in a sexual sin and brought the woman out to be humiliated. This was less about her and more about them trying to trap Jesus. If He said that she should be punished according to the Old Testament laws, then people would think He wasn't loving; but if He didn't acknowledge the laws, the Pharisees could say He was a false teacher.

As always, Jesus stepped forward into what appeared to be a no-win situation. He first did it by pausing and writing in the sand. No one knows why He did this or what He wrote, but it showed that the Pharisees weren't in control of the moment. Remember that the next time someone bullies you into a quick response; you can take your time to respond.

When Jesus did speak again it was to ask that they hold themselves to the same standards of being sinless that they wanted to hold the woman to. The Pharisees became stuck in their own trap and walked off while Jesus remained behind. He was the only sinless person who could have condemned the woman but instead offered grace and told her not to purposefully sin again. He did this not by calling her bad names, but through decency.

Some people give you the benefit of the doubt. Others try to benefit by doubting you. Nothing anyone says to you matters more than what Jesus says to you. He sees our faults but is more interested in our potential. What if as His followers we were known for that too? Do you see what He sees?

THERE IS HOPE

If someone is upset with you, hope that it's for the same reasons people got upset with Jesus.

Would you have said anything else to the woman, the people watching, or the Pharisees?

- ***IF*** there is one life-giving thing a friend of yours needs to hear, what is it (and do you think God wants you to share it)?
- ***WHAT IF*** a friend told you something life-giving? What might it be?

312: Party Time

***IF** you could throw a million-dollar party to celebrate anything, what would you celebrate?*

***WHAT IF** you could choose ten people from history to attend your party?*

READ IT: LUKE 15:1–32

After a major sporting event like the World Cup, Super Bowl, or World Series, it's a special time for all the players and fans who were gripped by the competition. Strangers end up giving each other hugs and high-fives. Fans who were cautious to believe their team would pull it off end up dancing in the street together. Neighbors run out of their homes to cheer and set off fireworks while soaking in the moment. Clearly, it's party time.

Jesus said that situations like these are a small glimpse of what happens when a lost person gets saved and enters into the kingdom of God. The three stories He told are about someone who had given up all hope but found out that it wasn't the end of the story. The lost sheep may have gotten eaten by wolves before the shepherd found it; the lost coin may have rolled into a deep crack never to be found; the lost son may have figured he'd gone too far for his dad to take him back. But in each situation, each was found—and a celebration took place.

God wants us to know that there is always hope, for it's not just the winners who get to celebrate. Heaven isn't just for one group of people but for *anyone* who confesses their sin and trusts in Jesus to save them. It would be a shame for people to try to be good their whole lives and feel like all their hard work and enthusiasm came up short in the end. That doesn't have to happen, for in Christ outsiders are invited to become insiders and losers can become winners. Clearly, it's party time.

THERE IS HOPE

Your imperfection doesn't change God's affection. Through reflection, change direction to feel His connection, protection, and resurrection.

When have you found something you thought was lost forever?

- ***IF*** you could find something someone else lost, what would it be?
- ***WHAT IF*** this week you helped a spiritually lost person find Jesus?

313: Friends for Life

***IF** you could instantly fall asleep, what would change about your nighttime routine?*

***WHAT IF** you could make others fall asleep or wake up instantly?*

READ IT: JOHN 11:1–7, 17–44

If Jesus was on social media, what would His friend list look like? Picture your name being on it—not because you sent Him a request but because He sent one to you. He would regularly read your updates, comment on your photos, laugh along with the good things you laugh at, and affirm the mission He gave you. How would that feel?

Mary, Martha, and Lazarus were good friends with Jesus. Picture what that would've been like back then or even today. You'd be tight with one of the most famous miracle workers around, and thousands of people followed Him. You'd think that if a loved one was sick He'd be up for doing you a solid favor.

Only Jesus didn't do that miracle of healing for Mary, Martha, and Lazarus. He took His time coming so that by the time He arrived Lazarus was officially dead and in the tomb for four days. The Lord was up to a more significant miracle to reveal His authority over death, but it made Mary and Martha sad and frustrated. We may feel the same way when God does something larger or more confusing than the miracle we ask for.

Before you think that's the end of the story and you're just supposed to deal with it, consider the shortest verse in the Bible. John 11:35 lets us know that "Jesus wept." Despite knowing the big picture and His plan to resurrect His friend Lazarus, Jesus took the opportunity to grieve. Sure, He doesn't just give resurrection and life, but is the Resurrection and the Life. Yet He let His heart break for the loss of His friend.

Never doubt God's heart. Those who saw what Jesus did for Lazarus still had to choose to believe. Jesus isn't just a friend during life; He's a friend *for* life—eternal life.

THERE IS HOPE

Jesus doesn't make everything feel right: He makes everything begin to become right, be it on this side of life or in eternity.

What can we learn from this about how to face death or help the people we care about face death?

- ***IF*** Jesus takes the time to weep when He's sad, what does that mean for you?
- ***WHAT IF*** what we studied today is meant to prepare us for some time in the future when we will face a tough loss? What should we remember most?

314: Bucket Lists

***IF** you lost a friend because money came between you somehow, how would you feel?*

***WHAT IF** a year later your friend came back and gave you a thousand dollars?*

READ IT: LUKE 19:1–10

Ever heard of a bucket list? It's all the things you hope to do before you die, be it skydiving, driving a Porsche, or a really important goal like "eat five whole burritos in one sitting." Although a bucket list acknowledges death, it's more about what you'll do with your life.

As Jesus journeyed toward Jerusalem where He'd spend His last days before dying, He stopped in the town of Jericho. Perhaps "one more transformation" was on His bucket list, for He connected with a wealthy Jewish man named Zacchaeus who served as a chief tax collector for Rome. This job made Zacchaeus unpopular, since he could use Roman soldiers to take money from people. For all his wealth and power, though, Zacchaeus needed to see Jesus.

Many people were pleasantly surprised that evening when the infamous tax collector started handing out money. He determined to pay back four times the original amount of what he'd cheated anyone out of. There's no record of Jesus telling Zacchaeus to do any of this, but clearly the man was changed after spending time with the Lord. It's a great reminder that no one is a lost cause.

Experiencing grace doesn't mean we don't make something right that's been wrong. It's one thing to say you're sorry and another thing to start fixing things. Zacchaeus took it further by being generous instead of only paying back what was expected.

People will sense your faith through your actions. As Zacchaeus blessed others, Jesus made it clear that it was because salvation had happened. Perhaps it's easier to write someone off or try to forget about what's owed, but making amends is an opportunity to give a relationship a future. Put that on your bucket list.

THERE IS HOPE

Jesus doesn't just want you to be sorry. He helps you to be changed.

What might it mean to make things right with someone you've said something about or taken from in the past?

- ***IF*** Jesus seeks out people who make mistakes, what does that mean for us?
- ***WHAT IF*** we created a family "bucket list" together?

315: Weekly Recap

***IF** there was a real town where cartoon characters lived and did all the things you see them do on TV, would you want to visit it?*

***WHAT IF** when you crossed into that town you became a cartoon character?*

One of the scribes approached. . . . he asked him, "Which command is the most important of all?" Jesus answered, "The most important is, 'Listen, Israel! The Lord our God, the Lord is one. Love the Lord your God with all your heart, with all your soul, with all your mind, and with all your strength.'" (Mark 12:28–30)

CATCH UP

- Who or what made you laugh recently?
- How did life feel easy or hard this past week?

RECAP

- What stood out to you from what we've read together, talked about, or attempted to do together over the past week?
- What thoughts or questions do you have from today's Bible verse?

GROW TOGETHER

- What might be the main thing God is trying to tell our family today?
- What if we did something new together or returned to a good habit to live out what we're learning? What might that be?

OPEN UP

- In what ways are you struggling in life or experiencing something hard?
- If we were to confess something to God as a family, what might that be?

PRAY

- Who is Jesus to you today?
- Who would be willing to close our time with a simple prayer?

THERE IS HOPE

PURPOSE

Part of being human means wondering about the point of life and your role in it. You started warming up to this the first time you asked an adult, "Why?" You may have thought it was just about trying to understand the reason something was the way it was, but it was actually your first of many steps in realizing you have a choice in how you respond to everything you're presented with. Whether or not we take ownership of a value or task someone else tries to hand us is one huge way we begin to discover our purpose.

There have also been moments in your life when you've had to figure out what to do with things that seemed meaningless. As you felt like you wasted your time on a situation or took a certain subject in school that didn't seem like it had any practical value for your life, you again asked, "Why?" That one-word question this time wasn't about understanding how something worked, but whether you were going to invest any work into it.

God doesn't want to leave you hanging on this. Jesus spoke about His purpose and ours before He died and later again as He rose. That's something you don't want to skip over, by the way. Anyone who can predict His own death and resurrection and pull it off is worth paying special attention to.

So ask your questions about why things are the way they are or why you're considering doing something. One of God's greatest gifts is allowing us not to live life merely for ourselves but for something greater. Asking big questions can lead us to big answers.

Just as Jesus had a purpose of transformation on earth, so has He given us the purpose of being His church and transforming the entire world.

316: Jesus Christ Superstar

***IF** rocks could talk, what do you think they would say?*

***WHAT IF** rocks could also move around and were eager to help you in any way?*

READ IT: LUKE 19:28–44

At the beginning of rock concerts an emcee gets everyone excited with a few rounds of saying "Make some noise!" and "I can't hear you!" Soon the crowd is screaming *"WOO!"* without really knowing what *"WOO!"* means. Finally the superstar comes up on stage and has everyone's attention.

Companies try to get us excited for their products too. We may not run through a grocery store shouting *"WOO!"* over ramen noodles, but we do hope for a good experience with what we buy.

We're regularly at risk of treating Jesus the same way. We'll want Him to pump us up with *"WOO!"*-level excitement or guarantee that if we buy whatever He's selling that we'll have a good experience. This could have been the situation when Christ made His way into Jerusalem and crowds of people cheered for Him (something Zechariah 9:9 had spoken about centuries earlier, down to the colt Jesus rode).

Like any celebrity or product, there's more to Jesus than what we've been exposed to. He's not a mere celebrity, nor is He a product. He certainly deserves red-carpet treatment like when the Jews shouted "Hosanna!" (perhaps without some people really knowing what "Hosanna" meant—a phrase that used to mean "Save me!" but came to mean "Salvation has come!"). Except Jesus wasn't entering in to do what they expected Him to do. The Jewish people wanted Him to overthrow Rome, but He came to overthrow sin.

Be careful not to turn Jesus Christ into a superstar you only cheer for in excitement. He is Lord and deserves our praise, but also our commitment, especially when His larger purpose doesn't equal what you expect. Follow Him with purpose.

THERE IS HOPE

God will enter into places where people cheer for Him, but also places where people misunderstand and eventually reject Him.

What affects the level of passion you're willing to have for God?

- ***IF*** we only supported each other as a family when we were excited or feeling at our absolute best, what would life around our house be like?
- ***WHAT IF*** we consider how Jesus knew He was going to be betrayed yet went into the city anyway? What can we learn from Him about commitment?

317: Politically Correct

***IF** every Tuesday the government came to take your fifth favorite item, how would you change what you owned or bought?*

***WHAT IF** the government always took your top favorite item (not including living things or your home)?*

READ IT: MARK 12:13–34

Is it okay for Christians to salute their country's flag? What about running for an office in government? Is it possible to say the Pledge of Allegiance without it becoming more important than our pledge to follow Jesus? Should a church have a flag in its building?

Welcome to faith and politics. There are various hot topics, like valuing unborn children who are alive in pregnant mothers, or taking care of the poor who have no access to food, shelter, or medicine. Each can cause intense disagreements among people of faith who value everything and everyone differently.

Jesus spoke a parable to the Pharisees to show them what was happening in their hearts. Jewish listeners knew that a vineyard was a symbol of Israel and that those in the story who were in charge of it were like the religious leaders. The way they treated the vineyard and the vineyard owner's son was Christ pointing out how they would one day kill Him to hold onto the power and authority they thought was theirs.

Angered by this, they tried to trick Jesus with a political hot topic. He didn't have an issue talking about these matters, and instead of arguing as a critic or patriot He spoke from the soul. His answer brilliantly left more people thinking than clapping.

Wouldn't it be great if that's how we took part in politics? Some people will try to win your vote by saying what's popular, while others will try to cast you aside by narrowing our faith down to one stance on one topic. Every issue in the world is a way of seeking God's heart and trying to reflect it. When you don't know what to say (or are about to just say what you always say), pause to put your hope in Jesus and share the larger story.

THERE IS HOPE

Whoever our "Caesar" is these days, Jesus is still on the throne and the government is still on His shoulders.

What do you think about some of the political topics mentioned or other ones not mentioned?

- ***IF*** you knew something was a trick question, would you answer it?
- ***WHAT IF*** every question was a chance to ask a better question in response?

318: The Royal Treatment

***IF** you had a device that let you instantly sort things into any categories you wanted, what would you use it for?*

***WHAT IF** the sorting ended up being a system that only you understood?*

READ IT: MATTHEW 25:31–46

You can call it "being spoiled" or "getting the royal treatment." It's when others go out of their way to make you extra special, like being a dinner guest of someone who makes sure you and your family feel all kinds of consideration in the food, activities, and the time that were offered.

Remember someone behind one of these good, cared-for experiences in your life. Maybe you get to drink a homemade smoothie, ride a horse around a farm, or watch a fun movie on someone's big screen. As you remember, pay attention to how you feel about that person. You've probably sorted them out to be someone special you'd want to bless back.

God is not that different; He sees all the things we do or don't do for others. Just like you have warm affection for those who are kind and loving to your family, He is looking to be warm and affectionate toward anyone who cares for those He cares about (which is everyone in the world). He also sorts out those of us who do nothing and allow the mistreated or poor to stay stuck in their mistreatment and poverty.

Part of our purpose in life is to help those who are in need. Donating money is great, but God is looking for real care that lifts others up. The little things are the big things, for we do to Him what we do to His family.

As you're sorting out your life, pay attention to the lives of others. No human being on this planet is meant to be just "scenery" to you. Give someone the royal treatment they deserve as a fellow child of the King.

THERE IS HOPE

Helping others see what God sees in them is one way God helps you sort out what He sees in you.

Why might Jesus want us not just to believe in Him but actually to live out our faith? What's on the line?

- ***IF*** you could share one truth from the Bible with a friend, what would it be?
- ***WHAT IF*** your life is meant to tell that truth to your friend in how you live?

319: Food for Thought

***IF** every food was crunchy, would the foods you like change?*

***WHAT IF** every liquid was also crunchy?*

READ IT: MARK 14:10–31; JOHN 13:1–15

Why does food bring people together? Sure, the stuff is great (even when it isn't), but there's more to it. Some of the best belly laughs, passionate thoughts, deepest gratitude, and most powerful breakthroughs have taken place around a plate. It's also where we work through misunderstandings, because eating keeps us sitting together long enough to work it out. Meals offer "food for thought" one way or another.

Now put yourself around the table with Jesus at His last supper before He was arrested and led to die on the cross. Just like around meals in your home, not everyone understood the conversation (and maybe some weren't fully paying attention). He used the bread and cup from the Passover meal to help them get a sense of how He would sacrifice His body and blood for our sin. Still, not everyone understood it.

So Jesus washed the disciples' feet. People have for centuries guessed about why He did this, but the Lord made it clear that it was so they'd know He loved them in a way that would endure beyond any misunderstanding. Days later as the disciples sat down after denying or running away from Jesus, they likely slumped over in embarrassment (as we all do) with their hands on their heads. In that position, they'd naturally see their feet—the very feet Jesus washed to let them know He loved them. What He did at dinner gave them "food for thought" in the future.

Countless people need to know in advance that when they blow it they're still loved. Remind them of this over a meal where you can naturally bring up what they mean to you. You don't need to literally wash their feet afterward, but humbly serving them or giving a considerate gift can start that message.

THERE IS HOPE

Jesus said heaven is like a banquet (Matthew 22). God enjoys putting together feasts of food for us where He does the catering and hosting.

What do you think it would be like to eat a meal with Jesus? What would you talk about?

- ***IF*** you could have Jesus prepare any meal for you, what would you choose?
- ***WHAT IF*** you could prepare a meal for Him?

320: Friendly Fire

***IF** you had a robot who looked like and acted like anyone you chose, who would you choose?*

***WHAT IF** the robot wasn't completely loyal to you?*

READ IT: MATTHEW 26:36–56

Part sport, part fun, part war, part fashion show (when it's over). We're talking about paintball. It's a completely unpredictable activity of advancing, waiting, and diving for cover. There's also the matter of friendly fire when someone on your team shoots at you, thinking you're the enemy. When it happens you may have to take the hit and walk off the field that round.

On the night Jesus was arrested, He had plenty of friendly fire to deal with. Judas, one of the twelve disciples, led a mob to seize Christ. In this moment Jesus said one of the more frightening words for us to hear as His followers. He called Judas a "friend."

Stay there a moment. Have you ever considered yourself "a friend of God"? Does that mean you're at all like Judas? What about friendly fire—have you ever taken a shot at God, thinking He's the enemy? Just as Jesus took the hit from Judas and walked off the field for that round, He may let you attack Him without firing back.

It's a wakeup call that any of us could be like Judas when we'd rather use Jesus for our own purposes than follow Him for His purposes. Or maybe we're like Peter, who attacked a soldier thinking that's what Jesus wanted, only to then watch Jesus heal the wounded man. We do this today when we use the Bible to attack others and discover Jesus wants to *transform* others.

You may not always know what Jesus is specifically asking of you, but He's always looking to do life with you and through you. Being His friend does mean some days we'll get it wrong, but it also means that many days we can get things right. Even better, we can help others get right with Jesus and call Him a friend too.

THERE IS HOPE

This is how friendship is defined: Jesus, the night He was to be betrayed, knelt down and washed all His disciples' feet, including the feet of Judas.

How would you describe what Jesus is to you: familiar acquaintance, casual buddy, good friend, or something else?

- **IF** a close friend betrayed you, would you be up for the friendship continuing?
- **WHAT IF** we told Jesus right now in a family prayer what we like about Him?

321: Challenge Accepted

***IF** you could create a new form of organic life, what would it be like?*

***WHAT IF** you had to create another form of organic life to feed it?*

READ IT: JOHN 19:16–37

This may be the hardest devo for you to read. Challenge accepted? The problem is you've already heard about the cross of Christ. You may be so familiar with the fact that Jesus died for you that you overlook how special this is.

To add to the challenge, the big day we celebrate it is called "Good Friday." We might wonder, "How can a day of such sadness be *good*?" The answer is that Jesus is involved and turns it into something more. His death brings about tears but can also inspire real joy and newfound freedom from sin.

Think about Jesus' death another way—like that of an organ donor. When someone's body parts save the lives of other sick people, there can be both heartache and happiness from the same thing. The big difference is Jesus didn't just save a few lives by donating His kidneys or liver but offered all of Himself to save us from sin.

The greatest miracle that day may have been that His death didn't look like a miracle. Instead of legions of angels swooping in to rescue Jesus, they watched Him rescue us. Instead of the Father snubbing us for how we snubbed Him, He subbed His one and only Son in our place. Instead of Christ skipping over the pain and jumping into the resurrection, He walked through the pain to prove He'll walk with us through whatever we face. Instead of Jesus dying for only certain people, He died for all (including the ones who literally killed Him). Check out 2 Corinthians 5:15; Hebrews 2:9; 1 John 2:2.

How amazing is Jesus' love? Through His sacrifice, any further sacrifices were no longer needed. Through His death, any further death was no longer the end. He saw our need for a Savior and said, "Challenge accepted."

THERE IS HOPE

The cross answers the question, "Does God love me?" Jesus is dying to let you know how much you matter to Him!

What's a story you remember about a scar you have or a time you got hurt?

- **IF** people who didn't know you looked at you to try to figure out the kind of person you are, what might they guess?
- **WHAT IF** you knew nothing about Jesus but saw Him on the cross? What would you guess about Him just from sight alone?

322: Weekly Recap

IF your blood could cure cancer, what would you do?

WHAT IF others found out and forced you to sit in a hospital each day to give blood?

"Do not let your hearts be troubled. Believe in God; believe also in me. In my Father's house are many rooms; if not, I would have told you. I am going away to prepare a place for you." (John 14:1–2)

CATCH UP

- Who or what made you laugh recently?
- How did life feel easy or hard this past week?

RECAP

- What stood out to you from what we've read together, talked about, or attempted to do together over the past week?
- What thoughts or questions do you have from today's Bible verse?

GROW TOGETHER

- What might be the main thing God is trying to tell our family today?
- What if we did something new together or returned to a good habit to live out what we're learning? What might that be?

OPEN UP

- In what ways are you struggling in life or experiencing something hard?
- If we were to confess something to God as a family, what might that be?

PRAY

- Who is Jesus to you today?
- Who would be willing to close our time with a simple prayer?

323: Yes! Yes! Yes!

***IF** you could add a holiday to the calendar, what would it be or celebrate?*

***WHAT IF** you could eliminate a holiday?*

READ IT: JOHN 20:1–31

Without checking any nearby device, what's today's complete date? Go ahead and say it out loud. Then say your complete birth date. Then say as many important dates from history as you can in twenty seconds.

One huge thing all these dates have in common is each reflects the reality of Jesus! Every time we say or reference a year we note that it's been around that long since Christ walked the earth. Unlike other people who claimed to be God, He came back from death to prove He is who He said He is. *YES! YES! YES!*

So why does Easter for some people end up being about biting the ears off chocolate bunnies or wearing fancy clothes to church? We can be like people who encountered the resurrection back when it happened:

- *Those who dismiss Jesus:* People who think they've seen enough of Him and nothing else is worth seeing.
- *Those who like Jesus:* Anyone who cheers for Him in holiday moments but adds, "Don't expect much more than that."
- *Those who follow Jesus:* Real-deal believers who are Christ-centered and outward-focused.

The resurrection isn't just something that happened but is something that is still *happening*. Jesus is just as much alive today, and he makes little "resurrections" happen in us and around us. If you're sad about something like Mary was, the resurrection says you aren't stuck there anymore. If you've run from Jesus and felt like that was the end of the relationship, notice Jesus pursuing you with life. Individuals, marriages, families, churches, and communities can all get a fresh start! What are you waiting for? Resurrection awaits! Spread the Word! *YES! YES! YES!*

THERE IS HOPE

Jesus Christ makes hope, second-chances, and eternity touchable.

What does the resurrection mean to you personally?

- **IF** you saw Jesus alive back then, what would be the first thing you'd say?
- **WHAT IF** something in your life you think God is done with is something He isn't yet done with? What might that be?

324: Peek-A-Boo

***IF** you had to explain why you did something you did an hour ago, what did you do and why did you do it?*

***WHAT IF** that reason was the reason why you did everything?*

READ IT: LUKE 24:13–35

Ever been jealous of people in the first century? They saw Jesus walk the earth as He taught, healed, cared, and more. They watched our unpredictable Hero bend down to serve, flip over what people believed, challenge the judgmental, and slow down to give anyone hurting real hope. They may have even heard Him crack a joke or make funny noises with His lips that caused kids to giggle.

Centuries later, we act like we don't know how to find Jesus. Sometimes, like the men on the road, we're temporarily prevented from seeing Him, yet moments later we realize He was with us all along. It usually happens when we're so busy being frustrated with God for not answering our questions that we fail to hear Him offering answers to questions we haven't yet asked.

People in the first century would likely be jealous of how we have the living words of God written down and collected for anyone to read. We are always one reach away from powerful truths that invite Jesus to speak into our lives from every direction. We don't have to wait for Him to walk into our town on tour, but can be as inspired reading about His resurrection as they were while seeing it.

Maybe it's not God who's playing peek-a-boo with us. Maybe we're the ones who play peek-a-boo with Him.

How giddy do you think Jesus was as He ate bread with the two men at dinner right as they realized it was Him? How giddy is He to create miracles of changed lives, households, careers, education, free time, issues, beliefs, and everything else today? It's amazing to consider how it's still possible to come next to Jesus, and how Jesus still comes next to us too.

THERE IS HOPE

Whether you notice God or not, He's there and notices you.

How many times this week do you think you've been in a big moment with God without realizing it?

- ***IF*** you were stuck on an island for thirty years and could have either a one-time hug from someone or a letter from them, which would you pick?
- ***WHAT IF*** reading the letter somehow felt like a hug from that person?

325: Point of Entry

***IF** you could instantly be anywhere right now, where would that be?*

***WHAT IF** you had to pay money to take regular transportation back?*

READ IT: JOHN 20:19–31

If a baby hands you a rubber phone, you "answer it." If a toddler makes you a meal out of plastic fruit, you "eat it." These moments are each a point of entry into a relationship with a person; by playing together in real life you figure out what is in that person's mind. If someone else walked in on you, they wouldn't have the context you'd gained.

Thomas struggled when he didn't see Jesus resurrected like the other disciples did. Since the moment had come and gone, he questioned the experience. This wasn't imaginary play, though. It really happened. So Thomas basically said, "I'd like to believe that, but it feels like my only option is to see it for myself."

Can you relate? Sometimes we miss what happens at church and can't connect to what people describe God did. Other times when we haven't felt a breakthrough with Jesus we start making arguments against Him.

Thomas has famously been labeled a doubter despite having incredible moments of faith. He had said it was good to go with Jesus to see Lazarus's funeral despite the threat of being attacked along the way by critics (John 11:1–6). His questions also prompted Jesus to declare, "I am the way, the truth, and the life. No one comes to the Father except through me" (John 14:6).

Thomas had it in him to trust what he couldn't see, but perhaps his sadness got in the way of seeing what was possible. When the daily grind wears us down, we can feel the same way—as if there is no point of entry to see Jesus like we once did or others have.

When Jesus did appear to Thomas, He added that the best point of entry is through faith in Him. The true stories others tell about Him help us claim it when we realize God does way more than what our eyes can see.

THERE IS HOPE

God speaks to you personally and through His community. You can't be everywhere, but He is. Track Him somewhere.

Have you ever grown your faith in something by pushing through a big doubt?

- ***IF*** you missed out on seeing Jesus as Thomas did, what would you say?
- ***WHAT IF*** everyone you know doubts the next big thing God does in your life?

326: Grow and Go

***IF** you suddenly woke up and there was an extra level to your home, what would be your first three reactions?*

***WHAT IF** you discovered a homeless person living in that extra level?*

READ IT: MATTHEW 28:16–20

You know one of the hardest problems for Christians? Helping people know we actually follow a risen Savior and aren't just moral or spiritual people. "I heard you were religious," they may say, minimizing it all.

The disciples who saw the risen Jesus had minimizers around them too. Even they wondered, "How did this just happen?" How inspiring that the Bible doesn't ignore this but records it. Remember, questions help you take ownership of something so you can share it with others. It's a "grow and go" mentality that supports what Jesus said in Matthew 28:

- *Authority exists, and Jesus has it.* You can enter into any situation where others seem to be in control knowing that they ultimately aren't.
- *Go!* It's up to us to make the next move that lets others experience God through us. We give them reasons to say yes.
- *Make disciples who make disciples.* Move past just getting people to say a salvation prayer by helping others follow the Lord daily.
- *Teach them everything.* Like Jesus, we receive people where they are and speak truth that guides them out of sin and into life.
- *Have faith.* When all this doesn't seem to be working, trust that God is always working beyond what you see.

Jesus invited a group of doubters and non-doubters into a relationship with Him—not into religion. Even if you feel you don't "know enough" to share Jesus, He's given you the authority and command to do it. So grow and go, letting others see you as more than a good or spiritual person. Where you are isn't random; it's your personal mission field for people to see Jesus through you!

THERE IS HOPE

We get to help spiritually dying people find life in the resurrected Jesus. We do this not just for a victory but from a victory.

In what ways is each day an opportunity to share Jesus?

- **IF** others around you knew more about the faith journey you're on, what might they ask you?
- **WHAT IF** we truly claimed the authority Jesus gives us? What can it look like?

327: Participation Award

***IF** a head coach of a sport you don't play wanted to recruit you, what would you say?*

***WHAT IF** someone dared you to play the last professional sport you watched on TV?*

READ IT: JOHN 21:1–19

How do you feel about participation awards in team sports? The person who sits on the bench gets the same recognition as someone on the field.

With Jesus, a participation award is Him looking to "award" us with purpose based on where we are. We see it in the original language He used with Peter, who had denied Him three times the night of the big arrest (John 18:13–27). Twice Jesus asked Peter if he had unconditional love for Him, and twice Peter replied that it was obvious he just had a friendship love for Him. So Jesus adapted the third time. In our language it might look like this:

> *Jesus: Peter, are you all in on your love for Me?*
>
> *Peter: Jesus, you know I'm Your friend.*
>
> *Jesus: Peter, I'm talking about all-in love. Do you have it for Me?*
>
> *Peter: Jesus, it's obvious that I'm nothing more than a friend.*
>
> *Jesus: "So, Peter . . . you're My friend?"*
>
> *Peter: (sighs) Apparently that's who I am.*
>
> *Jesus: Then be My friend. Help others be My friend.*

Jesus took what Peter said out of embarrassment to raise up a strong leader. Because Peter had returned to his fishing job likely thinking his only option was his old life (which is what we may do if we feel defeated following Jesus), Christ met him there and blessed him with a massive catch of fish. And then Jesus offered, "Come . . . have breakfast."

When things are hard or embarrassing, Jesus is nearby. He'll meet you on the bench before He calls you off of it. He'll take what you're using to avoid Him as a way to find Him. He'll reward your participation with purpose!

THERE IS HOPE

Jesus can turn what looks to be a "failure" of Him dying on the cross into a victorious resurrection. So, what can He do in your life?

When have you failed in a way that was pretty embarrassing?

- ***IF*** you made a big mistake that hurt someone and then that person invited you over to eat breakfast, what would you do?
- ***WHAT IF*** that person said your mistake could be used to help others grow?

328: Be the Church

***IF** you could merge two businesses together so their products were available in the same place, which would you bring together?*

***WHAT IF** each product from each business fused with a product from the other?*

READ IT: ACTS 1:1–11

A colorful flower emerges out of a crack in a sidewalk littered with trash. A kitchen full of dirty dishes is overtaken by a warm sunrise beaming through the window. Both reveal beautiful things in not-so-beautiful places.

The church is the same way. Jesus has power over death and could have stayed around to lead things Himself. He instead had the wild idea to trust us knowing that we'd sometimes be ugly to each other. Jesus has faith in His church being inspirationally beautiful despite its not-so-beautiful days.

He doesn't leave us alone in this, though. The disciples may have felt excited to change the world after seeing Christ alive, but He told them to get rooted together through the Holy Spirit. He promised we'd do greater things than Him, in fact (John 14:12, 26). So Jesus did just that, leaving the realm of earth and fully trusting us to step into our purpose together.

Essentially, church is a perfect Jesus idea created for imperfect Jesus people. People will at times let you down when you expect them to lift you up, and you'll do the same to them. In these moments, borrow some faith from Christ to keep believing in the church like He does. In fact, He cares about church way more than you do and won't give up on us or His idea. We can learn so much from Him on this.

So embrace your purpose by embracing church. Do it with the Holy Spirit instead of good intentions or excitement. He'll remind you that we aren't here to just "be fed" but to learn how to feed ourselves and others spiritually. Church gives you a chance to see God in things you don't like, in people you don't get along with, and in choices you wouldn't naturally make. What a beautiful thing in an ugly place. Be the church!

THERE IS HOPE

Jesus believes in the church, and you believe in Jesus, which means you can believe in what Jesus believes in—the church.

What do you expect out of church? How does that match up with what Jesus said about church?

- ***IF*** you could have changed Jesus' decision about leaving earth, would you? Why?
- ***WHAT IF*** we focused on what to give to the church versus what to get out of it?

329: Weekly Recap

IF *soccer involved using two balls at the same time, would you like it?*

WHAT IF *instead of normal balls you got in huge inflated ones like balloons?*

"If you love me, you will keep my commands. And I will ask the Father, and he will give you another Counselor to be with you forever. He is the Spirit of truth. The world is unable to receive him because it doesn't see him or know him. But you do know him, because he remains with you and will be in you. I will not leave you as orphans; I am coming to you." (John 14:15–18)

CATCH UP

- Who or what made you laugh recently?
- How did life feel easy or hard this past week?

RECAP

- What stood out to you from what we've read together, talked about, or attempted to do together over the past week?
- What thoughts or questions do you have from today's Bible verse?

GROW TOGETHER

- What might be the main thing God is trying to tell our family today?
- What if we did something new together or returned to a good habit to live out what we're learning? What might that be?

OPEN UP

- In what ways are you struggling in life or experiencing something hard?
- If we were to confess something to God as a family, what might that be?

PRAY

- Who is Jesus to you today?
- Who would be willing to close our time with a simple prayer?

330: A Gathered Church

***IF** you could be on a sports team with the best players or your best friends, who would you choose?*

***WHAT IF** you could pick either the smartest kids or your closest friends to work on a school project?*

READ IT: ACTS 1:12–20

People call it "splitsies" to make it sound fun, but it's risky to gather with others for food and assume everyone will pitch in to pay. If you end up stuck with the bill or feel the portions were off, you'll rethink the next invitation.

Any friendship or community involves risk, though. Things can be great for a while until you naturally get overlooked, like when everyone except you spontaneously decides to see a movie. Other times it'll feel like someone didn't consider you on purpose. All of this can add up and create lasting hurt.

About 120 disciples gathered after Jesus ascended (a small number compared to how many Jews lived in that region). Judas had betrayed them, but rather than being guarded with each other they took a risk to value Jesus and His purpose. That's the same reason why we gather today as a local church—to "huddle" so we can take the field together as a team.

Some people you know may pull "splitsies" with your church. They'll go from church to church, grab portions for themselves between different congregations or youth groups to feed their needs at the expense of everyone else. They take, but they don't give by getting involved. This isn't cute and leaves others "holding the bill" of responsibility to launch ministries and cover classes. All this can add up and create lasting hurt.

Don't quit gathering as a church because of a "Judas" or "splitsies." Jesus created a community of believers on purpose to live with purpose. When we don't gather we miss out on how the church is alive and at work in our world despite the fact that we may feel like a small group at times. When you're guarded, separation is strengthened. When you take a risk to be open, community is birthed.

THERE IS HOPE

Ever struggle with your church's people or leaders? They may have had to muster up all their courage and faith just to show up. Be graceful.

What's your favorite part about gathering with other Christians as a church?

- ***IF*** it were up to you to decide who would be in our church, would you want to?
- ***WHAT IF*** you could be a pastor or teacher of a church?

331: An Organized Church

***IF** you worked in a restaurant and had to invent a new recipe every day, how long do you think you could keep it up?*

***WHAT IF** you were required to invent three new recipes a day?*

READ IT: ACTS 1:21–26

You're going on a picnic. What food will you bring? Where will you go? Questions like these don't have to be stressful. After all, you're going on a picnic! You have the freedom to add some organization to it.

We don't have to fear organization in the church either. The disciples paused to be wise after the failure of Judas created an opening for a new "twelfth" leader. They wanted someone who had been a witness of Christ's ministry and resurrection, and so they identified a man named Matthias.

The method the disciples identified this through was odd, though. "Casting lots" was like flipping a coin, only people believed that God made His will known through the way things turned out. Ironically, this is the last time the Bible mentions anyone ever casting lots because the Holy Spirit clearly came to guide us. That doesn't mean what the disciples did was wrong, but that through what they organized God revealed His will.

And that's kind of the point. Many things that happen in a church are someone's best guess at what it means to honor God. A worship leader may pick songs that members don't personally care for. A youth pastor may organize a trip that students criticize. On and on, it's easy to pick at the decisions of others or claim they aren't biblical, and yet in the Bible itself we see Christian leaders making their best guess at something to help organize the church.

People say they aren't a fan of "organized religion" yet quickly complain when a church seems disorganized. What if we instead offered our best God-honoring ideas and honored the ideas of others to make things better? Jesus doesn't need us to fix His church, but He does give us the freedom to have fun adding some organization to it.

THERE IS HOPE

God put us together for the best ideas, the best accountability, and the best purpose!

Ever organize anything? Talk about it.

- ***IF*** others offered to help you but had different ideas, how would you respond?
- ***WHAT IF*** you could organize something for God today? What would it be?

332: A Spirit-Led Church

***IF** you could only eat food from one other culture all next week, which culture would you pick?*

***WHAT IF** everyone only ate that food for that week?*

READ IT: ACTS 2:1–41

Christianity has some phrases that confuse others, like *salvation*, *blood of Christ*, and *inviting Jesus into your heart*. There are fancier ones too, like *sanctification* and *atonement*. This language is our attempt to sum up things the greatest Teacher shared in simple language (even though the people who heard Him often didn't understand Him). As you look at His ministry, it feels like any big breakthroughs people experienced were usually less about a big word Jesus said and more about His authority to say it.

For this reason (and many others) the Holy Spirit began living inside of Christians. Before this He only blessed certain people for a certain time, like when King Saul first came to power. Now the Holy Spirit can enter into any person who genuinely receives Christ as Savior and Lord. He gives us counsel and authority to speak on God's behalf so we aren't trying to sound spiritual on our own. When God wanted His people to speak to others, He helped them. When He inspires you to share Him with someone, He'll help you too.

This change began during a feast called Pentecost as people from different tribes and cultures came to celebrate. The Spirit spoke through the disciples to make sure every person could hear the message of Jesus in that individual's own native language. When they scattered as changed people, they lived out God's original purpose in Genesis for us to be fruitful and multiply.

By talking with the Holy Spirit and following His leadership, transformation can make sense out of applying the Bible. Over time you'll feel like a glass of water that has been filled and can't help but overflow. Being Spirit-led will allow other people to come to Jesus simply by catching something truthful through the authority you share it in.

THERE IS HOPE

The Spirit didn't come to give us goose bumps but growth. He won't do all the work for us but will work in us and through us.

What questions do you wonder about when it comes to the Holy Spirit?

- **IF** someone asked you to describe the Holy Spirit, what would you say?
- **WHAT IF** you could see the Holy Spirit in you or others?

333: A Devoted Church

***IF** you could remember everything you'd ever seen, read, or heard, how would that help you in life, school, or at work?*

***WHAT IF** you could repeat what you'd memorized but never understand it?*

READ IT: ACTS 2:42–47

A great professional football coach named Vince Lombardi was known for helping his players think straight. Once when his team lost a game they should have won, Coach Lombardi called a practice the very next morning. He began by holding a football high enough for everyone to see. "Gentlemen," he said, "this is a football!" He went on to explain some of the other basics of the game they should devote themselves to.

Keep in mind, Lombardi said this to professional athletes who already played football well. It'd be like saying, "Chef, this is a pan" or "Actor, this is a script." You might wonder why a seasoned coach would waste time doing this, but Lombardi didn't see it that way. His team ended up with three consecutive world championships.

The first-century Christians devoted themselves to core values like studying the teachings of Jesus through church leaders, regularly gathering together, eating with each other, seeking God in prayer, making sure there were zero needs among them, and praising the Lord daily. They could have avoided all this by making excuses about why none of this was necessary, like "We just led thousands of people to the Lord. We're good." Instead these amazing Christ-followers took the time to "hold up the football" and say, "Let's commit ourselves to the basics. We need to keep deepening our faith if we ever hope to widen it." It was a natural decision with supernatural purpose, and they reached new people every day.

We serve the same God who blessed them through their devotion. How is He looking to bless us? What would a radical "this is a football" type of conversation and commitment from your family look like?

THERE IS HOPE

The church exploded with growth when Christians exploded with commitment. Casual Christianity is for slackers. A rooted faith bears fruit.

Name one beautiful thing about Christianity that you wish more people could see, even if just for a moment.

- ***IF*** Jesus were to stand before our family today to hold up something symbolic He wanted us to focus on, what might He hold up?
- ***WHAT IF*** everybody in the world could be presented with this same symbol?

334: A Revealing Church

***IF** everytime you cooked a meal someone else got the credit for it, how would you feel?*

***WHAT IF** that same person got the credit for anything good you did in your life?*

READ IT: ACTS 3:1–10; 4:5–22

What are you really good at? Making omelets? Dancing? Wrapping presents? Drawing? Yodeling the alphabet? Whatever it is, when is the last time you gave credit where credit is due? Each of us discovered our talents and got better at them through the influence of others. God Himself played a part in revealing our talents and their purpose too.

For example, you may feel completely at ease speaking in front of others and claim, "I was born to be on stage." Or you could instead say, "God's given me this confidence not to worry about the crowd." It's all about revealing that we're not the source of our successes, but that Christ is.

Peter and John did this as they compassionately stopped to help a crippled man. Through the Spirit of God in them and the name of Jesus as their authority, they claimed a healing over him that changed his condition. Everyone who saw it became interested in Peter and John, as if the healing had come solely from them. Rather than accepting credit, the apostles pointed everyone to Jesus. They kept this up after being questioned by the Jewish leaders who tried to get them to stop talking about the Lord, only they wouldn't stop revealing who He was and how He was at work.

Revealing Jesus doesn't mean you lose yourself in the process but that you don't make the focus about you. You can take a compliment without saying, "No, I'm garbage. I'm nothing." God created you with *purpose*, and if someone notices it, you're to count it as an encouragement. Receive it graciously, and then "regard Christ the Lord as holy, ready at any time to give a defense to anyone who asks you for a reason for the hope that is in you" (1 Peter 3:15).

THERE IS HOPE

Your greatest ability is your availability. Your coolest story isn't about your glory. You're most exceeding when you're revealing.

Who do you know personally or have seen publicly who knows how to give credit where credit is due?

- ***IF*** you owe a few people a thank-you for something, who might that be?
- ***WHAT IF*** no one ever thanked you or gave you credit for your help?

335: An Awkward Church

***IF** whenever anyone cheated in a game the ground underneath them would break apart, how often do you think people would cheat?*

***WHAT IF** instead anytime a person cheated they lost an inch of their height?*

READ IT: ACTS 5:1–11

Picture yourself in a large church group about to sing a worship song. Just as everyone begins praising God, someone starts singing the theme song to a children's television show. This person begins quietly, but slowly builds to a loud level. How would everyone react to this? Awkward, right?

You may have a similar feeling if a friend or family member asks to play a game with you, only halfway into the game you discover he was cheating the whole time. He was the one who asked you to play! Awkward again.

Ananias and Sapphira made a big deal about giving the church a big gift of money after selling some property. No one asked them to do this, but they wanted to make it look like they had given it all while secretly keeping a portion of the money back for themselves. Peter, filled with the Spirit, identified the lie and confronted them. Ananias and Sapphira immediately fell over dead. Awkward?

When deception is discovered, the impact upon those who find out is usually dramatic. Cheating and lying in church circles especially affects everyone because it makes people question whether Christians can be trusted. No matter how many excuses we come up with to justify what we did, the Lord holds us accountable. Galatians 6:7 states, "God is not mocked. For whatever a person sows he will also reap."

Any church is going to have awkward moments, but hopefully not on purpose. Doing something selfless-looking to hide your selfishness may fool people for a moment, but you'll eventually be found out. Nobody wants to be around a lying show-off, but everyone is looking for people of honor. It's a part of our purpose as His church.

THERE IS HOPE

You can't bluff God. He calls us to live in Him rather than pretend.

How would you describe in your own words what Ananias and Sapphira did wrong?

- ***IF*** someone lied to you over money as Ananias and Sapphira did to the church, how would you respond?
- ***WHAT IF*** you had to guess if Ananias and Sapphira were Christians or not?

336: Weekly Recap

***IF** every time you opened your closet a small lizard would jump out, would you open your closet?*

***WHAT IF** you would be flooded with popcorn anytime you opened your closet?*

When they had prayed, the place where they were assembled was shaken, and they were all filled with the Holy Spirit and began to speak the word of God boldly. (Acts 4:31)

CATCH UP

- Who or what made you laugh recently?
- How did life feel easy or hard this past week?

RECAP

- What stood out to you from what we've read together, talked about, or attempted to do together over the past week?
- What thoughts or questions do you have from today's Bible verse?

GROW TOGETHER

- What might be the main thing God is trying to tell our family today?
- What if we did something new together or returned to a good habit to live out what we're learning? What might that be?

OPEN UP

- In what ways are you struggling in life or experiencing something hard?
- If we were to confess something to God as a family, what might that be?

PRAY

- Who is Jesus to you today?
- Who would be willing to close our time with a simple prayer?

337: Courage Under Fire

***IF** you could remove pain from one situation in your life, what would it be?*

***WHAT IF** to do this you had to intensify the pain in another area of your life?*

READ IT: ACTS 6:8–15; 7:57–60; 8:1–3

You've probably not had much experience with volcanoes. Not the delicious kind made out of mashed potatoes and gravy, but the *stay-away-from-the-lava* kind. If you have personally seen one, you likely kept some distance, for hot lava and living people don't go together.

Let's say people ignored this fact and started building homes next to active volcanoes. They'd put themselves, their families, and anyone they invited over at tremendous risk of death. If you said something against it, they might get angry and call you judgmental. You'd have to decide if you had the courage to speak up and save lives.

Stephen was a Christian who spoke about the destructive power of sin. He didn't let the possibility of being attacked or criticized stop him from sharing bold truth to people whose lives and relationships were on dangerous ground. They couldn't match the wisdom the Holy Spirit spoke through Stephen, so they threw stones at him to kill him.

It's sad to say, but Christians around the world today still brutally die like this for their faith. Others face people making fun of them or ending relationships over Jesus. It's natural for us to fear what will happen to us if we speak against the hot-lava-like power of sin to people who keep building their lives on it.

Find courage through what else happened to Stephen. He saw Jesus more clearly by making Jesus clearer to others. He also glimpsed what happens when Christians die as his life ended and he entered into an incredible heaven that lasts forever. And while Stephen didn't know it, one of the men who witnessed Stephen's death would become one of the greatest Christian leaders. There is hope in every sacrifice you make.

THERE IS HOPE

Our willingness to fall over for Jesus will help others get on their knees before Him. Have courage under fire.

What do you think of what Stephen went through versus what you face as a Christian?

- ***IF*** someone you spoke to yesterday described Jesus based only on what you've told them about Him, what would they say?
- ***WHAT IF*** today were your last day to tell that person anything else?

338: Vision

***IF** the only way to protect a special item was to trust a complete stranger with it, would you?*

***WHAT IF** that person was someone who had broken your trust before?*

READ IT: ACTS 9:1–31

Have you ever tried on a pair of eyeglasses belonging to another person? Odds are it will make things blurrier for you since your eyes won't be working as they normally would. In rare instances, though, you might unexpectedly find yourself seeing more clearly by taking on the vision they have, not realizing you needed glasses yourself.

Saul felt his life come in and out of focus until Jesus provided new perspective. Saul had been attacking Christians like a terrorist, all based on beliefs about Christ that weren't true. After encountering Jesus in a vision, Saul had to humbly get help from some Christians so the rest of the church would receive him as a changed man (1 Corinthians 15:1–10). Saul eventually became known as the apostle Paul, and would go on to claim, "if anyone is in Christ, he is a new creation" (2 Corinthians 5:17).

There's no denying what happens when people finally put on the right pair of glasses. It's utterly astounding as they see what they've been missing their whole lives. Every intricate detail up close or far away becomes clear. They can see differences in two objects of the same color next to each other and tell people apart in a crowd. It's like they had their eyes closed but now they're opened!

Our relationship with Jesus is similar. Sometimes life is really blurry and we know we need sight to find the way. Other times we think we know better than God and refuse to see life as He does. When we finally admit our need for Him it's like a covering over our eyes has been lifted and we can see the world as it truly is (along with how awesome God is). Christianity is more than just "finding Jesus"—it's about discovering Jesus again, and again, and again.

THERE IS HOPE

Through Jesus, blurriness becomes sight; enemies become allies; regrets become wisdom; reactions become responses; haters become healers.

What might it have been like for the early church to have Saul become a Christian?

- ***IF*** someone who treated you like an enemy started treating you like a friend, how would you respond immediately and over time?
- ***WHAT IF*** that person no longer treated you as an enemy but still let you down at times?

339: On a Mission from God

***IF** you could change a kids' menu in any restaurant, what would you put on it?*

***WHAT IF** you could only list one item?*

READ IT: ACTS 13:1–12; 14:21–28

Who isn't fascinated by the school lunch lady? The stereotype is a woman wearing a stretchy hair net, rubber gloves, and an apron covered with yesterday's "meatloaf surprise." She'd be armed with an ice cream scoop, ready to plop some rice pilaf onto your tray.

Maybe your local cafeteria worker doesn't fit this description, but it's a good bet that yours knows how to feed people. Day in and day out, this person gets you the right number of tater tots while sneaking in some "green stuff" you would've skipped (it's called a vegetable, by the way).

Early Christians like Paul and Barnabas went out as missionaries to bring the message of Jesus to others, like serving up "spiritual food" to whomever was open to it. They wanted everyone to be fed spiritually and learn to feed others, so they established churches from city to city to keep up the work. Along the way they confronted evil, revealed truth, and raised up leaders. Like a typical day for the lunch lady, not everyone liked what was scooped out, while others couldn't get enough of it.

Jesus said meeting the needs of others leads to an awesome reward (Matthew 10:42). There's nothing like helping someone be transformed by Him and get plugged into His family. Just imagine how many new congregations could be formed in your area if you went out and pursued nonbelievers instead of waiting around and hoping they walked into your church building on their own.

We're on a mission from God. The world is hungry, and we have food for their souls.

Strap on your hair net, rubber gloves, and apron (whatever those symbolize) and quit loafing around about the surprise we get to bring into the world!

THERE IS HOPE

Sometimes a mission field looks like a remote part of the world. Most often it looks like what's in front of you right now.

What part of our culture or world do you think really needs a genuine transformation through Jesus?

- ***IF*** you could be a key person who brings Jesus to that place, would you go?
- ***WHAT IF*** you could spend ten minutes with just one person to tell him or her about a new life in Jesus Christ? Who would it be?

340: Learning the Lyrics

***IF** your favorite song disappeared and you could only remember that it existed but nothing else about it, how would you feel?*

***WHAT IF** your least favorite song disappeared too?*

READ IT: GALATIANS 1:18–19; ACTS 15:1–21; JAMES 1:1

THUMP. THUMP. THUMP. THUMP. You've heard cars drive by that seem to be playing the "all-bass channel." If those songs had lyrics, you wouldn't know it. And then other vehicles drive by with people singing along to quieter music you can't hear. As it is, you still have no sense of the lyrics.

Jesus had a half-brother named James who used to blend into the background. Though the two of them shared Mary as their mother, James was the son of Joseph and Jesus was the Son of God. Try to understand how hard it must have been for Jesus' siblings to believe that He was the Messiah (which they initially didn't: Matthew 13:55–56; John 7:3–5). It was like the Lord was singing along to lyrics no one else could hear.

At some point James tuned into the truth and realized that he'd been wrong not to believe in Jesus. He saw his half-brother resurrected and was present when the Holy Spirit came at Pentecost (1 Corinthians 15:1–7; Acts 1:14). James believed and received, eventually describing himself as a servant of Christ. He became a key leader in the Jerusalem church.

The "lyrics" Jesus sings into the world are available to everyone (regardless of spiritual "singing ability"), but someone has to slow down to help them hear. Like James, some people on the outside won't easily tune in to what God's singing inside us. So don't turn faith into a private thing but instead roll the windows down and turn the volume up on what Jesus is doing in you. Pretty soon we'll have a royal jam session of new people singing melody, old singers adding harmony, and the whole world feeling the beat. *THUMP. THUMP. THUMP. THUMP.*

THERE IS HOPE

You don't have to be perfect to share about a perfect God. In His kingdom even "off-key" singers can hit all the notes.

What song do you think Jesus would crank up if He drove around town?

- ***IF*** you were with Him in the car, would you sing along?
- ***WHAT IF*** you were a famous singer and could share anything with the audience in between songs? What would you talk about?

341: Work It Out

***IF** you could touch a menu and cause a price to lower but it would also increase another price on the menu, would you do it?*

***WHAT IF** another person used that on you, and your bill ended up costing more?*

READ IT: ACTS 15:36–41; JAMES 4:1

Winning. This idea is everywhere. Ads tell you what you need to do to look better than others: "Change your body. Buy more stuff. Earn a bigger check." The idea is not just that you can be better than anyone else, but you can know better than anyone else. This attitude fuels every argument in our homes, community, and world.

Paul and Barnabas got caught up in winning a weird argument about who should travel with them on their missionary journey. They each wanted someone of good character who wouldn't distract them from their purpose. Somehow while trying to figure that out, though, they missed a larger purpose: "How good and pleasant it is when brothers live together in harmony!" (Psalm 133:1).

Like others in the Bible who were flawed or fell short in a situation, we're not meant to use their disagreement as an excuse to hold grudges or be fine when Christians walk away from each other. There's nothing in this passage that tells us this is okay. God did graciously allow both men to keep serving Him, but a real loss happened here. The one upside is neither Paul nor Barnabas wrote letters to churches to "tell their side" of things, but each went on to do the mission work they both agreed was worth doing.

That's a good tip in tricky situations you face with other Christians. Find something that keeps you growing spiritually so God can work in your heart and do His will to help in that tense relationship. When a brother or sister in the family of God lets you down, don't let it define your faith in God; let your faith in God define how you work it out with that brother or sister.

THERE IS HOPE

It's possible not to see eye-to-eye with someone without poking out their eyes. Invite Jesus to give you vision on what to do next.

Who have you seen do a great job at working out conflict or stopping it from starting?

- **IF** there were one lesson to learn from that person, what would it be?
- **WHAT IF** you could give some advice to Paul and Barnabas? What do you think they'd need to hear?

342: Spirit Smoothie

***IF** you could have an endless supply of three foods and two drinks, what would you choose?*

***WHAT IF** you had an endless supply of all food and drinks?*

READ IT: GALATIANS 5:16–26

Let's get one thing straight—a smoothie is not a shake. That's like saying a steak is a burger (and don't you dare bring up "steak-burgers"). Shakes are liquid desserts in a cup, but smoothies are a heavenly helping of delicious goodness blended together to create world peace. All of that's true, except for the world peace part . . . although a worldwide smoothie break might get us started.

Smoothies come from different fruits that blend into one refreshing, delectable drink. You could add water, juice, crushed ice, or milk, but at its core a smoothie flows from its natural ingredients. Some drinks out there claim to be smoothies, but they're made of syrup and sugar.

Similarly, having a genuine relationship with Jesus means we gain the "fruit" of being in a relationship with Him. We get love, joy, peace, patience, kindness, goodness, faith, gentleness, and self-control from the Spirit all at once. It would be like God handing you a smoothie instead of different pieces of different fruit. He'd say, "This is all yours, all at once. Drink up!"

That's the key, by the way. It's one thing to be handed something to drink that is absolutely yours and another thing for you to make the most of it. It'd be a drinking crime to let a smoothie go bad, but it's spiritually worse to have the Holy Spirit make so much available to you that you don't use.

Maybe you aren't naturally patient or gentle, but the Holy Spirit within you has those characteristics and will help you claim them. So instead of reaching for artificial ways to sweeten your life, let the Spirit inside you blend into you. Hmm . . . maybe it is the key to world peace.

THERE IS HOPE

The first sin involved a literal piece of fruit, but the fruit of the Spirit helps us overcome sin.

How might seeing or not seeing the fruit of the Spirit in others give you a sense of where they are with God?

- ***IF*** we get all this from God at once, why does it take time to see fruit in us?
- ***WHAT IF*** a friend said they were a Christian but didn't have this fruit?

343: Weekly Recap

***IF** you had special gloves that would give you the strength of ten men but would only work an hour each day, how would you use those gloves?*

***WHAT IF** you could use these gloves all day but would get quickly tired when the gloves were on?*

My dear brothers and sisters, understand this: Everyone should be quick to listen, slow to speak, and slow to anger, for human anger does not accomplish God's righteousness. (James 1:19–20)

CATCH UP

- Who or what made you laugh recently?
- How did life feel easy or hard this past week?

RECAP

- What stood out to you from what we've read together, talked about, or attempted to do together over the past week?
- What thoughts or questions do you have from today's Bible verse?

GROW TOGETHER

- What might be the main thing God is trying to tell our family today?
- What if we did something new together or returned to a good habit to live out what we're learning? What might that be?

OPEN UP

- In what ways are you struggling in life or experiencing something hard?
- If we were to confess something to God as a family, what might that be?

PRAY

- Who is Jesus to you today?
- Who would be willing to close our time with a simple prayer?

344: What a Ride!

***IF** you could change one thing about getting older, what would it be?*

***WHAT IF** you could change one thing about being young?*

READ IT: ACTS 17:1–4; 1 THESSALONIANS 4:1–18

How are your bike-riding skills? Remember what they used to be? Riding a two-wheeler started as riding a four-wheeler. These "training wheels" help us all learn to sit and pedal but aren't meant to stay on forever. As you realize you can't go places or at a speed others can, you might ask for the wheels to come off. Or others around you help you notice when you've learned the basics and only have the wheels on out of habit versus actual need.

The first churches began like a bike with training wheels; each one got people pedaling into a new faith with Jesus. They needed encouragement to keep growing, so someone like Paul would send them a letter of God-inspired truth. The church in Thessalonica received two letters like this to guide them through fears and struggles while reminding them Jesus would return again to bring heaven and earth together forever. Being told it was time for "sanctification" meant, "Time to take the training wheels off of your faith. You can now enter into new exciting places at a new pace with God. You'll also be able to journey with others like you never have before!"

That's another thing similar to the day you ride a two-wheeler. Just as you don't want to keep a set of training wheels on longer than needed, you don't want to delay your next growth step with God. As 1 Thessalonians 5:19 challenges, "Don't stifle the Spirit."

Like bike riding, growing in your faith involves a combination of time, practice, decisions, and help from others. One day you'll fall down, yet another day you'll do some wheelies. One day you may find that you're in a place to help younger Christians learn how to pedal and balance. What a ride!

THERE IS HOPE

Maturity happens through choices and not time alone. Otherwise you just end up repeating your first year of faith every year that follows.

In your own words, what do you think it means for someone to take the "training wheels" off their faith?

- ***IF*** you never learned anything new about God but became fully faithful to everything you've already learned, how much growing could you still do?
- ***WHAT IF*** growing in your faith is filled with more "get tos" than "have tos?"

345: Dimples

***IF** all the balls used in every sport became golf balls, what would be different about some of your favorite sports?*

***WHAT IF** the golf balls were also cameras that captured the game for the audience?*

READ IT: ACTS 18:1–4; 1 CORINTHIANS 1:18–31

There are two kinds of golf: the kind where you cart around on grass, and the kind involving a windmill and a mechanical alligator. Both involve awkward attempts to get a ball in the hole. You may end up thinking, *I'm going to mess this up. This is going to end badly. Who am I to even try?*

Something golf and life have in common is that what looks foolish actually has a purpose. Case in point: those silly looking bumps on the surface of a golf ball minimize the air resistance it faces while traveling. Most balls will actually travel twice as far and as fast because of these "dimples." Something that appears foolish or useless is actually super important.

That's one of the first things written to the church in Corinth. It was a rich city that was a hub for sports, business, government, and pagan worship. Christians living there might feel they had zero chance to make any kind of a difference.

Can you relate? Do you ever feel foolish or useless in trying to change things? It's actually less about who we are and who God is in us. First Corinthians 1:27 says, "God has chosen what is foolish in the world to shame the wise, and God has chosen what is weak in the world to shame the strong." That includes you and me knowing we'll always be imperfect in how we share about our perfect Savior, yet doing it anyway.

Like the dimples on a golf ball, what appears to be "useless" or "foolish" in us is more important than you realize. Give God your strengths and your weaknesses as you step up to take your best swing. You not being smooth all the way around is just another way the Lord helps you soar. Smile and show your dimples.

THERE IS HOPE

Everybody fails by just watching.
With Jesus, nobody fails by trying.

Have you ever felt like you made a big difference doing something?

- ***IF*** you knew God could use you no matter what, what would you try doing?
- ***WHAT IF*** on your very worst day you can still change a life for the better?

346: The Gift of the Line

***IF** whenever you did something tough, your skill or strength in that area would double, how would that affect the way you approach tough things?*

***WHAT IF** you only grew in skill or strength if you asked for help?*

READ IT: 1 CORINTHIANS 6:1–20

How many gifts have you received throughout your life? What about the ones that didn't show up in a wrapped box? Don't overlook things like the forgiveness of a friend, being spared from an accident, the smile of a baby, food in the fridge, and so on. Overlooking them could cause us to misuse them.

One big gift God gives us is a kind of line that exists for all of humanity. He describes it by saying on one side of the line is sin and death, but on the other side is Jesus and life. We choose which side we'll live on when it comes to everyday matters like working problems out with each other, deciding if certain temptations will define us, how we approach sex, and so on.

The Christians in Corinth who first heard this lived among people who did whatever they wanted as if the line didn't exist. The Greek religion urged people to act this way, so the Christians needed a reminder that they didn't have to end up like everyone else.

Some people view God as trying to limit them when He cares enough to state the truth. If you were given a car as a gift and the person who gave it to you explained the right way to operate it so you didn't injure anyone, you'd be grateful. Why not view the line God gives us like this?

The Lord wants us to hear things like "Run from sexual immorality!" He also wants us to see that our identity isn't meant to be found in a sin, like the people who "*used* to be like this." The gift of the line reveals that Jesus makes transformation possible and helps us avoid sin in the first place. That's a gift you give to God, others, and yourself, for "You are not your own . . . you were bought at a price."

THERE IS HOPE

Every gift God gives us has His love and purpose behind it.

What makes a gift a gift?

- **IF** people always used the gifts you gave them in ways they shouldn't, how would you feel?
- **WHAT IF** the way they misused those gifts hurt others you cared about?

347: Fitting In

***IF** you could create your own line of toys, what would it be?*

***WHAT IF** everyone decided they would buy nothing but your toys?*

READ IT: 1 CORINTHIANS 12:4–27

Jigsaw puzzles are quite the challenge to put together. You might start building using the outside pieces, but the inside pieces matter too. It is frustrating to discover you're missing pieces when you are about to finish a puzzle.

The body of Christ (another way to describe the church) is like a puzzle where every piece is needed. If one part holds back or goes missing, the whole thing is incomplete. Between those who do things on the inside and others who are more noticeable on the outside, everyone matters (including you).

The Holy Spirit adds to this by giving us spiritual gifts to build up the church and serve others. They're different than natural abilities because they come to us after we become a Christian and are revealed as we grow with God. We all can invite people into our homes, but someone with the spiritual gift of hospitality helps others feel the presence and love of God in how everyone is welcomed and cared for. A teacher can say something inspirational, but people with the spiritual gift of teaching end up uniquely revealing Jesus as they teach. And so on.

So if the Holy Spirit has given you a unique capability to help complete the puzzle, and if using those gifts satisfies you, why not take the time to identify and use these gifts? Each of us has enormous potential to lead God's kingdom to another victory, but none of us by ourselves is as powerful as we are as the church. Show what Christ can do in this world when we pull together as His body. The Lord has shaped you for His purpose. You don't have to worry about fitting in . . . you already do.

THERE IS HOPE

When we see a great need that's bigger than us, we can do something about it—because our big God put something big in us.

What is something you see in your family members that you think is more than an ability, but is a spiritual gift?

- ***IF*** you could better learn how God uniquely gifted you, would you want to?
- ***WHAT IF*** we each held back in adding to God's church? What would be the impact of our family alone doing this? And then what if we didn't hold back?

348: Backup

***IF** you got a free bouncy house as a gift but it was always filled with spaghetti and meatballs, would you want it?*

***WHAT IF** you had to eat the food while you jumped?*

READ IT: 2 CORINTHIANS 6:14–18; 1 KINGS 11:1–3

A line you'll likely hear in action movies or police shows is "I need backup!" It's how characters admit that the situation is dangerous and they need the *right* person to help them. The right person is the key. If the only backup is a person who can't keep up or who isn't on their side, the character will be distracted instead of helped.

We also know the importance of "backing up" a computer. This involves copying your files somewhere safe so if your system breaks or is attacked, you can retrieve it from a trustworthy source. Using a bad hard drive will obviously backfire.

Our relationships with other people are meant to offer us backup. Especially in dating and marriage, God wants us matched up with people who match our faith. Being attracted to someone who believes differently is a red warning light—not a green light. Giving in leads to the same heartbreak many people we've read about in the Bible experienced. Why invite that into your life?

We all long to "belong" with someone. At the same time, we also want our lives to have the right purpose. One of those desires will lead the other, whether we look for love and lower our standards or honor God and let Him guide us into lasting relationships. Yes, people we find super attractive need Jesus. If the only reason they say they're interested in Him is to date you, though, then they aren't setting Him up to be Lord—they're following you.

The starting place in any courtship is making sure the other person is solid with Jesus. God's dream is for your benefit—that you'd be connected to people who give you backup versus those who set you back. May you willingly receive and promote this without lowering His standards.

THERE IS HOPE

If we allow our relationships to be led by God, we're trusting in the ultimate Deliverer, Counselor, and Strengthener.

How might strong feelings or attraction confuse us from seeing things the way they are?

- ***IF*** you felt attracted to someone who didn't share your faith, how would you make sure you didn't start lowering God's standards or dream for you?
- ***WHAT IF*** that person promised to go to church as long as you dated?

349: Ninja Grace

***IF** everyone's legs were springy and could jump great heights, how would life change?*

***WHAT IF** everyone had stretchy arms instead?*

READ IT: ROMANS 6:1–14; 8:31–39

Are you a ninja around the house? Kitchen ninjas try to complete all their food prep before the microwave hits 00:00. Homework ninjas set a timer and race to get it all done in an hour so they have more free time after dinner. Nighttime ninjas turn off all the lights and run up the stairs superfast to then turn, completely stare into the darkness and shout, "I'm not afraid of you!"

Fun, right? Just keep in mind that you aren't under any law that says you need do these tasks this way. That's up to you.

The book of Romans shares how God's laws that were given under Moses no longer were required of Christians. The various Jews and non-Jews who become believers needed to hear this so they could fully live in God's grace (without using that grace as a reason to sin). They could do some of the old tasks that the law once required of them, but they no longer needed to because Christ fulfilled that law for them.

There are practices meant for Christians to take part in, though. They add to our relationship instead of burdening us, like being baptized as a believer as a statement of your faith. You do this also to make known how you want the help and encouragement of others so you can turn away from sin and your old way of doing life to grow into the adventure Jesus has for you.

You may have some great ninja-like skills for how to handle any sins you're tempted by, but trusting in God is better. He embraces you in your worst moments and celebrates you in your best moments. He'll even help you face the darkness and shout into it, "I'm not afraid of you!"

THERE IS HOPE

Sin holds you down. The law yells, "Get up!" Grace scoops you into the arms of Jesus, who raises you into transformatión.

What are some things you enjoy doing that help you get stuff done in life or grow in faith?

- ***IF*** you didn't do these things, what would change in God's love for you? (Hint: It's a trick question: nothing would change!)
- ***WHAT IF*** Jesus walked in on you doing something that deepens or widens your faith? What do you think He'd say to you about it?

350: Weekly Recap

***IF** ten little insects floated around you and helped you do things, would you find that encouraging or annoying?*

***WHAT IF** just one insect followed you every day to mess you up somehow?*

We always thank God, the Father of our Lord Jesus Christ, when we pray for you, for we have heard of your faith in Christ Jesus and of the love you have for all the saints because of the hope reserved for you in heaven. You have already heard about this hope in the message of truth, the gospel that has come to you. (Colossians 1:3–6)

CATCH UP

- Who or what made you laugh recently?
- How did life feel easy or hard this past week?

RECAP

- What stood out to you from what we've read together, talked about, or attempted to do together over the past week?
- What thoughts or questions do you have from today's Bible verse?

GROW TOGETHER

- What might be the main thing God is trying to tell our family today?
- What if we did something new together or returned to a good habit to live out what we're learning? What might that be?

OPEN UP

- In what ways are you struggling in life or experiencing something hard?
- If we were to confess something to God as a family, what might that be?

PRAY

- Who is Jesus to you today?
- Who would be willing to close our time with a simple prayer?

351: Whatever

IF *ice cream never melted, what would eating ice cream be like?*

WHAT IF *ice cream did melt but only in sections you licked?*

READ IT: COLOSSIANS 2:6–10; 3:1–17

Let's say a typical ice-cream sundae represented your life. Some people think God should be at the top of everything like a cherry. That sounds right when you hear people say things like "Put God first in life."

Colossians 2–3 points out a deeper reality about how He isn't meant to only be first over your life, but *first in all things*. It's saying, "*Whatever* I do, God, I'll do it for You." Symbolically, God is less like the cherry topping a sundae and more like the spoon you use to eat *every* bite of life. For example:

- With money: "God, I tithed. The rest is mine," versus "God, I tithed. Any wisdom about what's left?"
- With chores: "God, I did my part," versus "God, I did my part. How else can I serve?"
- With school: "God, get me through the test," versus "God, equip me through this to bless You back with it."
- With family: "Everyone is cranky. I quit," versus "Everyone matters. I'm still all-in and will lead them to You."
- With beauty: "God, I look good. Selfie time!" versus "God, my body is Your body. Help me take care of it and be modest with it."
- With faith: "God, wow me," versus "God, how can I wow you?"

Putting God first in all things means instead of just turning to Him about some things we follow Him in everything. We take on a "whatever" attitude that opens us up instead of shuts us down. By all means, plop the cherry on top and recognize He is over everything.

THERE IS HOPE

There are two ways to begin your day, and both get a conversation with God started: "Good morning, Lord" or "Good Lord, it's morning."

How do you build a sundae?

- **IF** each part of the sundae represented your life, what would symbolize what?
- **WHAT IF** we each took a moment in prayer to specifically invite Jesus into each of these parts of our lives, one by one?

352: The Human Factor

***IF** you could see through all physical objects, what would you do?*

***WHAT IF** you could only see through all non-living things?*

READ IT: COLOSSIANS 2:6–10; 3:1–17

Politicians can be amazing forces for good in God's hands, but they can also get pretty nasty with each other. Edwin M. Stanton was one of Abraham Lincoln's earliest adversaries, and Stanton regularly let him know it. He called Abe horrible names and compared him to a gorilla. Lincoln never responded to any of it until he became president and needed a secretary of war. He chose Stanton believing (and telling everyone) that he was the best man for the job. It takes a real leader to turn a tension into a triumph.

The short, God-inspired letter called Philemon shares a tension that Paul tried to heal between two people. Onesimus used to work for Philemon but ran away to escape punishment for a theft he was accused of. He then began serving Paul who had been put in prison for his faith, and during that time Onesimus received Jesus as Savior and Lord. Since everyone was all now a part of the family of God, Paul tried to get Philemon to forgive what had happened so a fresh start could begin.

Philemon had the same challenge we face when someone offends us—not to view that person through the hurt but remember there's more to him or her than what's on our minds. It's owning the human factor.

Everybody is somebody Jesus Christ gave His life for. If you won't see someone you're at odds with in this way, then something in your own relationship with God is broken. We don't need to quickly dismiss our hurts if what happened is truly terrible, but be honest—how many times do we get permanently mad over forgivable things? Don't become so blind about where you think you are with Jesus that you refuse to walk over to someone else to love and forgive them.

THERE IS HOPE

You rarely will stumble over something you've put behind you.

Who needs forgiveness?

- ***IF*** people never forgave you, how would that affect who you are over time?
- ***WHAT IF*** there were a way to feel what an unforgiven person feels? Do you think that would change how quickly you offer forgiveness?

353: Made-Up Words

***IF** there were no curse words,*
how would the world change?

***WHAT IF** there were no rude talking or gossiping of any sort?*

READ IT: EPHESIANS 4:17–32

Did you know that words can be made up? Some people got so tired of saying "gigantic" and "enormous" that they created "ginormous." This slang eventually became an official word in the dictionary in 2007. That's a little scary.

People have that impact on each other, as whatever "made-up words" we speak can sound official and become a part of us. That's why you're surprised by the thoughts that rise up to pop out of you when you're angry. The input of others into you over time impacts what comes out of you now.

The church in Ephesus was in a city where people of different morals (or lack of morals) regularly traveled through. Those who lived there worshiped a pagan goddess.* All that sin and opinion colliding in one place made it challenging for Christians to stay on track with God. They constantly were handed "made-up" words and values influenced by culture.

What's in Ephesians 4 for them is also there for us. Spending time with Jesus and His words renews our minds and gives us something more to draw on than what others have handed us. He won't love you any less if a swear word comes out of your mouth, but it doesn't need to. Your words can instead tell others about His love if you store them up to speak on purpose and with purpose.

Words create life and steal life. They can also stay in us; so speak up or walk away from bad language, dirty jokes, or harmful attitudes that can put stuff in you that you don't want leaking out. Taking responsibility right away blesses you later and introduces others to the Word of God—Jesus Christ.

* Ephesus built everything around the worship of a false fertility goddess they believed provided all things—money, health, family and so on. The temple they built to her (where multiple inappropriate things happened) was so massive that it became one of the seven wonders of the entire world.

THERE IS HOPE

Using nasty words is nasty. To change your shocking talking, change your stinking thinking.

List several ways bad words or negative language can come out of us.

- ***IF*** you said whatever you felt all the time, what would you lose?
- ***WHAT IF*** you changed one of the ways negative thoughts or words come into your life? What would that be?

354: Family Reunion

***IF** you could choose an animal species that would from now on have all of its members wear a hat, which one would you pick?*

***WHAT IF** the species you chose inspired a cartoon that you got to be a voice actor in?*

READ IT: EPHESIANS 5:15–33; 6:1–11

Family reunions can feel like a reality show. You're all given wild tasks like, "Show up with food made from scratch that people will actually eat" or "Sit at a four-person card table with sixteen other people." You play board games in a living room with furniture protected by plastic zip covers. A chat about the news can turn into a heated political disagreement. But then the smile on a toddler sitting on the lap of the oldest person in the room reminds everyone why we do this in the first place. So much of our family habits are caught more than taught.

Enter the wisdom of God through His letter to the Ephesians. The Lord doesn't want us guessing at the different relationships in a family or us learning from bad examples in the world. Picture a homeless man who ends up sleeping on the ground outside because he doesn't know how to read a sign on the building he's sleeping in front of, which is inviting him in for a meal and a bed. That can be us.

People in the first century had "caught" some ideas about marriage and parenting that were horrible. The picture the Bible paints instead is breathtaking. Husbands are to love their wives like Christ loves and gave Himself up for the church; wives are to honor their husbands back by looking for ways to add to what he's doing versus criticize; parents are to raise their kids up tenderly; kids are to waste no time in respecting their parents who are looking out for them.

Ironically, so much of this is *taught* more than it's caught. Someone has to be the first one to say, "I'll do my role whether or not anyone else does theirs." Only then can others by seeing your example feel invited into this family reunion.

THERE IS HOPE

Family is more than keeping sinks clean, laundry baskets empty, and cupboards full. It's how you change the world, beginning in your home.

Define what *family* means to you.

- ***IF*** you were given a job description for your role in the family, would you want to read and follow it or would you rather do your own thing? Why?
- ***WHAT IF*** you could add or get rid of a family tradition of your choosing?

355: Spoiler Free

***IF** you could enter any one episode of a TV series, which one would you enter?*

***WHAT IF** you were on the show for a whole season, starting at episode one?*

READ IT: PHILIPPIANS 3:10–21; 4:8–9

When it comes to new movies, it's hard to keep a secret. Just walking down the toy aisle of a store will spoil a movie's plot through the merchandise alone. Toss in all the trailers and by the time we see the film we have a detailed expectation of what it's "supposed" to be like. It's not easy to be spoiler free in a culture that wants to expose itself.

But you can. It is possible to avoid ads, stay off of certain websites, ask friends to stop talking about what they've heard, and anything else that won't ruin you experiencing the film for what is actually is. This is true for movies and so many other areas of life. You *can* pursue being spoiler free.

The Philippians needed this encouragement. They'd seen the apostle Paul end up in jail for his faith after being a superstar to them. The God-inspired letter they received was Paul's way of saying, "Forget what you've seen. Don't focus on negativity or even on me. Focus on Jesus."

This incredible wisdom still applies. To avoid letting life spoil you, root yourself in Christ. Practicing self-control in small things like entertainment offers small wins that remind you how God's idea for purity is genius. Sure, some people around you won't think twice about spoiling things that should be saved for the right moment, like sex before marriage. But notice how we're culturally losing our innocence and eliminating childhood when we don't need to.

Entertainment relaxes our guard and hands us values we normally would run the other way from. Rather than wondering, "Can I handle this?" ask, "What gift will God give me if I don't take part in this?" There is a real joy after waiting and not ruining something ahead of time. Live spoiler free.

THERE IS HOPE

There's always a way out of temptation, starting with not heading in.

Define what makes something "inappropriate."

- **IF** a movie was "inappropriate" but you liked other parts of it, would you stop watching or try to get used to the bad parts?
- **WHAT IF** the way you view movies reflected the same values you use when approaching bigger problems or temptations?

356: Leadership

***IF** every door in the world opened as you touched it, how would you use this power?*

***WHAT IF** a camera always captured whatever door you opened so you'd never be able to use this power privately?*

READ IT: 1 TIMOTHY 3:1–13; 4:12; 2 TIMOTHY 4:1–5

Leadership means different things to different people. Some picture a person in an official role who makes big decisions that affect countless others. Others imagine an everyday person who steps forth when something needs to be changed. Leadership can refer to a family member who takes care of other family members or a kid in your neighborhood who's always organizing games for other kids. In a nutshell, leadership happens when one person (or more) changes something that otherwise wouldn't have changed.

Timothy grew under the leadership of Paul, but had a mother and grandmother who taught him the Hebrew Scriptures and later became Christ-followers (Acts 16:1–5; 2 Timothy 1:1–5). By the time God inspired Paul to write the letters of 1 Timothy and 2 Timothy to him, Timothy was around thirty years old and taking on a big leadership role. The letters were meant to remind him about what honoring God as a leader looks like so Timothy could get the right people around him.

Becoming a leader is a process like that. You don't become a healthy one overnight by reading, studying, or making decisions without any help. We all need a "Paul" in our lives who is ahead of us in some way and can mentor us; we need peers around us to spur us on with encouragement and accountability; and we need someone like a "Timothy" who can benefit from what we've learned.

Everyone is a leader, whether it's in how they're taking people forward on purpose or urging people backward by being lazy. Figure out how one or both of those are true in your life before you miss the opportunity to do something great. What the Bible and God's church offer us is the best place to start. Set a GOAL: Go Out And Lead.

THERE IS HOPE

God has a plan. You have a part, and it's your part. Step up.

Finish this sentence: "I personally lead others by . . ."

- ***IF*** you could lead anything in the world, what would you want to lead?
- ***WHAT IF*** leading people to do the right things causes them to treat you in wrong ways? How can we stay faithful when it's not easy or popular?

357: Weekly Recap

***IF** you were paid one thousand dollars to exercise one hour a day for a month, would you?*

***WHAT IF** you were paid one hundred dollars instead?*

Watch out, brothers, so that there won't be in any of you an evil, unbelieving heart that departs from the living God. But encourage each other daily, while it is still called today, so that none of you is hardened by sin's deception. For we have become companions of the Messiah if we hold firmly until the end the reality that we had at the start. (Hebrews 3:12–14)

CATCH UP

- Who or what made you laugh recently?
- How did life feel easy or hard this past week?

RECAP

- What stood out to you from what we've read together, talked about, or attempted to do together over the past week?
- What thoughts or questions do you have from today's Bible verse?

GROW TOGETHER

- What might be the main thing God is trying to tell our family today?
- What if we did something new together or returned to a good habit to live out what we're learning? What might that be?

OPEN UP

- In what ways are you struggling in life or experiencing something hard?
- If we were to confess something to God as a family, what might that be?

PRAY

- Who is Jesus to you today?
- Who would be willing to close our time with a simple prayer?

THERE IS HOPE

ETERNITY

We have a unique relationship with trees every fall. Depending on where you live in the world, you may be one of those who struggle with the love-hate relationship of watching the leaves change colors. On one hand, it's breathtaking to see the red, purple, orange, and yellow hues color up the trees on a street. On the other hand, you know that someone (likely you) is going to have to take care of all of those leaves as they fall to the ground.

The deeper secret is that these fall colors have been there all along. We may be so used to seeing green leaves during the spring and summer months because of the chlorophyll trees produce, but each leaf's true color is buried underneath it during that time. As the seasons change, some beautiful truth comes to light.

Romans 1 tells us that creation shows us a deeper truth if we simply pay attention. In this case, the analogy couldn't be clearer. There is a deeper reality to the world we live in than what we see with our eyes right now. Jesus will come again in all of His full glory and take us into the realm of heaven where we will see colors and more that we didn't even know existed. It means some changes on our end now along with some meaningful work, but the view is quite spectacular.

One day heaven and earth will come together forever, and God's people will live with Him forever.

358: Look!

***IF** you had your own island floating in midair, what would you use it for?*

***WHAT IF** you could decide its size up to a mile and have anything you wanted on it?*

READ IT: REVELATION 1:1–20

Have you ever visited a restaurant based on someone describing its food to you? To help you to understand what you hadn't yet experienced, they connected it to what you know. For example, "Look, you've had tacos before, but these are like someone gave your stomach a hug from the inside." You might've thought, *That's just an expression.* Then you finally sat down to eat the tacos and were so moved that you thought, *That kind of does feel like a hug on the inside.*

The book of Revelation is full of wonderful images that let us glimpse how heaven and earth will one day come together forever. It was all revealed to John (one of Jesus' original twelve disciples) who as an old man was banished to an island because of his ministry. There he was quickly caught up into heaven through a vision where he experienced Christ in a glorified, heavenly form.

Imagine how hard it was for John to describe everything. Rather than saying, "There were no words" he did his best to write down what everyone could learn. We may wish that Revelation wasn't so puzzling to read, but it's a challenge to use natural words to describe something supernatural. At least John didn't say, "Look, seeing Jesus was like someone giving your stomach a hug from the inside."

To help us understand eternity, the first thing Jesus told John was how we have some work to do "now." All that "purpose" we're called to is happening from now into eternity. For all the guesses about what Revelation is about, it actually tells us in the first verse: "the revelation of Jesus Christ." That doesn't just mean Jesus is the One who gave it to John, but that it's a revelation *of* and *about* Jesus. Look!

THERE IS HOPE

Everything good in life is ultimately about Jesus. Everything bad in life is ultimately a rejection of Him. Either way, Jesus is everywhere.

What are some things you wonder about when it comes to heaven or eternity?

- ***IF*** you could interview one person in heaven about heaven, who would it be?
- ***WHAT IF*** heaven had all the things you like doing? What if it didn't?

359: Soundtrack

***IF** you could choose one song to replace the singer's voice with your voice, what song would you pick?*

***WHAT IF** whenever that song played in your voice, everyone everywhere sang along?*

READ IT: REVELATION 2:1–11; 3:1–13, 22

You've probably watched your favorite movie more than once. How familiar are you with its music? The right soundtrack tunes you into the story, whether it's epic, quirky, gentle, or intense. You wouldn't want music usually found in a romance movie in a kids' cartoon (or the other way around) because the story and the soundtrack should cooperate.

The seven churches Jesus spoke to in Revelation 2–3 all needed words of correction and encouragement about the way the story they said they were living didn't match the "music" coming out of them. First Corinthians 13:1 says they were like a "clanging cymbal." Jesus wanted them to realize that their actions directly impacted eternity. Some of their "music" wasn't showing others the message.

The same is true of us with living out God's story in the world. You may also be bold enough to ask, "Jesus, if You wrote me a letter like You did these churches, what would You tell me?" He may remind you of who you're created to be or what you're doing that no longer serves the right purpose. Paying attention to this can help you find the motivation to change.

Consider how we sing songs in church and how the right ones sung on-key can help tune you into the story of God. As the church we're God's soundtrack to lost people when our "music" (how we live) better shows others the message. If we say we're following Jesus yet live according to the world's funky rhythm in one or more areas of life, we make things choppy and confusing. Your life *is* a song, whether it's epic, quirky, gentle, or intense. How off-key or in-tune you live really can change the world.

THERE IS HOPE

The conduct the world is waiting for gets played like a song when the church quits playing around with Jesus and lets Him conduct.

What would be a great soundtrack during big moments when you are sharing Jesus?

- ***IF*** you were shown a five-minute video of all the worst things in the world (including things that had never been seen), how would that affect you?
- ***WHAT IF*** people like us letting Jesus work in our lives changed enough of the world that even just one of those stories could be different?

360: It's All Real

***IF** God offered to do a miracle that could be viewed by everyone in the world, what would you ask Him to do?*

***WHAT IF** everyone saw the miracle but it couldn't be captured on film?*

READ IT: REVELATION 4:1–11

Ever made a mess that seemed impossible to clean up? Like major, monster-sized chaos where everything seemed lost? Throughout history, huge oil spills in the ocean or worldwide wars made it seem like nothing would ever change.

Check this out—the first thing John saw in heaven was a throne with someone on it. Notice who that is (God) and who it isn't (like, anyone else). There is real authority and power that everyone and everything must answer to, and He says the mess we've made of things will change. After giving us all kinds of time on earth to do something about it, He will do the last part of it.

Hope is real. It's all real! Being nervous about how things might turn out pulls you out of things that need you now. Hope, on the other hand, reminds you of what is worth fighting for. We can say, "Lord, I know one day You'll set the world right. I want to help things move that way today."

Decide to have hope in God's authority and what He hopes in. That includes you, His church, the people under your roof, others you've argued with, and relationships you think are over. Decide to have hope, even if only for the next ten minutes. And in that time let God show you what He says is possible. It's all real!

Revelation reminds us that the Lord is the Lord. When time and history as we know them end and we enter into the realm of eternity, God will be there. It'll be like when you're getting a great big hug from someone and are so overwhelmed with the joy of being there in that moment that it's like time doesn't exist. We get to experience a unique warmth and new relationship with God like that!

THERE IS HOPE

Through hope we let our Jesus-centered faith in what we can't yet see produce Jesus-centered love and action that others can see.

What is something wrong in this world that you're looking forward to God one day transforming?

- ***IF*** we all will answer to God one day, what does that mean to you?
- ***WHAT IF*** God's waiting because He has something for you to do today "not wanting any to perish but all to come to repentance" (2 Peter 3:9)?

361: The Lion and the Lamb

***IF** you could domesticate any animal to live with you, which one would you pick?*

***WHAT IF** all the members of that species became domesticated?*

READ IT: REVELATION 4:1–11

Professional baseball games often invite non-players for something fun on the field, like running the bases or standing on home plate. But imagine a young kid being picked to bat against a major league pitcher who instead of tossing a slow pitch whipped out his fastest ball! It'd be a strike for sure that would leave the kid crying out for help.

Now picture one of the greatest hitters ever stepping up to take the place of that kid. Everything would change as people thought, *This guy can do something!* As the ball came in and the bat swung hard to drive the ball out as a homerun, the stadium would erupt with praise as the great player and the kid ran the bases together, like a lion and a lamb.

We've read about Jesus dying on the cross in history, but Revelation shares what He does for us in eternity. In the ancient world a scroll represented life-changing information that was sealed until a person with authority said it was to be opened. No one seemed able to open this one, so there was an awkward pause in heaven that made John weep. Then a loud announcement said that a Lion had the power to do it, only as John turned to look he instead saw a Lamb. Both of these images pointed to Jesus coming in power yet also sacrificing Himself. All of heaven erupted with praise as the Great Messiah and Savior stepped forth as that Lion *and* Lamb.

This is who we sing worship songs to. *This* is why we pray with honor. Jesus is both tender and powerful for us, yet protective and fierce against our enemy. Let Him be all of who He is in your life!

THERE IS HOPE

Jesus is so concerned about where you've been, where you are, and where you're going that He did something about all three.

Why do you think Jesus is known as both a Lion and a Lamb? What other animal could you describe Him as?

- ***IF*** you could have any specific animal personally know Jesus like you do, which animal would you pick?
- ***WHAT IF*** you could make one other person today know Jesus like you do?

362: Hell

***IF** you had to watch criminals around the world facing a judge, what might you change in your own life afterward?*

***WHAT IF** one of the criminals being sentenced was someone you knew?*

READ IT: REVELATION 12:1–18; 19:11–16; 20:1–15

Morse code has saved the lives of countless people. It's an old system of communication that assigns letters to dots and dashes so a sender and a receiver can exchange a message. Morse code is typically sent by tapping noises out, but it's also been used by prisoners of war who blinked out messages on camera.

Reading about the war in heaven has a code that the ancient world understood. The "woman" represented Israel, the "child" represented Jesus and the "offspring" represented the non-Jewish Christians. On the other side, the "dragon" represented Satan, the "beast of the sea" represented an Antichrist (who would claim to be God returning back to earth), and the "beast of the earth" represented a human leader who promotes the Antichrist.

Also notice that the lake of burning fire where God's enemy ends up is a place made for Satan and his demons. God doesn't want any person there, but we can choose it by default if we refuse to join the winning side. God won't force us to love Him or go to heaven if we don't want to.

But He also doesn't want anyone to be lost. Can you decode how He's fighting for you and everyone who has ever existed to come into relationship with Him? This has to be the context for any conversation about hell. Jesus created a way to pull the evil and sin out of this world. Hell says there will be a day when the force behind every lie, abuse, argument, assault, arrogance, torture, and wound will end. Amen?

God is not trying to send us to hell—He's trying to keep us out of it. You'd never recognize it if you didn't know the code, so help Him help others decode it.

THERE IS HOPE

If you're not a Christian, this world is the only heaven you'll know. If you are a Christian, this world is the only hell you'll know.

How could our view of life and how we spend our time change if we understood heaven and hell better?

- ***IF*** you could visit heaven for an hour, what might change about your life?
- ***WHAT IF*** you visited hell for five minutes? How would your life be different?

363: Heaven

IF *leaves flew up instead of falling down, what would that be like?*

WHAT IF *grass was always the perfect height and snow didn't land on the ground?*

READ IT: REVELATION 21:1–14; 22:1–17

The day has come. A groom and a bride-to-be face each other, each saying their vows. Everything is changing. It's a time for celebration!

In the ancient world there was a bit more to weddings as the man and woman would commonly be apart from each other before the wedding. It may have been that the groom was coming from far away or was using the time to create a place for them to go to together once they were married. He could literally show up at any moment and the wedding party would have to be ready to meet him, but a good groom would give a hint as to when everyone should be ready.

One day Jesus will cross a great distance to become one with His bride, the church. Heaven is the place He's prepared for us, a realm so awesome that even our deepest imagination cannot even penetrate how cool it is. God promised us that we go to heaven if we believe and receive Jesus. When we follow Him and His teachings, we reveal we're ready for Him to come.

As awesome as you think that is now, you will be completely blown away by how much better it will be. God's Son *will* return, Satan *will* have his ultimate defeat, and heaven and earth *will* become one. When they merge, we won't sit on clouds with harps. We will take part in the world the way it was supposed to be, see each other without problems between us, and have a face to face relationship with the Lord!

So if God made all of this for you to enjoy, what reason do you have not to say yes? What reason do you have not to share it with others? Spread the word! Everything is changing. Heaven and earth are becoming one before everyone's eyes. It's time for a celebration!

THERE IS HOPE

Heaven is full of answers to prayers you didn't know to pray for.

What do you think of heaven?

- ***IF*** you could pass out three passes to heaven to friends who could go there for a meaningful visit, who would you hand them out to?
- ***WHAT IF*** you had to guess when heaven and earth will come together?

364: Weekly Recap

***IF** our culture swapped the role of forks and spoons, what would you do?*

***WHAT IF** we had to use the fridge as the freezer and the freezer as the fridge (and you had to start putting ice cream in the fridge, etc.)?*

"Watch out that you are not deceived. For many will come in my name, saying, 'I am he,' and, 'The time is near.' Don't follow them. When you hear of wars and rebellions, don't be alarmed. Indeed, these things must take place first, but the end won't come right away." (Luke 21:8–9)

CATCH UP

- Who or what made you laugh recently?
- How did life feel easy or hard this past week?

RECAP

- What stood out to you from what we've read together, talked about, or attempted to do together over the past week?
- What thoughts or questions do you have from today's Bible verse?

GROW TOGETHER

- What might be the main thing God is trying to tell our family today?
- What if we did something new together or returned to a good habit to live out what we're learning? What might that be?

OPEN UP

- In what ways are you struggling in life or experiencing something hard?
- If we were to confess something to God as a family, what might that be?

PRAY

- Who is Jesus to you today?
- Who would be willing to close our time with a simple prayer?

365: Now What?

***IF** you could choose one age you could be and always stay, what age would it be?*

***WHAT IF** it meant never having memories that lasted beyond a year?*

READ IT: 2 PETER 1:3–21

So, you made it to the end of this book. You might be thinking, *Now what? We finished the book, so we're all done, right?* Seems like a common idea.

But you're not common, are you? You've glimpsed the Trinity, owned your Heritage, realized the Enemy, considered the Revolution, dealt with Ego, remembered your Identity, felt the *Shhh* . . . and then met the Hero, embraced the Opportunity, taken on your Purpose, and gotten excited about Eternity! You've discovered that just because you finish your stay on earth doesn't mean God is done with you yet.

So why should you be done with what you've learned when it still has much more it can do for everyone? What great idea is the Holy Spirit urging you to act on to help people have a relationship with Jesus and spread what you received?

That *could* involve this book. You could go through it with someone else as a disciple making disciples, perhaps with a neighbor or by sending a copy to someone. You can return to it when God seems distant to remember that He isn't. Whatever you do, finishing this book has not finished your journey through the Bible. There is still much left in both of you.

One day the invisible world that is more real than the one we can see will be revealed. Jesus will return as a leader and judge, bringing a final end to injustice and the evil forces behind it. All things will be restored into a new heaven and earth under Him, so that the triune God and His people can once again live face to face—unashamed. Death will be no more, broken relationships will be made whole, and you'll experience the reality of love to the *nth* degree forever. What do you say to giving people a glimpse of that reality?

THERE IS HOPE

Don't turn down a chance to change the world because your calendar is full. Momentum tomorrow comes from momentum you put into today.

Now what?

- ***IF*** we did a great thing this next month based on all this, what would it be?
- ***WHAT IF*** that great thing would be to do a regular/daily/weekly thing?